THE THEORIES OF DECENTRALIZATION
AND
LOCAL GOVERNMENT:

IMPLEMENTATION, IMPLICATIONS, AND REALITIES. **A GLOBAL PERSPECTIVE**

THE THEORIES OF DECENTRALIZATION
AND
LOCAL GOVERNMENT:

IMPLEMENTATION, IMPLICATIONS, AND REALITIES. **A GLOBAL PERSPECTIVE**

Edited by
Kwame Badu Antwi-Boasiako and Peter Csanyi

Stephen F. Austin State University Press
Nacogdoches ◆ Texas

For information address:
Stephen F. Austin State University Press,
1936 North Street, LAN 203
Nacogdoches, TX 75962

sfapress@sfasu.edu

Book Design: Laura Davis and Troy Varvel

LIBRARY OF CONGRESS CATALOGIN-IN-PUBLICATION DATA

Theories of Decentralization and Local Government: Implementation, Implications, and
Realities. A Global Perspective / Kwame Badu Antwi-Boasiako and Peter Csanyi—1st ed.
p.cm.
ISBN 978-1-62288-038-6

I. Title

First Edition: 2014

TABLE OF CONTENTS

FOREWORD

Local self-government is a key element of the political system of liberal democracy and is considered a civilization advance plus a theoretical and practical ingredient of every modern democratic political system. The most straightforward definition of local self-government states that this is the level of government closest to citizens, hence its task of representing the meaning and standpoints of locality. The implementation of local self-government is a demanding task, which primarily refers to the division of powers between the state and local communities. One can only speak of local self-government if the state recognizes local communities their legal existence, confers on them the right to decide on certain issues which it does not interfere in and provides them with necessary resources for managing these affairs. The true role of local self-government thus lies with the vertical division of power. The division of power between the state and local communities' curbs state (center's) authority so as to reduce the possibilities of its alienation and abuse. The system of local self-government within a democratic state enables certain public services to be more efficient and having better performance than would be the case if all power was centralized.

The term "decentralization" embraces a variety of concepts, which must be carefully analyzed in any particular country before determining if projects or programs should support reorganization of financial, administrative, or service delivery systems. Decentralization—the transfer of authority and responsibility for public functions from the central government to subordinate or quasi-independent government organizations and/or the private sector—is a complex multifaceted concept. Different types of decentralization should be distinguished because they have different characteristics, policy implications, and conditions for success. In decentralization, systematic efforts are being made to delegate to the lowest levels all authority except that which can only be exercised at the central points. Decentralization is delegation not from one individual to another but delegation to all units in an organization.

Local self-government performs the activities intended for strengthening national identity and enhances cooperation between local communities and citizens and local authorities. It is crucial for democratic character of a state that democracy is protected and works in the smallest units of government, i.e., local communities. Nevertheless, one cannot omit a yet another, certainly significant fact regarding the role of local self-government, or, to put it more appropriately, local democracy within modern democracies. Local democracy is a mechanism that, even in utmost centralized systems, contributes towards the decentralization of power and to mitigation of centralistic attempts at all-encompassing control of life from a single center of power, as it was already stressed by De Tocqueville.

Local self-government and with it the principle of subsidiarity, which has to be stressed, as it demands that competences be delegated from the level of state to the lowest possible level of government, is enacted in municipalities and, in most states, in other, i.e., wider, higher communities of local self-government. Hence, the primary task of local self-government is the transfer of decision-making on matters of local-level significance (i.e., matters concerning all inhabitants

7

of a local community) to the local level. Local self-government functions as the decision-making power at the lowest possible level or unit, meaning that local community acquires the status of self-government, of autonomy.

New book "The Theories of Decentralization and Local Government: Implementation, Implications, and Realities. A Global Perspective" by editors Kwame Badu Antwi-Boasiako and Peter Csanyi brings fresh perspective to the debate and comparative analysis of vertical division of power, i.e. processes of decentralization and relations between central and local (self) governments. The multiple author book is not just one of many similar around the globe, as it encompasses contributions from many different academics from not only different countries, but also different continents and even more importantly, very different political traditions and cultures; this way, the book deepens and strengthens the knowledge about the role of local governments in the contemporary world, and brings new value to the discussions on the relationship between decentralization and development.

Miro Haček
University of Ljubljana

Chapter One

Introduction: Decentralization from Global Perspective

Kwame Badu Antwi-Boasiako and Peter Csanyi

Introduction

It is our great pleasure, as editors, to present this book on Decentralization and Local Governments. We hope that this publication, which is one of the first of its kind, will help deepen and strengthen knowledge about the role of local governments in the contemporary world, and will enrich national and international discussions on the relationship between decentralization and development. The present book clearly shows that the world is undergoing a quiet democratic revolution. Therefore, even if important aspects of this process have yet to be accomplished, especially in countries in conflict (in the Middle East, Asia and Africa) local democracy is gaining momentum all over the world: from the settlements in the Americas, through the African savanna villages to the towns of Eurasia.

"The modern debate about decentralization and the optimal size and structure of government begins with the perceptions of the failings of the modern state. Proponents of decentralization condemn the impotence and waste of centralized government, and seek to invigorate it and focus its efforts; the ills of corruption, clientelism and political alienation are often regarded as the natural by-products of a bureaucracy distant in space and rendered insensitive, inefficient, and inflexible by its size. Policy failure in the sense of sub-optimal choices is diagnosed as resulting from poor information and incentives that are skewed away from ideal outcomes." Faguet (1997:1). Reformers advocate the decentralization of political authority and public resources to sub-national levels of government as a general cure for these ills, operating through the reduction of government to more manageable dimensions, thereby making it responsive and accountable to the governed. The decentralization debate is both broad and often frustratingly imprecise. Arguments for and against decentralization frequently assume the character of sweeping, cross-disciplinary claims about the effects of administrative measures on the quality and efficiency of both government and social interaction.

In administrative reforms anywhere, the search for an optimum vertical territorial structure of government and for optimum government areas has always been a highly relevant issue. As a rule, institutions of government are designed to act on more than just one geographical level - they are organized into several territorially defined tiers. Besides the national administrative institutions, there exist institutions operating at subnational levels as well - typically a regional (intermediary) level and local level. The need for such a multi-tiered structure has been supported by two lines of arguments, each referring to a different aspect of a modern state.

First, as bureaucratic organizations, governments have to deconcentrate some of their functions along the geographical scale in order to attain higher efficiency, both internal administrative efficiency and efficiency of service provision. Deconcentration is understood as a process whereby governmental functions are shifted downward within the hierarchical system of state bureaucracy, yet without weakening the vertical hierarchy of the system - deconcentrated units remain vertically subordinated to central authorities (Illner, 1998). It is argued that deconcentrated units of government, being nearer to the field of their operation than the core units, can act with a better knowledge of situations, can better communicate with the parties involved, and are better disposed to implement administrative decisions.

"Second, central governments decentralize some of their functions to subnational governments in order to support their legitimacy. Decentralization means the devolution of functions of state to autonomous territorial governments that can act, within the scope of decentralized functions, on their own behalf, without recourse to higher standing authorities. Decentralization may be based on two alternative theoretical models, each expressing a different philosophy of state building. One argument (e.g., classical nineteenth-century conservative ideologies) is the top-down reasoning that views local and regional government as being derived from a central authority, enjoying the level of autonomy that was granted to it by the central state and promoting state interests on a local level." Illner (1998:9). Alternatively, the existence of a "local state" (the political form of a local or regional community) can be explained and supported by federalist bottom-up arguments (e.g., liberal theories of government): the local state as a political form of local or regional community is primary, while any higher-level governments are derived from it and enjoy discretions ceded to them from below.

In a fact, decentralization played a major role in the democratic development of many Western societies from the United States of America to Spain. These governments also tend to have a high quality of governance. Achieving good quality governance in developing nations seems to be the new goal of donor agencies. However, the means of achieving it is a difficult task (Nyíri, 2003). Decentralization is identified by many as a crucial factor contributing to good governance. Nevertheless, the role of decentralization in development is complex: it is an agent of change as well as a target of it.

Decentralization is usually underpinned by functional arguments, again drawn from different theoretical/ideological contexts: it is maintained that a decentralized government promotes citizen participation; is more responsive to the concerns of citizens and more able to find solutions acceptable to them; provides opportunities for the development of a new elite; is a counterweight to the authoritarian state; gives an opportunity to experiment with new structures and policies; is most effective and efficient in delivering services to meet local needs; creates a sense of place or community; and is an element of "civil society" or a bridge linking civil society to the central state. It is, therefore, the efficiency, the effectiveness, and the concerns surrounding the legitimacy of the government that stand behind territorial deconcentration and decentralization. In practical terms, irrespective of theoretical and political underpinnings, territorial decentralization and deconcentration are manifested in the way two principal issues concerning the territorial aspect of government are dealt with: (1) the number, character, competencies, and mutual relations of territorial tiers of government and (2) the character, number, and concrete delimitation of areas of government representing each tier (Taylor, 1993). It is the approach toward solving these two issues, as well as the theoretical and political embedding of the approach, that is the focus of the decentralization debate in the world.

Probably the most important issue behind decentralization is "the subsidiary" principle. The principle of subsidiarity conveys that public administration should operate on the lowest possible level, to achieve optimum quality. Closer to citizen it is expected that administrators and managers can better understand specific local needs and are able better to react to them. Decentralization as the co-ordination mechanism for the public provision of goods and services represents an attempt to overcome information weaknesses involved in central co-ordination (Melumad, Mookherjee and Reichelstein, 1995). When there is intergovernmental collaboration, then principals placed lower down know better how public programs can be made to run efficiently. From the economic point of view, decentralization is generally desirable from the viewpoint of efficiency and local accountability. These criteria must be balanced with other elements, such as spatial externalities, economies of scale, overall fiscal efficiency, regional equity, redistributive responsibilities of the government.

Based on these facts, decentralization is generally accepted as the important or main public administration reform in any country. However, it shall be stressed that decentralization is the tool with important potential, but also with some limitations. As there are not just positive reform mechanisms, also decentralization has to be introduced with respect to concrete reform environment, to avoid "unexpected" negative consequences of its implementation. Decentralization may for example increase direct and indirect costs. Except of costs, decentralization may be limited by insufficient local capacities - too small government units are expected to suffer from lack of competence and expertise, but also from lack of resources (Nemec, 2007). Expected positive impacts of decentralization might be reversed also by so called transaction costs. Increased local activity means more voices, sometimes contradicting each other – it could be hardly expected that there is any government intervention with only positive impacts to all affected. To handle large scale of different interests is not simple, as well-known, ideal mechanism of collective voting does not exist in reality.

Decentralization and the principle of subsidiarity are very much based on the assumption that they would further revive local democracy and stipulate a higher level of participation of citizen in local issues. However, this relation is "both-sides" relation. Decentralization may help to create modern governance system, but its implementation has to respect the level, to which principles of openness, participation, accountability, effectiveness and coherence have been already achieved, too. Current "quality" of local democracy in world countries differs in many aspects from what are the reality in given countries, and this fact shall be respected in the processes of decentralization. Each of the chapters in this book uniquely discusses how decentralization is theoretically and physically implemented in a given geographical and political unit around the world.

In chapter 2, Ahmed Mansour looks at *Decentralization Policy in the Sudan: Control and Participation.* According to him the issue of decentralization has become a catchword for both academicians and practitioners. Recent moves towards democratization in the developing countries have granted the issue of decentralization a priority status in the agenda of public policy of these countries; Sudan is not an exception. This chapter explains some theoretical concepts of decentralization before delving to discuss the process of decentralization in the Sudan. It traces the issue of decentralization in Sudan by providing from the outset different meanings decentralization chief among which is the taxonomy presented by the United Nation Development Program (UNDP) and the World Bank. The UNDP taxonomy is consistent with the World Bank four types of decentralization that includes political decentralization, administrative decentralization, market decentralization and fiscal decentralization. Whereas political decentralization is related in the literature to democratization and self- government market decentralization is associated with privatization and divesting the public sector. Mansour further explores the socio-economic context of the Sudan and provides an overview of the legal evolution of the policy of decentralization during the different military and democratic regimes since the independence of the country in 1956.

Although ethnic and religious diversity in the Sudan and its vast size indicate the necessity for decentralizing government and administration the trend has been always a reluctant central government to transfer power to sub-national units. The post- independence regimes adopted a plethora of political ideologies that covered all the shades of the political spectrum and ranged from right and left of center liberal/capitalist thought to leftist/socialist and ending with all shades of Islamic fundamentalism. However, the different post-independence regimes, and irrespective of their type or ideological orientations, were not able to endow the country with the needed political stability necessary for social and economic development. Some of the recent attempts to restore order achieved by the last military governments sustained short lived periods of stability before they were disrupted by their makers.

However, Sudan was governed as a unitary country before independence and, despite a series of post-independence decentralization policies, remained effectively a unitary centralized state. Despite abundance of lip service to the contrary, the center has always been reluctant to devolve real power and authority to flesh out popular participation of the marginalized areas to enable them to participate in policy making The solutions to address the problems of size and diversity have been sought first in the principles of administrative decentralization to the Provinces and, later, in the creation of Regions to which powers have been formally devolved. The application of the principle of administrative decentralization to the Provinces culminated in the establishment of Peoples Local Government in 1972. Regional Self Government was conceded to the Southern Region in 1972, following the Addis Ababa Agreement, to be annulled ten years later. Regions were created out of the Northern Provinces by the Regional Government Act of 1980, and powers devolved to the Regional Councils were actually found only on paper.

The inexorable trend since independence has therefore been toward granting greater administrative responsibilities to sub-national entities without effective devolution of fiscal and economic power. In many cases these measures were dictated by unavoidable administrative necessities and satisfaction of legitimate aspirations of the diverse ethnic and cultural populations in those sub-units. In conclusion, the chapter contends that the overall reluctance to decentralize explains the incidence of civil wars and separatist tendencies in the country. This state of affairs resulted in separating the South from the North and expected to lead for more demands of separation by other marginalized regions in Darfur and the East. The concept of decentralization could be apply to any form of politics as discussed in chapter three.

Hong Pang discusses the politics of copyright in China in **Chapter 3.** *Centralized Commitment vs. Decentralized Enforcement: The Politics of Copyright Protection in China.* Pang argues that since the early 1980s, the central government of the People's Republic of China has made a series of commitments to protect intellectual property rights (IPRs), bilaterally with the United States and multilaterally by signing several international agreements. Following these international commitments were a series of legislation and policy-making efforts by the national legislature and bureaucracy, which have made Chinese intellectual property protection laws and regulations consistent with the international standards specified in the Trade-Related Aspects of Intellectual Property Rights Agreement (the TRIPs Agreement). However, until today, China is still criticized heavily and persistently for its inadequate protection of IPRs. Using the principal-agent theory, this chapter examines how the decentralized structure of enforcement, both administrative enforcement and civil enforcement, compromises the effectiveness of implementation of those international commitments made by the central government in copyright protection. Given the decentralized structure of copyright enforcement and lack of effective controlling mechanism available to the central government, the local enforcement agencies have fewer pressures and incentives to protect copyright and are easily penetrable to their local interests and considerations as well as their institutional and bureaucratic agendas and priorities.

Chapter 4 presents: *The Past and Present of Decentralization: Local Administration in the Hashemite Kingdom of Jordan.* Abdulfattah Yaghi discusses different aspects of the history and present of decentralization and local administration in the Hashemite Kingdom of Jordan (Jordan). He covers the geographical, historical and cultural background of the country, foundations of decentralization, status of centralization and decentralization, developments in the public administration and municipal administration systems, laws of local administration, and challenges facing the progress decentralization in the country.

Jordan is located in the heart of the Arab World. Modern Jordan was established in 1921 as a constitutional monarchy. Today, the Jordanian society is a unique composition of all different peoples who migrated and lived in the country bringing with them different

13

cultures and experiences. The total population of Jordan is more than five millions. Ancestors of the Jordanian people built several famous ancient states, but the most remarkable ones were the Nabateen Kingdom, Moab Kingdom, Maania State, and Amoon Kingdom. Each one of those states were famous for its administrative structure, which created an administrative culture that laid the foundations for the administrative advancements during the Omayyad Empire during the middle ages. The Omayyad Empire relied on developing unique systems for decentralized governance and local administration of its vast territories, including Jordan.

For a long time, Jordan was divided into three districts (Sonjoks): Ajloon district in the central west, Balqa district in the north, and Kerak district in the south. Today's administrative system in Jordan borrowed several segments of laws that were used by the Ottomanian Empire during the four hundred years prior to the independence in 1921 in addition to utilizing territorial division that was used by the ancient Omayyads. In 2007, the Jordanian government adopted a new municipal law, which has better democratic features than the old laws. Specifically, the new law recognizes the importance of popular vote and substitutes the old partially-elected municipal councils with fully-elected municipal councils. In addition, the law responses to people's demands for better transparency and accountability in local government by establishing better rules for accountability.

Yaghi again looks at *Decentralization in the United Arab Emirates* in **Chapter 5** where the different aspects of decentralization in the United Arab Emirates (UAE) are presented. He provides a brief history of the state and society in the UAE, origins of decentralization, oral history of decentralization, contemporary governance, structure of federalism, local administration system, and inter-governmental relations. Like Jordan, the UAE is an Arab state located on the southern shores of the Arabian Gulf. Although it declared independence in December 2, 1971, the country has developed steadily to become an important commercial center. One of the biggest challenges to the UAE government and society is demographical imbalance between citizens and expatriates where citizens only make less than 20% of seven million people who live in the country. Today, the is a federal union of seven emirates (states), namely AbuDhabi, Sharja, Ras Al Khaima, Dubai, Fujera, Ajman, and Om Al Quwain. Each emirate is composed of several localities.

Two major factors helped maintaining decentralization during the past three hundred years and helped creating autonomy of the different parts of the UAE, namely the tribal culture (kinship) and coherence within the Arab Emirati society. Therefore, traditions remain till today a significant component of the society and its bid for development. Today, the state continues to be influenced by nets of kinship, where relatives are trusted and given important political and administrative positions in federal as well as local governments. However, while kinship is important, it does not provide those public officials with automatic immunity against legal questioning of their decisions and actions. The UAE is moving steadily toward more good governance practices where accountability laws are emphasized over kinship.

Authority in the UAE's local administration has always been communal or family-based. The ruling families in all seven Emirates relied on their family ties and family recognition to extend their legitimacy over a particular territory and the people who lived within that geographical and social domain. Potentials and challenges of these realities shape the contemporary structure and practices of local administration, especially when seeking higher levels of transparency and accountability.

Chapter 6 takes us to Central America: *The Segundo Montes Community and the Politics of Post-war Desires.* José Neftalí Recinos examines the trends and status of decentralization in Central America. According to Recinos efforts are being made by agencies such as the United Nations Development Program (UNDP) and the United States Agency for International Development (USAID) to monitor the processes of improving and strengthening municipal governments in the isthmus since the early 1990s. Results from these studies have identified El Salvador as the country with more decentralization projects in Central America. The purpose of this chapter, however, is to contextualize the experience of a group of repatriates that in 1990 left the refugee camp of Colomoncagua, Honduras, to settle in northern Morazán and form Comunidad Segundo Montes (CSM)— Segundo Montes Community—. This community was expected to bring into fruition the glorified transforming ideals of the revolution and to validate the utopian landscape as a possible social reality through a participatory model of democracy in a post-war scenario that did not take into account adverse external impediments stack against such a project. The failure to establish a system of sustainable development under the flag of utopia, did not preclude the community to implement decentralization policies and give continuity to principles such as self-governance, community problem-solving, and popular participation. This attitude has permitted CSM to surge from adversity and become, if not an economic model, a precedent for other communities. Therefore, CSM is the convergence of stories and history, of ideology and praxis, of symbols and processes, of desires and reality.

Next Peter Csanyi utilizes the traditional definition of decentralization as he looks at *Decentralization and Local Governments in Europe/Central Europe* in **Chapter 7.** Decentralization is defined in accordance with US foreign aid programs as a transfer of responsibility for planning, management, and resource raising and allocation from central government and its agencies to: (a) field units of central government ministries or agencies, (b) subordinate units or levels of government, (c) semi-autonomous public authorities or corporations, (d) area wide, regional or functional authorities, or (e) non-governmental private or voluntary organizations (Rondelli, 1984). Accordingly, the basic types of decentralization are the following: 1. Deconcentration; 2. Delegation; 3. Devolution; and 4. Privatization. Decentralization has often been rhetoric and not a reality. Announcing decentralization did not only brought in foreign aid but it also pacified internal opposition. However, action rarely followed rhetoric. Today, one can see that it nearly impossible to judge decentralization solely relying on political documents.

After the collapse of the Soviet Union, there was not only rhetoric of decentralization in Central European countries, but real efforts were made to implement some forms of it. Still, the efforts remained largely at the level of deconcentration and delegation while real devolution of power to the local level only happened half-heartedly, especially with issues concerning finance. Spain, in contrast, implemented a high rate of political and financial decentralization that led to territorial pluralism with an impressive division of power. Quite interestingly - and proving how formal framework and reality often do not match, the actual decentralization was deeper than its constitutional mandate in Spain. The Spanish decentralization is more of a result of real politics than official state rhetoric or constitutional issues. The European countries, today, are embarked on a new phase of territorial reform, distinct from that of the 1960s and 1970s. Not all states are similarly affected by this process –some in fact have remained outside of it. In essence, these reforms are concerned with strengthening municipal and intermunicipal frameworks, the trend towards regionalization, and problems related to the organization of urban areas. On the other hand, levels of local funding are not consistent with the increase of local government functions in most countries. Moreover, the relatively simple two-tier local administration system (and even in certain countries only one tier of decentralization, the municipality) has evolved into a more complex system with a greater tendency towards regionalization.

Most countries have a system of local government for two reasons: as a manifestation of local democracy and a provider of local services. As an instrument of local democracy, councils of elected politicians make decisions on behalf of local communities, thus serving to safeguard against central government domination. The strengths of local government as a democratic instrument are its closeness to the population, its elected status, its accessibility and the opportunity it provides for public participation in the democratic process. The European Charter on Local Self-Government (Council of Europe, 1985) signed by most European countries recognizes local government as an integral part of a democratic regime. If we look at the reforms of regional administration in Central Europe: Czech Republic, Slovakia, Hungary and Poland, the most of them suggested an adaptation to similar regional structure, as in the European Union. It was obvious that a degree of convergence was also taking place in these countries, which were not members of the European Union in the 1990s and already ten years after the fall of communism in Eastern Europe, a stable and often sophisticated framework of political and free market economic institutions was established in most of the countries of former Eastern bloc, especially in Central European countries. However, the systematic reform of the administrative system lagged behind, although the absence of administrative reforms means the continuation of one of the most severe legacies of the socialist system.

In the upshot the systemic administrative reform in all four Central European countries (Czech Republic, Slovakia, Hungary and Poland) indicate on similar developments. At the beginning of the nineties there was radical decentralization facilitated by the formation of self-governing administrative units at lower level of communes. However, gradually the further administrative reform was either stopped or impeded and the re-centralization appeared. Thus, only ten years after the transition began the second wave of reform in all four countries: districts and regions have appeared.

The literature on decentralization is most of the time discussed as a concept, which tend to address political administration but the theoretical concept is better understood when it is applied to a given geographical or political unit so in **Chapter 8** Peter Csanyi looks at the specifics of decentralization by discussing *Local Governments in the Czech Republic and Slovakia*. The creation of modern, democratic and effective local/regional, self-government system is still one of the main issues of public administration reforms in Central and Eastern Europe (CEE). Nevertheless the basic legal and financial basis for local self-governments was created in most of CEE countries (especially in all accession countries) very soon. Already in 1990, in countries like Czech Republic, Slovakia, Hungary, and Poland, the first local democratic elections were held. There was a set of new laws on local self-government, respecting basic criteria for this level of governance, as defined by the European Charter of Local Self-Government.

The Czech Republic and Slovakia introduced regions and regional self-governments as missing links between central and local government on the one hand, between state administration and self- government on the other. In the wake of the democratic transition in Czechoslovakia, the national committees ceased to function as organs of Communist party rule on the regional and local level. Whereas democratic local self-government was established already in 1990, the new democratic elites did not create institutions of general territorial administration on the regional level. This was mainly due to the complexity of administrative reform and the lack of political consensus over the constitutional status of regions, the need for regional self- government and the administrative division of the territory. In the early 1990s, governments were preoccupied with re-organizing and dissolving the Czechoslovak federation as well as with economic reforms to create a market economy. The resolve to introduce "higher territorial (self-administrative) units" was declared in both constitutions of the new republics emerging in 1993, but attempts to realize these units failed until 1996-97. In both countries, the laws on regional self-government were preceded by laws that defined the new territorial-administrative division. In March 1996, Slovakia's parliament adopted a law dividing the country into eight regions ("kraje"). The parliament also created regional offices of state administration as bodies of general territorial state administration and attached several de-concentrated units of sectoral state administration to these new "integrated" offices. In the Czech Republic, the constitutional law on the creation of 14 regions ("kraje") was adopted between October and December 1997. The self-governing institutions, their competences and resources and their relations with local self-government and state administration were codified in subsequent years. The competences and relations between the institutions were gradually adjusted in both countries during the last 15 years.

For the purposes of Eurostat, Slovakia is divided into five NUTS (Nomenclature of territorial units for statistics) area levels, NUTS 1 being the whole territory of Slovakia; NUTS 2 being four large regional units (Bratislava, Western Slovakia, Central Slovakia and Eastern Slovakia); NUTS 3 being the eight regional self-government territories; NUTS 4 being 79 state government districts; and NUTS 5 being the local self-government level (2,892 local governments). The territorial organization of Slovakia has been subject to many political debates and changes. Even the current system of eight administrative regions and four NUTS 2 regional units does not copy the traditional ethno-cultural division among different territories of Slovakia. The most recent change, in 2006, was the abolition of eight regional state governments and the transfer of their powers to 79 district state offices. This change was meant to save administrative costs. It, however, did not have the expected financial impact, since most of the agenda and employees were transferred elsewhere rather than eliminated. In the light of this, further political debate, and possibly changes, may be expected.

In Slovakia, the municipality is the basic unit of local administration, which is an independent and legal body. At the subnational level, the public administration has a system of self-government and a system of state administration. The reform of public administration has as objective to give more responsibilities from the central government to municipalities.

The Constitution of the Czech Republic anchors the division of the Czech Republic into lower (municipalities) and higher (regions) territorial self-government units. Regional self-government is formed by 14 regions, including the City of Prague (which is at the same time a municipality and a region). Municipalities administer their territories within the framework of independent competence. Besides, they execute delegated competences on behalf of the state. Within their self-competence, all municipalities and towns have equal rights and obligations. Execution of the delegated competences depends on the size of the municipality and the territory it administers. Municipalities are divided into three groups, according to the scope of delegated competences. "Classification of regional statistical units - CZ-NUTS" replaced the existing Nomenclature of Regions and Districts.

Miranda-Recinos takes us to Latin America where in **Chapter 9** *Economic Empowerment for Women in Petac and Tizimin, Yucatán Mexico* is discussed. In this chapter she examines and presents qualitative data on women's economic empowerment participating with two non-governmental organizations in Yucatán: *Mundo Rural* in Petac and *Ayuda para Ayudar* in Tizimin. These foundations use microcredit to provide women with opportunities for access and participation in economic processes, consequently, as delineated here, making them an integral part of social and political structures. Many discussions at global forums have been centered on the need to deliberate on a concrete plan of action to the persistent and abysmal issue of poverty. Microcredit has been sought as a favorable tool to alleviate poverty, and to empower women economically through the use of small loans. In this case, decentralization at a local level resulted in the delivery of financial services to populations habitually excluded from the traditional banking system. However, the controversies surrounding the microcredit industry and the validity of the contribution to women's empowerment are points of debate. As it will be articulated in this essay, the worked performed by *Mundo Rural* and APA present an example of constructive practices and affirmative results of women living in these communities.

Another way of understanding decentralization is through federalism where states have their own laws, taxes, and the autonomy for certain administrative decision. Lee Payne in **Chapter 10** critically examines *Decentralization in the United States of America*. The federal and State governments are in fact but different agents and trustees of the people, constituted with different powers, and designed for different purposes. The adversaries of the Constitution seem to have lost sight of the people altogether in their reasoning on this subject; and to have viewed these different establishments, not only as mutual rivals and enemies, but as uncontrolled by any common superior in their efforts to usurp the authorities of each other. These gentlemen must here be reminded of their error. They must be told that the ultimate authority, wherever the derivative may be found, resides in the people alone, and that it will not depend merely on the comparative ambition or address of the different governments, whether either, or which of them, will be able to enlarge its sphere of jurisdiction at the expense of the other. Truth, no less than decency, requires that the event in every case should be supposed to depend on the sentiments and sanction of their common constituents. Many considerations, besides those suggested on a former occasion, seem to place it beyond doubt that the first and most natural attachment of the people will be to the governments of their respective States (Madison, Federalists #46).

Decentralization is a double edge sword as it ensures accountability and probity at the local level. However, it could encourage corruption when political dynasty is well established at the local level. Heather Wyatt-Nichol and Ed Gibson in **Chapter 11** *have Perspectives on Corruption*: *"He who pays the piper."* Corruption is historical and global, existing in every society regardless of time and place. However, the extent and impact of corruption ranges from various acts of transgression in some societies to being deeply imbedded in the institutions of others. The consequences of corruption also vary from a mere loss of money for a few individuals to the loss of lives for entire groups of people. This chapter examines perceptions of corruption across various countries in Africa, taking into account the hegemonic discourse of Western nations, and offers contrasting instances of corrupt acts in U.S. municipalities.

Among African countries, there are numerous examples of corruption that contribute to social injustice across the continent. For example, the Democratic Republic of Congo is a major oil producer in sub-Saharan Africa yet 70 percent of the population lives in poverty. In addition, one third of the oil revenue is unaccounted for. Similarly, Angola annually produces over $1 billion (American dollar – USD) of oil – of which 25 percent is unaccounted for. The majority of the population lives on less than one dollar per day. In the Nigerian Delta, oil and gas account for 85 percent of government revenues, but two-thirds of the population lives in poverty.

An institutional perspective has been used as the framework for anti-corruption reforms in Africa. Studies have found that corruption is less likely to occur in affluent countries and more likely to occur in countries under authoritarian regimes with valuable natural resources. There is also a common perception in the literature that corruption is less likely to occur in democracies due to factors such as freedom of the press, a well-informed public, equality, and openness. When power is centralized, there is both motive and opportunity for corruption. Ayittey (2005) asserts, "The centralization of both economic and political power turns the state into a pot of gold that all sorts of groups compete to capture. Once captured, power is then used to amass huge personal fortunes, to enrich one's cronies and tribesmen, to crush one's rivals, and to perpetuate one's rule in office" (48). Research has demonstrated a relationship between corruption and centralized structures that afford discretion only among top leaders (Antwi-Boasiako & Bonna, 2009; Joaquin, 2004; Meagher, 2001). Considered a necessary element of democracy, decentralization is correlated with economic growth and deemed an indirect means to minimize corruption when transparency and participation are included in reform efforts . Yet decentralization, if it is to have effect, must provide for true independence of action and perspective, lest the corrupting influences of concentrated economic and political power find and exploit the ethical vulnerabilities of decentralized units of government.

The many branches of decentralization include deconcentration, delegation. and devolution. Public policy, which incorporates inputs from the governed in most cases trumphed but locals sometimes have to get into political wars with central governments. James Newman confronts such a duel in **Chapter 12** where *Devolution of Water Policy in the American South: The Case of the ACT and ACF Water Wars* is discussed at length. This case study considers devolution of policy formulation of water allocation in the American South. Absent of federal water policy the region developed a water policy on an ad hoc basis. As population in the region grew, the need for a region-wide water policy developed. Because of a legacy of a water use policy reflecting an abundance of freshwater, little regulation existed in 1990 when a rash of lawsuits filed on behalf of states and water users regarding surface water allocation. A moratorium with lawsuits was reached as parties entered into interstate compact negotiations with the goal of attaining a regional water policy within the region's two primary river basins, the Alabama-Coosa-Tallapoosa, and the Apalachicola-Chattahoochee-Flint. Over time, the negotiations failed, lawsuits resumed and the region entered into ad hoc policy development in regards to water allocation. This case study explores devolution of water policy to the state and local level and the role interest groups play in formulating this policy.

Africa by all accounts is struggling with democracy desipte the democratic waves across the continent lately. Kwame Asamoah in **Chapter 13** examines *Implementation of Decentralization in Ghana: Issues and Challenges.* He argues decentralization is a vital tool in governance and for this reason, the government of Ghana in 1988 introduced a decentralization program based on governmental values such as empowerment, equity, stability, accountability and checking of rural-urban drift. This program was designed to accelerate growth and equitable spread of development in rural communities as well as urge these communities to participate in decision-making that relates to the overall management of development in their districts. This study, therefore, investigates the implementation challenges and major issues affecting decentralization in Ghana.

He see decentralization as a means of transferring power and resources from the national governments to sub national governments or to administrative units of national governments. Decentralization has been categorized into four forms, which are deconcentration, delegation, devolution, and privatization. Decentralization as a developmental policy is aimed at bringing governance to the doorsteps of the citizens in every nation. This, therefore, depends largely on the modalities and implementation of the policy- decentralization. How the various institutions are well resourced in terms of powers and capacity to be able to operate freely, the human resource capabilities, and their abilities to turn around things in favor of their nation in a competitive global environment.

Although the decentralization policy in Ghana has achieved some impressive successes, there are still some major challenges which have to be addressed. These include but not limited to the appointment of Metropolitan/Municipal/District Chief Executives, some elements of re-centralization, and logistical constraints. It is recommended that Metropolitan/Municipal/District Chief Executives must be elected. The logistical constraints must also be seriously addressed to enable District Assemblies to function effectively. The Assemblies must be given enough autonomy to use the District Assemblies Common Fund based on locally planned objectives, priorities and projects in order to meet the needs of the local community. This would encourage the concept of administrative responsibility where the Assemblies would be accountable and responsive to the needs of the local people in service provision.

In **Chapter 14,** Minerva Cruz looks at decentralization in health policies as she focuses on two geographical areas. *Medicaid: The Decentralization of Health Policies in the United States and Puerto Rico* examines the decentralization of health policies in the United States and Puerto Rico. Specifically, it provides an overview of decentralization of policies involved with the medicaid program in the United States and Puerto Rico and examines how the Program works under the American federal system. Medicaid is a health program, created by the Social Security Amendments of 1965, to cover the health care needs of individuals and families with low-income in the United States. Puerto Rico has been a territory of the United States since 1898. In 1917, Puerto Ricans became citizens of the United States, and by 1952, the country became a Commonwealth (Estado Libre Asociado in Spanish). This means citizens of Puerto Rico are entitled to most of the benefits enjoyed by citizens of the states, including medicaid.

Medicaid operates in a decentralized manner. In a decentralized system, the power of decision making is shared between the higher and lower levels. For example, the Federal government creates a program and establishes general guidance for its administration, but states and territories are allowed to decide about their specific criteria for eligibility. However, it appears that the federal government utilizes different criteria to allocate funds to Puerto Rico, compared to the states. The disparity of funds for the medicaid program limits the Puerto Rican government's ability to provide the health services needed in the country.

Puerto Rico does not receive a typical state's share in federal contributions for its medicaid program. On the contrary, Puerto Rico's medicaid program operates under a financial 'cap' created by the federal government. Because of the federal spending caps applied to the territories, the Puerto Rican government is unable to offer certain health care services under its Medicaid Program that states may offer. Cruz describes services provided by the medicaid program in Indiana, a state within the United States, and compares them to the ones provided in Puerto Rico. She argues that to implement the program successfully, the American Federal Government should support its localities by making adequate financial resources available to its localities. The Federal Government shares the administration of the program with states and Puerto Rico, but maintains the power to control the financial resources to the Program. She defines decentralization and discusses the division of power between the federal government and localities. Then, it provides an overview of the medicaid program in Puerto Rico and the United States.

Other policies discussed in this book, which have nothing to do with the health industry is Economic Development (ED). Under a federalist political system, the central government has very little impact, if any, in the local and state levels. In **Chapter 15**, Alexandra Tsvetkova examines Cluster Policies in the U.S. States: The Effects on Job Creation and the Number of Firms in Four High-Technology Industries. ED policies in the U.S. are designed and implemented at all levels of government. Although the national government participates in ED projects in various states and localities, lower levels of government are better suited to shape economic performance in their jurisdictions, as policy-makers at those levels are more perceptive to local demands, market signals, and are effectively disciplined by political pressures.

The results of ED efforts at state and local levels depend on many factors and may drastically differ depending on specific circumstances. The analysis in this chapter distinguishes between clusters and cluster policies and estimates their effects on population-adjusted employment and population-adjusted number of firms in four U.S. high-technology industries during the 1998-2004 period. The results suggest that clusters have a significant positive effect on employment and the number of firms in two industries, aerospace & defense manufacturing, and software design, development & publishing. There is no statistically significant relationship in computer & electronic component manufacturing, and biotechnology & biotech research industries. State cluster initiatives appear to have no effect on employment in all four industries of interest. As for the number of firms, cluster policies are not a significant predictor of this variable in software design, development & publishing, computer & electronic component manufacturing, and biotechnology & biotech research. In aerospace & defense manufacturing, cluster policy initiatives are negatively related to the population-adjusted number of firms.

The chapter demonstrates opportunities and limitations of state government policies in economic development. State governments have the freedom to devise and put into action a wide range of ED programs in accordance with their needs and resources. This does not guarantee the ability to shape economic landscape of any industry in a desired way. Cluster initiatives appear to be an example of ED policies that, despite the reported success of clusters and much guidance provided to policy-makers, have yet to prove their positive effects on job creation and firm formation.

The concluding chapter, *Public Administration, Decentralization, and Elections in Africa: Ghana, A Case Study,* seeks to examine administrative responsibilities of locals in democratic Africa. As Kwame Antwi-Boasiako argues in **Chapter 16**, to fully understand public administration, decentralization, and governance in Africa, one has to study each of the over fifty countries on the continent. Despite the similarities in the form of administration in Africa both military and democratic administrations, one should expect conspicuously distinct differences employ by each country and regime. That is, the evolution of public administration in Africa would be a collection of traditional and contemporary administrative history of each country. Africa is very deficient in recorded history as outsiders documented greater part of its history. Such deficiency in the data makes it difficult in the chronological and/or longitudinal analysis of public administration and governance in Africa. But public administration and governance in Africa "has been with us as long as recorded history" (King and Chilton 2009: 29). The Great Empires of Africa and Ancient Civilizations including Egypt, China, and Rome did require their citizens to build cities and other public goods such as roads and palaces as symbols of unity and power. Similarly, traditional administrative leaders in Africa also utilized communal labor for public projects while contemporary political leaders rely on taxes to build public goods.

The administrative process required leaders the need to plan, organize, staff, direct, coordinate, report, and budget. Luther Gulick in the 1930s referred to this administrative process as POSDCORB. In fact, Gulick's acronym had been in existence even before recorded history therefore the POSDCORB concept is not a new phenomenon to traditional societies and administrations. The great empires had fully understood the concept of decentralization as conquered cities, tribes, and villages did control themselves but took instructions from a central authority (the conqueror). The conquered were also made to pay taxes for the upkeep of the central authority, a concept the European colonial powers adopted to rule the conquered colonies in Africa and elsewhere. Public Administration therefore is a process of manipulating the human capital to increase productivity to improve our environment for a better quality of life. So administration is not a new phenomenon in African history as the kings, chiefs, and opinion leaders did plan, organize, mobilize, and got their subjects ready for communal labor including fighting wars.

The diverse nature of how decentralization has been discussed in this book presents a global perspective on its implementation. Though the theoretical narratives of decentralization as promoting political empowerment have their doubts, the actual implementation of the concepts will remain an academic conundrum as the various political systems provide different interpretations of decentralization. The concept succeeds when it is closely related to its designing principles of finance, transparent decision-making, identifying local priorities, and effective accountability at the local level. The difficulty in applying these principles is influenced by the constitutions and policies of the various countries and societies. While decentralization and central government activities are not zero sum game, there is the need to balance decentralization policies with central government activities to ensure effective and efficient governance. We argue here that one of the main reasons for global decentralization is democratization in former socialist and colonized countries where the old political structures continue to crumble.

References

Antwi-Boasiako, K., & Bonna, O. (2009). *Traditional institutions and public administration and democratic Africa.* Bloomington, IN, Xlibris.

Ayittey, G.B.N.(2005). *Africa unchained: The blueprint for Africa's future.* New York: Palgrave Macmillan.

Faguet, Jean-Paul (1997). Technical Consultation on Decentralization. *Decentralization and Local Government Performance.* FAO, 1-17

Illner, M. (1998). Territorial Decentralization: An Obstacle to Democratic Reform in Central and Eastern Europe?. *The Transfer of Power. Decentralization in Central and Eastern Europe.* Local Government and Public Service Reform Initiative, 7-43

Joaquin, E.T. (2004). Decentralization and corruption: The bumpy road to public sector integrity in developing countries. *Public Integrity* 6(3) 207-219.

Marcou, G. and Wollmann, H. (2008). Europe. *Decentralization and Local Democracy in the World.* United Cities and Local Governments – First Global Report, 128-166

Meagher, P. (2001). Devolution, quality of governance and corruption. Center for Institutional Reform and the Informal Sector, University of Maryland. Retrieved January 15, 2011 from http://www.iris.umd.edu/Reader.aspx?TYPE=FORMAL_PUBLICATION&ID=7 60f4bad-62f0-4659-b631-b6a849552a6d

Melumad, Nahum, Mookherjee, Dilip and Reichelstein, Stefan (1995). Hierarchical Decentralization of Incentive Contracts. *Rand Journal of Economics* 26 (4) 654-672

Nemec, J. (2007). Decentralization reforms and their relations to local democracy and efficiency: CEE lessons. *Uprava, letnik* 5 (3) 7-40

Nemec, J., Bercik, P. and Kuklis, P. (2000). Local Government in Slovakia. *Decentralization: Experiments and Reforms.* Budapest. LGI Books, Open Society Institute 297-343

Nyiri, Zs. (2003). *Decentralization and Good Governance: Ten Years of Hungarian Experience.* Storrs-Mansfield. University of Connecticut Press.

Surazka, B. et al. (1997). Towards regional government in Central Europe: Territorial restructuring of postcommunist regimes. *Government and Policy* 15 (4) 437-462

Taylor, P.J. (1993). *Political Geography.* Harlow: Longman. Third edition.

Chapter Two

DECENTRALIZATION POLICY IN THE SUDAN: CONTROL AND PARTICIPATION

Ahmed Mustafa Elhussein Mansour

Key words: decentralization, Sudan, diversity, policy, political regime

Introduction

In recent decades, the issue of decentralization has become a catchword for both academicians and practitioners. Moves toward democratization in the developing countries have granted the issue of decentralization a priority status in the agenda of public policy of these countries. In its ideal-type academic models, decentralization looks as a benign scheme that aims at empowering the populace and burgeoning popular participation. However, there are always conflicts between the intentions of pure academic goals of decentralization and the agenda of the ruling elites concerning the goals of decentralization and its role in the process of modern governance.

Countries with high levels of ethnicity and ruled by central elites, whose legitimacy is based on control of societal economic and political resources, decentralization may represent a menace to that legitimacy in that it may lead to fragmentation of power and division among ethnic groups. This fact actually summarizes the experience of the Sudan and its different political elites, notwithstanding their political orientation, and their policies of decentralization. Irrespective of the type of political regime, multi-party or military, the Sudanese political elites have always been reluctant to effectively decentralize the polity.

Moreover most military governments in the Sudan and some developing countries, whose popularity is weak amongst the populace, may seek to enhance their popularity and control by using paper decentralization projects as symbolic devices to camouflage their real aims and intentions of achieving central control. The paramount goal is promoting support for the regimes through mass mobilization rather than involving them in policy and decision-making. However, being the largest in term of size and the most diversified country in Africa, Sudan has always proved ungovernable through centralized arrangements. This fact led to the adoption of ambitious policies of decentralization with proclaimed objectives of encouraging popular participation and end up hiding actual goals of controlling that participation.

The Meaning of Decentralization

Decentralization is not a moot intellectual concept because it has practical as well as theoretical connotations to both scholars and practitioners irrespective of their country or political background. It has supporters from the left and right of the political spectrum. Contemplating on the British political scene, Lawton and Rose (1994, 57) argue that

> Decentralization has supporters from all parts of the political spectrum. On the left it is believed that it will encourage political participation, and on the right it is believed that it will get the central state off the backs of individuals and allow greater individual choice.

Decentralization is doubtless related to many themes of administrative reforms in both developed and less developed countries alike. It represents the backbone for many modern paradigms to reform the public sector performance such as total quality management, empowerment, organizational reengineering, reinventing of government and good governance (Osborne and Gaebler, 1992; Morgan and Murgatroyed, 1994; Bendell, et al. 1994). It is not astonishing at all that there is voluminous political science and economics research that purported to explain this global drive for decentralization (Rodden, 2004).

Since independence of many developing countries, decentralization has become a catchword for reformers from any breed and continued to be in high vogue. It is also an overused concept rendering ambiguity and difficulty in its definition. In simple terms decentralization refers to the transfer of political and administrative powers from a center to its peripheries. However, the word used to refer to many meanings ranging from the administrative to the social spheres. Consider, for example, the following plausible definitions. In administrative literature the word is used to refer, at both state and organizational levels, to the distribution of administrative functions or powers of a central authority among several local authorities or departments. In development economics the word is employed to refer to the process of redistributing and reallocation of industry and an urban population to rural areas. In modern neo-classical economics, the word actually means the transfer of government decision making to the free paly of markets.

In sociology, the term decentralization is used to denote social processes in which population and industry moves from urban centers to outlying districts. The word is also used in a more general sense to denote the dispersal of a center of concentration such as *decentralizing* a university complex. In public management decentralization is the transfer of power away from the central government to local branches or governments. However, simply defined, decentralization may be conceptualized as "a shift of authority towards local governments and away from central government, with total government authority over society and economy imagined as fixed" (Rodden, 2004: 482).

Centralization and Decentralization

Usually decentralization is conceptualized as an antinomy to centralization. Centralization is the act of consolidating power under a central control through a process in which important decision-making is concentrated on the top of the organization or the state thereby subjecting all important actions at the lower levels to the approval of central bodies. The popular motto "*centralization is bad, decentralization is good*" has become a universal platitude. The popularity of the motto is based on certain perceived benefits of decentralization that range from " economic efficiency, improved public services to more participatory government" (Falleti, 2010: 1).

However, decentralization is not a free lunch because with more decentralization problems of co-ordination of organizational activities became salient and may prove more expensive in cost-benefit logic. Nevertheless, centralization is not all evil and many writers, especially in traditional management and economic thought, are able to list benefits to it similar to those of decentralization (Tinbergen, 1954; Kindleberger, 1996). For example, at the national level, centralization may help to preserve state and national unity against separatist tendencies flared by ethnic or religious diversity. It may also help to achieve efficient control over scarce national resources and its fair and just allocation to different regions in the state.

The realization of the assumed benefits of centralization and decentralization may be obstructed in practice by socio-economic and political realities. In many cases in developing countries decentralization schemes may be used to tighten up the grip of central government over localities and centralization may be modified to a great extent by actual ethnic fragmentation, country size and poor communication and transportation systems. Therefore, it may be appropriate to think of centralization and decentralization as theoretical categories by which the actual patterns of authority relationships became clear. However, the popular motto "centralization is bad, decentralization is good" is an oversimplification of reality since decentralization does not mean the transfer of all powers to lower levels in the organization. It is not possible to have a completely decentralized entity because this means, in fact, complete independence in which the entity is no longer a single one. For example, at organizational levels, administrative (managerial) decentralization may involve only

> a systematic delegation of authority at all levels of management and in all of the organization. In a decentralization concern, authority is retained by the top management for taking major decisions and framing policies concerning the whole concern. Rest of the authority may be delegated to the middle level and lower level of management (Management Study Guide, 2011).

This means that the question is not either centralization or decentralization because every state or organization needs a specific mix of the two. The right mix of centralization and decentralization is contingent upon the nature and purposes of the organization. The degree of centralization and decentralization can be affected by many factors including the nature of operations, number of subordinate units, size of a concern, availability of resources, and subordinates competency. The larger the size of an entity, the more suitable a decentralized structure is (Management Study Guide, 2011). Hence it may be appropriate to think of pure centralization and pure decentralization as extreme points in a continuum and all possible organizational configurations are located on different positions in this continuum. Evidently, in reality there is no entity, which is exactly positioned in either of the two extremes. Therefore, the description of an entity as decentralized or centralized is relative to whether its location is close to either of these extremes. One predicament encountered here is related to the methods of accurately measuring the degree of centralization and decentralization. Attempts to address this problem concentrated mainly on fiscal power and to lesser extent policy and political powers (Hankla, 2008). Since the latter is difficult to measure accurately, transfer of fiscal power may offer a plausible though inexact measure of actual transfer of power.

The Taxonomy of Centralization-Decentralization Continuum

The idea of the continuum prompted traditional writings on the subject to classify the different points in the continuum into categories that signify different degrees of mixes of centralization and decentralization. These categories include centralization, concentration, de-concentration, administrative decentralization, territorial decentralization, functional decentralization and devolution (Taamna and Abdelwahab, 2005). Whereas, the first three categories represent points located more or less near the extreme of centralization in the continuum, the other categories are points poisoned differentially close to the other extreme of decentralization. Historically, concentration was the norm when the functions of government were limited to the preservation of internal and external security and the collection of taxes. De-concentration is a modified form of centralization and involves the transfer of certain administrative functions to department or field units with the central government retaining the actual decision making and overseeing powers (Taamna and Abdelwahab, 2005). These arrangement may include minimal or no citizens' participation in the form of formal elected bodies. In this arrangement, citizens' participation may be indirect through existing *de facto* traditional or tribal organizations (see for example, Elhussein, 1989).

On the other hand, in administrative decentralization the government delegates some of its functions on planning and resource allocation to field units. In this sense administrative decentralization is a form of decentralizing the administrative function from the central administrative units to local elected or non-elected units with the central government playing the role of a watch dog and retaining the privileges of supervision, audit and direction (Taamna and Abdelwahab, 2005). In territorial decentralization, central government powers in certain areas are transferred to autonomous units that are entrusted with performing certain local functions. This form of decentralization is embodied in the

French system of local administration as opposed to the British system of local government. Functional decentralization is exemplified by public corporations, which are specifically designed to carry out certain economic and commercial functions away from the control of central bureaucracies. However, these corporations are not completely free from central government supervision (Taamna and Abdelwahab, 2005).

Unlike all the above categories of decentralization, devolution or political decentralization is a constitutional arrangement in which government authorities- legislative, executive, and judicial- are constitutionally divided between central governments and states, republics, cantons or local governments. The extreme form of devolution may be found in federal states and in its extreme existence it is exemplified by con-federal arrangements (World Bank, 2011).

The Bureau for Development Policy, which is part of the Management Development and Governance Division in the United Nations Development Programme (UNDP) (September, 1997), developed, as part of its efforts to promote decentralized governance and strengthening capacity for people-centered development, a similar taxonomy of four types of decentralization. These are autonomous, subordinate, semi-autonomous, and divestment units. Subordinate types include concentrated and de- concentrated types of power transfer in which field units are subordinated to central government units. In this type the central government delegates limited policy, financial, and administrative functions to field units, which depend in their financial resources and inputs on central government allocations. This type also represents the least autonomous model of decentralization. Examples of this type include central government ministries' units in different territories of the state.

In the semi-autonomous type, field units enjoy limited autonomy in which central governments delegate partial authority and some functions to field units through laws and contracts. The generic model of power transfer in this type is based on delegation rather than devolution. Delegation of power in this type refers to the transfer of the government decision-making and administrative responsibilities in specified errands to semi-autonomous field institutions such as state-owned regional and urban development projects, under indirect central control. In delegation, central bodies retain responsibility and power to oversee the actions of lower units. By contrast the central government in the autonomous type devolves completely some of its functions to local units such as governorate, district municipality or other forms of local government and bestows on them legal identity as autonomous decentralized units.

Devolution of power in the autonomous type is different from delegation in the semi-autonomous type. For example, in delegation the central government unit responsible for budgeting delegates certain budgetary functions to a local government body. Nevertheless, the central unit retains the authority to revoke decisions taken by the field unit. Devolution is wider in scope and local units' responsibility increase in this case. On the other hand, in delegation the field units remain answerable even for the acts of subordinates to their superiors (Management Study Guide, 2011). Divestment is actually a recent concept, which refers to transferring power to units outside the formal governmental system and is not considered by some writers in public administration as related to decentralization *per se* (Taamna and Abdelwahab, 2005). Divestment takes place when certain government functions are deferred to voluntary, non-governmental organizations or private enterprises. In many cases divestment takes place through outsourcing or outright privatization of government entities and corporations. Table 2.1 below summarizes the major characteristics of different types of decentralization as related to the concept of governance. Mansour (2007 and 2008) distinguishes between two types of privatization: macro and micro privatization. Whereas macro privatization refers to transfer of public ownership to the private sector, micro privatization involves the use of business management tools, such as total quality management in the public sector.

2.1: Characteristics of Different Types of Decentralization

Type of Unit to Which Authority is Transferred	Aspects of Governance Transferred or Shared			Generic Pattern of Authority Transfer
	Political (policy or decision making)	Economic or financial resource management	Administration and service delivery	
Autonomous lower-level units	Devolution	Devolution	Devolution	Devolution
Semi-Autonomous lower-level Units	Delegation	Delegation	Delegation	Delegation
Sub-ordinate lower-level units or sub-units	Directing	Allocating	Tasking	De-Concentration
External (nongovernmental) units at any level	Deregulation	Privatization	Contracting	Divestment

The UNDP taxonomy is consistent with the World Bank (2011) four types of decentralization that includes political decentralization, administrative decentralization, market decentralization, and fiscal decentralization. Whereas political decentralization is related in the literature to democratization and self- government (Treisman, 2007) market decentralization is associated with privatization and divesting the public sector.

One justification for decentralization is that it is necessary to encourage popular participation in decision-making. Fiscal decentralization is imperative for meaningful popular participation. Therefore, administrative and fiscal decentralizations are complementary to political decentralization. In the absence of fiscal decentralization, political and administrative decentralization became disguised exercises in central control. Nevertheless, some economists believe that popular participation may be at variance with economic growth, which requires centralized control over scarce economic resources (Elhussein, 1983; Linder, 2009; Ezcurraand and Rodriguez-Pose 2009). Empirical research is not conclusive regarding this assertion. It equivocally illustrates that fiscal decentralization maybe in sometimes harmful and still in others positive to economic growth (Ezcurraand and Rodriguez-Pose 2009; Rodriguez-Pose Ezcurraand 2010). However, political scientists tend to view popular participation as an end in itself (Sabatier, 1995). Unfortunately, most decentralization policies in Africa, and especially Sudan, are involved in decentralizing legal powers (responsibility) without concurrent transfer of fiscal and economic power (authority) rendering them as classical examples of "responsibility without authority."

In many cases formal definitions and studies of centralization and decentralization, especially those undertaken by traditional management theorist and economist, fail to capture the political dimension involved in their practical application (See for example Al-Teraifi, 1987; Lalvani, 2002; Hankla, 2008; Ravallion, 2009). Since decentralization policies involve transfer of power, politics is inevitable in praxes of any type of decentralization even at the most basic levels of bureaucratic organization let alone a locality or a national government (Montero, 2001; Albino, 2006; Falleti, 2010).

The Socio-Economic Context in Sudan and the Need for Decentralization

The diversified socio-economic context of the Sudan, which is characterized by regional pressures, economic inequalities and ethnic and religious hybridity, led to significant demands for subnational recognition and participation, which have often challenged the centralized tendencies of both military and multi-party regimes in Sudan (Feqley, 2010). Sudan was the largest country in Africa. This sentence is expressed in the past tense because the information it conveys is no longer correct after the declaration of the Republic of South Sudan in the 9th of July 2011 forming the state number 193 in the United Nations. No doubt this tragic development is an outcome of misguided policies of decentralization and centralization in the Sudan. Nevertheless, the historical fact regarding the huge geographic area of the country is still relevant to the discussion of the policy of decentralization in the Sudan. With an area of 2.5 million square kilometers, Sudan, before the cession of its southern region, is the largest country in Africa. (It is now the second in Africa after Algeria and the third in the Arab World after Algeria and Saudi Arabia). Its strategic geographical location serves as a melting pot for Arabic and African cultures by linking the Arab world to Sub-Saharan Africa.

This complex configuration is compounded further by the fact that Sudan's shared borders with 9 Arab and African countries thereby dividing different ethnic groups across its political boarders and adding a complex myriad of different ethnic composition. This geographical fact made the country the most diversified country in Africa. In the North the country is populated by Nubian and Arab races with Arabic as the main language of communication. In the West, Bedouin Muslim Arab tribes coexist with numerous Muslim African tribes. The South is populated by predominantly Christian and pagan African tribes. The East contains a mixture of Arabic and African tribes. This mosaic structure of races and religion is made more complex by the hybrid of languages and local dialect diversity. Within each race numerous tribes with different cultures, traditions and dialects coexist. Consequently, the country lives under racial, lingual, religious and political diversity. The different regions and localities enjoy a great diversity of cultures, ethnicities, resources and folkways. Religious and ethnic divides together with failed leadership have led to prolonged social strife in Sudan (Collins, 2008). This renders the management of the country from the capital Khartoum unfeasible and also explains the spread of the contagious civil strife in the Southern, the Western (Darfur) and the Eastern regions- the so-called marginalized regions (Jok, 2007).

Moreover, the divisive aspect of that diversity is further confounded by economic realities, which worked to polarize the so-called marginalized regions and flare the war against North-dominated central governments. Economically, the country is classified as among the low-income countries with an average per capita income of $300. In 2010 the country's score in the Human Development Index (HDI) of (0.505) positioned it at the rank of 139 out of 177 countries for which the index was calculated (Human Development Report, 2010). Despite the chronic deficiency of accurate data on levels of family consumption or income in money terms, Sudan has always suffered from high levels of poverty and unequivocal social inequality. In the last decades of the 20th century and the first decade of the 21st century, this rising trend of poverty and inequality has led to mounting rates of urbanization. For example, the 1993 census indicated significant increase in urban population from below 20% in 1956 to approximately 36% in 1993 (Census, 1993). The country Capital, Khartoum, received the majority of migrants to urban areas who settled in shantytowns encircling the major cities and especially Khartoum. A report on migration published in 1996 shows that Khartoum received daily approximately 1000 displaced migrants from different regions. Munzoul Assal (2008) noted this state of affairs;

(In) February 15, 2008 — Sudan is one of the fastest urbanizing countries in the world. Population figures show that the country was already 40% urbanized in 2005—and that figure excludes the displaced of Darfur and the large numbers of unregistered migrants and squatters in Khartoum. Darfur today is approximately one third urban, one third rural and one third displaced. Even with the most optimistic scenarios for peace and stability, the majority of Sudanese—including Darfurians—will soon be living in cities. This is a pathological urbanization—it is occurring without social integration.

Beside regional civil strife and political instability, the major factor behind this rising rates of urbanization is the concentration of government services in the Capital and main urban centers. Although Sudan's urban centers and cities are relatively better off than rural areas, significant inequality prevails even within these urban areas. The levels of urban poverty and inequality are expected to increase with the incidence of flooding, drought, conflict, displacement and civil strife in different regions leading to more migration to urban centers. A prominent Sudanese scholar from Darfur and a distinguished politician diagnosed the problem in the following terms:

> Therefore, if we want to look for the real causes behind this failure to bring security and political stability we should stop thinking in terms of democratic or non-democratic government or capitalistic-communistic bases. We should look at the basic socio-political and geographical structure of our country. It is there that we can find the reasons why we failed to achieve the security and stability we so badly need (Diriage, 2010).

In this context it is not astonishing at all that the demands of separatist movements in the South, Darfur, and the East, which claim to have been historically marginalized by the center, revolve around issues of division of authority and economic resources; that is decentralization. Although these socio-economic facts reveal the dire need for a decentralized polity, Sudan has remained, effectively though not legally, a unitary state with all ultimate powers effectively claimed by the institutions of the North-dominated central governments. With the exception of Ustadh Mahmoud Mohammed Taha (1909-1983) and his Republican Party, as well as the Sudanese Communist Party, most Northern elites and political parties failed to acknowledge the merits of decentralization for national unity. Whereas the Southerners' demands on the eve of independence for a federal system was seen by these elites as divisive and disruptive to national unity, (This was exemplified by the slogan "no federation in one natation, down…down colonization"), Taha swam against this current and advised outright federalism.

As early as 1955, before the formal independence of Sudan, Taha (1955), in acknowledgement of Sudan diversity and size, argued in a famous book entitled, *The Principles of the Sudanese Constitution,* for the adoption of a federal system in the Sudan. Taha's Federal proposal suggested the establishment of five self-governed states (*Wilaiyat* sing. *Willaiya*) comprising the middle, western, eastern, northern, and the southern regions: Nowadays, three of these regions represent the sources of conflict and civil strife in the Sudan. Each of these five *wilaiyat* were to be subdivided into two districts to be granted a degree of self-government limited only by its ability to practice it. From the outset the central government should work to qualify these states and districts to shoulder more power and be ready to devolve needed powers and authorities to them whenever they are ready. Self-government in each *wilaiya* was to be based on a hierarchy of village, city, districts and states elected councils. This constellation of councils at all levels was to be free in carrying out its responsibilities in accordance with the law with no or minimal interference from any of the other senior levels or the central government. The latter could interfere only in cases of necessities stipulated by the law. The importance of Taha's proposal to this chapter is that most post-independence polices of decentralization in Sudan have borrowed one or the other of its basic principles and proposals without proper acknowledgement of Taha's efforts. Unfortunately, these attempts appeared to be a futility as recent civil wars in the South, Darfur, and the East clearly illustrate (Prunier, 2008; Cockett, 2010). This led Diriage (2010), a Darfurian Politician, to conclude that:

> Over the past thirty years a number of attempts have been made to devise permanent constitutional arrangements for the Sudan which would secure peace, stability and economic progress. The most notable of them were the draft Constitutions of 1956 and 1957, and the Constitution of 1973 together with the Southern Province Self Government Act of 1972. They have been without success.

An Overview of the Legal Process of Decentralization Policies in Sudan

The legal process of decentralization in Sudan can be traced in four distinct phases. The first phase covers the period between 1889 and 1951. The second phase starts in the 1951 and ends by 1971. The third phase extends from 1971 to 1991 and the fourth phase covers the period between 1991 to the present. It is interesting that each of these phases has witnessed different types of political regimes and different elite political orientations and ideologies. The first phase represents the British colonial rule, which reigned until 1956 when the country gained its political independence. A multi-party system dominated by religious sectarianism continued until 1958 when it was overthrown by the first military coup d'état, which was subsequently overthrown by a popular uprising in 1964. The short lived previous sectarian multi-party system was revisited following the uprising in 1964 to be overthrown by the second military coup d'état in May 1969, which was again removed in 1984 by another popular uprising that reinstated the previous multi-party system. This last regime lived until 1989 when it was obliterated by a third military coup d'état in June 1989.

The legal unfolding of decentralization policies in the Sudan before and after independence travelled all the way from different types of centralization to different types of decentralization spanning almost all points in the continuum of centralization-decentralization and UNDP taxonomy. Legally speaking, the process of decentralization in the Sudan is embodied in a set of laws. The first law that provided for organizing central local relations was the Local Government Act of 1951, which mimicked the British system of local government. This act established two layers of government: central government and a web of local governments. The latter was categorized into five different hierarchical levels that determined the financial and administrative functions of each level. The first military rule (1958-64) supplanted the 1951 Act with the Provincial Administration Act of 1960. The latter introduced two apparatuses at the local level: a central government representative (always drawn from the Army), with a job title of director, and a local government representative with a job title of inspector. Both offices reported to the Ministries of Interior and Local Governments respectively. The chief goal of the system was to help overseeing local control and security and to facilitate central ministries operations in the provinces. It was a system of semi-autonomous de-concentrated administration. No effective popular involvement was engrained in the system.

A major shift in the legal process of decentralization occurred in 1972 when the second military rule (1969-1984) introduced the People's Local Government Act of 1972. This Act repealed the 1951 and the 1960 Acts and established two-tier system that provided for a Peoples Executive Council at the provincial level. The Regional Local Government Act later replaced this system in 1980. The Constitution of 1973 was amended to incorporate the new system and former provinces were integrated to form five regions in the North and one in the South. Consequently, the country administration consisted of three levels: national, regional, and local. The latter consists of the local councils established by the previous Peoples Local Government Act of 1972. The regions became formally autonomous legal entities with legal personality, budgets and elected legislative councils (Taamna and Abdelwahab, 2005). However, in cooperation with the parallel units of the sole governing party, the Sudanese Socialist Union (SSU), the system proved to be a machine for control rather than popular participation. The regime also employed functional decentralization and created a hybrid of public corporations. However, after President Nemairy's (1969-1985) sudden decision to divide the Southern Region into three autonomous regions, the Civil War broke out again bringing the whole system down in a popular uprising in April 1985.

The short-lived multi-party system (1985-89) contributed little to decentralization efforts and was sooner ousted by the third military coup d'état in June 1989. In its first Republican Decree of 1991, the new regime adopted a federal system of government. This trend was consolidated in a series of decrees and laws of local government in 1995. Accordingly a two-tier system of government was established consisting of federal and state levels. Finally, the new Constitution of 1998 added a web of local government and neighborhood committees controlled by the National Congress (NC), the dominant governing party.

The new system is not very dissimilar from the previous regional government system. Like the previous system, the ruling party utilized the new system to control the localities as machines of mass mobilization. Although, the Constitution of 1998 transformed the system of governance in the Sudan from regional autonomy to federal governance (Taamna and Abdelwahab, 2005), localities were effectively under the control of central elites through the nexus of local councils, neighborhood committees and the NC units at different levels. Moreover, the government experienced intensive efforts of divestment using extensive privatization, deregulation, and outsourcing combined with abhorrent levels of corruption. The dynamic operation of the different phases of the process of decentralization in the Sudan is discussed below to show how the formal legal beautiful shapes of decentralization policies were defiled by unhealthy politics and extensive political mudslinging.

The Colonial Legacy: De-concentration through Sub-Ordinate Lower- Level Units

Robert Collins (2008), unveils Sudan's history in two hundred years to argue that many of the present problems have been woven in its past. Sudan was under Turkish rule as part of the semi-autonomous Egyptian monarchy until 1885 when the Mahdist revolution ousted the Turks and established a fundamentalist Islamic rule that survived until 1899. The British recaptured the Sudan from the Mahdist Regime, in 1899 in the name of the Khedive of Egypt. Britain signed with Egypt the Condominium Agreement that provides for joint British-Egyptian administration of the Sudan. According to the Agreement the British Queen nominates the Governor General of Sudan to be appointed by the Khedive of Egypt. Consequently, the Governor General was in all instances selected from British personnel (Collins, 2008). Under the Governor General at the center there were three Secretaries responsible for all governmental functions and reporting to the Governor General. Those are the Administrative, Financial, and Judicial Secretaries. The three secretaries were always drawn from British personnel. However, since Egypt itself was under direct British influence, the latter effectively ruled the Sudan by proxy to the Khedive from 1899 until independence in 1956. Hence, Sudan was not in strict legal terms a British Colony; it was part of the Kingdom of Egypt.

The *zeitgeist* (sprit of the time) of this era is: control through the existent tribal patron-client networks and indirect limited popular participation based on the infamously pragmatic British doctrine of indirect rule This doctrine was guided by two principles; these are cost-effective administrative system and effective control of the people. Cost-effectiveness led them to device a very simple military-like bureaucracy and to divide the country into nine *mudeeriyat* (governorates), which represents the central administration in the localities. On top of each of these governorates there was a *mudeer* (governor) reporting to the Administrative Secretary who was a direct subordinate to the Governor General in Khartoum. The governorates themselves were subdivided into small inspectorates called *markaz* (center) with a British inspector at the top. Subordinates of Inspectors were drawn at first from Egyptian cadres and few Sudanese. Following a pro- Egyptian rebellion of the Sudanese military officers in 1924, all Egyptian personnel were expelled from the Sudan and henceforth all subordinate administrative cadres were drawn from the graduates of Gordon Memorial College, which was established in 1909 by the British rulers to man the colonial bureaucracy.

The imperatives of control led the British to reinvent the system of tribal rule. To achieve effective control and reduce the costs of administration, the British facilitated the then existing tribal system and consolidated it in the form of the so-called "native administration," which survived until 1996 when it was abolished by the first military coup d'état (Nemairy's regime). The system of native administration was a target of attack to the nationalist movement, led by Gordon Memorial College graduates, following the establishment of the Graduate Club in 1935. The nationalist saw the system as a colonial device to keep the educated class away from the political administrative affairs of the country. Tribal chiefs became the local agents for the colonial central government and were

36

granted tremendous powers in the local affairs of their tribes. They were entrusted with administrative and judicial functions including collecting taxes and presiding over tribal courts. Ironically, by designing this system for the Sudan, the British colonial rulers abandoned their tradition decentralized local governments to the more centralized Continental-French system of local administration. However, on the eve of political independence, the British rulers issued the Local Government Act of 1951, which was designed along their local government traditions. Notwithstanding this fact, the new local government system served to institutionalize the previously informal system of native administration: tribal chiefs became councilors. It is worth noting here that the patron-client relationships between tribal chiefs and their allowed limited degree of popular participation. Before independence, the British modified their system of rule and implanted in the Sudan a Westminster political system and a Whitehall administrative system. Like in other African countries, The The Sudan's soil proved to be too hot for the two implanted systems.

The Multi-Party Systems: Fiascos of Fragmented Decentralization

It is worth noting here that the Sudanese nationalist movement evolved around the two Condominium powers, Britain and Egypt, and clustered later into two major movements with two contrasting schemes for independence: the pro-independence and Unionist schemes. Whereas the Unionist political parties, the predecessors of the present Democratic Unionist Party (DUP), supported union with the Egyptian monarchy, the pro-independence Umma (Nation) Party supported the establishment of a Sudanese monarchy led by the Mahdi son; closely tied to Britain. The popular base of the two parties was derived from the two major religious sects: the Khatmiya, led by Almirghani family, and the Ansar, led by the Mahdi family; this explain the sectarian nature of post-independence political activities. The only political party, which then called for complete independence of Sudan from both Egypt and Britain is the Republican Party (later renamed the Republican Brothers) led by Ustadh Mahmoud Mohammed Taha. Two other small ideological parties were formed: the Sudanese Communist Party and the Muslim Brotherhood, the predecessor of the Islamic National Front, which took over political power following a *coup d'etat* in June 1989. These parties, together with the Labor Movement and small Sothern and Nubian parties represented the major active actors in the three short-lived Sudanese multi-party systems.

The experiences of the three multi-party systems (1953-1958; 1964-1969 and 1985-1989) were not at all impressive. With regard to local government and decentralization, their contributions were minimal. The three systems, dominated mostly by religious sectarian politics, looked with awe to demands of decentralization in the form of a federal system mainly originating from the Southern Region. The first multi-party system 1953-1958, which was dominated by religiously sectarian type of politics, was eventually overthrown by a military coup d'état in 1958. The October Revolution of 1964 successfully displaced the first military regime and replaced it by a short-lived technocratic civilian government. The sectarian political party leaders prematurely overthrew the technocratic

37

civilian government in less than a year.

The 1965 national elections reinstituted the previous sectarian multi-party system, which lasted for less than five years before it was ousted by the second military coup d'état led by Major General Nemairy (May Revolution) in May 1969. The latter ruled for 16 years before it was also overthrown by a second popular uprising in April 1984 (April Uprising). An interim government summited by a self-appointed military council and a Civil Cabinet was formed. The mandate of this interim government, which lasted for one year, was to prepare the country for popular elections, which again reinstated the old sectarian multi-party systems. The present Islamite military government of Omer Elbashir in in June 1989 saw no hope in sectarian multi-party systems.

The political activities of the multi-party regimes concentrated on national government and ignored questions of central-local relations. They mostly operated through the inherited systems from previous regimes. In fact, serious attempts were espoused by the last multi-party regime to revive the system of native administration after being abolished by the May Regime in 1969 (Elhussein, 1987). Treatments of instability in the South, which started in 1955, were left to the Army. Negotiations with Southern rebels, especially in the third multi-party system, were aborted by national mudslinging, political maneuvers, and electoral competition. Therefore, the experiences of the multi-party systems regarding the policies of decentralization can be summarized as fiascos of fragmented centralization. Whereas the government operations and activities were concentrated in the Khartoum, the lack of communication and size of the country, civil wars, and ethnic diversity kept most areas outside the effective control of the central government. Ironically, it is the periods of military rule that witnessed real, albeit, unsuccessful attempts at decentralization to address unrest in the marginalized regions.

Military Rule and Drives for Control and Participation

Military rule in the Sudan, lacking in popular bases, usually inclines toward centralization and control camouflaged by ambitious project of decentralization. Therefore, the two military regimes in the Sudan (Nemairy's May Regime 1969-1984 and Elbashir's government 1989-until present) were the ones, which were forced to decentralize power, and also created more chaos and instability. Policies of decentralization in the forms of autonomous regional government for the South or formal federalization of the political systems emerged as tools for controlling localities and mass mobilization to promote the popularity of the regime in Khartoum.

This opaque conclusion is relevant to Nemairy's People's Local Government and regional government as well as the present regime policies of local government and federalization. These policies ultimately led the country to disintegrate into two separate countries by the Declaration of the Independence of the Republic of Southern Sudan in July 9 2011. In fact, the decentralized systems of Peoples' Local Government (PLO in 1972), Regional self-government (1980) adopted by Nemairy's regime and the federalization policy (1998) adopted by the present military regimes, have been forced on the two regimes by international pressures including geographical and political circumstances. In fact, the two regimes did defile their decentralization policies to serve their own interests in centralizing political power in the hands of the ruling elites in Khartoum.

Sudan has experienced a plethora of different types of governments and political ideologies. Political instability has been the norm in Sudan since its independence from Britain in January 1956. The country has witnessed a series of continuous civil wars and political turmoil (Johnson, 2003). On the eve of its independence a bloody civil war broke out between the Southern region of the country and the North. After substantially damaging episodes and massive collateral havocs the war stopped in 1972 after the signing of the Addis Ababa Accord (AAA) between the Southern rebels and the central government of the May regime (Nemairy's regime 1969-1984). After ten years of fragile peace, the civil war broke out again in 1983 following the decision of Nemairy to annul the backbone article of the AAA, which established self-government in the South as a unified and autonomous region. In outright violation of the Accord, the central government acted without the consent of the Southerners and decided in 1983 to divide the Southern region into three autonomous regions.

The present Islamite regime inherited the Sothern civil war, but successfully added new hot spots of bloody civil wars at Darfur in Western Sudan and the Eastern regions. The major driving forces that fuel these wars are the aspirations of local people for equal shares from the country's wealth and self-government. The three regions are actually the most underdeveloped with no real local participation in policy making in governance. It is the contention of this author that the problem of political instability and civil wars in the Sudan are closely associated with the issues of power and resource, i.e. centralization and decentralization. These issues have become later the focal points in negotiations between all regional rebels and different regimes in Khartoum.

Nemairy's Semi-Autonomy for Lower Level Units: The Myth of Participation

Nemairy's regime took over power in May 1969 and appeared at the outset wearing a socialist cloak showed at first sympathetic concerns for the Southerners demands for self-rule and decentralization of political power. Therefore, motivated by its leftist orientation, the first move of the regime was to abolish the system of native administration. After an aborted military coup in 1972, led by the communist members in the revolutionary council, the regime made a 180 degrees shift toward the right (Elhussein, 1983). The regime was then dominated by intellectual pragmatists, Nasirites (pro President Nasir of Egypt) and Arabist factions (Niblock, 1974). Accordingly, and as a result of the declining popularity of the regime after 1972, the government established the Sudanese Socialist Union (SSU) as the sole political party and adopted in 1972 and 1973 three major schemes of decentralization: (1) the Peoples Local Government Act (1972) and regional autonomy for the South (1972); and (2) regional autonomy for the whole country (1980); and (3) the Constitution of 1973.

The Constitution of 1973 described the Peoples Local Government Councils as institutions of local government devised to encourage popular participation and to shorten the administrative shadow of the center. However, the actual praxis of the system unveiled the heavy hand of the center, which determined and closely oversaw the activities of the sub-national entities by denying them real fiscal decentralization. The Province Commissioners, who were appointed by the President from the cadres of the SSU and answerable to the President, were utilized to subject the Local Councils to detailed fiscal control and intervention from Khartoum. Moreover, the Peoples Local Governments established in the Northern Region were deprived of the needed resources to shoulder the responsibilities bestowed on them.

Administratively, the local councils were kept under the detailed control by the Ministries in Khartoum through the Province Commissioners and the tight political grip of the SSU local units. Although the PLO provided for an elected Provincial Executive Council, the Commissioner and the field SSU units directly controlled the council. The interesting development here was the domination of the old tribal chiefs, now transformed into merchants, and local merchants over the operation of local councils. The regime permitted the tribal chiefs come-back after the success of the latter to resist and sabotage central government activities in their tribal domains and localities (Elhussein, 1983). In 1980 the whole system of PLO was brought under the Regional Autonomy Act of 1980 without any significant changes.

As a result of the devastating civil war in the South and international pressure, the laudable Addis Ababa Agreement of 1972, forced Khartoum to concede a greater measure of autonomy to the Southern Provinces by considering the Southern Provinces as a unified entity. Initially, unlike the Peoples' Local Government units in the North, the agreement provided for wider powers for the new autonomous entity and endowed it with more resources. These new arrangements for the South were recognized in the Constitution of 1973. However, despite the agreement and the constitutional arrangements, the actual implementation of the agreement unveiled the intentions of Khartoum to deprive the agreement of its beef. This was evident in the subordination of the Southern government by the central government in Khartoum and the violation of the agreement by the president himself. The president moves and arbitrary decisions from 1980 onwards support this conclusion. Contrary to the agreement stipulations, the President dissolved by a republican decree in 1980, 1981 and 1983 the elected Southern Assemblies and Governments. Moreover and following the discovery of oil in the South, Khartoum government attempted to change the boundaries of the Southern Provinces. Finally, this trend culminated in the President arbitrary Decree of 1983 that restored the South to the pre-Addis Abba Agreement status by dividing the Regions into three autonomous Regions.

These violations attest to the real central government intentions behind its declared goals of decentralization and regional autonomy. Despite the fact that formal goals of decentralization policies, as expressed in the Constitutions, agreements and declared laws and regulations, vowed to provide for popular participation and self-government, the praxes of these policies have proved the lack of the political will to respond to the desires and needs of ordinary people in both the North and South.

The best example of lack of efficiency and lack of responsiveness to the needs of the regional people are demonstrated by the fact that the previous Government refused to admit that there was famine in the Sudan until early 1985 when the Governor of Darfur had already submitted a comprehensive report to the Government in Khartoum and to all embassies and international organizations as early as October 1983. Even after admitting that there was famine in the country, the Government played an insignificant role in making sure that the food that was given to the country by the world reached the hungry people in the Western and Eastern part of the country (Diriage, 1989).

The result of all this, is to enhance the burgeoning seeds of mistrust and the situation deteriorated to trigger the revival of civil war in the South and dissatisfaction in all other marginalized regions with a form of government, which is so lacking in stability, efficiency or responsiveness to the needs of their peoples. To add oil to fire and to achieve central control by terror, President Nemairy declared in September 1983 the application of Islamic Law (Sharia) in all parts of the country. The application of the Sharia Law intensified the war in the predominantly Christian and pagan South. This Law, which is congruent with the Islamite orientations of other sectarian political parties in Sudan, was adamantly opposed, from a modernized Islamic perspective, by the Republican Brothers, led by Ustadh Taha, (who dubbed this Law as September Laws) as endangering national unity and non-Islamic. Consequently, the government in January 18, 1986 publicly executed Taha. This abhorrent incident, together with atrocities committed under the umbrella of the September laws, ignited a popular uprising in the North in March-April 1985 that led to the demise of Nemairy's regime.

The May Revolution regime was succeeded by the third short-lived multi-party system (1985-89). The coalition governments under this system indulged in political wrangling and indecision regarding the Southern civil war and paid little attention to issues of decentralization and local government. In fact, they attempted to revive the defunct system of native administration (Elhussein, 1987). Shortly after the leader of the Unionist Democratic party reached an agreement with the Southern Peoples' Liberation Movement (SPLAM) in the South, political power was taken over by the third military coup d'état led by Major General Omer Elbashir on behalf of the National Islamic Front (NIF) led by Dr. Hassan Turabi: the National Salvation Revolution (NSR). The NIF was adamantly against the agreement because an agreement was reach in it to abolish September laws: the mantra of the Islamite movement. Consequently, the military faction in the movement engineered and carried out the successful military coup that aborted the third multi-party system.

Devolution and Divestment: Autonomy, Decentralization and Diversity

Major Elbashir's NSR in 1989 brought to the fore an Islamite elite. The new regime espoused a clear commitment to establish an Islamite rule and applied the Sharia Law to the whole country. This development shed more new oil to the already flaring civil war in the South. The civil war, which was conceptualized under previous regimes as a civil strife between rebellious southern groups and the central government, became under the new Islamite government a sacred *jihad* (holy war) against Southern *kafirs* (non-believers) (Johnson, 2003).

In the North the new regime introduced a new federal system to the whole country. According to this new system the country is divided into 27 *wilaiyat* (states) with a *wali* (governor) on top of them. The *wali* was granted the status of a cabinet minister and reported directly to the President. The *wilaiyat* were subdivided into *muhafazat* (governorates) toped up by a *muhafiz* (governor). The *muhafazat* (governorates) were in turn subdivided into *baladiyat* (municipalities) led by a *mu'atamad* (mayor). A nexus of Peoples Committees in villages and cities neighborhoods were established. Members and supporters of the National Congress (NC), the governing party, to oversee and promote support for the regime, manned all these institutions and different local councils are subjected to close supervision by party units and government bureaucrats. In move to weaken the President and his faction's grip over localities, the Turabi faction called for the direct election of *walis*. This factor, *inter alia*, led to the ousting of Turabi and his faction from government in famous rift in the NC.

The decentralization moves under this regime included extensive divestment efforts under the program of Economic Liberalization which, dismantle the public sector by privatizing and selling almost all government corporations, established by the May regime, to the regime supporters. Although the move of divestment was inspired by the global trend toward privatization, it was calculated to create a business class to enhance the regime popularity and establish strong constituency for the regime.

With pressure from the West and the African states of the organization of Intergovernmental Authority on Development (IGAD), the Islamite regime signed a Comprehensive Peace Agreement (CPA) in 2005 with the SPLM in Nifasha, Kenya. The CPA paved the way for the forging of an Interim National Constitution (INC) that distributed and divided power between a national unity government and a local self-ruled southern government. The INC and CPA, which were integrated in the Interim Constitution, acknowledged the need to provide for new governance arrangements to achieve peace and development. Thus, the CPA made decentralized governance its focal point to encourage devolution of central agencies powers and functions to serve the cause of decentralization. The CPA also provided for an Interim Constitution for Southern Sudan interim self-government. Accordingly, the South was given a self–government, headed by the leader of the SPLM. The Head of the Southern self-government also serves as first Vice President in the national government (ReliefWeb, 2011).

The interim constitution for Southern Sudan, together with the interim National Constitution, adopts clear provisions that established decentralized governance arrangements in Southern Sudan. These arrangements have organized decentralized governance in Southern Sudan in three layers. These include the layers of government of Southern Sudan, the state government, local government and local counties. These decentralized arrangements can be categorized under two headings: political decentralization and administrative decentralization. Political decentralization involved the formation of representative organizational and management structures; allocations of functional powers and participation of decision-making. Provisions were made to promote accountability and enhanced horizontal and vertical inter-governmental coordination (UNDP, 2006).

Administrative decentralization, on the other hand, involves devolving administrative decision making to the three layers of local government in the South, i.e. from the interim South government to states and from the latter to local governments. In their turn local governments assigned certain administrative functions to *Payams* and *Bomas* (traditional tribal authorities and structures). It also involves defining administrative/management and decision-making competencies across all levels of governance, functional allocations and responsibilities, and civil service. It also involves managerial and fiscal decision-making (UNDP, 2006). In practice, the SPLM government maintained firm grip on all levels of local government. The diversified nature of the ethnic Southern Region made it difficult to control the entire region effectively (Selassie, 2009).

However, the ambitious goal of decentralized governance in the North and even more in the South was effectively stymied by the weak capacity of the administrative system and the inefficiency of its two main national training institutes for civil servants. The Management Development Center (MDC) and the Sudan Academy for Administrative Sciences (SAAS), as demonstrated by an assessment study undertaken by UNDP in 2006 (UNDP, 2006). In co-operation with the Sudanese Government of National Unity, the World Bank agreed to carry out a project designed to decentralize public sector, and to assist in building its capacity to shoulder post CPA implementation. The project, which was entitled "*Decentralization and Capacity Building Project* (PSCAP), was funded by a Multi-Donor Trust Fund. The project officially began in 2008 by establishing a Project Implementation Unit (PIU) to oversee daily coordination and supervision of the project. These moves were complemented by a joint venture of UNDP and UK Department for International Development to enhance PSCAP aim of improved decentralization. The joint venture included activities of job design, job description, and specification as well as restructuring government ministries. It also indulged in capacity development process for the national training institutes; and provides the needed assistance that strengthens the operational capacity of the PIU (UNDP, 2010).

The most important and significant aspect of CPA is granting the South the right for self-determination at the end of the interim period. After a worldwide plebiscite in Sothern Sudan, in which the issue of separation from the North scored 98%, resulted in the emergence of Southern Sudan as an independent state. Finally, decentralization in the Sudan unfolds itself into disintegration.

Conclusion

The chapter starts by explaining some theoretical concepts of decentralization before delving to discuss the process of decentralization in the Sudan. Although ethnic and religious diversity in the country and its vast size indicate the necessity for decentralizing government and administration the trend has been always a reluctant central government to transfer power to sub-national units. The post-independence regimes adopted a plethora of political ideologies that covered all the shades of the political spectrum and ranged from right and left of center liberal/capitalist thought to leftist/socialist and ending with all shades of Islamic fundamentalism. However, the different post-independence regimes, and irrespective of their type or ideological orientations, were not able to endow the country with the needed political stability necessary for social and economic development. Some of the recent attempts to restore order achieved by the last military governments sustained short lived periods of stability before they were disrupted by their makers.

However, the Sudan was governed as a unitary country before independence and, despite a series of post-independence decentralization policies, remained effectively a unitary centralized state. In spite of abundant lip-service to the contrary, the center has always been reluctant to devolve real power and authority to flesh out popular participation of the marginalized areas to enable them to participate in policy making (See for example, Albino, 2006; Feqley, 2010). The solutions to address the problems of size and diversity have been sought first in the principles of administrative decentralization to the Provinces and, later, in the creation of Regions to which powers have been formally devolved. The application of the principle of administrative decentralization to the Provinces culminated in the establishment of Peoples Local Government in 1972. Regional Self Government was conceded to the Southern Region in 1972, following the Addis Ababa Agreement, to be annulled ten years later. The Regional Government Act of 1980 created regions out of the Northern Provinces, and powers devolved to the Regional Councils were actually found only on paper.

The inexorable trend since independence has been toward transferring some administrative functions to localities without decentralization of effective fiscal and economic decision-making power. In many cases these measures were dictated by political expediency rather than by deliberate intentions to satisfy legitimate aspirations of the ethnically and culturally diverse populations in those localities. In conclusion, the chapter contends that the reluctance to decentralize explains the incidence of civil wars and separatist tendencies in the country. This state of affairs resulted in separating the South from the North and expected to lead for more demands of separation by other marginalized regions in Darfur and the East.

References

Albino, O. (2006). *Power and democracy in the Sudan: How decentralization hurts*. Blooming-ton, Indiana: Authorhouse,

Al-Teraifi, A. A. (ed.). (1987). *Decentralization in Sudan*. Dryden, NY: Ithaca Press.

Bendell, T., Boulter, L. and Kelly, J. (1994). *Implementing quality in the public sector*. London: Pitman Publishing.

Cockett, R. (2010). *Sudan: Darfur and the failure of an African state*. New Haven, Connecticut: Yale University Press

Collins, R. O. (2008). *A history of modern Sudan*. London: Cambridge University Press

Colin M. and Murgatroyed, S. (1995). *Total quality management in the public sector*, Bucking-ham: Open University Press

Diriage, A.I. (1989). *A New political structure for the Sudan*. Published in the Proceedings of Bergen Forum on "Management of the Crisis in the Sudan: Some Basic Issues" 23-24 Feb-ruary, 1989. Retrieved on 26-April-2011 from: http://www.fou.uib.no/fd/1996/f/712001/backahme.htm.

Elhussein (1983). *Decentralization and participation in rural development: the Sudanese experi-ence*. Unpublished Ph.D. Thesis. Manchester: the Vitoria University of Manchester

Elhussein. A. M. (1989). *The revival of native administration in the Sudan: a pragmatic view*. Public Administration and Development, (Britain), 9 (4).

Falleti, T. G. (2010). *Decentralization and subnational politics in Latin America*, London: Cam-bridge: Cambridge University Press (reviewed by Maria C. Escobar-Lemmon. the Journal of Federalism.(2011)

Feqley, R. (2010). *Beyond Khartoum: A history of subnational government in Sudan*. Law-renceville, New Jersey: The Red Sea Press.

Hankla, C. R. (2008). *When is fiscal decentralization good for governance?* The Journal of Fed-eralism 39 (4) pp. 632-650

Jok, M. J. (2007). *Sudan: race, religion and violence*. London: Oneworld

Johnson, D. H. (2003). *The root causes of Sudan's civil wars*. London: James Currey Human Development Report, 2010. Retrieved on 1-May-2011 from: http://hdrstats.undp.org/en/countries/profiles/SDN.html

Kindleberger, C. P. (1996). *Centralization versus pluralism*. Copenhagen: Copenhagen studies in economics & management

Lalvani, M. (2002). Can decentralization limit government growth? A test of the Leviathan hy-pothesis for the Indian federation, *The Journal of Federation*, 32 (3) pp. 25-45

Lawton, A. and Rose, A. (1994). *Organization and management in the public sector*. London: PITTMAN Publishing.

Linder, W. (2009). On the merits of decentralization in young democracies. *The Journal of Federalism*, 40 (1) 1-30.

Mansour, A. M. E. (2007). Public policy and privatization: The case of the Qatari experience. *Public Administration and Development*. 27 (4) 283-91.

Mansour, A. M. E. (2008). The impact of privatization on the United Arab Emirates (UAE) federal public sector. *International Public Management Review* (IPMR) 9 (2)

Management Study Guide. (2011). *Centralization and decentralization*. Retrieved on 1-May-2011 from: http://www.managementstudyguide.com/centralization_decentralization.htm.

Niblock, T. C. (1974). A New political system in the Sudan. *African Affairs*, 73(293).

Munzoul Assal (2008). *Urbanization and the future of Sudan*. Retrieved on 1-May-2011 from: http://www.ssrc.org/blog/category/darfur/

Osborne D. and Gaebler, T. (1992). *Reinventing government*. New Delhi: Prentice-Hall of India

Prunier, G. (2008). *Darfur: A 21st century genocide*, NY: Cornell University Press

Ravallion, M. (2009). *Decentralizing for federal antipoverty program: A case study for China*. The World Bank Economic Review, Published by Oxford University Press on Behalf of the International Bank for Reconstruction and Development. pp. 1-30.

ReliefWeb, (2011), *Sudan's other war*. Retrieved on 26-April-2011:from: http://reliefweb.int/sites/reliefweb.int/files/reliefweb_pdf/briefingkit-623cb28ffd7a0c9a44c97b20c65fdc68.pdf on 26-4-2011.

Republic of the Sudan, *the (1993) Census*. Khartoum: Sudan

Republic of the Sudan, *the (1973) Constitution*. Khartoum: Sudan

Republic of the Sudan, *the (1998) Constitution*. Khartoum: Sudan

Rodriguez-Pose, A. and Ezcurra, R. (2009). *Decentralization of social protection expenditure and economic growth in the OECD. The Journal of Federalism* 41 (1) 146-157.

Rodriguez-Pose, A. and Ezcurra, R. (2010). Is fiscal decentralization harmful for economic growth? Evidence from the OECD countries. *Journal of Economic Geography*1-25.

Rodden, J. (2004). Comparative federalism and decentralization: on meaning and measurement. *Comparative Politics*, 36 (4). 481-500.

Sabatier, P. A. (1995). Political science and public policy. In Stella Z. Theodoulou and Matthew, A. C. (eds.). *Public policy: The essential readings*. Upper Saddle River, New Jersey: Prentice Hall.

Selassie, Z. G. (2009). *Southern Sudan: Volume II: Final Report, October 2009*. Retrieved on 26-4-2011 from: http://www.goss-online.org/magnoliaPublic/en/ministries/Finance/Non-Oil/mainColumnParagraphs/0/content_files/file/Non-Oil%20Revenue%20Study%20of%20Southern%20Sudan.pdf.

Taha, M.M. (1955). *The principles of the Sudan's constitution*. Omdurman, Sudan: the Republican Brothers. Retrieved on 29-July-2011 from: http://www.alfikra.org/book_view_a.php?book_id=4,

Tamna, M. M and Abdelwahab, S.M. (2005). *Alhukum Al Mahlli fi Alwatan Al Arabi and Itigaahat Al Tutweer (Local Government in Arab Nation and Approaches to Development)*, Amman: the Arabic Organization for Administrative Development

Tinbergen, J. (1954). *Centralization and decentralization in economic policy*. Amsterdam: North Holland Pub. Co

Treisman, D. (ed.). (2010). *The Architecture of government: rethinking political decentralization*. New York: Cambridge University Press. (reviewed by Robert Agranoff, The Journal of Federalism 38(4) pp. 739-741)

United Nations Development Programme (UNDP). September, (1997). *Management Development and Governance Division, Bureau for Development Policy, Decentralized governance programme: Strengthening capacity for people-centred development*. Retrieved on 26-April-2011 from: http://www.pogar.org/publications/other/undp/decentralization/decenpro97e.pdf.

United Nations Development Programme (UNDP) (2006). *On centralization in Sudan*. Retrieved on 26-4-2011from: http://www.sd.undp.org/doc/governors%20forum/Decentralized%20Governance%20FAST%20FACTS%20SHEET%20Rev%20Sept%202008.pdf.

United Nations Development Programme (UNDP) (2010). *Support to public sector, Decentralization and capacity building project (PSCAP)*. Retrieved on 26-April-2011 from: http://www.sd.undp.org/projects/dg15.htm.

World Bank. Decentralization Thematic Team. (2011). *What is decentralization?* Retrieved on 26-April- 2011from: http//www.ciesin.colombia.edu/decentralization/English/General/Different_forms.html.

Chapter Three

CENTRALIZED COMMITMENT VS. DECENTRALIZED ENFORCEMENT: THE POLITICS OF COPYRIGHT PROTECTION IN CHINA

Hong Pang

Key words: decentralized enforcement, China, copyright protection, local governments, legislation

Since the early 1980s, the central government of the People's Republic of China has made a series of commitments to protect intellectual property rights (IPRs), bilaterally with the United States and multilaterally by signing several international agreements. Following these international commitments were a series of legislation and policy-making efforts by the national legislature and bureaucracy, which have made Chinese intellectual property protection laws and regulations consistent with the international standards specified in the Trade-Related Aspects of Intellectual Property Rights Agreement (the TRIPs Agreement). However, until today, China is still criticized heavily and persistently for its inadequate protection of IPRs. Using the principal-agent theory, this article will examine how the decentralized structure of enforcement, both administrative enforcement and civil enforcement, compromises the effectiveness of implementation of those international commitments in copyright protection.

Centralized Commitments and Legislation

The Chinese odyssey of providing protection for copyright is largely a story of making international commitments by the central government, implementing those commitments, being detected inconsistent and unsatisfactory, making more international commitments, and implementing new commitments. This cycling process has been propelled by the central's desire to further integrate with the world economy, the exogenous incentives to admit China into the international economic regime, and the foreign pressures to strengthen IPR protection. The initial impetus to legislate for copyright protection in China came from the need of normalizing and sustaining trade relationship with the U.S. since the end of 1970s. Chinese central government made a general promise to "take appropriate measures" to protect copyright[1] in its Bilateral Trade Agreement and Memorandums of

Understanding with the U.S. and finally performed this promise by promulgating *the Copyright Law* in 1990. Then it was in order to address the deviations of *the Copyright Law* from the international standards, China issued *the Regulations for Implementing the Copyright Law* and *the Regulations for Computer Software Protection* in 1991 as well as *the Regulations for the Implementation of International Copyright Treaty Provisions* in 1992. China also quickly acceded to *the Berne Convention for the Protection of Literary and Artistic Work*s in 1992 and *the (Geneva) Convention for the Protection of Producers and Phonograms against Unauthorized Duplication of their Phonograms* in 1993.

Thereafter, under the close surveillance of foreign industry associations (especially those from the U.S.), with the looming threat of trade sanctions by the U.S. under the Special 301[2], with the bait of admitting China into the World Trade Organization (WTO) (before 2001[3]) and the pressure of being found non-complying with the TRIPs Agreement in front of the WTO Dispute Settlement Body (DSB) (after 2001), the Chinese government and legislature have made continuous efforts to strengthen copyright protection. *The General Provisions of Civil Code* (1986) confirmed IPRs as one of the civil rights while *the Criminal Law* (1997) added criminal penalties for copyright infringement on a commercial scale. *The Copyright Law* and the regulations for implementing it have been revised.[4] Six judicial interpretations (JIs, "*sifa jieshi*") related with copyright protection have been issued by the Supreme People's Court (SPC, "*zuigao renmin fayuan*").[5] A series of regulations and measures have been announced either by the State Council ("*guowuyuan*") or the National Copyright Administration of China (NCAC, "*guojia banquan ju*"), such as *the Regulations Regarding Transferring Cases of Suspected Crimes of the Administrative Law Enforcement Institutions* (2006), *the Measures for Administration Enforcement in Copyright* (1997, 2003 and 2009), *the Measures on the Payment of Remuneration to the Copyright Owners of Audio Products*" (2009), and *the Circular on the Use of Legal Software by Governments at all Levels* (2004).

After this series of legislating, revising, and clarifying, legislative protection for copyright has been significantly strengthened in China. Barriers to national treatment within the administrative enforcement system have been removed. The types of copyright infringements which are subject to administrative enforcement as well as the forms of administrative enforcement have gradually increased. It became possible for copyright holders to have judicial review of the final administrative decisions. Provisional remedies, such as preliminary injunctions, have been made available to copyright holders. The principles of collecting fines upon copyright infringement were stipulated and the maximum fines increased. Statutory damages became available, for any case in which actual damages cannot be determined. Use unauthorized software in a commercial environment has been made a civil liability. The monetary thresholds required for criminal prosecution have been lowered, a numerical copy threshold was added, and the measures of calculating the monetary value of infringing products were further specified. The copyright owner's rights has been extended, for example, to include the right of transmission over information network, and how the copyright laws and regulations would be applied in the copyright cases over information networks has been further specified.

In the past three decades, Chinese central government has made a series of international commitments to protect copyright and Chinese administration, legislature and judiciary have codified these commitments into laws, regulations and policies, which have been aligned with the key principles of the TRIPs Agreement. This centralized commitments and legislation and policy-making could have an impact on the IPRs enforcement in China since at least they provide the principles, standards and measures to enforce the rights. However, unfortunately, the authority and discretion of actual enforcement lie not in the hand of central policy makers and legislators, but in the hand of local enforcers. It is doubtful whether the local governments, with different interests to put into calculation, could have the same level of commitment as the central government.

Decentralized Enforcement

Administrative Enforcement

Administrative enforcement is public enforcement based on the public authority of various government agencies, in contrast with civil enforcement, which is private enforcement through individual civil actions in courts. Different from the IPR holders in other countries in the world, the IPR holders in China have highly depended on and continue depending on administrative bureaus and procedures as the primary means of enforcing their IPRs in China, despite the recent moves towards greater use of judiciary enforcement as discussed below. A comparative study by Dimitrov (2009) showed that administrative enforcement is disproportionately widely used in China to provide IPR enforcement, with as many as twelve different bureaucracies with IPR enforcement responsibility and with administrative cases outnumbering non-administrative ones by a hundredfold in 2004.[6] For instance, in the area of copyright protection, there are four major bureaucracies in charge of enforcement, which include the NCAC, the General Administration of Press and Publication (GAPP, "*guojia xinwen chuban zong shu*"), the Ministry of Culture (MOC, "*wenhua bu*"), and the State Administration of Radio, Film and Television (SARFT, "*guojia guangbo dianying dianshi zong ju*").[7]

Administrative enforcement has continuously been the most appealing means for IPR holders within the Chinese IPR enforcement system largely because it is relatively more cost-efficient, much quicker, and more morally consistent with the Confucian and Socialist ideology characterized with the Chinese culture, which emphasizes collective rights over individual rights,[8] than pursuing the pirates and infringers through courts. Comparing to the civil enforcement, which requires complainants to supply evidence, administrative enforcement carries the weight of government support, resources and authority. However, the continuing prevalence of piracy and infringement of copyright[9] still stands in a sharp contrast to the seemingly large number of enforcement agencies and cases and the popularity of administrative enforcement.

To solve this perplexing puzzle, we have to probe the nature of administrative enforcement, the decentralized structure of bureaucracies in charge of copyright enforcement, and the ensuing inefficiency resulting from local protectionism. Administrative enforcement is not familiar to the observers of IPR protection in the U.S., where IPR holders almost entirely rely on civil and criminal procedures for enforcement.[10] According to China's *Copyright Law*, administrative agencies could take actions, including "order[ing] the person to discontinue the infringement, confiscate[ing] his unlawful gains, confiscate[ing] or destroy[ing] the copies produced through infringement" and even "impose[ing] a fine", where "public rights and interests are impaired".[11] However, the contents of "public rights and interests" are never specifically defined and, furthermore, acting on behalf of "public rights and interests" sounds incompatible with the essence of private interests embedded in IPRs, although some government officials commented that "public rights and interests" could be understood to include "preserving the normal market order"[12] so that the private interests of protecting private IPRs could align with the public interests.[13]

In practice, this ambiguity leaves a huge leeway up to the enforcement authorities, especially the local ones, when they are acting to protect "private interests" in the name of serving "public interests". Once an IPR holder formally brings his or her complaint to the local administrative authorities, those authorities then solely control what action they can take. How would they act if the infringer is an enterprise who contributes a lot to the local economy and tax revenue? How would they act if the infringer is a state-owned enterprise (SOE) who is operating in a vital industry? How would they act if the infringer is a government bureau? How would they act if they face with an array of retailers carrying their small luggage of pirated CDs and DVDs and running into the alley upon a raid investigation, given that selling those products is only one of the limited options they have to make a living after being laid off as an aftermath of economic reform and depriving the very means could be a potential source of social instability? Apparently a lot of considerations, including those for economic development, tax revenue, social stability, have been factored into the calculation of "public interests" besides protecting privately-owned IPRs for the purpose of "preserving the normal market order". Given the fact that the power and the voice of indigenous innovators are still generally week in China, protecting private IPRs has hardly been given a substantial weight in the agenda of local governments. They can arbitrarily make a decision not to actively pursue a certain case, or to postpone or even suspend action on it, or to impose a negligible fine on the infringers.

The decentralized structure of bureaucracies in charge of IPR enforcement further worsens the inefficiency problem of administrative enforcement. Before we move on to the bureaucratic structure specifically for copyright enforcement, a literary sketch of Chinese bureaucracy warrants itself. As shown in Figure 1, the Chinese bureaucratic system follows a pyramid structure. Underneath the central government, there are four levels of local governments[14], which include provincial governments[15], prefecture governments[16], county governments[17], and township/village governments[18] lying from the top to the bottom. Each level is composed of certain numbers of smaller pyramids. At the center, the top of the small pyramid is the State Council and each cell at the bottom of the small pyramid represents a ministry, which is the functional unit within the central government. This structure of the central government is duplicated (although not completely, as shown in the copyright administration discussed below) at each lower territorial and administrative layer. At the local levels, the top of the pyramids is the local government leadership while each cell at the bottom of the pyramids now represents the functional unit called "bureau" at the corresponding local levels[19].

3.1: The Decentralized Structure of Copyright Enforcement Agencies in China

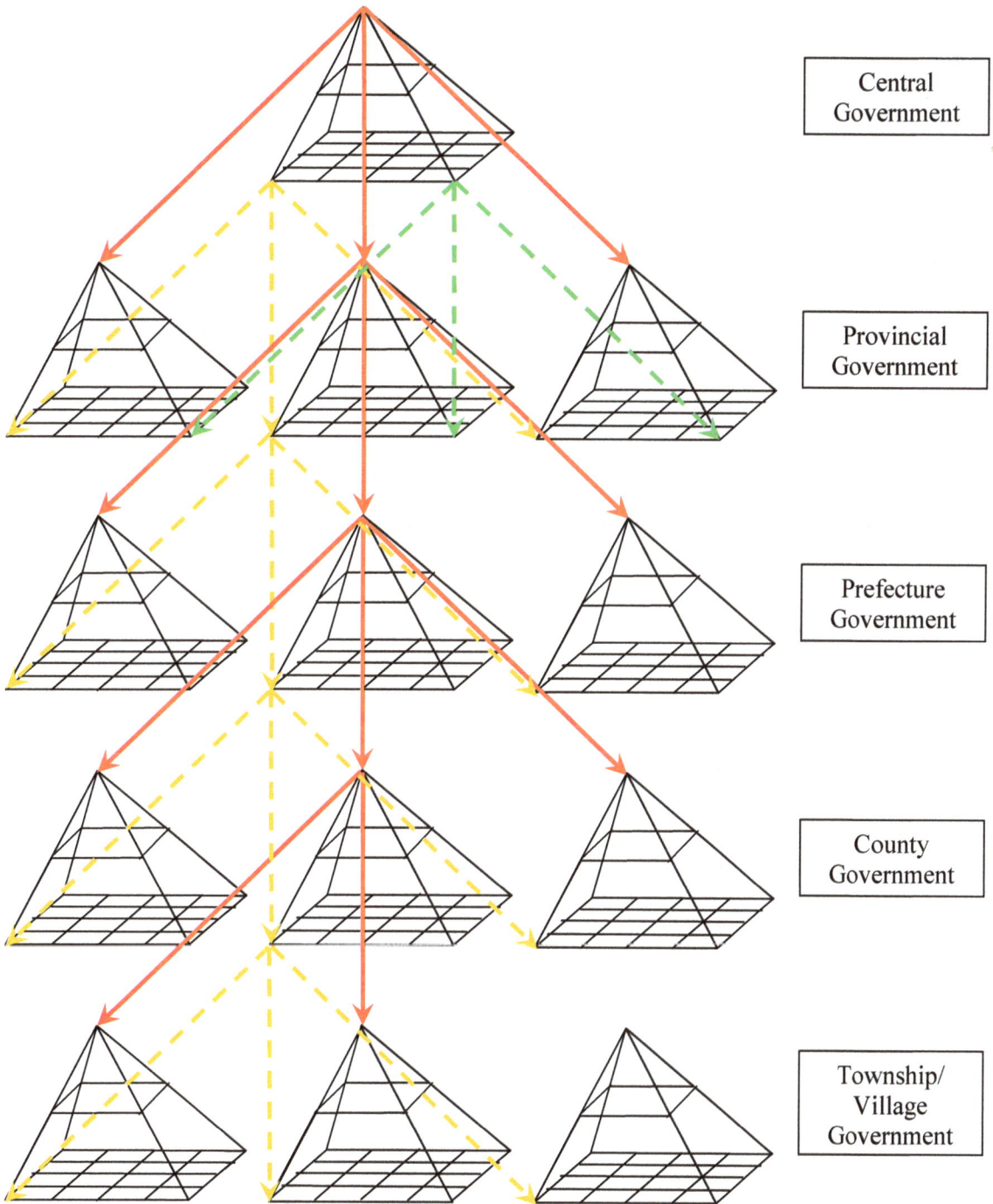

Within this pyramid structure, several rules of the game need to be followed. The rule No. 1 is that a government agency has no authority to enforce commands to the agency at its upper rank, nor can government agencies at the same rank issue orders to each other. The rule No. 2 is that a government agency at each rank can only issue orders to the government agency within its own jurisdiction, either territorial or functional, of one rank lower. Therefore, orders are issued along three different pathways vertically from the top to the bottom: (1) from the leadership at each layer to the leadership at one layer lower (represented by the red solid line connecting the tips of the pyramids across adjacent levels in Figure 1), (2) from the local leadership at each layer to the functional units within its territorial jurisdiction (roughly represented by the black solid line connecting the tip and the bottom cells of each pyramid in Figure 1), and (3) from the functional unit at a certain layer to the corresponding functional unit at one layer beneath it (represented by the dotted line connecting the bottom cells of the pyramids across adjacent levels in Figure 1). However, the orders along different pathways carry different weights. Given that the government leadership at a certain level has the authority to appoint or remove the leaders of the local governments of one rank lower as well as the directors of various functional bureaus within its own territorial jurisdiction while the functional departments at certain level has no authority to appoint or remove the directors of the functional departments of one rank lower, the first and the second pathways along which any order was issued are called "leadership relations" ("*lingdao guanxi*") with "binding orders" while the third one is called "professional relations" ("*yewu guanxi*") with "non-binding orders". That is exactly why they are represented by solid line and dot line respectively in Figure 1. Another thing worth to note is that although Figure 1 seems to suggest that the functional units at a certain level are of a higher rank than the government leadership at a lower level, they are actually of the same administrative rank. As a result, the functional units at a certain level cannot enforce commands the government leadership at a lower level.

Keeping this general picture in mind, let us take a look at how this bureaucratic structure and the rules of the game apply to the copyright enforcement agencies specifically. Among the four major bureaucracies of copyright enforcement mentioned above, NCAC and MOC are the mainstay. NCAC and its local subordinates seem to be the agency specialized in copyright management and enforcement. However, several loopholes have restricted the power and efficiency of NCAC. Firstly, although nominally NCAC (represented by the cell at the lower right corner of the top pyramid in Figure 1) is an agency enjoying the relationship of "one organization, two signboards" with GAPP, which is directly affiliated to the State Council[20], and therefore at the ministry rank, essentially it is only one of the departments ("*si*", department under a ministry) subordinate to GAPP. Similarly, the provincial copyright bureaus (PCBs, "*sheng banquan ju*") (represented by the cell at the lower right corner of the pyramids at the provincial level in Figure 1) are only one of the departments ("*chu*", department under a bureau) nestled within the provincial press and publication bureaus (PPPBs, "*sheng xinwen chuban ju*").

Secondly, NCAC itself does not have the manpower and the capacity to enforce copyright. Although NCAC has a department ("*chu*", department of a "*si*" under a ministry) for copyright enforcement[21], this department never has more than four personnel and, for two decades, the primary responsibility for copyright enforcement has rested with local officials. At the provincial level, each PPPB, which is sharing their title of "bureau" with PCB, has a department normally called the "Department of Copyright Management" (PDCM, "*banquan guanli chu*"). If you carefully read through the description of duties and responsibilities of these departments, you can easily find out that they emphasize more on the function of "management" rather than "enforcement". For instance, among the twelve responsibilities specified for the PDCM of Hebei Province, only four of them can be barely counted as for copyright "enforcement".[22] In another word, the officials in PDCMs are either not working full-time on copyright enforcement or the number of personnel working full-time on copyright enforcement is even smaller, given that there are only four to five people in total at the PDCMs.[23]

Thirdly, the copyright administration, even though it is subordinate to the press and publication administration and even though it mainly focuses on copyright management rather than enforcement, never extends to the lower levels of bureaucratic structure. Below the provincial level, the copyright administration (as well as the press and publication administration as its host bureaucracy) is largely subordinate to the cultural administration headed by the MOC at the center (represented by the cell at the lower left corner of the top pyramid in Figure 1) and the Departments of Culture at the provincial level (PDOCs, or "*sheng wenhua ting*", a functional unit of cultural affairs and industries at the provincial level, represented by the cell at the lower left corner of the pyramids at the provincial level in Figure 1). Although some prefectures [24] ever had their own independent copyright bureaus (along with the press and publication administrations as their host bureaucracies) before, most of these bureaus have been merged into a hybrid bureau called "Bureau of Culture, Radio, Film and Television, Press and Publication (Copyright)" at the respective prefecture (PBCRFTPPC, "*wenhua guangdian xinwen chuban (banquan) ju*", represented by the cell at the lower left corner of the pyramids at the prefecture level in Figure 1) since 2005.[25] The function of copyright management and enforcement is further fading out at the county level where the function is taken on by the hybrid bureaus called "Department of Culture and Sports" (CDOCSs, or "*wenti ju*") or "Department of Culture and Broadcasting" (CDOCBs, or "*wenhua guangbo ju*") at the county level (both represented by the cell at the lower left corner of the pyramids at the county level in Figure 1) and "culture station" at the township/village level ("*wenhua zhan*", represented by the cell at the lower left corner of the pyramids at the township/village level in Figure 1). This is exactly why the green dotted lines connecting the NCAC at the lower right corner of the top pyramid and the PCBs at the lower right corner of the pyramids at the provincial level in Figure 1 stop at the provincial level.

Then who is the enforcement team on the ground? It is the cultural market management units and cultural market investigation teams inside the cultural administration at each local level. These units include the Departments of Cultural Market (Management) at the provincial level ("*wenhua shichang (guanli) chu*") and the Divisions of Cultural Market Management at the prefecture and county level ("*wenhua shichang guanli ke*"). The cultural market investigation teams were all over the territory up from the provincial level down to the county level with the cultural market enforcement at the prefecture and county level as the main focus. These teams might carry different names such as "general investigation team" ("*jicha zongdui*"), "investigation team" ("*jicha dui*" or "*jicha dadui*"), or "investigation detachment" ("*jicha zhidui*") of cultural market (for simplicity, all abbreviated as ITOCMs).[26] These teams were in charge of copyright enforcement on the ground as a part of their functions given the fact that copyright administration almost did not reach below provincial level.

Since 2003, an institutional reform has swept these ITOCMs and still continues up to date. In this institutional reform, the function of copyright enforcement was deprived from the local copyright administrations[27] and transferred to the local ITOCMs at respective levels.[28] After the reform, these teams were renamed as "comprehensive administrative enforcement teams of cultural market" (CAETCMs, "*wenhua shichang zonghe xingzheng zhifa dui*"). The institutional reform helped the local ITOCMs to claim the authority over copyright enforcement which has been left out before and made them the exclusive entity of copyright enforcement at the local level.

Besides that, there is no significant change in copyright enforcement. "CAETCMs" are just another name of "ITOCMs", given that they are actually composed of the same group of personnel. CAETCMs still emphasize more on its enforcement function in cultural market rather than copyright protection, given that they were established on the basis of former ITOCMs, which were themselves spin-offs of the cultural market management units at each local level. These cultural market management units were originally entitled to supervise the "cultural market", which encompass any venue where cultural products are traded, such as bookstores, periodical vendors, audio-video retailers and wholesalers, cinemas and theaters, karaoke parlors, recreation centers, Internet café, crafts and fine arts galleries, and antique markets.[29] Apparently, some copyright-related products, such as software, are not a part of the cultural market. At the same time, cultural enforcement agencies are more enthusiastic in concentrating their fire on the cultural products with pornographic, antigovernment or antiparty orientation. Furthermore, these ITOCMs and CAETCMs are either administrated by the local cultural bureaus as one of their departments or directly subordinate to the local government. In any case, they are financed by the local governments at respective level.

To conclude, the NCAC, which is supposed to be the least influenced by local interests and economic and social considerations other than copyright protection given its own institutional agenda and interests, cannot effectively manipulate the behaviors of local enforcement teams and personnel. According to the principal-agent theory, the problem of slack agent is inherent by nature in any delegation relationship and can only be attenuated to some degree by using certain control mechanisms by the principal. However, as the principal of copyright enforcement, the NCAC is feeble in maintaining and wielding those controlling mechanisms upon the agent of copyright enforcement. Firstly, in order to enforce copyright on the ground, the NCAC has mostly relied upon the local cultural market enforcement teams (especially below the provincial level), who generally carry different institutional agendas and priorities in enforcement activities. Before the aforementioned institutional reform in which the function of copyright enforcement was deprived from the local copyright administrations and transferred to the local ITOCMs, copyright holders can either resort to the local copyright administrations (if there are) or to the local ITOCMs. However, after the institutional reform, the opportunity of "forum shopping" for the copyright holders disappears and so does the possibility of competition between different agents.[30] Secondly, although the NCAC can issue orders (although non-binding) to the PCBs and monitor their activities, it cannot easily and effectively do that upon the local cultural market enforcement teams, which essentially exist in a different functional jurisdiction from the copyright administration. What makes the situation even worse is the fact that copyright administration has been generally regarded as half-step lower in rank than press and publication administration and therefore cultural administration of the same level. Last but not the least; NCAC cannot effectively punish the slack behaviors of local cultural market enforcement teams. Besides the aforementioned difficulties resulting from functional jurisdiction and administrative rank, NCAC has no authority in determining personnel appointment and financial allocation for the local cultural market enforcement teams while the local governments do. Therefore it is not surprising to see that copyright enforcement is marginalized in local cultural market enforcement activities as long as the infringing products have nothing to do with pornographic, antigovernment or antiparty orientation. The lower the local enforcement teams along the bureaucratic structure, the more likely they sway toward the local interests under the financial and personnel control of the local government.

Civil and Criminal Enforcement

Although the current international IPR regime does not place any obligation upon countries, including China, to establish a special judicial system for IPR enforcement, China has made great efforts in institutional establishment in order to strengthen the adjudication of IPR cases in the past two decades. One such effort is to establish specialized IPR sections in Chinese court system to try all IPR cases since 1993. China has taken the initiatives to establish such specialized IPR sections for the purpose of improving the quality of adjudication of IPR-related cases and ensuring timely, consistent and quality application of IPR laws, especially considering that IPR-related cases are normally characterized with specialty and technicality and therefore require judges to have necessary scientific and technological knowledge and even knowledge of foreign languages. The specialized IPR sections were firstly established at several big cities at the coastal region, such as Beijing, Shanghai, Guangdong and Jiangsu, and then expanded throughout the country. The specialized IPR section at the Supreme People's Court was formally established in 1996.[31] Up to 2006, there had been 172 specialized IPR sections, 140 specialized IPR collegiate panels, and 1667 specialized IPR judges throughout Chinese court system, although most of them are located at the level of SPC, all Higher People's Courts (HPCs, "*gaoji renmin fayuan*"), and Intermediate People's Courts (IPCs, "*zhongji renmin fayuan*") in the capital of provinces and other large cities.[32]

Another effort in institutional establishment is to streamline the adjudication of IPR-related cases in the courts. Before, the newly established specialized IPR sections could only accept and hear all civil IPR cases but not the administrative and criminal IPR cases according to the instruction from the SPC. Since 2006, some of these specialized IPR sections have undergone judicial reforms called "three-trial-in-one" ("*sanshen heyi*"), which try to integrate all adjudication activities for civil, administrative and criminal cases together under the specialized IPR sections or the specialized IPR collegiate panels.

Despite all these efforts of institutional establishment, the deep-rooted institutional structure in which the judiciary resides has not changed much throughout the years and has kept undermining its independence and efficiency to protect the rights of IPR holders. In this institutional structure, courts heavily depend on local governments and people's congresses for operation funding, salary and benefits, as well as appointment and promotion. Although courts are also subject to the instructions, activity reviews, and personnel reviews by the courts at higher level, especially the SPC, this vertical supervision and management is thwarted by the horizontal supervision and management by the local polity.

As shown in the Figure 2, there are four levels of courts in China: the SPC, HPCs, IPCs, and Basic People's Courts (BPCs, *jiceng renmin fayuan*).[33] HPCs are provincial-level courts in the capital of provinces, directly administrated municipalities, and ethnical autonomous regions. IPCs are those established for several districts inside a directly administrated municipality or those established in municipalities and prefectures inside a certain province or ethnical autonomous region. BPCs are those established in counties and urban districts. Specialized IPR sections, if there is such a section in a certain court, are one of the four sections of civil division.[34] Courts at each level are financed by governments at the same level. They depend on local governments for funding to cover the cost of court buildings, office supplies, computers and other equipment. Judges' and staffs' welfare and benefits, such as housing, salaries, bonuses, and insurances also come from financial budget of the local governments. This financial dependence makes courts penetrable to the interference of the local government officials into the adjudication of cases, including IPR-related cases, especially when the cases are administrative litigation or related with local companies in commercial disputes, and implicit or explicit pressure from the local governments upon the judges to rule in favor of administrative agencies or local companies who are of significant impact on the local economy.

3.2: Institutional Structure of China's Court System and Its Relationship with the Legislature and the Administration

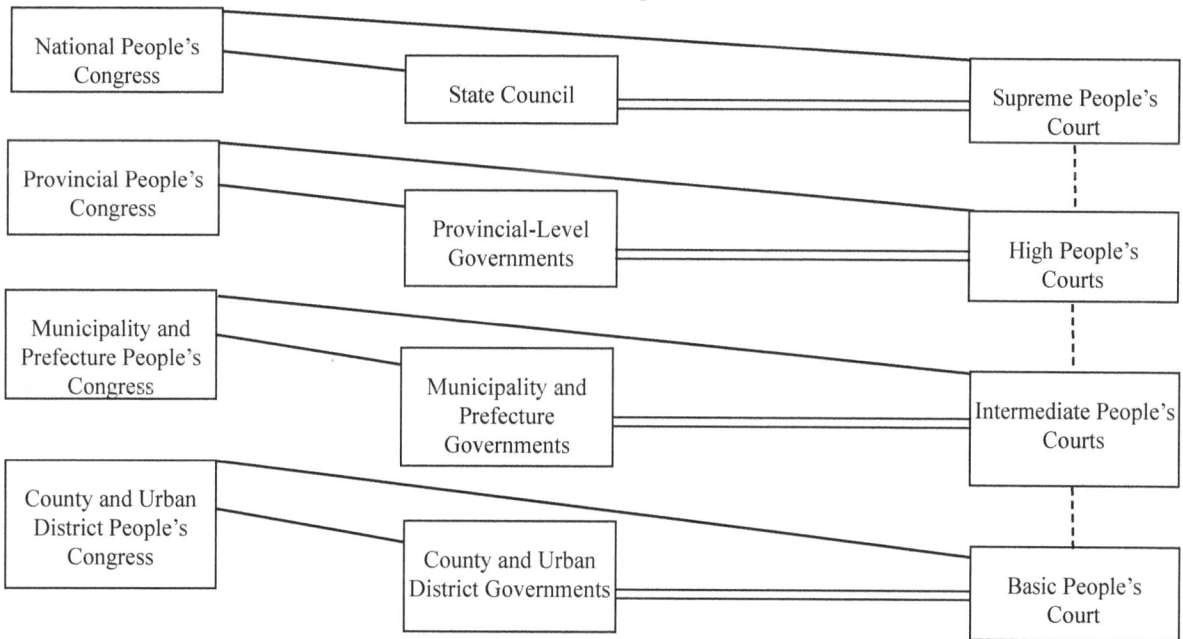

P-A Relationship with Principals Controlling Agents through Financing Means

P-A Relationship with Principals Controlling Agents through Personnel Appointment, Review and Promotion

P-A Relationship with Principals Holding Loose Control over Agents

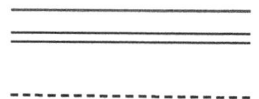

At the same time, the courts are also administratively and institutionally accountable to the people's congresses at the corresponding level that create them. Different from the U.S. where the judiciary, the legislature and the executive branch enjoys the equal standings in the polity and therefore could check and balance each other, in China the National People Congress (NPC) is the highest organ of state power and creates both the executive branch and the judiciary. The judiciary (as well as the executive branch) reports its works to the People's Congress at the same level and receives its supervision. In general, People's Congresses are responsible for appointing and removing judges of the courts at the same level. More specifically, the president of a court is appointed or removed by the People's Congress at the same level, while the appointment or removal of the vice president, members of adjudicative committee, division chiefs, deputy division chiefs, and judges is proposed by the president of the court and approved by the standing committee of the People's Congress at the same level.[35] Although higher courts may also play a role in the appointment, promotion and disciplining processes of judges (especially senior ones) in lower courts, the role of higher courts is more marginal than that of local people's congresses since higher courts can only make suggestions to lower courts to annul an appointment or to refer annulling the appointment to the people's congresses at the lower level, once they find a certain appointment goes against the *Judge Law* (*faguan fa*).[36]

Besides, courts are also supervised by the courts of higher level, although the supervision is more indirect and thus marginal. The SPC generally provides guidance to lower courts throughout the country by promulgating JIs, issuing internal regulations, setting policies, and deciding cases that have quasi-precedential value. These JIs, regulations, policies and juridical decisions are announced nationally and required to be studied and followed by the courts of lower levels. At the same time, courts at lower level frequently make inquiries to courts at higher level for advice regarding difficult issues in particular cases presented to the courts at lower level. Courts directly supervise the activities of lower courts by reviewing their decisions in appeal. As far as adjudication of IPR-related cases is concerned, those JIs, adjudication decisions of quasi-precedential value, and judiciary advices made by the SPC, which are the least subject to the threat of local protectionism and therefore more likely to be based on legal reasoning and merits of the cases, have positive influence on IPR protection. However, lack of direct means of rewarding and punishing, either through financial allocation or personnel management, courts of higher level are less powerful principals to the courts of lower level as agents than local governments and local people's congresses and therefore feeble to constrain the influence of local protectionism.

Conclusion

The Chinese history of copyright protection in the past three decades has been characterized by a cycling process of making international commitments by the central government, implementing those commitments through legislation and policy making by the central legislature, administration and judiciary, finding inconsistency and dissatisfaction on paper and in practice, and making new international commitments again. Changes in copyright protection in China have largely clustered at the level of central government and at the area of legislation and policy making. Those changes reflect the commitment of Chinese government to improve copyright protection in China. However, given the decentralized structure of copyright enforcement agencies, including administrative and judicial ones, it is highly doubtful whether the local governments of different levels have commitments at the comparable level with the central government. Those local governments do not face with foreign pressures and incentives related with copyright protection as the central government, but they are easily penetrable to their local interests and consideration as well as their institutional and bureaucratic agendas and priorities. As copyright enforcement is still much tied to these local interests embedded in the decentralized structure of administrative and judiciary agencies, copyright enforcement may not consistently meet international expectations. Thus, if China's copyright enforcement is to improve significantly, it will have to arise from the local officials and judges.

ENDNOTES

1   See Agreement on Trade Relations between the United States of America and the People's Republic of China (1979), available at http://tcc.export.gov/Trade_Agreements/All_Trade_Agreements/People_China.asp, accessed on Jul. 28, 2012. The original test reads as "[b]oth Contracting Parties agree that each Party shall take appropriate measures, under its laws and regulations and with due regard to international practice, to ensure to legal or natural persons of the other Party protection of copyrights equivalent to the copy right protection correspondingly accorded by the other Party".

2   The "Special 301" provision of the 1988 Omnibus Trade and Competitiveness Act gave the U.S. President authority to retaliate against foreign countries that violate IPRs of the U.S.'s citizens and companies. Special 301 requires the US Trade Representative [USTR] to identify, within 30 days of issuing the National Trade Estimates Report, "those countries that deny adequate and effective protection of intellectual property rights, or deny fair and equitable market access to the United States persons that rely on intellectual property rights." At the end of every April, the USTR publicizes an annual Special 301 Report, listing countries where the treatment of IPRs fails to meet the U.S. standards, based on the nominations by several industry associations. Countries are listed in one of the three categories, with increasing severity of their IPRs infringement: Watch List, Priority Watch List, and Priority Foreign Countries. Especially, if a country is identified as "Priority Foreign Countries", the USTR has 30 days to decide whether or not to conduct a formal investigation that could lead to trade sanction. Besides the three categories of priority monitoring, the USTR also announces which countries are under Section 306 monitoring for their compliance with bilateral intellectual property agreements signed with the U.S. and which countries are under the Out-of-Cycle Reviews by the USTR in the annual USTR Special 301 Report. See Sell 1998.

3   In 2001, China was admitted into the WTO.

4   *The Copyright Law* has been revised twice. The first time was in 2001, for the purpose of making China's copyright law consistent with the TRIPs Agreement. The second time was in 2010, for the purpose of following the ruling of the WTO DSB as for a case in which the U.S. complained against China on certain measures affecting the protection and enforcement of IPRs. *The Regulations for Implementing the Copyright Law* and *the Regulations for Computer Software Protection* were revised in 2001.

5   There are three JIs dealing with copyright protection over information network. They are *Judicial Interpretation on Several Issues Regarding the Application of the Law to Adjudicate Copyright Cases over Information Network* in 2000, 2003, and 2006. There are two JIs dealing with criminal protection. They are *Judicial Interpretation on Several Issues Regarding the Application of the Law to Adjudicate Cases of Criminal Disputes on Intellectual Property Rights* in 2004 and 2007. The other one, *Judicial Interpretation on Several Issues Regarding the Application of the Law to Adjudicate Cases of Civil Disputes on Copyright* in 2002, is dealing with civil protection.

6   In contrast, administrative enforcement is virtually never used in the U.S. while in most countries there is relative parity between administrative enforcement and enforcement provided by the courts, the police and the customs, taking Russia, Taiwan, Czech and France as examples. See Dimitrov 2009.

7   Among these bureaucracies, NCAC is largely the same unit as GAPP. Nominally, the two enjoy the relationship so-called "one organization, two signboards". Essentially, NCAC has remained one of the departments subordinate to GAPP.

8   Thomas 2007.

9	For instance, the piracy rate for business software in China has been astonishingly high at the level of over 80% since the mid of 1990s until recently, with the world average decreasing and fluctuating around 40% during the same time period.

10	Dimitrov 2009.

11	See the Copyright Law of the People's Republic of China ("*zhonghua renmin gongheguo zhuzuoquan fa*"), which was revised and issued on Feb. 26, 2010, Article 48. For the full text in Chinese, see http://www.china.com.cn/policy/txt/2010-02/27/content_19484098_4.htm, accessed on Jul.17, 2012. For the full text in English, see http://www.wipo.int/wipolex/en/text.jsp?file_id=186569, accessed on Jul.17, 2012.

12	However, again, the meaning of "the normal market order" is never defined explicitly.

13	Interview 08202009BJ.

14	China's Constitution (1982) specifies that there are three levels of local governments, including provincial governments, county governments and township/village governments. However, in practice, a lot of cities have been established to administrate counties. In some autonomous regions, there are also autonomous prefectures administrating autonomous counties. These cities and autonomous prefectures gradually form a new level of administration, which is called prefecture. See http://news.xinhuanet.com/ziliao/2004-10/29/content_2153676.htm, in Chinese, accessed on Jul.19, 2012.

15	The governments at provincial level include those of provinces, autonomous regions, or municipalities directly governed by the central government. See http://news.xinhuanet.com/ziliao/2004-10/29/content_2153676_1.htm, in Chinese, accessed on Jul.19, 2012.

16	The governments at prefecture level include those of regions/prefectures, autonomous prefectures, prefecture-level cities (which are cities directly governed by a provincial government), or leagues (which are an administrative division of the Inner Mongolia Autonomous Region). See http://news.xinhuanet.com/ziliao/2004-10/29/content_2153676_2.htm and http://news.xinhuanet.com/ziliao/2004-10/29/content_2153676_4.htm, in Chinese, accessed on Jul.19, 2012.

17	The governments at county level include those of counties, autonomous counties, county-level cities (which are cities directly governed by prefectures or prefecture-level cities), municipal districts (which are underneath cities), banners (which are an administrative division of the Inner Mongolia Autonomous Region), autonomous banners, special zones, forest zones, and etc. See http://news.xinhuanet.com/ziliao/2004-10/29/content_2153676_3.htm and http://news.xinhuanet.com/ziliao/2004-10/29/content_2153676_4.htm, in Chinese, accessed on Jul.19, 2012.

18	See http://news.xinhuanet.com/ziliao/2004-10/29/content_2153676_5.htm, in Chinese, accessed on Jul.19, 2012.

19	Some of the functional units at the provincial level are called "bureau" or "*ju*", while some of them are called "*ting*".

20	For the composition of the State Council and its functional units, please see http://www.gov.cn/gjjg/2005-08/01/content_18608.htm, in Chinese, accessed Jul.19, 2012.

21	The other three departments inside NCAC are "Comprehensive Department", "Copyright Department", and "International Department". For the composition of NCAC, see http://www.ncac.gov.cn/cms/html/309/3520/List-1.html, in Chinese, accessed on Jul.20, 2012. This was also confirmed by Interview 10222009BJ.

22	These four enforcement responsibilities are "to participate in drafting of local copyright-related rules and regulations and enforcing them", "to inspect the implementation of copyright laws, regulations, and rules as well as the international copyright treaties which China has signed on", "to investigate and crack down copyright infringement", and "to arbitrate copyright disputes". Management responsibilities are "to administrate copyright-related international exchange and cooperation", "to approve the establishment of the provincial subordinates of copyright collective management organizations and to monitor and direct their activities", "to direct the activities of copyright-related social organizations", "to administrate copyright registration and statutory licensing", "to mediate copyright-related international exchange and cooperation, and to monitor and direct copyright trade", "to administrate the registration of contracts for importing books and audio-video products", "to administrate record filing for copyright licensing and transfer", and "to participate in drafting development plans for copyright-related industries". See http://www.hebeichuban.gov.cn/gkjs/zzjg.jsp, in Chinese, accessed on Jul.20, 2012.

23   Interview 09072009BJ.

24   Some examples include Taiyuan and Jincheng in Shanxi Province, Shenyang in Liaoning Province, Guangzhou and Shaoguan in Guangdong Province, and Shijiazhuang in Hebei Province. This is different from the description by Mertha (2005), who thought there is no copyright bureau at all below the provincial level. The situation of Shijiazhuang is based on interview 10172009SZ. The situation of others is based on personal research of the websites of the respective bureaus, with webpage information on file.

25   Ibid.

26   It is relatively hard to tell the specific rank of a certain team from its name.

27   The reform even proceeded in those local copyright administrations which had been exercising the function of copyright enforcement before the reform. For example, Beijing Press and Publication (Copyright) Bureau lost its authority in copyright enforcement to the Beijing General Team of Administration Enforcement in Cultural Market in 2005. Interview 08262009BJ.

28   Other functions which were transferred to the local ITOCMs include those enforcement functions which formerly belong to the radio, film and television administration as well as the press and publication administration.

29   The boundary of cultural market and cultural administration's enforcement authority is always under debate and continuous adjustment. However, we can gain some basic ideas about it from the official brochure of these agencies. See "Culture Market Enforcement in Beijing" ("*Beijing wenhua zhifa*"), a brochure published by Beijing General Team of Administration Enforcement in Cultural Market, on the author's file.

30   Interview 08262009BJ.

31   Zhipei Jiang, 2008. "The Establishment and Development of The Intellectual Property Trial Division in the Supreme People's Court" ("*zuigao renmin fayuan zhishi chanquan shenpanting de sheli he fazhan*"). See http://www.chinaiprlaw.cn/file/2008111013833.html, in Chinese, accessed on Feb. 27, 2012).

32   Ibid.

33   For the structure of Chinese judiciary system, please see it at http://news.xinhuanet.com/ziliao/2003-08/13/content_1024723.htm, in Chinese, accessed on Mar.15, 2012

34   Other sections of civil division in a court include one for marriage, family and real property, one for contract and torts, and one for maritime and foreign investment disputes. Besides civil division, other substantive divisions of a court include criminal, administrative, case filing, judicial supervision, petitions and appeals, juvenile and enforcement sections. See Peerenboom 2002.

35   *Judge Law*, Article 11, see http://www.gov.cn/banshi/2005-05/26/content_1026.htm, in Chinese, accessed on Mar.15, 2012.

36   *Judge Law*, Article 14, see http://www.gov.cn/banshi/2005-05/26/content_1026.htm, in Chinese, accessed on Mar.15, 2012.

References

Dimitrov, Martin K (2009). *Piracy and the State: The Politics of Intellectual Property Rights in China*. Cambridge. Cambridge University Press.

Mertha, Andrew (2005). *The Politics of Piracy: Intellectual Property in Contemporary China*. Ithaca. Cornell University Press.

Peerenboom, Randall (2002). *China's Long March toward Rule of Law*. Cambridge. Cambridge University Press.

Sell, Susan (1998). *Power and Ideas: North-South Politics of Intellectual Property and Antitrust*. New York. State University of New York Press.

Thomas, Kristie (2007). "The Fight against Piracy: Working within the Administrative Enforcement System in China." In *Intellectual Property and TRIPS Compliance in China: Chinese and European Perspectives*, ed. by Paul Torremans, Hailing Shan and Johan Erauw, pp.85-106. Cheltenhum, UK. Edward Elgar.

Chapter Four

THE PAST AND PRESENT OF DECENTRALIZATION: LOCAL ADMINISTRATION IN THE HASHEMITE KINGDOM OF JORDAN

Abdulfattah Yaghi

Key words: decentralization, local administration, Jordan, municipalities, public administration

Geographical, Historical, and Cultural Background

The Hashemite Kingdom of Jordan (Jordan) is an Arab state that is located in the heart of the Arab World. Jordan's neighbors include Syria, Saudi Arabia, Palestine, Iraq, and Israel. Although the country is ancient, the modern state was established in 1921 as constitutional monarchy. Jordan has a very homogenous society within which several diverse sub-communities exist, such as East Jordanians, West Jordanians (aka, Jordanian Palestinians whom were forced by the Israeli occupation to flee Palestine in 1948 and 1967), Circassians/Sharkas, Chechens (who were forced to flee their land after Russia occupied it in the early 1900s), Iraqi refugees (since 2003), Syrian refugees (during 1980s and 2011), Armenians immigrants from Southern Russia, and some Egyptians, Lebanese, Saudis (Amer, 2010; Al Khalayla, 2013).

Jordan was established as the land of freedom and a place for those who were prosecuted because of their race, ethnicity, religion, or political beliefs (Ghawanmeh, 1982; Al Qaryotee, 1989). The Jordanian society welcomed all immigrants and refugees who sought a safe haven in Jordan from aggression. Older comers soon assimilated and joined other elements of the society in welcoming newcomers. This is why many Jordanians like to call themselves Al Murabeteen, meaning those who were dedicated to wining freedom. Further, many politicians and thinkers call Jordan the Land of Emigrants and Supporters (Muhajereenwa Wa Al Ansar), meaning those who migrate to live free and defend others who need support. Highlighting these facts attempt to show the demographical composition of Jordan, which had a direct impact on local administration. Today, the Jordanian society is a unique composition of all different peoples who bring with them different cultures and experiences. The total population of Jordan is more than five millions, excluding all recent refugees from Iraq and Syria since 2006 (see, Jordan's Department of Census, 2004). Table (1) shows the distribution of Jordan's population in different regions.

4.1: Distribution of Jordan's Population in 1994 and 2004

Governorate/City	Total Population in 1994	Total Population in 2004
Amman	1,576,238	1,939,105
Balga (Salt)	276,082	344,985
Zarga	639,469	774,569
Madaba	107,321	129,792
Subtotal of Central Region	**2,599,110**	**3,188,751**
Irbid	751,634	925,736
Jerash	123,190	153,650
Ajloon	,94,548	118,496
Mafrag	178,914	240,515
Subtotal of Northern Region	**1,148,286**	**1,438,397**
Karak	169,770	204,135
Tafela	62,783	75,290
Maan	79,670	92,672
Aqaba	79,839	101,736
Subtotal of Southern Region	**392,062**	**473,833**
All Totals	**4,139,458**	**5,100,981**
Source: Jordan's Department of Census (2004). http://www.dos.gov.jo/dos_home_e/main/index/htm		

Although the Kingdom was only established in 1921, the Arabs have inhabited Jordan for over seven thousand years. During this long history, Jordanians built several famous ancient states, but the most remarkable ones were the Nabateen Kingdom, Moab Kingdom, Maania State, and Amoon Kingdom. Each one of the aforementioned states was famous for its administrative structure, which created an administrative culture that laid the foundations for the administrative advancements during the Omayyad Empire in the middle ages. For example, Diwan (Court), budget, and mailing system were well-established during the Nabateen Kingdom (Yaghi, 2008a). Most ancient Jordanian states developed decentralized systems according to which Jordan was divided into several territorial districts. The king appointed rulers of each district. From a religious point of view, it is believed that Prophet Abraham (the Father of all Arabs) and Prophet Moses lived in Jordan for some time. Jesus, son of Mariam (Mary), was baptized in the River Jordan (on the western boarders of the Kingdom). Most importantly, Prophet Mohamed blessed Jordan in authentic narrations in which he mentioned the city of Amman in well-documented heritage (Hadith).

Before and until Islam reached Jordan, Natural Syria- of which Jordan was part- was under the brutal Roman occupation. Centralized Roman rule lasted for over five hundred years, when policies of the central government resided in Rome, have dictated all decision making with which representatives of the Roman Emperor in Jordan (Natural Syria) had to deal.

The Arabs liberated Jordan in the seventh century. After the decisive battles of Mouta and Yarmouk, they defeated the Roman armies and pushed them back toward the north. Since then, Jordan realized its role as a center of the Islamic and Arabic culture as it is located between the Holy Lands in Palestine (Jerusalem in particular) and Hijaz (Mecca and Medina). During this era, several administrative units were established and the Caliphate residing in Damascus delegated most administrative and financial authority to his deputies who resided in Jordan. Local norms and traditional Majlis (councils) continued to be part of the decision-making process. It was during this golden age of the Arabic state when governmental decisions intertwined with the Jordanian Arabic culture, which has been accumulating and developing for centuries. City councils, village councils, and tribal councils were always essential to the success of the state.

During the Ottoman era (1500-1921), Majlis or councils were less important to the governing process than they were before the Ottomans (Bayyat, 2003). However, more decentralization was developing under the Ottoman wali (representative of the Emperor). In fact, the current system of local administration relies on the heritage of the Ottomans according to which Jordan was divided into districts. A superintendent, who appoints several deputies overseeing a certain number of localities, governed each district. There was an appointed Mokhtar for each neighborhood or village, who signed contracts, issued birth certificates, and documented marriage and divorce cases. Each Mokhtar was equipped with enough power to establish local councils to advise him. However, not all Mokhtars did that.

In 1921, the Arab Revolution led by the Hashemite gained independence from the Ottoman Empire and soon after the Hashemite established new independent administrative units, such as the agriculture, road, and custom departments. In 1958, a modern constitution was adopted under the late King Talal Bin Abdulla Al Hashemi. The constitution outlined progressive foundations for administrative and political decentralization. For example, civil liberties and political participation were recognized and protected as part of the new government philosophy of pluralism. For decades, the late King Hussien Bin Talal was heavily engaged in the efforts of modernization and improvement of public administration as well as all public institutions in the kingdom. During the reign of King Hussein, a cabinet level department (Ministry) was created for administrative development. The current King Abdulla Bin Hussien launched several initiatives to energize public administration and encourage decentralization, as a practical response to national development needs (Ghawanmeh, 1982; Abu Sowailem and Salah, 1996).

Foundations of Decentralization

Decentralization has always been significant in the Jordanian political and administrative culture. In ancient times (before liberation from the Romans), centralization of government was perceived as an unusual governance practice. Indeed, most parts of the country had their own type of councils that managed their daily affairs. The representative of the Jordanian ancient Kings (Ammonites, for example), Roman Emperors, and for brief time the Persian Kings ruled Jordanian territories based on a regional representative. They made the headquarter of the regional administration either inside the Jordanian lands (such Ammon city, Kerak, and Petra) or in neighboring territories, such as Damascus, Jerusalem, and Baghdad.Amman, the capital city of modern Jordan, remained an important town during the early Islamic periods. However, Kerak city and some other cities gained more significant roles in managing the country's affairs. During the Ottomanian era (Ottomanian Jordan: 1516-1916) Jordan was part of Sham District (Welayat Al Sham Shareef) where Damascus was the capital of the district's local government (Bayyat, 2003; http://www.discover-syria.com/bank/6399).

Just before the demise of the Ottomanian Empire during the First World War, Jordan was divided into three districts (Sonjoks): Ajloon district in the central west, Balqa district in the north, and Kerak district in the south (Farhan and Sokkar, 2002). Each district established several departments. Those departments were responsible for managing education, healthcare, markets, and other domains of the public sector. All three districts were supervised by Wali (governor), who was an appointed representative to the central government in Istanbul, but resided in Damascus, in today Syria (Mahaftha, 1989).

Upon the defeat of the Ottoman Empire in WWI, Britain colonized Jordan. Leadership of Jordan promptly transferred from Damascus in Syria to Jerusalem in Palestine. In 1920, the representative of Britain (superintendent) met in Salt city with representatives of Jordanian communities. The meeting resulted in establishing several local governments in Kerak, Salt, and Ajloon cities. Each local government established a consultative council to manage the district's affairs. The colonial British government appointed one representative to oversee each one of the three governments (Al Musa, 1971; Al Maani and Abu Faris, 2000). Those governments played their administrative roles until the establishment of the new central government after the independence of Jordan in 1921 (for which Jordanians and free Arabs had fought).

Public Administration After 1921

After the declaration of the Emirate of Trans Jordan (later the Hashemite Kingdom of Jordan), the new government faced confusing situations related to two realities. Firstly, the new state did not have clear boarders. The surrounding areas of the capital city, Amman, were parts of other bigger and stronger neighboring regimes such as Syria, Iraq, and Najd and Hijaz (now Saudi Arabia). This situation burdened the new government in Amman and made it difficult to make decisions or organize areas that other states might claim.

Secondly, the new state did not have an established administrative system. Therefore, the government borrowed several segments of laws that were used by the Ottomanian Empire. In addition, the Jordanian government relied heavily on norms-based laws (tribal and social laws). Norms were not written in most cases, yet, but they had strong influence over people (Al Farhan and Al Sukkar, 2002).Law and order according to the norm-based laws was different from those set by modern laws. Nevertheless, norms were sufficient at that time to help the government run the daily affairs of cities and towns.

When King Talal ruled for about a year (September 1951 to July 1952) a new constitution was adopted and the structure of public administration become well organized (Abu Nowwar, 2000). When late King Hussien came to power in 1953, modernization of the state accelerated. The era of the current King Abdulla continues to witness more building and developing of the state, based on previous accomplishments during the last four decades. Thus, it is safe to judge that public administration in Jordan is progressing, yet still evolving.

Centralization and Decentralization

Jordanians never stopped searching for better ways to administer their state. For over eighty years, the government continued to implement new policies aiming at improving (1) services provided to citizens, (2) accountability measures through clear channels of responsibility, and (3) the relationships between people and their government. These three goals make the platform of the today's government. The collective effort of the government to reform public administration and ensure accountability is labeled "good governance." Pursuing good governance is an emerging philosophy of the government and is the measure according to which the cabinet's performance is judged (Yaghi, 2008b).

The environments of public administration in Jordan contributed, in encouraging the government to seek better public administration practices. The most significant environmental factor was the composition of the Jordanian society itself. Al Musa (1971) and Abu Sowailem and Salah, (1996) noted that segments within the Jordanian society complained in early stages of the statehood. Many public employees back then were not Jordanian nationals; rather they came from Syria, Lebanon, Iraq and many other countries. Those feelings contributed in creating a sense of nationalism in public administration, thus there was an urging need to reform laws that regulated hiring and employment in so early stage of the state building. At the same time, nationalism in public administration ignited a movement of enlightened civil servants who carried the banner for reform.

Al Farhan and Al Sukkar (2002) noted that centralization in managing the public sector in Jordan was rooted in the Ottoman's July 23, 1913 law, which was adopted by the Turkish Etihadeieen Party (Unionists who overtook powers in the Empire). The law was titled "The Law of Managing Districts." This law vested most decision-making authority in the hands of districts' governors. Thus, the law aimed at strengthening centralization and allowing little room for citizens' participation. The law also gave governors certain powers to exercise discretion in political issues within the district. Therefore, the governing approach was centralized, but yet decentralized in the sense that the central government in Istanbul gave governors and their appointed representatives a wide range of authorities, which seemed more like delegation of power. Some governors used their discretionary and delegated powers wisely, while others did not (such as Jamal Pasha "El Saffah," governor of Sham-Damascus district of which Jordan was part).

The dilemma of centralization and decentralization in Jordan between 1920 and 1930 did not only limit the natural development of public administration, but also hindered municipalities' efforts to empower citizens. Specifically, the British mandate over Jordan has failed to create a national administrative system that is autonomous and effective. On the contrary, Britain abused its power as a colonial state and encouraged different regions in Jordan to disintegrate thus the administrative system remained neither institutionalized nor capable of inventing needed methods to manage the country effectively (Al Farhan and Al Sukkar, 2002; al Khalayla, 2013). It was not until 1946 when the Jordanian national government liberated the country from the British colonialism and built strong administrative tradition. The new administration continued to progress institutionally and mature impressively until now.

Municipal Administration

Municipal or local administration in Jordan can be considered among the best-practiced systems of governance in the Arab World and its surroundings (AWIS). The concept of local governance (decentralization management of regions) has emerged as a natural development of the Jordanian history (Yaghi, 2008b). Arabs in Jordan have developed an over of two-thousand-year old system of regional governance. Cities, towns, and nomadic tribes all had well-established systems of self-governing. With some variations, Jordanians as the descendents of ancient Arab groups such as Ammonians, Moabians, Phoenicians, and Maonians, retained traditional systems based on norms and family-based loyalty (kinship).

Communities, large or small, have always had councils of elders. Those councils played legislative, judicial, and executive roles in managing the affairs of each region. Although membership in such councils was self-proclaimed and in some instances was inherited, no member was able to retain his or her position without legitimate means. In other words, public approval was needed to maintain legitimate council authorities. Some citizens and communities socially alienated members who were incompetent. Such punishment could be severe for council members, who failed to uphold justice and impartiality in their decisions. All groups, urban and nonurban citizens in Jordan, practiced this form of local governance.

In the early 1920s, some laws were crafted and enforced to better managed municipalities. Al Zubi (1992) and Ghawanmeh (1982) noted that Jordan was divided into three districts, namely Salt (Balga), Ajloon, and Karak. An appointed representative (Mutasarrif) for the Prince of Trans Jordan headed each district. In order to ensure effectiveness in the capital city, Amman, each district was divided into (1) precinct (Kaeim maqameyiah) headed by a Superintendent (Kaeimmaqam), and (2) departments (Moderiyat) headed by an administrator/manager (See Figure 1).

In 1923, a new administration law was enacted by the government according to which Jordan was divided into six districts, namely Amman, Salt, Karak, Madaba, Jarash, and Irbid (Al Farhan and Al Sukkar, 2002). The law gave the government more liberty to create as many precincts as needed. Managing each district was given to the governor of district (named Administrative Ruler), a judge, an accountant, and a secretary (letter and communication officer). In addition, the government established a court system with a number of employees staffing each unit. Each district was to have a council to manage its affairs and be headed by a person appointed directly by the central government. Employees affiliated with the council would be elected and/or appointed by the district (Al Qaryotee, 1989; Abu Sowailem and Salah, 1996).

Al Maani and Abu Faris (2000) noted that in 1925 the government gave local administration units some specific responsibilities to oversee buildings, construction projects, healthcare services, roads, and other basic needs of people living within the jurisdiction of each district and unit. In 1938, the Municipalities Law mandated that at least half of all municipal council seats should be elected directly by people. The composition of central and non-central administrative practices had gained popular support because it succeeded in reconciling norms-based laws with modern administrative laws. People in localities were able to a certain extent to find themselves in the new governance approaches. In other words, the government's approach did not entirely rule out people's long-lived norms and traditions. However, the coming twenty years would witness several attempts to organize and reorganize local administration.

4.2: Local Administration in the 1920s and 1930s in Jordan

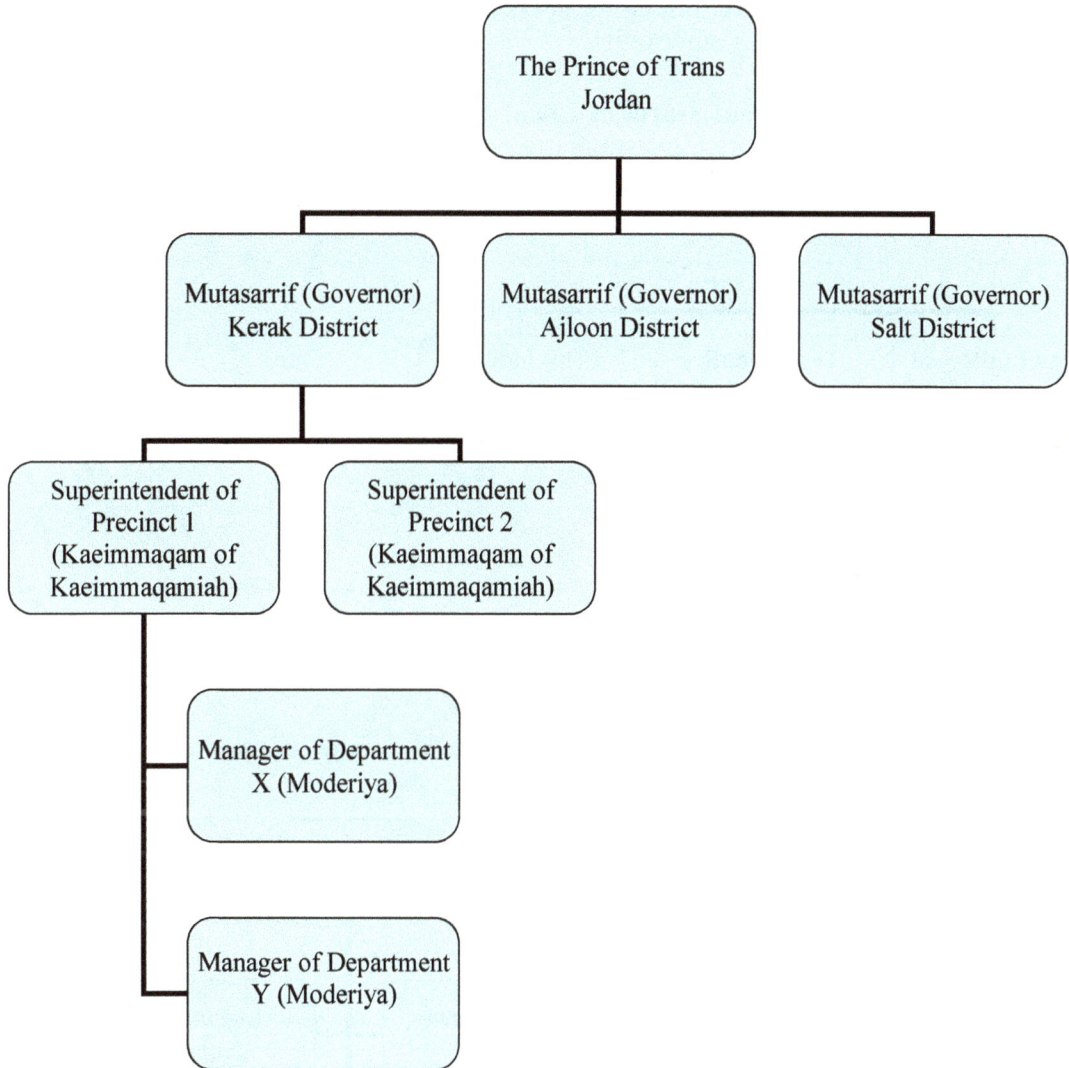

The Prince of Trans Jordan

Mutasarrif (Governor) Kerak District

Mutasarrif (Governor) Ajloon District

Mutasarrif (Governor) Salt District

Superintendent of Precinct 1 (Kaeimmaqam of Kaeimmaqamiah)

Superintendent of Precinct 2 (Kaeimmaqam of Kaeimmaqamiah)

Manager of Department X (Moderiya)

Manager of Department Y (Moderiya)

Modern Local Administration in Jordan 1954-2007

The Jordanian local administration system is currently organized as part of the executive branch of the government. Figure (2) shows the relationship between the central government in Amman and other units.

4.3: Current Status of Local Administration in Jordan

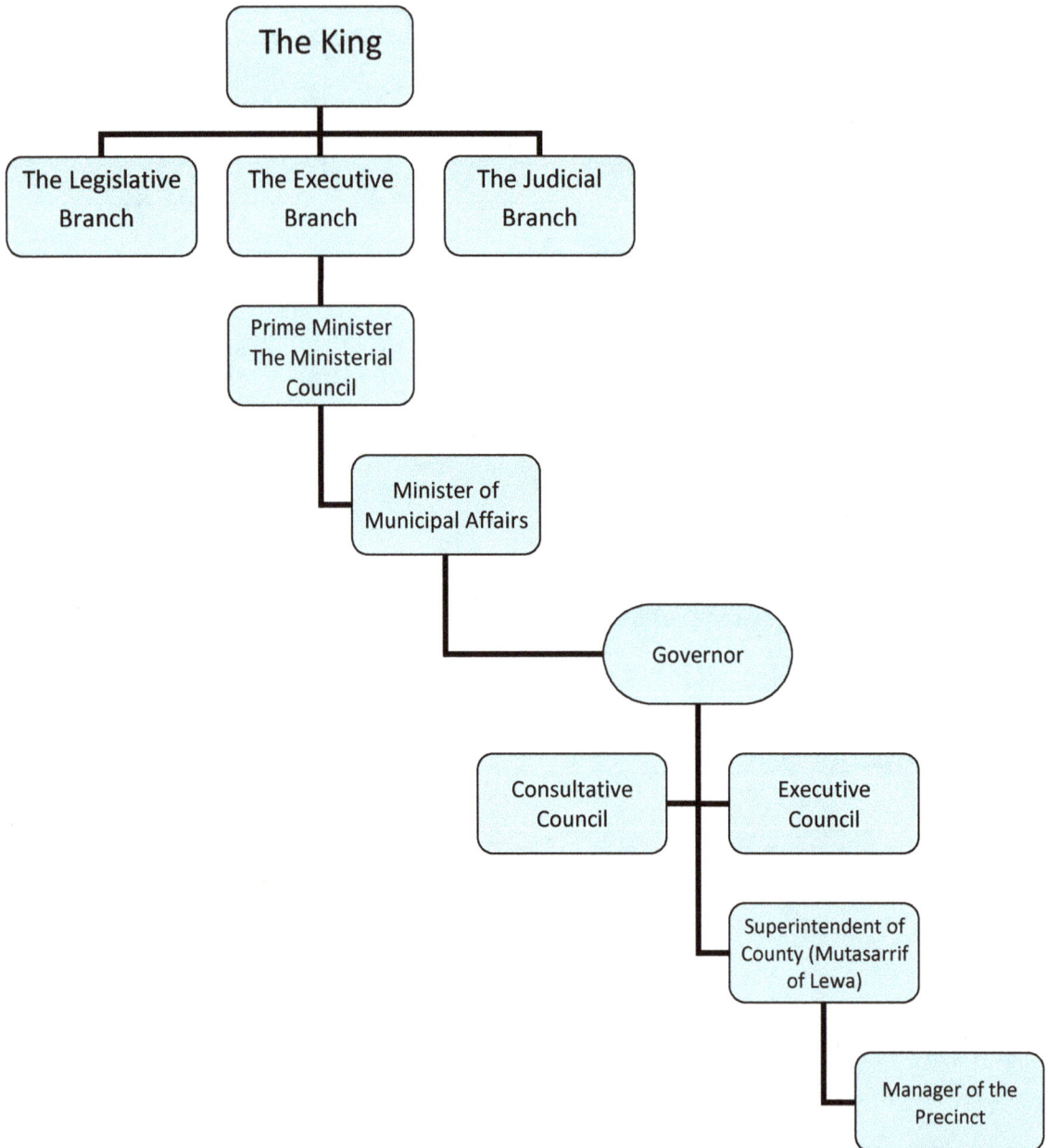

```
                        ┌──────────────┐
                        │   The King   │
                        └──────┬───────┘
          ┌────────────────────┼────────────────────┐
   ┌──────────────┐    ┌──────────────┐    ┌──────────────┐
   │The Legislative│    │ The Executive│    │  The Judicial │
   │    Branch     │    │    Branch    │    │    Branch     │
   └──────────────┘    └──────┬───────┘    └──────────────┘
                        ┌──────────────┐
                        │Prime Minister│
                        │The Ministerial│
                        │   Council    │
                        └──────┬───────┘
                          ┌──────────────┐
                          │  Minister of │
                          │Municipal Affairs│
                          └──────┬───────┘
                                  ┌──────────────┐
                                  │   Governor   │
                                  └──────┬───────┘
                    ┌─────────────────────┴──────────────┐
              ┌──────────────┐              ┌──────────────┐
              │ Consultative │              │  Executive   │
              │   Council    │              │   Council    │
              └──────────────┘              └──────┬───────┘
                                        ┌──────────────────┐
                                        │ Superintendent of│
                                        │County (Mutasarrif│
                                        │    of Lewa)      │
                                        └──────┬───────────┘
                                            ┌──────────────┐
                                            │Manager of the│
                                            │   Precinct   │
                                            └──────────────┘
```

Presently, governors are the head of twelve governorates, namely: Amman, Irbid, Ajloon, Jarash, Salt (Balga), Zarga, Madaba, Kerak, Tafela, Maan, Aqaba, and Mafrag. Governors are not only representatives of the central government, but also the head of public administration within their governorates (top bureaucrats or first civil servants). Very often, a governor is called the Administrative Ruler to signify his or her managerial as well as political roles in maintaining law and order and ensuring effective governance. The philosophy of the government is to delegate more authorities to local units. The following sections explain the various levels of local government in Jordan.

Levels of Local Government before 2007

Governorate Level

Governors are appointed by the king based on the nomination of the Prime Minister and the recommendation from the Minister of Interior. We see here that the political role of governors stems from the follow-ship relationship of governors to the Minister of Interior instead of following the Minister of Municipalities. If the Minister of Municipalities appointed governors, their administrative roles then would have more priorities in their work. It is obvious that mandating governors to report to the Minister of Interior aimed at emphasizing their affiliation with the executive branch of government and their role as representatives to the security apparatus (Al Farhan and Al Sukkar, 2002; Al Zubi, 1995). This is why governors were often called "Administrative Rulers" suggesting that they have ruling powers that go beyond the managerial functions. The Rulers here have the power to adjudicate conflict, supervise civil service within their governorates, make necessary decisions to implement public policy, and most importantly supervise law enforcement within the jurisdiction of each governor.

The Governorate Executive Council is a smaller version of the Ministerial Council with a major difference in the scope of jurisdiction of each council. While the Ministerial Council is responsible for running the entire country, the Executive Council is only responsible for running the affairs of one governorate. Each governorate has an Executive Council to aid the governor in making executive decisions and managing public policies. Each Council is composed of the governor (Chair), deputy governor, head of police force, and directors of all executive departments (directorates) in the governorate (Al Lateef, 1992; Al Obwa, 1991).

Of course, executive departments or directorates are mini-ministries. Each central ministry in the capital city, Amman, operates branches of it in every single governorate. Public administration experts can also view this form of administrative decentralization as centralization of the executive authority. Instead of managing the local municipality affairs directly by the central government residing in Amman, the Jordanian government elected to create another form of centralization, which took a form of what we can call "administrative concentration." According to this system, each ministry establishes branches in all twelve governorates and delegates to them certain necessary authorities to serve people. Therefore, instead of traveling to Amman from villages, towns, and cities, citizens can contact directorates close to them and within their own municipal unit to finish business with the government. Figure (3) explains this concept of administrative concentration. In some cases where a problem or a case could not be resolved on a governorate level, it could be transferred to the central government (the Ministry). The same applies on the county (Lewa) and precinct levels (Mudereya).

The Governorate Consultative Council is composed by the governor (Chair) and no more than twenty-five members appointed by the Minister of Interior, based on the recommendation of the governor. Membership of this council is left to the discretion of the governor, but based on an established norm; members are selected among parliamentary senates and representatives of the governorate, heads of major municipalities within the governorate, and other well-known figures. The responsibilities of this council include providing the governor with insights and wise opinions about various issues of policy implementation and management within the governorate (see, Al Zubi, 1992; Al Khalayla, 2013).

4.4: Example of Administrative Concentration in Jordan

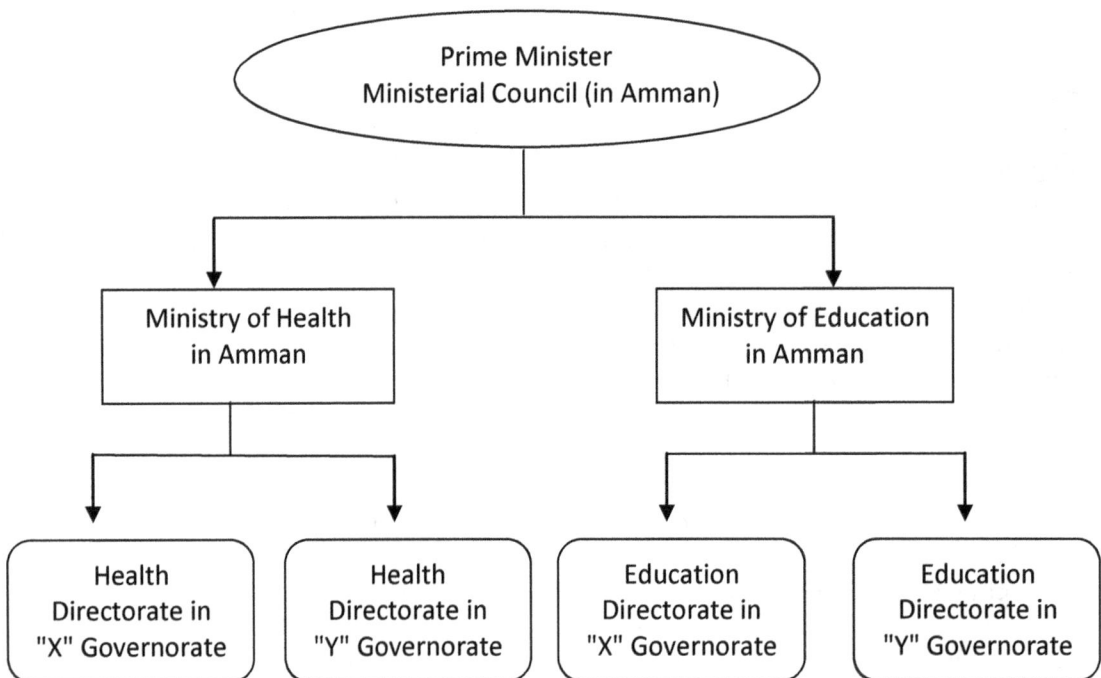

76

County Level

Al Farhan and Al Sukkar (2002) assert that according to the Administrative Cadet System of 2000, number 37 and 38, county superintendents should have at least three years of experience in the Interior Ministry and should also have a bachelor degree as a minimum requirement for appointment. We can see that the law has recognized the position of superintending as a serious post according to which the Superintendent is the head of the civil service system within the county. Therefore, this person should possess needed skills, knowledge, and expertise to handle huge responsibilities.

The County Executive Council is similar to the one on the governorate level. The most important difference however is the jurisdiction, which is narrower in the county than the one in the governorate. The Superintendent is the Chair of the council and members are appointed to include the head of the police force and head of all administrative departments in the county.

The County Consultative Council has similar functions of that on the governorate level, but with smaller jurisdiction. The council is composed of the Superintendent (Chair) and at least fifteen members appointed by the governor, based on the nomination of the Superintendent (Mutasarrif) for three years.

Precinct Level

Manager of the Precinct is the head of the civil service system within the precinct. The manager should have a public service in the Ministry of Interior for at least three years and should have a bachelor degree in any major. Because precincts are the closest level of governance to citizens, managers face a tremendous amount of casework to finish, thus they have to spend a considerable time with their constituents. In other words, precinct managers have an executive nature, because they deal with people directly. The advantage of working as precinct manager is the strong rapport, which managers can develop with wide constituencies. The people, therefore can easily notice the effectiveness of the manager's work! Precincts have neither executive nor consultative councils because there is a relatively limited need for such councils.

Contemporary Law of Local Administration in Jordan

As discussed earlier in this chapter, decentralization took different forms in Jordan. Indeed, the development of local administration has followed the changes in the political culture of the Jordanian society. Therefore, those developments were motivated by the needs of the society to improve public administration and municipal services (Al Naeem, 2006; Al Zubi, 1984; Al Shaikhali, 1983; Amer, 2010).

In this section, I will compare two main laws of local administration in Jordan, which signify the two cultures of Jordan's government and people during two periods: before and after 2007. The first law is Municipal Law number 29 issued in 1955 (the old law).

This law reflected the service-delivery paradigm according to which the government is concerned by providing basic services, which people needed and demanded. The second law is Municipal Law number 14 issued in 2007 (the new law). This law came as the Jordanian society matured and moved away from merely demanding municipal services to expect democratic governance and participation in making municipal changes. The government's enactment of the new law places local administration in the center of economic and social development by delegating more authorities to local councils.

Because the new local administration law is the cultivation of over eighty years of developments, it is essential here to briefly summarize some of the most important developments of local administration in the past decades chronologically before comparing the two laws:

- March 4th, 1925: The Municipal Law used provisions from Ottoman laws after incorporating new and progressive articles such as those on accountability and effectiveness.

- The Municipal Law number nine in 1938; introduced the concept of elected members in municipal councils and it identified length of term for municipal councils, which was four years.

- Municipal Law of Village Management number 5 in 1954; this grand law for village administration was valid until 2007. It regulated all aspects of managing villages and structuring their councils.

- Municipal Law number 29 in 1955; this grand law for towns and city management was valid until 2007. However, it has been modified and ratified several times during the years 1955 and 2007. It was a comprehensive law that regulated all aspects of municipalities that were larger than villages.

- Municipal Law number 14 in 2007; this is the most recent development of local administration, which came about as a response to public demands and governmental efforts to upgrade and overhaul local administration. This law regulated municipalities and villages and incorporated provisions on local development, elections, good governance, and financial issues.

Comparison between the Old and the New Municipal Laws

It is essential to analyze the new municipal law so that we can understand the new philosophy of the government in managing localities. To this end, I will classify changes bases on eight important components, namely council membership, leadership, termination, elections, role of women, voter's age, vacancy, and council responsibilities.

4.5: Comparison of Old and New Municipal laws

#	Compnent	Old Municipal Law (Municipal Law number 29 in 1955)	New Municipal Law (Municipal Law number 14 in 2007)
1	Council Membership	Half is elected directly by people, and half appointed by the Prime Minister following the nomination by the Minister of Municipalities.	The people elect all members.
2	Council Chair	Appointed by the Prime Minister with recommendation of the Minister of Municipalities.	Elected by the people.
3	Termination of the Council		All municipal councils are considered dissolved three months before the new municipal elections. The Municipalities Minister appoints special committees to run the localities until new councils are elected.
4	Elections		All municipal elections occur in the same day in the Kingdom.
5	Females		At least 20% of council members should be reserved as quota for females.
6	Voters' Age	Voters should complete the age of nineteen years old (19) before the election day.	Voters should complete the age of eighteen years old (18) before the election day.
7	Vacant Seats		If a female seat becomes vacant as a result of death, termination, or resignation of a female council member, the candidate who gained the second largest votes during the election will be appointed to fill the vacant seat.
8	Responsibilities of the Council	- Water - Public manners - Establishing clinics and midwives centers - Establishing public defense (police force for disasters)	- Water is not included. - Public manners is not included - Establishing healthcare institutions is not included - Public defense is not included

Analytical Notes

We notice from the previous comparison that the new municipal law has better democratic features than the old law. By recognizing popular elections (general elections) as substitute of the partially elected approach, the new law gives constituents the ultimate power to choose council members who show promising qualities. From the government's perspective, the fully elected council approach relieves the central government from the burden of peoples' direct criticism. It instead leads to directing people's complaints to the council itself. Very often, people and opposition parties in Jordan blame the central government for the difficulties that face municipalities. In particular, people complain that some municipalities are inefficient in providing basic services to residents. In addition, some people complain that municipal councils deplete financial resources without doing enough for the localities. Because the government appointed fifty percent of council members according to the old law, it was convenient to blame the appointed members for any malfunction in the municipal management. Since the new law mandates that all council members and its Chair be elected directly by the people, people themselves will be responsible for electing the best candidates.

Reducing the age of eligibility-to-vote from nineteen to eighteen aimed at encouraging a wider group of people to participate in running their localities. The Minister of Municipalities in 2007 noted that the new system would add 150,000 new voters, mostly young people who would become eligible to vote (Akher Khabar, 2013). Practically, younger voters are expected to influence the outcomes of municipal elections, because this group of citizens may have different ideas and aspirations than what older people may have. In other words, younger people may expect different things from their candidates, which in turn can energize municipal elections and lead to better municipal work.

Although quotas may not be fully democratic as an abstract concept, considering the sociological and political background of Jordanian municipalities, women needed a legal mandate to encourage them to run for public office and empower them to challenge male runners. Twenty percent of all municipal seats are reserved now for women, which brings a new blood to local administration and reflects wider interests, needs, and demands of the people. It is expected that quota provisions in the law could be eliminated in the future if women were capable to run and win elections in free competition.

Increasing political participation by women and young people may be seen as advancement towards more reforms not only in public administration but also in causing and managing local economic, political, and social development. Mobilizing women and young people would require better efforts by municipal candidates to present diverse platforms. The old and typical platforms would not be sufficient to attract those voters.

The new law takes away three old, major responsibilities from municipalities. Providing water and maintaining its network is no longer a municipal work, the privatization of this sector kept providing water in the hands of private companies. As for public manners, the changes in people's culture make it unacceptable for the municipal council to monitor people as it used to do some fifty years ago! It was natural for the society to expect the council to control public dress, behaviors on the roads, and general manners, because many towns back then had suspicions about the role of government and how being in one state would affect their local conservative values. In other words, during the 1950s, people wanted some guarantees that their values and norms were well protected in light of the fast growth of towns which led to mixing native town citizens with others, coming from other towns in Jordan. Development of small towns was accompanied by more liberal values, social and political changes. Thus, it was natural for a large segment of the population to demand such assurances from the municipal councils. Such assurances are now less important, thus they are absent in the new law. Lastly, public defense force has developed greatly in the past fifty years. Presently, there is a well-established, well-equipped and trained institution for public defense. The Jordan Public Defense (El Amnul Aam) is a unit within the Ministry of Interior and is staffed by a large number of well-trained civil servants. Public defense now handles all catastrophes, relief activities, firefighting, and many other responsibilities. It was unfeasible in 2007 to leave such important work fragmented and handled by various municipalities.

Conclusion: Challenges of Local Administration in Jordan

Several challenges affect the future of local administration in particular and centralization in general. These challenges are not obstacles as much as opportunities for government and society alike to improve their practices of decentralization. There are increasing demands for better transparency and accountability in governmental work. After about four years of practicing local administration based on the 2007 municipal law, people living in various localities started assessing the experience of fully elected councils. Therefore, there are voices that demand tougher laws for accountability and transparency. The central government is too responsive to those demands, but improving local administration is mutually beneficial for both, the government and citizens. It is increasingly important for the central government as well as local administration institutions to adhere to the best practices of good governance. Local administration and the outcomes of municipal councils, the closer satisfy the more people the government will be to achieving good governance.

Some of the most significant challenges are economic development and political participation. Jordanians are inter-dialoguing about the role of decentralization (i.e., local administration) in stimulating economic development within their own localities. More and more people are criticizing municipal councils for their lack of independence, even under the new municipal law. Ordinary citizens, as well as elites, expect more efforts by local councils to self-engage in economic planning and partnerships with the private sector and the central government to implement progressive economic policies, such as new industrial zones, enterprises, and encouraging investments. The least local councils should be doing is building infrastructure that is needed for economic development. Most roads and transportation system were built by the central government. Unfortunately many localities added nothing to those roads. Some municipalities do not even maintain the highways and roads that the central government built in and around their towns. Financial difficulties and lack of professional knowledge to manage town's resources stand behind this weakness.

Energizing locally based economic activities within each locality is another challenge. Unfortunately, some municipalities depend heavily on the central government, so they facilitate, though indirectly, immigration of their citizens from localities to city centers. Some towns have been losing population continuously for decades. Unless municipal councils implement strong policies to energize people and partnership with them, negative immigration may continue, thus hurting localities and their development. As dependency on the central government remains a fact, economic development policies remain ineffective. One approach, which the government so far has adopted, was establishing special zones and economic zones aiming at encouraging local people and local institutions to take the initiative to develop their own areas. The outcomes of such policies remain to be seen and evaluated.

References

Abu Sowailem, Khamis and Salah, Mamoon. 1996. Local administration system in Jordan. Forum on local administration- Cairo.

Akher Khabar. 2013. The text of the new Jordanian municipal law. Available: http://www.akherkhabar.net/content/view/18908/44 (accessed on Feb 26, 2013).

Al Khalayla, Mohamed Ali. 2013. *Local administration and its application in Jordan, UK, France and Egypt*. Amman: Dar Al Thaqafa.

Al Lateef, Basheer. 1992. *Evaluation of distribution of municipal services in Jordan east wadi*. Unpublished Master's Thesis University of Jordan. Al Maani, Ayman and Abu Faris, Mahmood. 2000. Local administration, principles and application. Amman: University of Jordan.

Al Musa, Suliman. 1971. Establishing the Emirate of Trans Jordan 1921-1925. Amman: Jordanian Press.

Al Naeem, Abdula. 2006. Decentralization and local administration in the Arab Countries. Riyadh: Arab Institute for City Development.

Al Obwa, Majed. 1991. Institutionalization of municipalities in Jordan. University of Jordan, master thesis.

Al Qaryotee, Mohamed. 1989. Improving productivity of local councils in Jordan. Al Rafideen.

Al Shaikhali, Abdul Kader. 1983. Theory of local administration. Amman: Arab Organization for studies and Publications.

Al Zubi, Khalid. 1992. Formulation of local councils and impact on council's effectiveness. Amman, Maktabat Al Thaqafa.

Al Zubi, Khalid. 1995. Municipalities in Jordan from legislation. Forum on the role of accountability in municipal development, July 25-27, 1995. Aqaba, Jordan, p. 10-11.

Amer, Adil. 2010. Toward developing local administration law. Amman: Dar Al Adala wa Al Kanoon (als available online at: http://justice-lawhome.com/vb).

Bayyat, Fadil. 2003. Examination of historical studies of Arabs under the Ottomanians (Dirasat Fee Al-Tareekh Al Arab fee Al Ahd Al Otmanni). Beirut: Al Madar Al Islami Press.

Farhan, Amal, and Sukkar, Abdulkareem. 2002. Public administration in Jordan between theory and practical experience. Amman: Dar Al Shorooq.

Ghawanmeh, Yousof. 1982. The civilization history of Jordan during Mamluki ear (Hadarittareekh al Ordon fee al Asr al Mamluki). Amman: Dar Al Fikir for Publishing. http://www.discover-syria.com/bank/6399, accessed on April 21, 2011. Jordan's Department of Census. 2004. Early Results of the General Census. http://www.dos.gov.jo/census2004/page1.htm

Mahaftha, Ali. 1989. The Modern history of Jordan. Amman: Jordan Book Center www. amanjordan.com, accessed on March 3rd, 2011.

Yaghi, Abdulfattah. 2008a. Using Petra simulation in Teaching Graduate Courses in Human Resource Management: A Hybrid Pedagogy. Journal of Public Affairs Education, Volume 14, Fall Issue 3, pp. 399-412.

Yaghi, Abdulfattah. 2008b. Good Governance Practices in Jordan and Georgia. International Journal of Rural Management, January/December, 4: 47-65.

Note: Most of the listed references are in Arabic and the translation was made to accomodate the language of the chapter.

Chapter Five

DECENTRALIZATION IN THE UNITED ARAB EMIRATES

Abdulfattah Yaghi

Key words: decentralization, United Arab Emirates, political system, local administration

Introduction

The United Arab Emirates (UAE) is an Arab state on the southern shores of the Arabian Gulf. Although it declared independence in December 2, 1971, the country has developed steadily to become an important commercial center. Emiratis (local citizens of the UAE) have long been known for their strong trade relationships with Europe, Asia, and Africa. The UAE is the second largest economy in the Arab World after Saudi Arabia. One of the biggest challenges to the UAE government and society is demographical imbalance between citizens and expatriates where citizens only make less than 20% of the total population, which is over seven million.

In this chapter, I will focus on exploring the cultural foundations of governmental decentralization in UAE. The major concepts of the chapter are (1) administrative decentralization is an old and new practice within the UAE society, (2) decentralization has always been an important factor in shaping the modern state of UAE and the federal system, and (3) administrative and political decentralization are connected. In order to discuss these concepts, I will start by addressing the history of the state and society.

Brief History of the State and Society of UAE

During the sixteenth to the eighteenth century the UAE was known as the "Coast of Oman." Then, European invaders called it the "Coast of Pirates." During the late nineteenth century and early twentieth century, the region was called the "Coast of Reconciled Emirates." In 1971, after the declaration of independence from colonial Britain, the region was named "United Arab Emirates (UAE)." The new state established a federal union of seven emirates (states), namely AbuDhabi, Sharja, Ras Al Khaima, Dubai, Fujera, Ajman, and Om Al Quwain.

Local culture is an important part of the past and present of the UAE. Although Persian and European invaders, such as the Portuguese, Dutch, and British, have fought Arab Emiratis fearlessly for centuries, and dominated the area for quite long time, Emiratis were able to retain a great deal of communal autonomy. Two major factors helped maintaining such autonomy, the tribal culture (kinship) and coherence within the Arab Emirati society. The family structure of the society was the glue that maintained the integrity of the Emiratis' cultural core. Social coherence has always been an important factor in shaping the UAE state and society. Today, the state continues to be influenced by nets of kinship, where relatives are trusted and given important political and administrative positions in federal as well as local governments. Kinship, however, does not provide those public officials with automatic immunity against legal questioning of their decisions and actions. The UAE is moving steadily toward more good governance practices where accountability laws are emphasized over kinship. Understanding the cultural aspects of the UAE government is vital to anyone who studies the public sphere in this country. We will see in the following sections how these cultural elements have left their imprint on all policy-related realities, including decentralization.

Origins of Decentralization in UAE

Before the origins of decentralization in the UAE are discussed, the concept is explained. Decentralization, in this chapter, refers to the practices of Emirati communities in selecting leaders from within the community and to develop governance system according to which the ruler and the people adhere to certain norms and legal criteria. These practices lead to establishing formal systems to manage local areas such as cities and towns and solve their problems without the need for the central government to directly involve in managing those affairs (Al Kobaisi, 1982).

The UAE society has strong networks of social and family relations. Local communities therefore are inter-connected by family relations (kinship). Regardless of the type of community, in which they live (e.g., rural or urban), people in the UAE since the ancient times have developed very sophisticated system of social traditions according to small communities maintained self-governance by selecting one of their members, called chief or sheik, to guarantee law and order for the entire community. Members of each community accepted the legitimacy of that leader and rarely challenged his authority. However, the sheik maintains his authority-to-rule by exercising high levels of wisdom, fairness, justice, and strength. Many sheiks that have failed to maintain their legitimacy have been forced to step down by their communities. Often, good sheiks retain the sheikdom within their own family (sons, grandsons, and so forth). However, the good legacy of a legitimate sheik was not sufficient for his successors to maintain legitimacy for their rule. Each sheik, whether he inherited power or not, should gain public approval. Popularity of a sheik was easy to observe through the level of support people show to that sheik, and by the extent to which a community was able to retain its coherence and mighty in defending its territory and people. Abu Basha (2002) asserts that Emirati ancestors have developed a system of governance based on their Arabic traditions and Islamic values. Solidarity amongst members of each community is crucial for the survival of each community and for the success of governing. Using money and wealth to gain leadership status in those old Emirati communities was not sufficient by itself to buy people's approval. Unless sheiks used their wealth and money to relieve the poor, pay for the defense of the community, and achieve welfare for the people, money and wealth were with little use.

Within the environment of decentralized governance, medieval Emirati society established two cultural practices, which remain valid until today, and Emiratis succeeded in maintaining unity and continuity. The practices are adaptability to change and traditional political system. The following section discusses these practices.

Adaptability to Change

It was obvious that ancient Emiratis have survived climate change that led to dissertation of the once a green forest region. By attaching oneself to a well-glued community (extended family), Emiratis succeeded in migrating from dry areas to settle in better areas where water and grass were available around the Arabian Gulf. They built communities that lasted for centuries and changed their life style several times to accommodate new environmental and geographical realities. Changes led to splitting one family or tribe into several communities, where each community practiced different crafts. For example, members of families such as Al Thaheri and Al Mansouri could be found working in Abu Dhabi as fishermen, cultivating land in Al Ain city, or practicing trade in Dubai. This social development was significant to the survival of people and to their needs, because people exchanged their products and complemented one the other.

Economically, Emiratis kept sheep and goats as their main livestock.. They then adopted camels and used them to travel across the Arabian Peninsula and the eastern shores of the Arabian Gulf (today's Arab Ahwaz occupied by Iran since 1924). When camels proved difficult to adapt to village life, rural Emiratis used cows and bulls as their main livestock and economic means to prepare land for cultivation. Emiratis who lived near the sea developed a sea lifestyle and became fishermen, plus they learned and mastered the craft of pearl hunting and collecting. Within a hundred years (during the 1700s and 1800s), Emiratis became the main exporters of pearls in the world. They developed a very sophisticated economy based on the pearl industry and trading - towns like Sharja, Dubai, and Kalba were main centers for pearl trading.

However, after Iran occupied Ahwaz (Arabistan) region in 1924 and after the Japanese discovery of artificial pearl, Emiratis lost their main source of income. They lost the eastern shores of the Arabian Gulf, where they used to practice pearl diving, at the same time when Japan stole their thunder and started selling manufactured pearl. In the early 1950s and during the 1960s, Emiratis adapted a new life style based on the discovery of oil . Today, Emiratis live in a very sophisticated and high-tech society, which was built using the wealth accumulated from selling petroleum (oil) and adapting public policies that invested in human capital.

The aforementioned changes and continuous adaptation of Emiratis, however, neither eliminated the core of their traditional communities (i.e., extended family and kinship values) nor did they end Emiratis' old crafts. In today's UAE, Emiratis work in modern industries in all cities, live as fishermen in coastal towns and trade fish just like old days, and cultivate land and harvest palm trees in addition to other crops.

Traditional Political System

Emiratis established four forms of political systems during the past five hundred years. Each political system served a particular era and thus achieved certain ends. Lets us first define "political system" and the Emirates context of this concept.

Political system is combination of interrelated patterns of decision making that affect a group of people through the practices of legitimate authority (Sharab, 1983). Based on this definition, we see that political systems are not always formal, and government in the sense of central authority with army and institutions is not always the best way to characterize political systems. Three elements however are necessary to establish a political system, authority, legitimacy, and decision-making power. Authority is the ability to enforce law and order. Power is the ability to compel change and get people to change their attitudes. Legitimacy is acceptance of power and authority.

In the UAE, authority has always been communal or family-based. Even in the modern state, the ruling families in all seven Emirates rely on their family ties and family recognition to extend their legitimacy over a particular territory and the people who live within that geographical and and social domain. Constitutional and legal legitimacy translates the will of the community (i.e., UAE society). Since authority is family-based, legitimacy of practicing authority is also communal in the sense that families, who have among themselves historical relationships and blood relations, form an alliance to defend their territory as well as to establish a hierarchy of law and order. On the top of such hierarchy, the ruling man (sheik) resides as the ultimate authority-holding figure in that territory. Here, authority transforms from a social authority (informal authority) of that sheik to a political authority (formal authority) according to which sheik becomes more of a ruler than a clan chief of a tribe.

Decision-making is the daily practice of leaders, who use decision making as a tool to exercise political authority. Through a series of meetings with wise men and elderly people in the community (Majlis), sheiks discuss problems, affairs, conflicts, and any matters that concern the members of the community. Verdicts are officially given by the sheik, even if a decision was made after a long process of deliberation and discussions with members of the Majils.

We mentioned before that Emiratis have established at least five major forms of political systems during the past five centuries. The first political system was the tribal system (tribal government) before the 1200s. During this era, a fragmented political system was built in the remote region of the Arabian Peninsula called today UAE. The functions of that system were straightforward and simple as the main goal of the tribal governments was to (1) defend the tribe against any external enemies, (2) constantly find new grazing locations for the tribe to migrate to with their livestock, and (3) maintain local peace within the tribe.

During the eleventh and sixteenth centuries (1200-1500), UAE communities were influenced by the strong Arab states in Iraq (the Abbasids) and in Oman, in addition to the Ottomanian Empire. However, because the geographical location of the UAE was remote and difficult to control, Emirati communities established a decentralized system according to which they maintained their tribal political system. However at the same time, they followed the leadership of the central governments in Baghdad and Masqat. At this stage, Emiratis established the second form of political system and they established a dual system according to which a central government existed and local authorities existed as well. The latter had to pay certain amounts of money to the central government in exchange for defending it and legitimizing the authority of local sheiks (Al Baz, 2001). Although, the relationship between central government and local authorities was nominal, Emirati communities have developed new skills and knowledge to deal with the demands and agendas of a central government, which they never experienced before in their history. Nevertheless, they succeeded in maintaining an acceptable level of autonomy for their communities while gaining the protection of a well-organized and well-established central government. We will see that all accumulated experiences of self-governance have benefited Emiratis later on, when they established the third form of political system, which was more autonomous than before.

The third political system was revolutionary in nature. After the collapse of the Yaorobi (Yaaribah) regime in Oman during the 1600s, many communities in today's UAE decided to secede from its union and affiliation with the Omani central government. Tribal sheiks were in a position, which enabled them to build their own autonomous mini-states. The strong alliance of Al Qawasim in Sharja might be one of the first groupings of Emirati communities, which declared independence from the Omani government. Instead of being loyal to a distanced government and pay tributes to it, Al Qawasim established their own political system based on tribal loyalty and alliance. The new system was effective and the newly established state was able to defend against European invaders for almost two hundred years. After that, the Omani government realized that it was impossible for Omanis to retain control over other communities in today's UAE, which led many tribes to declare independence. Bani Yas was another Emirati community that established its independent political system in Abu Dhabi and Al Thafra regions. Both political systems (Bani Yas and Al Qawasim) made the core foundations for the new Emirati statehood.

Despite the fact that those two main political systems were new and vulnerable to neighbors' attacks, they were able to defend themselves without the need for any central government. Indeed, the Al Qawasim and Bani Yas governments were strong enough to fight the British colonialists and Persian invaders, winning various battles.

The fourth political system established by Emiratis was a local government system under the British colony. The British aimed at dominating the trade routes in the Arabian Gulf, Arabian Sea, and the Gulf of Oman. Therefore, they were not interested in enforcing direct rule on Emirati communities. Instead, the British recognized local governments, which were long established by Emiratis before the British arrived in the UAE. The local governments in Abu Dhabi, Sharja, Ras Al Khaima, and Dubai retained authority over daily affairs with their people while the British government dominated foreign and economic affairs. For over one hundred years (from 1850s to 1971) the Emirati communities enjoyed a great deal of local autonomous and political independence under sever British colony, which preferred to watch how things unfold from distance rather than interfering in managing daily affairs of the people. Through establishing this fourth form of governments, Emiratis were trained to establish governmental institutions and adopt legal systems that remained valid even after the independence.

In the fifth form of political system, the Emiratis established a fully independent and federal state in 1971. Even in this most current form of political system, Emiratis found a way to consolidate their political experiences in creating a federal system with a central government that was not overly dominating local affairs. Under the current political system, Emirati towns and cities retain their own local administrative, political, and judicial institutions simultaneously with those federal institutions. However, the unification of the seven emirates was the most feasible solution to regain independence and build a modern state.

The Oral History of Decentralization in UAE

In order to understand decentralization in the UAE, I decided to conduct a very simple qualitative study, in which several older Emiratis were interviewed to collect an oral history of centralization in the UAE. I gathered first-hand information about centralization in pre-independence era. I conducted a field study, in which I trained a group of undergraduate interns and students on research methods skills, and led them to interview fourteen (14) man and woman who were between the ages of 62 and 78 years old. Those interviewees resided in Abu Dhabi, Al Ain, Sharja, Fujera, and Ras Al Khaima. The following table describes the demographics of the study panel.

5.1: Demographic of the study

Description	Number
Male	9
Female	5
Nomadic Background	4
Agricultural Background	5
Fishermen-based Background (from sea towns)	5
School-Educated	12
Uneducated	2
Total	14

The field-study was conducted from February 3, 2011 to June 5, 2011. All interviews were transcribed and information was analyzed by using content analysis method. Microsoft Word was used to store and analyze interviews and the gathered information. The following part of this chapter is devoted to findings from the field study.

Oral History of Decentralization Among UAE Elderly

For centuries the inhabitants of the UAE have been tied to two major ecological elements, namely water and grass availability. Being originally a nomadic society, Emiratis were accustomed to frequently moving from one area to another depending on the availability of water and grass for themselves and for their herds. The establishment of settled communities was not a priority for most Emiratis mainly because the arable land to which they had access was limited. There was no meaning of staying in one area permanently while there was no enough sustenance for the entire community. However, in the northern emirates such as Fujera and Ras Al Khaima, green lands existed near the mountains and were used for agricultural activities. Several communities settled in those areas and established the agricultural base of today's rural UAE. Those nomadic people who grazed their herds close to the seashores have gradually adapted their lives to the sea life style. Later, those small communities established sea villages in Abu Dhabi Island, Dubai, and Sharja in addition to many other smaller localities. Sea people worked in pearl diving and fishing industries. Ras Al Khaima and Sharja have created a great marine fighting power based on their sea skills. During the British war against the Emirates, Ras Al Khaima and Sharja owned a great fleet, which consisted of hundreds of big, locally built military, ships and vessels. This sea power deterred foreign invaders and caused them to change their colonial strategies in the region.

Analysis from the field-study confirmed what the previous and introductory discussion asserted. The three types of communities found in UAE were agricultural villages, fishermen towns, and nomadic communities (see, for example, Al Shaheen, 1997). Each one of those communities enjoyed a certain level of autonomy. By the nature of those communities, people lived too far from any central governments, thus lived free from government's direct dominance or control. Even the strong Omani Sultan, during the eighteenth century, was unable to rule the three types of Emirati communities, which led him to give up his claims of their lands. After the disengagement of the Omani government, Emirati communities knew an era of self-governance, which lasted until independence in 1971.

Nomadic communities were ruled by tribal sheiks who managed all aspects of the life of the tribe. The legitimacy of tribal sheiks was based on the sheiks' ability to solve problems, adjudicate disputes, and defend the tribe from foes. In most cases, the sheikdom was handed down from father to son. Legitimacy was also transferred from father to son, but it was almost impossible to maintain a strong legitimacy unless the sheik was able to prove his credentials and show his followers the worthiness of his rule.

In farm-based villages (i.e., agricultural), leadership was embedded in either a Mulla or the village Kabeer (elder). Mullas were religious figures who gained their authority by the wisdom they exercised in respecting the traditions and culture of the community as well as by being able to make sound judgments in intra- communal and inter-communal disputes. Intra-communal disputes require a delicate approach in which the Mulla must maintain impartiality yet solve problems that arise– usually amongst members of the same family. In inter-communal disputes, Mullas were expected to possess persuasive skills and the ability to work with other Mullas to solve conflicts that arise between two or more people from different villages.

Leadership practices in fishing communities were similar to that in agricultural villages. The two most significant differences however were, first, the existence of "Craft Councils". Craft Councils (CC) were gatherings of men who worked in the same industry or profession. Each council had an elected (chosen) leadership. CC had authority to make decisions that organized the practices of a certain industry as well as organize the relationship with the political governing authorities. The second difference was that craft or profession was the reason why people gathered in one council. It was not kinship or blood relationship, as the case in tribal culture that brought people together. Practicing similar tasks was the bond that kept those fishing communities together and helped them establish the industrial and commercial base of today's UAE.

Elderly Emirati viewed the role of the central government before the independence from the British colonial state as minimal. They asserted that there was no influence of a central government on their daily lives. Of course, the central government existed in deed, but because the Emirati society was well organized in the three communities (tribal nomads, fishermen, and agricultural), there was little need for a central government to intervene in regulating a society that was already regulated by councils and normative forms of governing bodies. In other words, nomads had their sheiks that functioned as rulers, judges, and social figures, rural villages had Mullas, and the councils regulated fishermen. In addition, the British rulers did not want to interfere directly in the administering of daily affairs within Emirati communities; neither they were interested in regulating their affairs. Thus, the philosophy and practice of the British colonialism in the Arabian Gulf region, including the Emirates, relied on using local culture to prolong its dominance over the region. Therefore, the British ruler strengthened local leaderships and tribal hierarchies to maintain domestic peace in the seven emirates. Hence, local leaderships were able for over one hundred years to maintain law and order, based on the legitimacy given to them by two parties - their followers (e.g., tribal communities and rural villages) and the treaties signed with the British colonial regime.

The Status of the Contemporary UAE Government

The political history of UAE made it easier for Emiratis in 1971 (year of independence) to transform the decentralized political system, which they inherited from their ancestors into a modern political system. Abu Dhabi government first introduced the federal system in the UAE. Sheik Zayed championed the efforts to unify the seven emirates and establish a modern state. The sheiks of the other six emirates were aware of the importance of unity, and they supported the federal proposal by the Abu Dhabi government.

Within the federal system, each emirate retained sovereignty over local affairs of the emirate. Some emirates retained a legal system, police force, and civil service system that were part of the federal system until today. While some emirates remain effectively submissive to the federal government, some emirates are significantly trying to distinguish themselves from the federal government (Al Shaheen, 1997).

The Structure of the Emirati Federal Government

The constitution of the UAE was adopted in 1971 as a temporary one, then it was adopted permanently in 1997 (Abu Basha, 2002; The Constitution of the UAE). The constitution created a federal system of three levels of political authority, namely the Supreme Council (SC), the Presidency (P), and the Ministerial level (M). The following chart shows this structure:

5.2: Organizational Chart of the UAE Federal Government

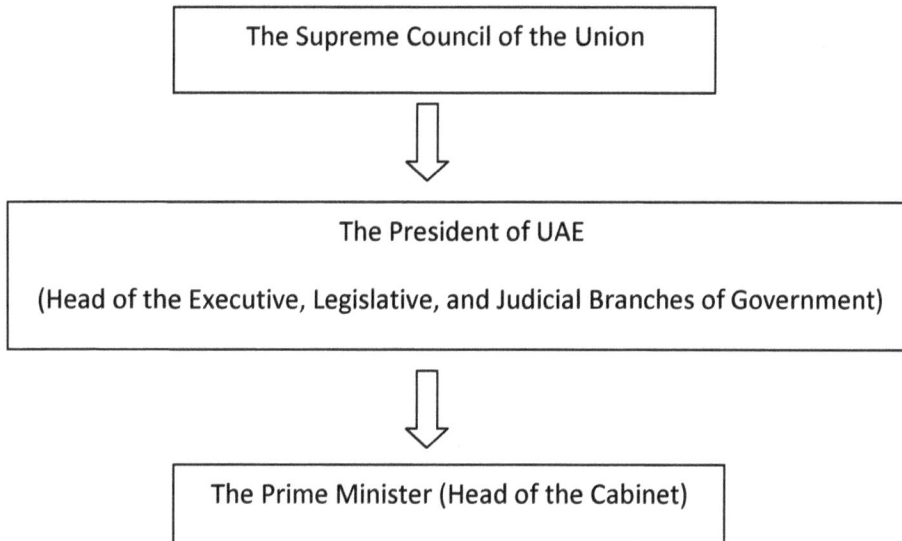

```
┌─────────────────────────────────────────────┐
│      The Supreme Council of the Union         │
└─────────────────────────────────────────────┘
                      ⇩
┌─────────────────────────────────────────────────────┐
│              The President of UAE                      │
│                                                        │
│ (Head of the Executive, Legislative, and Judicial     │
│           Branches of Government)                      │
└─────────────────────────────────────────────────────┘
                      ⇩
┌─────────────────────────────────────────────┐
│   The Prime Minister (Head of the Cabinet)    │
└─────────────────────────────────────────────┘
```

The UAE constitution did not specify responsibilities for each level of the three previous levels in the Emirati political system per se, but the practices of federalism in UAE for over forty years since the independence have established the current system divided in the aforementioned way (Ali, 1985). Division of labor in political decision-making has been evolving since 1971 and no specific pattern has yet settled to be final. The evolving federalism in UAE is a unique governance style according to which the relationships between various stakeholders are developing over years in a way that accommodates the needs of the country.

The Supreme Council

The constitution of UAE established a council of seven rulers, the rulers of all seven emirates. Membership on the council is automatic for any sheik that becomes a ruler of his emirate due to death or resignation of an incumbent ruler. While the Supreme Council is the ultimate stakeholder in all political and security-sensitive decisions, it plays a modest role in specific economic and social policy settings, which are left to the Prime Minster and his cabinet to handle (The Constitution of the UAE; Abu Al Majd, 1978). In addition, the SC rarely interferes in administrative or restructuring activities of particular agencies; as such, work lies within the domain of particular institutions under the presidency.

The UAE constitution did not set rigid roles for the Supreme Council. Instead, it listed a group of general but fundamental responsibilities of the SC. Those responsibilities were legislative, executive, and judicial. The following paragraphs discuss some of those responsibilities:

Approving and disapproving legislations: the SC can disapprove any piece of legislation that is submitted by the National Council (Parliament). If the Supreme Council or the President who is also a member of the SC disapproves any legislation, that legislation will not become a law. All members of the SC, therefore, must approve all legislation (before they become effective laws). May be, the most significant federal law that must be approved by the SC is the budget resolution (Al Hamid, 1990).

The SC enjoys three types of executive authorities. The President exercises some of these authorities directly, some, and the Prime Minister exercises some of them. The major responsibilities executed by the SC include the election of the President of the UAE by a majority vote in the SC. In addition, the joining of new states to the union must be voted on by the Council and must get unanimous vote. Responsibilities executed through the President of the UAE include: the declaration of war, declaration of state of emergency, appointment of the prime minister and cabinet, adopting general guidelines for all public policies, and dismissal of the National Council. As for responsibilities exercised by the cabinet and prime minster, the SC can appoint judges; accept resignation of judges, and sign treaties and agreements with other parties.

The President

The Supreme Council elects the President by the majority of five votes including the votes of Abu Dhabi and Dubai. The President can be elected for five years renewable for unlimited number of terms. If the Presidency is vacant due to the demise of the President or other reasons, the Deputy President should exercise the President's responsibilities until the new President would be elected within one month.

The UAE President is an executive position. Therefore, he exercises actual executive authorities including the approval or disapproval of amendments on any legislative bills sent to him by the National Council. The President reviews and signs all federal bills before they go to the Supreme Council for deliberation and approval. The President also issues decrees and federal executive orders within his realm of federal responsibilities. Since the President is a member of the Supreme Council, he chairs the council's meetings and calls members for assembly. Finally, the President is the commander in-chief and the head of the Defense Council, which includes the minister of defense, minister of interior, minister of foreign affairs, minister of finance, and the prime minister. Here we see that the UAE President has been given diverse responsibilities by the constitution as well as by the practices of federalism.

Prime Minster

The third level of authority in the previous chart is the position of prime minister. Prime Minister (PM) in UAE is an executive job, as it enables the Prime Minster to supervise the work of all members of the cabinet. The PM is responsible for ensuring that the policy guidelines set by the Supreme Council are met. It is his responsibility to nominate qualified candidates to fill vacant ministerial seats. The PM also coordinates the federal and local authorities to ensure best implementation of public policies.

Ministers or cabinet members are the executers of public policies in UAE. Each minister heads an administrative system, which has the capacity to run public domain. Civil servants are organized by flawed federal regulations mainly because the federal civil service system is still developing. Some local civil service systems could have been developed more than the federal civil service system, because local administration has been in existence for a longer time compared to the federal one.

Local Administration

Local administration in the UAE federal system occupies an important role as local authorities carry out all emirate-level affairs. Since UAE is composed of seven emirates, a ruler who is also the top civil servants within his emirate heads each emirate. Rulers delegate a wide range of authorities to others within the emirate. Rulers of each emirate enjoy a great deal of freedom in managing the affairs of the emirate, no matter how big or small an affair could be. The constitution has not limited rulers' authorities in any shape or form (Al Shaheen, 1997). The only limitation probably is the norms according to which each ruler has gained legitimacy of his ruling by the people of his emirate. The most significant administrative units that handle important local-level responsibilities are municipalities.

Municipalities in UAE are organized to serve people living within certain territories. Although there are eight major cities in UAE (Abu Dhabi, Al Ain, Dubai, Sharja, Ajman, Om Quwain, Ras Al Khaima, and Fujera), the complexity of administrative organization of each municipality varies from one city to another. For example, while Abu Dhabi and Al Ain have very sophisticated administrative units, other cities lack coherence and vision for better performance in the future.

Unfortunately, various municipalities are managed based on cultural norms and kinship rather than professional standards of management. This situation has led to poor performance within many units in each municipality. However, in the past ten years, Abu Dhabi has led the effort to energize and establish strong and decentralized local authorities and made customer satisfaction the major criteria to judge municipal success. The general framework for the administrative structure of municipalities in UAE follows the general framework as follow:

5.3: Structure of Local Administration in UAE

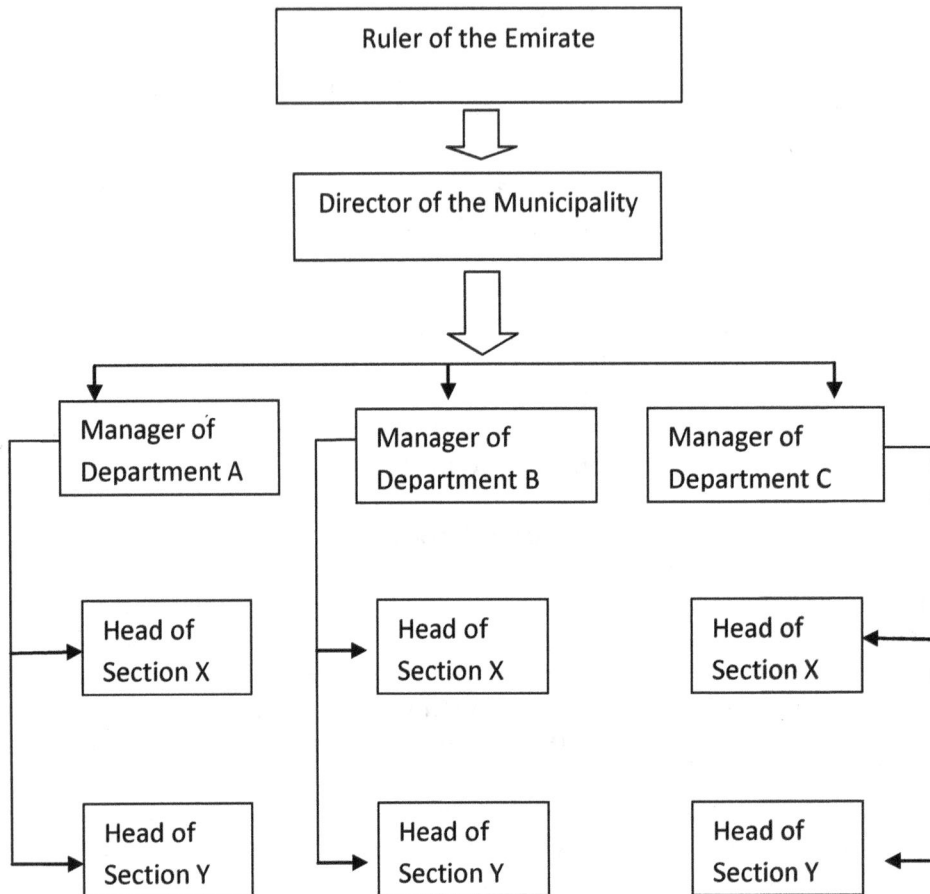

```
                    ┌─────────────────────────┐
                    │    Ruler of the Emirate  │
                    └─────────────────────────┘
                               ⇩
                    ┌─────────────────────────┐
                    │ Director of the Municipality │
                    └─────────────────────────┘
                               ⇩
```

Manager of Department A	Manager of Department B	Manager of Department C
Head of Section X	Head of Section X	Head of Section X
Head of Section Y	Head of Section Y	Head of Section Y

We notice that the structure of municipalities takes a rigid top-bottom shape. The absolute ruling authorities of the seven emirates enjoy gives then almost an absolute power in running their emirates. Therefore, the structure of municipalities fits within the tribal culture of the society, where limits of authority clearly separate one job from another. Despite the sophistication of some municipalities (such as Al Ain municipality) decision-making mechanisms still follow traditional frameworks. Managers seem to be reluctant to delegate authority or share power with others. This phenomenon is understandable within a tribal culture where personal dignity or family pride may interfere with professional performance, thus prevents a manger from working collaboratively and productively with others. The same can be said about the unitary way in which high-level decision- making is handled. Even in planning, we can see the fragmentation of municipal planning which led several cities to have poor planning and ineffective city development policies.

Another reality about local administration in UAE is the dependency of local departments on the central government. Even if the city has a long history of administrative record, some cities lack autonomy in deciding "what." Although high technology is used in big municipalities, some smaller municipalities are incapable of taking advantage of this technological advancement.

Administrative Structure on Emirate-Level

As mentioned earlier, the UAE's local administration is strongly connected by the will of the ruler of a particular emirate. Away from municipal administration, the following discussion highlights major developments of administration in Abu Dhabi, Sharja and Dubai emirates as examples of the seven emirates (Al Shaheen, 1997).

Emir's Council was the sole administrative unit in the Abu Dhabi emirate until 1965. The council was responsible for translating the policy agenda of the sheik into public programs. After 1966, the new sheik (ruler) of Abu Dhabi implemented a large-scale policy of administrative capacity building. He established modern agencies for finance, customs, defense, oil, justice, passport and naturalization, transportation, and many others. This reform policy was followed by the establishment of an urban planning council, which was charged with advising the ruler on best planning ideas. After the independence in 1971, and the formation the union, Abu Dhabi became the seat of the newly created federal government. Therefore, most emirate-level agencies became the nuclear units for state-level ministries. The UAE administrative system has benefited tremendously from the experience of the Abu Dhabi emirate in administrative organization and service providing.

Because the Abu Dhabi emirate is the largest and most influential emirate in the UAE, it took the initiative to establish several executive and legislative units to assist the ruler in making public policies and implementing them. Two major units reporting directly to the ruler were established, namely the Executive Council and the Consultative Council. While the Executive Council is a mini-ministerial council and considered a very effective institution in implementing all public policies as well as overseeing all executive agencies in the emirate, elitist members staff the council. Members of the council are appointed by the Ruler. Similarly, but less importantly, the Consultative Council plays a major role in advising the ruler on certain policy areas. This council has only a consultative authority and has no executive power. The ruler may or may not take the advice of this council.

Very similar to the developments in Abu Dhabi, Sharjah and Dubai (the second and third strongest emirates in the union) have established executive councils, consultative councils, and several emirate-level units. The economic advancement of these two emirates has led to establishing administrative units with executive power to handle commerce, security, safety, culture, and finance. All directors of these units are appointed by a decree issued by the ruler of the respective emirate. Thus, the rulers exercise direct and hierarchal authority over all administrative units.

Conclusion

In this chapter, we discussed various aspects of centralization, federalism, and culture in UAE. The UAE is a new state that was declared independent in 1971. The experience of federalism in UAE has proven fruitful despite challenges and obstacles. Some of the strengths of federalism in UAE includes: (1) The commitment of Abu Dhabi government and its ruling family to maintaining a strong federal state. (2) The economic capabilities of the UAE enable the federal government to generously distribute revenues of oil and commerce to other emirates. (3) The mutual threats that challenge all people in the UAE and unify them behind the federal government. Most importantly among these threats are the Iranian racist and expansionist agendas. Iran has not stopped dreaming about dominating all Arab states on the Arabian Gulf since the middle ages. Thus, all Emiratis feel compelled to unify against this devilish enemy. The imbalance of demographic composition of the UAE population makes all Emiratis on the same page in fearing the possibility that foreigners (mainly Asians such as Indians) overtake the country especially that local people only make less than 20 percent of the entire population in 2011. (4) Educated elites among the Emirati society have built a latent coalition of supporters of the federal government knowing that only a united country can survive amidst the ambitions of foreign powers to dominate smaller nations.

On the other side, some of the most serious threats to the federal system in UAE include: (1) The narrow thinking of several emirates and their elites to build a local capacity on the expense of the federal capacity. For example, some emirates insist on building separate and strong institutions that do not cooperate or coordinate with the federal government. (2) Some anti-federalism groups exist and hold stakes in the economy. These groups of individuals believe that an independent tiny emirate would benefit them better than a federal system where tougher checks and balances may exist - limiting their personal financial, political, and administrative ambitions. (3) Demographical imbalance may cause Asians and especially Indians and Pakistanis to cause damage to the culture, political system, and future of the state. It is increasingly obvious that the Arabic national language is pushed back to the benefit of expatriates' languages and dialects. Many foreigners refuse to learn the Arabic language using their numbers as a weapon to enforce a foreign culture. (4) Foreign security threats, especially Iran, perceive a strong federal UAE as a threat to their economic, cultural, racial, and military interests in the Arabian Gulf region. Such enemies have interests in weakening the federal government.

Decentralization in UAE is one element of federalism. There are three significant levels of administration in UAE, namely federal, emirate, and city levels. Each level has its own peculiarity and dynamics. However, the common denominator among the three levels is the tribal reality (United Nations' ESCWA, 2003). Despite all developments in UAE, public administration remains vulnerable to tribal cultural norms where kinship is more important than merit in hiring civil servants. In addition, tribal values may dominate the way some agencies operate leaving accountability measures marginal in affecting the agency's overall productivity.

The bright side of decentralization in UAE may be seen through the deeply rooted heritage of the UAE society. Since people lived for centuries in relative autonomy, they have developed clear traditions of running their own affairs without relying totally on a distanced government. This cultural element can enable cities and municipalities to champion a movement for administrative reform. Local authorities can sponsor many policy initiatives to energize the surrounding region and improve the life of the people.

References

Abu Al Majd, Ahmad. 1978. *The UAE: Comprehensive Examination*. Cairo: Institute of Arabic Research and Studies.

Abu Basha, Nabaweya Helmi. 2002. Social and Political Environment and its Impact on the United Arab Emirates. Abu Dhabi: Center for Research and Documentation.

Al Baz, Daoud Abdul Raziq. 2001. Political and Constitutional Decentralization in the United Arab Emirates. Journal of Legislation and Sharia Law, 15th issue.

Al Hamid, Said. 1990. The National Federal Council. Abu Dhabi: Dar Al Mutanabi for Publishing.

Al Kobaisi, Amir. 1982. Public Adminsitration in UAE. Sharja: Dar Al Khaleej Publishing.

Al Shaheen, Abdul Raheem. 1997. The System of Governance and Administration in the United Arab Emirates.

Ali, Shams Merghani. 1985. A Synopsis of Constitutional Law and Fundamentals of Constitutional Organization in UAE. UAE: Al Kods Publisher.

Sharab, Naji. 1983. The United Arab Emirates: Study of Politics and Ruling. Abu Dhabi: Al Etihad for Press and Publication. The Constitution of the UAE.

United Nations' ESCWA. 2003. Decentralization and its Emerging Role in ESCWA Region. E/ESCWA/HS/2001/3.

Most of the listed references are in Arabic and the translation was made to accommodate the language of the chapter.

Chapter Six

The Segundo Montes Community and

the Politics of Post-war Desires[1]

José Neftalí Recinos

Key words: decentralization, desire, utopia, El Salvador, Segundo Montes Community

Introduction

The Segundo Montes Community (CSM)[2] entails the virtuous illusions fluently articulated by the revolutionary discourse that sustained the armed conflict in El Salvador for more than a decade but also the specious ideological assertion of its possibility. A decentralization project in nature, CSM functions as a phenomenon beyond its political, social and economic implications: it is a symbol. The intrinsic value of this community is bound to its utopian intentions. The hard numbers, projections, and statistics drawn into the transfer of authority and responsibility to entities at a subnational level that started as a conscientious effort in Central America in the 1990s, prompt a definition of decentralization that does not apply to CSM since it lacks the peculiarities surrounding its unique nature and the purview to define its origins. Therefore, intertwined to the broadening efforts made to improve and strengthen the local government as a process of decentralized cooperation, the following pages will also direct its attention to the subjectivity that embraces a view of self-governance conjugated by desired ideals and expectations informed by reality in a post-war scenario.

Geovanny Díaz Pereira, mayor of the municipality of Meanguera in northern Morazán, El Salvador, was presented with the following question: After twenty years, how do you view the Comunidad Segundo Montes' initial project to create an alternative, egalitarian, popular economy? Mayor Díaz Pereira managed to assert that the conception of the economic model developed by the community back in 1990 was an impossibility:

> When we assembled a number of communally owned enterprises, it was not only the implementation of an economic model, it reflected the realization of a set of ideas in which we wanted to believed. Hence, the possibility of it working out was close to impossible. There we were, a small group of people confronting the capitalist machine of a nation (Díaz Pereira, 2011).

There is no doubt that, as an ideological experiment, the emergence of this decentralized community signified an alternative to an official economic system. Contrary to widely accepted assertions that "in most countries decentralization reflects a broader process of political and economic reform" (Litvack, 1998), CSM, a settlement of barely 1500 families then, articulated the desire to implement those compelling principles that would resonate with the revolutionary ideals. It dared to dream of being the model of an independent popular power that would promote and propel the development of the region, ergo, the norm for decentralization policy.

Limited decentralization policies were actually in place late in the nineteenth century in El Salvador and were dismantled after the coup d'etat in 1931 by General Maximiliano Hernández Martínez. Since then, centralization persisted as a form of state control at all levels for the next forty years of military rule (Bird, 2000). However, the presence of authoritarian/dictatorial regimes that restricted or stifled the voice of citizens in Latin America dates back to the Spanish and Portuguese colonies as a form of centralized political practice. This legacy only gave way to transitions of elected governments and other forms of decentralization during the 1980s (Tulchin & Selee, 2004)[3]. In the particular case of El Salvador from 1984 to 1989, during President José Napoleón Duarte's administration, the first steps towards decentralization were taken. In 1987, the Salvadoran Institute for Municipal Development (ISDEM) was legally established as the main arm of the Government of El Salvador (GOES) in local matters. During the administration of President Alfredo Cristiani (1989-1994), the government began the "Modernization of the State" program in 1990-1991 with the support of the United Nations Development Program (UNDP). The plan included decentralization, deconcentration and municipal development as important components of the process of modernization ("El Salvador country," 2004). Since then, El Salvador has established itself as the country in Central America with more decentralization projects according to studies conducted by the United States Agency for International Development (USAID) and UNDP, among others. Concomitant to this reality is the assertion of CSM as a project challenging an official economic system from the no place of utopia.

The politics of post-war desires

It was January 16th of 1992 when the Salvadoran government and the Farabundo Marti National Liberation Front (FMLN) under the auspices of the United Nations Secretary-General signed the Peace Accords at the Castle of Chapultepec in Mexico City. Time itself has undertaken the task to spell out the importance of such historical event. The extraordinary results of those agreements positioned El Salvador, a country lacking a democratic tradition and strong institutions, in a path to democratization[4]. In an era signaling the emergence of a new world order synonymous with new forms of imperialism at a global stage, this minute country, *El Pulgarcito de América*[5], became a high-profile case in an effort to transition a region, pummeled by twelve years of civil war, to a democratic State "without substantial alteration to the secular socioeconomic structure of injustice"

(Grenier, 1999)[6]. It is true that one cannot draw a parallel between formal mechanisms of electoral democracy and democratic values per se; nonetheless, beneath all conjectures, the Peace Accords remained a formidable effort from the warring parties to reconcile their positions under the prevailing circumstances and to accept the challenge of repositioning their individual points of contention in order to act on the demands for fundamental changes. A shift in their ideologies and dispositions was needed. It was imperative to set aside a notable intransigency in their dealings to put forth the implementation of a framework under which the war would be resolved.

In retrospect, looking at the process that brought about the end of the armed conflict in El Salvador, one cannot help to ponder the existential philosophical complexities that were negotiated; the level of consciousness displayed by both sides in signing the agreements that would allow political, economic, and military reforms in the country without alienating their respective supporters. The Peace Accords of 1992 also signaled the beginning of a new struggle over the direction of the nation in a post-war scenario, how would those efforts be channeled and in the service of whom. As Binford has noted, the battle lines were drawn from the beginning between two models of development:

> [O]ne model, developed in well-appointed suites in Washington, DC, or salons in Escalón and San Benito, and disseminated by an army of foreign service officers and bureaucrats, involves a commitment to private capital and the free market; the other, promoted by the Frente Farabundo Martí para la Liberación Nacional (Farabundo Martí National Liberation Front —FMLN) and popular organizations linked to it, is a more "participatory" model that combines collective and individual initiatives in the service of a diversified, ecologically sound system of production and distribution capable of meeting the basic needs (for food, housing, education, and health) of the broad masses of the population (1997:56).

Albeit a new confrontation of wills derived from this particular situation, one cannot forget that repatriated refugees who had fled the country's civil war in 1980 had already formed CSM in areas controlled by the FMLN in 1990 while the war was still being waged. It was an attempt to create a social and economic model of development that would resonate with the egalitarian socialist ideals promoted by the revolution. As an ideological project, it would function based in a model of participatory democracy and self-management principles that would put to the test a code of morals underlined by their discourse of unity, solidarity, and cooperation. It is noteworthy to consider that even before the peace agreements were reached CSM was functioning in spite of the traditional and formal national capitalist economic model. In other words: as a decentralized form of subnational government[7].

The efforts put forth by communities in territories controlled by the FMLN by the end of the armed conflict were once characterized by Father Rogelio Ponseele as a "mystical" endeavor that provided the opportunity to be part of something transcendental, to project oneself, to offer oneself for the good of society (López Vigil, 1987). However, lets not forget that this community, by the time of its repatriation, has to be framed in the absence of conflicting dogmatic ideologies —the Berlin Wall has crumbled, the Soviet Union has disappeared, in not so many words: the Cold War was over—. The popular mobilization rallying in favor of the scientific construction of an anti-capitalist, anti-imperialist, Leninist polity is not part of the discourse any longer. The chimera of revolution did not translate to truly profound processes of social, economic, and cultural change. It is the absence of a bipolar world, as sustained by Trigo that has "subsumed every single sociopolitical conflict and allowed for the formation of popular national blocs in order to carry out the pending national-democratic and social revolutions" (2004:7). It can be reasoned that during the civil war the utopian desires were inarguably necessary in the propulsion of subversive ideals, now those same utopian desires in a post-war stadium needed to be renovated and implemented as praxis, as a tangible and attainable project from which society would benefit. The FMLN recognized the organizational sources and collectivist ideology that were a key component of life in the warfront, as well as the many civilian organizations in northern Morazán which would contribute to the construction of an independent popular power that with time can successfully face the oligarchy and its allies (Villalobos, 1989). Principles such as self-governance, community problem-solving, and popular participation will become in the 1990s fundamental features in the implementation of decentralization policies (Bird, 2000).

Discourse shows all its malleable nature when it relates to FMLN's conceptions about a future based on the social experiences attained during the war. Such positioning illustrates a juxtaposition of an expired ideal that has lost its currency and one that predicates on the feasibility of its potential. The deferral of an independent popular power intends to validate the utopian landscape as a possible social reality. The ideological discourse here employed, not only pretends to advocate and reflect a reality of experience, but the suggestion that a new reality can be created. It cannot be ignored the mutually constituted relationship that exist between language, culture, and society; therefore any utterance reflecting on the responsibility to continue actively participating and pursuing a "grandiose, long-term social experiment" (Binford, 1997) can only corroborate how discourse is influenced and conformed by sociocultural circumstances but it can also shape and construct its own reality. After all, language is power and for Bakhtin:

> All words have the 'taste' of a profession, a genre, a tendency, a party, a particular work, a particular person, a generation, an age group, the day and hour. Each word tastes of the context and contexts in which it has lived its socially charged life... (1981:293)

Those individuals summoned to participate, to construct, and bring into fruition the glorified transforming ideals of the revolution, must do so conscious of the limitations, of the apathy, and the whole new set of societal attitudes characterizing the post-war[8].

Undoubtedly, the "socially charged life" that is the backdrop of revolutionary discourse in El Salvador is the result of decades of political violence, of inequality, of poverty. There is a multitude of reasons why many sectors of society felt the necessity or felt motivated, not only to articulate their inconformity with their social reality but also to unite in the effort to overthrow the government in power via a revolution. As stated by Salvador Samayoa:

> I believe that the people have different motivations for fighting than those acquired by a more sophisticated leadership. Politically, people have more rudimentary motivations: often *they simply have no choice*, like in the case of the peasantry, such an important component of the struggled in El Salvador, which joined the guerrillas *because it couldn't be in the other side, because their family were simply murdered*. They know since they were born that the Army is evil and that the guerrillas are against the Army[...] (qted. by Grenier, 1999, p. 82).

Joining the revolutionary struggle, as illustrated above, revolves around the absence of free will, lack of alternatives as well as preconceptions. This acceptance resonates with the notion that the insurgents became *la voz de los sin voz* —the voice of the voiceless. In spite of how popular such assessment might be, there were many factors that influenced peoples' decision to become actively engaged in warfare in support of the guerrilla. The decision of many to counter violence with violence was in direct result to the savagery of the Army, the constant raids at nighttime conducted by the death squads not only in urban areas but also on isolated villages that gave way to innumerable disappearances and assassinations. Many of us would think that people being affected by these egregious vicissitudes foreign to fortune, framed by a materiality of violence, would have had a clear vision, a homogeneous understanding, of the revolutionary process. Contrary to the latter assertion, due to contrasting backgrounds, in fact there was little sense of community (Ventura, 1990). Nonetheless, if there is one element that characterized the insurgency in El Salvador, it was its ability to evaluate and recognize that they could not remained oblivious and removed from the political conditions given rise outside their ideological and political world. At a particular moment, even the most extremist of factions were able to come together and visualize the necessity to redefine the armed struggle as a path to unity were democratic organizations and revolutionary forces converged (Jiménez C., Benítez M, Córdova M. & Segovia , 1988).

The vision articulated then by the left is reminiscent of those early stages when the possibility of a triumphal revolution would bring all aspirations to fruition. "Words" cites Rodolfo Cardenal when he evokes the political discourse of those days, "had become almost magical, having power in themselves, and therefore it was possible to disregard reality. For example the word socialism was understood in a utopian way..." (1987: 452). The participatory model of democracy envisioned in a post-war scenario can only be construed as the attempt to exert an ideal that had lost its currency at a global stage. All the same, it is this desire, this longing, this contradictory sentiment of nostalgia what will strive to accommodate a communal project, in charge of its own affairs, against a national capitalist model. According to Grenier "[t]hanks to radical priests and theology students, hitherto apathetic and conservative peasants and urban poor learned to identify the 'structural sin' of *capitalismo* and started to yearn for a politico-religious version of the promised land" (1999: 129). What determines the object of nostalgia is a temporal and spatial distance that separates the subject from that which is yearned. According to Jonathan Steinwand "the imagination is encouraged to gloss over forgetfulness in order to fashion a most aesthetically complete and satisfying recollection of what is longed for" (1997: 9). CSM, as a concept, clashes with reality since it does not recognize its own impossibility. There is no point of reference, the socialist bloc has crumbled, and the continuity of such ideals does not longer exist. Albeit this restorative nostalgic impulse is associated with a past lost, in the particular case of this community, is also signaling to a possible return. "The ultimate goal of nostalgic longing" argues Mario Jacoby, "is a condition, [...] a state of being which find symbolic expression in the image of paradise" (1985). Ironically, CSM's attempt signifies the return to a lost paradise —an ideological model framed by the reality of a post-ideological scenario— that only functions as an abstract nostalgic construct of a future promise.

Comunidad Segundo Montes and the impediments of reality

In 1991 I returned to my country: El Salvador. I had been living in the United States for the previous six years and within the broad context of the political changes taking place in the region mine was limited exclusively to the events dealing with my *patria*[9]. I had been following the war from afar and there was *no santo día* in which the news hour did not report on the gruesomeness of the conflict in El Salvador. I was young and must admit that I sympathized with the rebels' cause. In numerous occasions, I protested against the policies of my host-country in the streets of Los Angeles, San Francisco, Sacramento, and fantasized with the toppling of the U.S. sponsored government to return one day to the utopian scenario of a real popular democracy. Now, with the ceased-fire agreement between the Salvadoran Army and the FMLN, I just had to go back. I wanted to witness and experience first hand how organized grassroots communities were taking hold after being formed in refugee camps of neighboring Honduras. It was through the arrangements of a good friend that in August of that year I visited CSM[10].

Everything had a special significance. Nothing was devoid of symbolism. Even now, more than twenty years later, in a conversation held with Santos Sixto Vigil, an administrator for Fundación Segundo Montes (FSM) —Segundo Montes Foundation— his initial statement felt more like a verbalized introspection: "the first houses were built with the wood planks and tinplates we brought back from Honduras" (Personal communication, 2011)[11]. People here were survivors. They had spent ten years in a refugee camp in Colomoncagua where they had been subjected to constant intimidation. Nonetheless, they had also learned and accomplished many things under the assistance from international agency staff. Elizabeth Cagan captures in great detail how these people became a cohesive community, I cite *in extenso*:

The refugees were to spend almost ten years in the camp, creating a society that was in many ways utopian despite confinement and harsh conditions. Entirely dependent on goods supplied by outside agencies, the camp did not have a money economy; all resources were owned communally and distributed on basis of need. Work was performed for personal development or to directly satisfy community needs. As in many socialist utopias, gender equality was in evidence; women participated at all levels and in all capacities, studying and working alongside men, and serving on leadership bodies. These accomplishments came about through a strong ideological commitment to free women from traditional restrictions, which was reinforced by extensive services that socialized many of women domestic tasks. Children were cared for in day care centers and by "children's coordinators," who set up activities for kids before school and watched over them during the day; meals for the elderly or sick were prepared in nutrition centers, and tortillas were made in collective kitchens and distributed to each family. Like all goods and services in the camp, these were free and available to all who needed them. (1999: 177).

Replicating the same level of cohesion and organization in their new reality under the most daring of circumstances, underlined by the waging war, was never achieved. Nevertheless, confronted with the urgency of their situation and the necessity to transition from a subsidized economy, CSM set the framework for what they hoped would warrant a sustainable development. They tried to implement a number of communally owned projects[12] that would yield to a solid economic and financial base, hence, overcoming their condition of dependency[13]. Equally important, was the creation of a model that would preserve the guiding principles that fuelled the collective imagination during all those years of armed conflict.

Under these circumstances, CSM becomes a twofold prospect: one, it needed to address the urgency to put in place a project that would benefit the most immediate necessities of the whole community by creating local resources—a vital component of decentralization—; two, a project that must display for all to see, the origins of its foundations, the structural principles that allowed each of its member to overcome extraordinary adverse situations: exile, intimidation, poverty, etc. These common life experiences, these revealed values of solidarity and mutual cooperation, represented the decisive element that would make this project function in the margins of a dominant economic system. It is under the spirit of community and a participatory attitude that CSM created a handful of institutions to precede communal projects on housing, infrastructure, education, health, and commerce[14].

CSM's development resulted in an internal dynamical process of which a common and primordial objective would substantiate an administrative model guaranteeing high levels of coordination, planning, and organization. This model had to effectively negotiate the multiple and various needs of the community. It is undeniable that the high levels of engagement and social commitment by members of the community made possible the implementation of communal projects where they did not perceived any financial compensation for their labor; notwithstanding, the viability of CSM as an economic model had to be the result of its ability to create income-generating activities that would remunerate those participating families and individuals. Ironically, this monetary concept, essential to all capitalist logic, reversed those utopian practices they had enjoyed as refugees.

One has to question the feasibility of a community with limited resources that, without the managerial and technical capacity in place, would be able to promote change on a broad scale, in agreement with the transforming socialist ideals articulated by the FMLN. On the first few years, members in the community worked arduously on the implementation of different initiatives: the construction of housing by the residents themselves, the creation of schools holding classes under trees, daycare centers for children and the elderly, a communal medical center, as well as to set up the infrastructure of the five different settlements that form CSM[15]. The shoe and clothing factories, stockbreeding, the breeding of pigs, and the raising of chickens; as it were other minor projects such as a tinsmith's shop and pottery, represented and generated genuine, tangible expectations, the hope of the whole community to expand their level of production in order to develop their economic agenda.

Granted, during the first few years, many thought of the project embodied by CSM as a real possibility; nonetheless, legitimate concerns existed about the ability to establish a system of sustainable development. It seems that the revolutionary desires propelling these ventures overlooked the reality awaiting communally owned enterprises. The adverse external impediments were stacked against such undertaking. The most obvious: going against the traditional centralized national economic system of the country[16]. These incidents only substantiated the tradition of central government intervention and manipulation of community affairs. For members of the community these impediments were intentional and they found consensus in the belief that their projects were never going to operate as they initially intended. The failure to establish a competitive system of production forced members of the community to reassess their situation. They opted for a basic agrarian economy of subsistence farming. Confronted with the inability to create viable conditions to overcome all these external difficulties, CSM is reduced to a strategy that would allow its members stability through more realistic and simplified objectives[17].

A rallying community

I have planned to meet Mauricio Geovani Díaz Pereira, a young, educated, and charismatic politician from the FMLN —a romantic figure should I say— born in the refugee camp of Colomoncagua and now presiding as mayor of Meanguera. I have also arranged interviews with Lelin Ventura the director of SILEM and Dolores Benítez a representative *in situ* of Fundación Santiago y Segundo Montes —Santiago and Segundo Montes Foundation—[18]. My timeline also allows me to interview the trustee of Meanguera, as well as NGOs administrators working in CSM.

Twenty years have past and the community is no longer the hamlet that housed 1500 families of refugees on the predictable denouement of a twelve-year war. It has grown so much that it is hard to delineate where does one municipality ends and the next one begins from Jocoaitique and Meanguera to San Francisco Gotera, the department head. The road is now named *Ruta de Paz* —Peace Highway—. Walking the *Peace Highway*, one cannot help but to notice the discrepancies in construction from one house to the next. The bigger and better houses —I will find out later— belonged to members in the community with relatives living abroad[19]. During my stroll I talked casually with community members that never get tired of recalling in solemn voices their origins, their struggles; some of them, still attired with the red and black kerchief around their necks, loyal to their colors. They have seen it all. They evoke those first years with great fondness. They abound on their relations of how they had assumed the responsibility to push forward an ideological agenda that would prove impossible to implement. Nonetheless, they also felt the necessity to try, since it simply constituted a set of principles in which they believed and for which they fought an intricate and protracted war. They refer the stories of their original plan with nostalgia, but the mood changes when they are faced with the period of instability few years after the Peace Agreements. I notice doubt, resentment, antagonism and a plurality of versions regarding those years' events.

In the mid-1990s, Federación de Municipios del Istmo Centroamericano (FEMICA) — Federation of Central American Municipalities— and other national municipal government associations joined forces in pursuing of policy and reforms to improve the environment in which they were operating, and to provide services more effectively (International City/County Management Association, 2004)[20]. These attempts were a continuation of decentralization policies started under previous administrations and not always enjoying sufficient political volition. Working at the margins and after the fiasco of the initial economic production projects, it was of significant consequence to get the members of the community to participate in local development and test their resilience (Diaz Pereira, 2010). To its advantage, CSM already had in place a deeply committed and engaged group of citizens eager to participate in local governance and try to restore the initial vitality displayed on the outset of the community as a project. All the differences and frictions were push aside and civic committees were created in each one of the settlements as liaisons between the municipality and CSM (ventura, 2011).

One important aspect is the association and mutual assistance between the mayor's office and the different institutions representing and serving the community. Although, El Salvador does central government revenue transfers to its municipalities[21], CSM has not been extremely dependent on resources from the government to motivate investments on its own and attracting international donor agencies. There is even a partnership program among the mayor's office and the different communal and civil institutions where if there is a project, all entities involved, will work together in order to strengthen the chances of a positive outcome. CSM has not stop working on the improvement of its infrastructure and continues to push for an autonomous water supply system, a waste management system and improvement of local roads. All this projects are implemented as community owned projects in a decentralized cooperation format, where the donors provide all the equipment and material, the municipality provides the land or buy it if necessary, and the members of the community offer their unskilled labor without monetary remuneration. This particular situation not only tests a set of intrinsic values —unity, solidarity, and cooperation—, but also underlines the community's commitment to its development. The fact that some of the projects listed above have become feasible is due to the level of involvement and responsibility of the community members. Being able to have impoverish people donate their time without pay speaks volumes[22]. This act would be inconceivable in any other municipality in the country (Vigil, 2011). Also in conjunction with the mayor's office, universities such as Universidad Centroamericana (UCA) —Central American University — and The Escuela Nacional de Agricultura (ENA) —National School of Agriculture— have provided their assistance in the implementation of agrarian diversification in the community (Díaz Pereira, 2011).

Moreover, the turmoil generated by internal dissention in the mid-1990s provided the opportunity to amend their utopian initiatives and reassess their goals. Administrative and institutional weaknesses during those years of crisis prompted the lost of credibility and support from many international cooperating agencies. The different institutions in the community had to be restructured and were forced to develop new management strategies to gain the confidence and trust of the international donor agencies. FSM, which was established from the outset as the consulting organization to all projects by and for the community, stopped functioning as organizer and facilitator and became itself an executing agency (Vigil, 2011). As a result, FSM has been able to implement a variety of projects and inject itself in the community as never before. In 2006, FSM developed a strategy plan to be implemented in the next five years that focused on economic production projects —such as agriculture and microcredit—, citizen participation, gender advocacy, and raising environmental awareness ("Planificación estratégica 2006," 2006)[23]. Working in conjunction with different municipalities in northern Morazán —Meanguera, Jocoaitique, Torola, Arambala, and San Fernando— one of its many tasks is to change the peasant's mentality of single crop farming. Its assistance also focuses on the implementation environmental projects such as: organic agricultural production[24], planting of fruit and timber yielding trees as a reforestation effort and raising environmental awareness through teachers' workshops at ten different educational centers in the area of Meanguera and Jocoaitique. Under FSM's new guidelines and strategies, one of the main concerns is to address and solve the matter of self-sufficiency in the possible absence of donors in a near future. That is the main reason why FSM has invested in public transportation and the construction of an inn with restaurant service and a butterfly house[25]. FSM is also trying to offer its support by promoting active participation by the youth sector community. The Organización Casa Abierta (OSCA) —Open House Organization— is made up of university students trying to create political, social, and historical awareness, as well as to offer multiple job alternatives to stop youth from leaving the community.

In the area of education, CSM has excelled. Even during those difficult years in the 1990s when the Ministry of Education did not recognized the training of the popular teachers for lack of proper certification, they were able to keep it together. Teachers continued working without pay and were able to receive formal training and certification from the University of Girona, Catalonia, Spain. Today, CSM has the most prestigious High School out of the 26 municipalities in Morazán. In the fall of 2011, the Instituto Tecnológico Padre Segundo Montes (ITPSM) —Technological Institute of Higher Education Segundo Montes— opened its doors to the community. It was possible with the help of international cooperation and the administrative support of Santiago y Segundo Montes Foundation[26]. The ITPSM offers the students the possibility to study a career on Civil Engineering or Tourism and Hospitality. The necessity to develop the region's infrastructure and competent housing construction, as well as the bolstering of an incipient interior and foreign tourism industry, make these two fields attractive and also necessary. Equally important, is the certification in 2012 by the Ministry of Education declaring Jocoaitique ("Jocoaitique libre de," 2012) and Meanguera ("Meanguera libre de," 2012) as areas "libres de analfabetismo" —illiteracy free municipalities—. This echoes the success of a previous literacy campaign in the community. During the nine years in the refugee camp of Colomoncagua they were able to grow their literacy rate from next to nothing to 85 percent (Storm, 1992).

Conclusion

Many events have transpired since the refugees demanded their repatriation. Since then, the ideals forged by many years of struggle still remain intact in the psyche of many community members. The system that fed social inequality, to an extent, remains unchanged in El Salvador. Nonetheless, in CSM efforts have been made to give continuity to principles such as self-governance, community problem-solving, and popular participation, in other words, the organic structures behind their initial demands and goals. When in the 1990s national policies of decentralization were being promoted, as a form of strengthening democracy at all levels and sectors of society, CSM was already strong at the grassroots level. Working at the margins of a traditional centralized national economic system that won't allow for the implementation and functioning of their idealistic agenda, CSM managed to overcome ideological and institutional crises. Although, in its beginnings failed to establish a competitive system of production —a vital component of decentralization— the community was able, through the years since then, to underline its origins, its foundations, and the structural principles that allowed each of its members to surmount extraordinary adversity. The new generation is being educated to preserve the collective memory and the revered values of solidarity and mutual cooperation. After putting differences aside, there is tangible and quantifiable evidence that supports the community's success in many areas. Steps have been taken to promote viable economic production projects, the implementation of new citizen participation methods, gender advocacy, and the active support of environmental, ideological, and historical awareness.

In the limbo of a post-ideological era and the presence of a globalized society, CSM has been able to adapt. It recognizes the impossibility of the initial agenda — an island, an utopia, in between two municipalities in northern Morazán described it the young Mayor of Meanguera—, but hopes that a common and primordial objective should substantiate the necessity to implement an administrative model guaranteeing high levels of coordination, planning, and organization that would turn CSM the proponents of real and substantive change.

ENDNOTES

1   Research for this chapter was possible in part by a mini-grant from the Stephen F. Austin State University Research Enhancement Program.

2   The Comunidad Segundo Montes takes its name in memory of one of the Jesuit priests murdered in 1989. Dr. Segundo Montes was a sociologist in charge of the UCA's Human Rights Institute and one of eight persons assassinated on November 16, 1989 at the campus of Universidad Centroamericana José Simeón Cañas (UCA). This massacre was order by the Salvadoran Army. The victims were: Ignacio Ellacuría, Ignacio Martín-Baró, Segundo Montes, Juan Ramón Moreno, Amando López, Joaquín López y López (all of them Jesuit priests and scholars at the University), Elba Ramos (employee) and her 15 years old daughter Celina Ramos.

3   Decentralization efforts during the 1980s, according to Tulchin and Selee, have affected democratic governance in different countries and at different levels of societies. For example, in Venezuela, after the delegitimization of the two party system and the ulterior economic crisis, constitutional reforms were made and state and municipal governments were elected for the first time in 1989. In Mexico, the peso devaluation and the ensuing depression led the federal government to institute reforms at a municipal level in 1983. This act, granted municipalities a greater autonomy with new functions and resources. Eventually, the increasing local success of the opposition parties helped gradually dislodge the PRI from power. After two decades of military dictatorship, the economic crisis in Brazil urged political forces from left and right to promote decentralization to insure transparency, participation, and equity among its citizens. In Argentina, provinces recover authority with the return to democracy and increased their margin of influence through negotiations with the national executive during the 1980s. The arrival of Peronist president in 1990, coupled with fiscal crisis, led the federal government to transfer major responsibilities and resources to the provinces in the early 1990s. Although, decentralization of education and healthcare to the provinces were transferred without accompanying resources for these new responsibilities (2004:10).

4   The centralized government of El Salvador has worked in the context of reasserting and strengthening its authoritarian grip over the economic and political life of the country since the years of General Maximiliano Hernández Martínez. It has characterized itself by suppressing dissidence through violence (Bird, 2000).

5   *El pulgarcito de América* is the nick name that was given to El Salvador by Chilean poet and Nobel Laureate Gabriela Mistral in reference to its tiny size. It also has a literary connotation since it refers to the character in two of the fairy tales collected by the Grimm brothers: Thumbling and Thumbling's Travels.

6   Grenier characterizes the wave of democratization of Latin America in general during the decade of the 1980s as contradictory and fragile.

7   In 1992, after the Peace Accords were signed and reconstruction of the country began from an apparent more democratic frame of reference. The Salvadoran government and international organizations were behind a plurality of programs for community strengthening and citizen participation carried out by NGOs and other institutions in collaboration with the municipalities. Nonetheless, the Comunidad Segundo Montes remained independent and only merged into the municipalities of Meanguera and Jocoaitique until 1994 (Ventura, 2011).

112

8   The decade of the 90s is crucial for the Central America region. The media attention has subsided, the Sandinista project has failed, the war in El Salvador is over, and Guatemala finally fallows suit and signs a peace agreement. However, a sense of distrust towards governmental institutions, political parties and collective projects of social change has taken hold of the population in general. In addition, a new set of concerns, such as drug trafficking, juvenile delinquency, corruption, and violence become part of daily life in a postwar arena. At a cultural level, according to the scholars Werner Machenbach and Alexandra Ortiz Wallner, Central America experience a "normalization of violence". Ellen Moodie on the other hand, talks about a new coding of violence that rearticulates it from "political" to "common" and a new postwar social imaginary stemming out of the telling of crime stories.

9   A shift to democratic form of government through formal mechanisms of electoral democracy is view as a vehicle to contribute to better democratic governance in the region of Latin America during the 1980s (Tulchin & Selee, 2004).

10   In 1991, when I first visited this community, it was known as Ciudad Segundo Montes —Segundo Montes City—.

11   I also give in to nostalgia and started to remember walking through the different settlements, visiting several small factories and many other projects, sitting on a rock, together with a group of children, while a teacher dictated the day's lesson under the canopy of what I want to believe was a ceiba.

12   Initials projects in CSM reflected the technical training received in the refugee camp in Honduras. They established a clothing and shoe factories, a tinsmith's shop and pottery. CSM also attempted to get into stockbreeding, the breeding of pigs, and the raising of chickens. A series of unfortunate events created an economic crisis that brought forth the discontinuance of all projects.

13   There is one important aspect that has lingered for all these years among the members of the community. They believed their subsidized economy had encouraged a condition of *asistencialismo* —assistance mentality— that would interfere with their ability of self-governance.

14   Multiples community institutions were created: The Asociasión Comunal Segundo Montes— Segundo Montes Communal Association— (ASM), which was founded as the political front of the community since its repatriation and continues up to this day providing its services as a liaison between the community and the municipality; Fundación Segundo Montes —Segundo Montes Foundation— (FSM), it was established as the consulting organization to all projects by and for the community; Cooperativa Constructora San Luis —San Luis Cooperative Construction Company— (COCSAL), Sistema Local de Educación de Meanguera —Local Educational System of Meanguera— (SILEM).

15   CSM consist of five small communities: Los Quebrachos, El Barrial, San Luis, Hatos I, and Hatos II.

16   Elizabeth Cagan argues that the obstacles confronted by CSM amounted not only to the control and centralization of capital by El Salvador's economic system. She also observes that: Health promoters and educators who learned their skills in the camp were challenged by government ministries because they lacked proper certification. Unable to understand the complexities underlying these changes, many community members eyed the leadership with suspicion, assuming corruption was to blame (Cagan, 1999)

17   Mauricio Geovani Pereira Díaz, Mayor of Meanguera, adduces conjectures, administrative and institutional weaknesses as the reason for CSM crisis. For example, once the Peace Accords were signed, the community lost some of the gracing land to the rightful owners. The stockbreeding project suffered as a result. Also, the Policía Nacional Civil (PNC) —National Civil Police— and the Hospital

del Instituto Salvadoreño del Seguro Social (ISSS) —El Salvador Social Security Admisnistration Hospital— rescinded lucrative contracts to the shoe factory without explanations. Additional fiscal and permit issues made the functionality of these projects to collapse.

18 Santiago and Segundo Montes Foundation (Valladolid, Spain), was founded in 1994. From the beginning it concentrated its resources on the creation of basic communal infrastructures; later on, it concentrated its efforts on the area of public health, advancement of women, seniors and childcare centers, housing, sports, and education.

19 El Salvador leads the region in remittances per capita, with inflows equivalent to nearly all export income; about a third of all households receive these financial inflows. Remittances from Salvadorans living and working in the United States, sent to family members in El Salvador, are a major source of foreign income and offset the substantial trade deficit. Joaquín Villalobos mentions in his article *Popular Insurrection: Desire or Reality?* that the economy in El Salvador was "maintained by two artificial sources: economic aid from the United States, geared almost entirely to the war, and funds sent by Salvadorans living in the United States"(1989:8)

20 FEMICA, which was founded in 1991, led municipal government development in the region and functioned as a "reform initiator"; also, as a "reform facilitator" and as a promoter of municipal governance performance. Among the national associations, the Asociación de Municipios de Honduras (AMHON), Corporación de Municipios de la República de El Salvador (COMURES), and Asociación de Municipios de Nicaragua (AMUNIC) have been the most effective.

21 Only in Guatemala and El Salvador do central government revenue transfers to municipal governments comprise a notable percentage of central government revenues —6 percent— (International City/County Management Association, 2004).

22 Members affected directly from the project have to contribute the equivalent of $300 dollars in unskilled labor. This situation has benefited many unskilled workers in the community and created a source of income for many.

23 In 2011, FSM through a citizen consultation-workshop invited members from civil society and private NGO sector to evaluate the achievements, failures, strengths, and weaknesses from the previous plan in order to draft the new one that will extend from 2011 to 2020. Once the 10-Year Plan has been in effect for five years, FSM will conduct a follow-up citizen consultation to once again review and evaluate the needs, strength, and weaknesses of their work in Comunidad Segundo Montes. ("Fundación segundo montes," 2011).

24 Growers from the region of northern Morazán have been able to meet all the standards and requirements from Walmart and have been delivering their produce three times a week.

25 The area of northern Morazán is not only a destination for tourism in El Salvador but is also home for many Salvadorans living abroad that were displaced by the civil war.

26 onstruction process started on frebruary 24, 2010 with the signing of the contract between FSSM from Valladolid, Spain, and COCSAL (San Luis Cooperative Construction Company). The cooperation of all these financial institutions was transacted by SSMF: Spanish Agency for International Development Cooperation, Caja España — financial institution in Castilla y León—, Ayuntamiento de Valladolid —City Council of Valladolid—, Junta de Castilla y Leon — Castilla y León Regional Government—, Fons Catalá de Cooperació al Desenvolupament —Development Cooperation Catalonian Fund—, Caja Duero — financial institution in Slamanca and Soria—.

References

Bakhtin MM. 1981. *The Dialogic Imagination: Four Essays*, ed. M Holquist. Transl. C. Emerson, M Holquist. Austin: Univ. Texas Press.

Benítez, D. (2011, July 22). Interview by J. N. Recinos [Audio Tape Recording].

Binford, Leigh. 1997. "Grassroots Development in Conflict Zones of Northern El Salvador." *Latin American Perspectives*. 24.2 56-79.

Bird, S. L. (2000, May). Institutionalizing local democracy: Decentralization, municipalismo, and citizen participation in el salvador. , Miami. Retrieved (2011, December 18) from http://lasa.international.pitt.edu/Lasa2000/Bird.PDF

Cagan, Elizabeth. 1999. "Women and Grassroots Democracy in El Salvador: The Case of Segundo Montes." *Democratization and Women Grassroots Movements*. Jill M. Bystydzienski and Joti Sekhon, Eds. Bloomington and Indianapolis: Indiana University Press.

Cardenal, Rodolfo. 1987. Historia de una esperanza, vida de Rutilio Grande. San Salvador: UCA Editores.

Chambers, I. (1999, May). Decentralization and strengthening of local government. This document has been prepared by Project "Democratic Governance for Central America" CAM/96/001, as a contribution to the Panel on Transparency II consultative group for reconstruction and transformation of Central America, Stockholm, Sweden. Retrieved (2012, September 21) from http://www.iadb.org/regions/re2/consultative_group/groups/decentralization_workshop_1.htm

Civil society: Participation and transparency in Central America. (1999). This document has been prepared by Project "Democratic Governance for Central America" CAM/96/001, as a contribution to the Panel on Transparency II Consultative Group for Reconstruction and Transformation of Central America, Stockholm, Sweden. Retrieved (2012, September 21) from http://www.iadb.org/regions/re2/consultative_group

Díaz Pereira, M. G. (2011, July 22). Interview by J. N. Recinos [Audio Tape Recording].

Fundación Segundo Montes develops their 10-year strategic plan (2011-2020). (2011, April 11). Retrieved (2013, January 5) from http://voicesfromcsm.wordpress.com/2011/04/11/fundacion-segundo-montes-develops-their-10-year-strategic-plan-2011-2020/

García, D. (2011, July 21). Interview by J. N. Recinos [Audio Tape Recording].

Gonzáles Parada, José Ramón, and Juan Carlos García Cebolla. 2004. *Manual de evaluación para la cooperación descentralizada*. Madrid: Editorial Dykinson, S. L.

Grenier, Yvon. 1999. *The Emergence of Insurgency in El Salvador.* U.S.A.: University of Pittsburgh Press.

International City/County Management Association. The United States Agency for International Development, Latin America and Caribbean Division. (2004). *El salvador country report: Tendencies in decentralization, municipal strengthening and citizen participation in central america, 1995 -2003* (Cooperative Agreement No. LAG-A-00-98- 00060-00). Retrieved (2013, January12) from website: http://www.google.com/search?client=safa ri&rls=en&q=El Salvador Country Report Tendencies in Decentralization, Municipal Strengthening and Citizen Participation in Central America, 1995 -2003&ie=UTF-8&oe=UTF-8

International City/County Management Association. The United States Agency for International Development, Bureau for Latin America and the Caribbean. (2004). *Trends in decentralization, municipal strengthening, and citizen participation in central america, 1995–2003* (Cooperative Agreement No. LAG-A-00-98- 00060-00). Retrieved (2013, January12) from website: http://www.google.com/search?client=safari&rls=en&q=Tre nds in Decentralization, Municipal Strengthening, and Citizen Participation in Central America, 1995–2003&ie=UTF-8&oe=UTF-8

Jacoby, Mario. 1985. 1st Ed. 1980. *The longing for paradise: Psycologycal Perspectives on an Archetype*. Boston: Sigo Press.

Jiménez C., E., Benítez M, R., Córdova M. , R., & Segovia , A. (1988). *El salvador: Guerra, política y paz (1979-1988)*. . (1st ed., pp. 179-181). San Salvador: Graffitti.

Jocoaitique libre de analfabetismo. (2012, February 10). Retrieved (2013, February10) from http://www.mined.gob.sv/index.php/novedades/noticias/item/5405-jocoaitique-libre-de-analfabetismo.html

Litvack, J; Ahmad, J & Bird, R. 1998. Rethinking Decentralization in Developing Countries: sector studies. Washington, DC: World Bank.

Lopez Vigil, María. 1987. *Muerte y vida en Morazán: testimonio de un sacerdote*. San Salvador: UCA Editores.

Mackenbach, Werner, and Alexandra Ortiz Wallner. 2008. "(De)formaciones: Violencia y narrativa en Centro América." Iberoamericana: America Latina-España-Portugal 8.32 81-97. MLA International Bibliography. EBSCO. Web. 14 Nov. 2009.

Meanguera libre de analfabetismo. (2012, November 21). Retrieved (2013, February10) from http://www.mined.gob.sv/index.php/novedades/noticias/item/6004-meanguera-libre-de-analfabetismo.html

Montoya, A. (n.d.). La nueva economía popular ¿una economía realizable?. Retrieved (2013, January 26) from http://www.uca.edu.sv/revistarealidad/archivo/4e66397db7c3flanueva economia.pdf

Moodie, Ellen. *El Salvador in the Aftermath of Peace: Crime, Uncertainty, and the Transition to Democracy*. Philadelphia: University of Pennsylvania Press.

Planificación estratégica 2006 - 2010. (2006, September). Retrieved (2013, February 4) from http://fundacionsegundomontes.org/index.php?option=com_content&view=article&id=1 212:planificacion-estrategica&catid=109:biblioteca&Itemid=588

Stainwand, J. (1997). The future of nostalgia in friedrich schlegel's gender theory: Casting german aesthetics beyond ancient greece and modern europe. In J. Pickering & S. Kehde (Eds.), Narratives of Nostalgia, Gender, and Nationalism (pp. 9-29). New York: New York University Press.

Storm, J. (1992, September 22). Whyy films shed light on latin lands. *The Philadelphia Inquirer*. Retrieved (2011, March 18) from http://articles.philly.com/1992-09-22/ entertainment/26022346_1_peasants-whyy-abimael-guzman

Trigo, A. (2004). General introduction. In A. Del Sartro, A. Rios & A. Trigo (Eds.), *The Latin American Cultural Studies Reader* (1st ed., pp. 1-14). Durham: Duke University Press.

Tulchin, J. S., & Selee, A. (2004). *Decentralization and democratic governance in latin america woodrow wilson center report on the Americas.* Retrieved (2011, February12) from http://www.wilsoncenter.org/sites/default/files/ACF18E5.pdf

Ventura, L. (2011, July 19). Interview by J. N. Recinos [Audio Tape Recording].

Ventura, Miguel. 1990. "El Salvador: the Church and the Revolution." Challenge 1(2): 1, 8-11.

Vigil, S. S. (2011, July 21). Interview by J. N. Recinos [Audio Tape Recording].

Villalobos, J. (1989). Popular insurrection: Desire or reality?. *Latin American Perspectives, 16*(3), 5-37. Retrieved (2012, November 25) from Stable URL: http://www.jstor.org/ stable/2633863

Chapter Seven

DECENTRALIZATION AND LOCAL GOVERNMENTS IN EUROPE-CENTRAL EUROPE

Peter Csanyi

Key words: decentralization, Central Europe, local governments, development, local democracy

Decentralization played a major role in the democratic development of many Western societies from the United States of America to Spain. These governments of these societies also tend to have a high quality of governance. Achieving good quality governance in developing nations seems to be the new goal of donor agencies. However, the means of achieving it is a difficult task. Many as a crucial factor contributing to good governance identify decentralization. Nevertheless, the role of decentralization in development is complex: it is an agent of change as well as a target of it. As Vengroff notes "underdevelopment is both one of the problems that decentralization is supposed to address and a contributing factor to the difficulties and failures of decentralization programs." Vengroff (1994:5).

Decentralization is defined in accordance with US foreign aid programs as a transfer of responsibility for planning, management, and resource raising and allocation from central government and its agencies to: (a) field units of central government ministries or agencies, (b) subordinate units or levels of government, (c) semi-autonomous public authorities or corporations, (d) area wide, regional or functional authorities, or (e) non-governmental private or voluntary organizations (Rondelli, 1984).

Accordingly, the basic types of decentralization are the following:

1. Deconcentration; 2. Delegation, 3. Devolution, and 4. Privatization Decentralization has often been rhetoric and not a reality. Announcing decentralization did not only brought in foreign aid but it also pacified internal opposition. However, action rarely followed rhetoric. Today, one can see that it nearly impossible to judge decentralization solely relying on political documents. Stemming from his experience with African decentralization, Vengroff (1994) writes: "Findings on the impact of decentralization in developing countries have been quite mixed. Much of the inconsistency can be attributed to the fact that the correlation between 'formally' announced programs of decentralization and a serious and successful effort at its implementation is quite low, or in some cases nonexistent" (1994:5).

It could be argued that there are two major problems with decentralization programs. The first being that while there is a rhetoric of decentralization, what actually happens is centralization. Many countries believed in just the opposite of decentralization, i.e., it is the centralization of power that will achieve political integration and development. Secondly, even when decentralization was implemented, it rarely meant more than deconcentration or delegation. Real decentralization in the forms of devolution and privatization promotes good governance (Conyers, 1983 and Nyiri, 2003).

The Central European countries, clearly, do not fall into the first category. After the collapse of communism, there was not only a rhetoric of decentralization but real efforts were made to implement some forms of it. Still, the efforts remained largely at the level of deconcentration and delegation while real devolution of power to the local level only happened half-heartedly, especially with issues concerning finance. Spain, in contrast, implemented a high rate of political and financial decentralization that led to territorial pluralism with an impressive division of power. Quite interestingly - and proving how formal framework and reality often do not match, the actual decentralization was deeper than its constitutional mandate in Spain. The Spanish decentralization is more of a result of real politics than official state rhetoric or constitutional issues (Nyiri, 2003).

Local Governments

Territorial Organization

The European countries, today, are embarked on a new phase of territorial reform, distinct from that of the 1960s and 1970s. Not all states are similarly affected by this process –some in fact have remained outside of it. In essence, these reforms are concerned with strengthening municipal and intermunicipal frameworks, the trend towards regionalization, and problems related to the organization of urban areas. On the other hand, levels of local funding are not consistent with the increase of local government functions in most countries. Moreover, the relatively simple two-tier local administration system (and even in certain countries only one tier of decentralization, the municipality) has evolved into a more complex system with a greater tendency towards regionalization (Marcou and Wollmann, 2007).

The first such trend concerns territorial organization. The European countries seem to be entering a new phase of territorial reform that is significantly different from those of the 1960s and 1970s. Not all states are similarly affected by this development; some in fact remain outside of it. In essence, the new territorial reforms are concerned with strengthening the municipal and inter-municipal frameworks, the trend toward regionalization, and problems related to organizing urban areas. The reforms of the 1960s and 1970s set the scene for two contrasting approaches to local government: the council as provider of public services (epitomized by the United Kingdom), and the council as public body based on a community of local people (epitomized by France). The countries that followed the second approach did not undergo territorial reforms at the time, but since

119

the late 1990s these reforms are back on the agenda because of the now inescapable need to rationalize local government structures. Such reforms always aim at getting first-tier local governments to take on greater responsibilities, directly or indirectly, by giving them adequate capacity to do so. What has sometimes worked against this approach, however, has been an avowed policy of bringing local government closer to local people; after regime changes in Central and Eastern Europe, this localizing trend led to the break-up of many councils in the Czech Republic, Hungary, Slovakia, and the states of former Yugoslavia, like Serbia and Montenegro (Marcou and Wollmann, 2008).

The other important development in terms of territorial organization has been regionalization. Contrary to many assumptions, regionalization is much more a functional issue than an institutional one. Far more than a question of the number and character of institutions, regionalization concerns territorial policies adopted in response to problems that are neither strictly local nor national. Regionalization manifests itself very differently depending on the constitutional framework of each state, and on how it cuts across issues peculiar to that country. While it concerns urban organization in the Netherlands or institutional regionalism in Spain, regionalization takes many other forms as well. Sometimes it is a layer added to traditional intermediary authorities, without undermining them, as is the case with the French "department". These examples also serve to draw attention to the potential impact of regionalization at the municipal level. The organization of large urban areas, including their capital cities, is a key issue for all the European countries. Nor is this a particularly new issue. It has, however, come back under the spotlight in the past ten years. The problem remains one of how to structure and connect the different levels of urban organization while allowing for functional needs as well as the demands of democracy. Responses have varied, such as between adapting common law and applying specific regulations, between integration within a metropolitan authority and focusing on the city as a center.

Management and Elections

The second major identifiable trend concerns the management of local authorities, and their powers and responsibilities. Summarized, the powers and responsibilities devolved to local authorities are increasing, though states are tending to strengthen their control over local finance. With regard to powers and responsibilities in a strictly technical sense, local authorities have been affected by sector-specific developments as well as more general ones. Under the latter category, it should be noted how the general competence clause on their powers and responsibilities has found widespread application despite some resistance. The Charter's legal situation remains uncertain in Italy, Portugal, Spain and the United Kingdom, and there is an increasing tendency among local authorities to turn to the private sector to deliver public services; privatization has been less significant in countries with a long record of such outsourcing, including Belgium, France, Greece, Italy and Spain. Some countries have developed a system of delegated powers and responsibilities, in particular Austria, the Czech Republic, Germany, Hungary, Italy and Slovenia. This practice allows local councils to execute administrative tasks under state responsibility. Among the sector-specific developments, it is evident that local authorities are becoming increasingly involved in education as well as in public safety, though here central control is being reinforced in countries where the local councils and mayors already exercised broad powers.

Progress in public-sector management is evident throughout the European region, even in the newly democratized and decentralized countries that have benefited from various programs developed by international organizations, and through bilateral cooperation projects. The precepts of the "new public management" have been differently received among European countries, depending on individual public service traditions, but the increase in responsibilities and the accompanying rationing of resources intensified pressure on local authorities to find ways to rationalize their management.

Another major development affecting European local authorities concerns the dynamics of institutions and local democracy. Along with the steady progress made by local democracy, local government is further differentiating, regarding the relationship between an assembly and the executive body, between the design of the executive, the forms of election in use (e.g. increasing practice of direct election of mayors) and the place given to citizen participation. Despite the wide variety of processes and reforms involved, a common tendency can be identified: that of seeking to establish a political leadership that is clearly accountable to its citizens. Promoting local executive power, as distinct from the assembly, is widely regarded as a necessary means for strengthening political leadership and accountability, even where there is no direct election of a mayor, which is the case in the United Kingdom and the Netherlands. A presentation of the condition of local democracy in Europe, however generalized, must account for both common tendencies and the diversity of institutions and practices. The split between shared and distinct elements underlies territorial organization, powers and responsibilities, management and finance and local democracy (Marcou and Wollmann, 2008).

The election of local governments is a reality today in all countries. Moreover, there is a growing trend towards personalization of the executive power, principally through the election of mayors by direct universal vote. In other countries, the local executive consists of a council of members elected by direct popular vote; there are now steps being taken towards introducing a direct election system in countries where mayors are elected from within the municipal councils. Indirect elections of local councils at the intermediate level no longer exist. In to these developments, there is a growing tendency towards the professionalization of chief executive officers. Despite all the reforms, voter turnout at local elections is either declining or has remained low. Various forms of citizen participation have been provided for by the law, from citizen initiated referenda to other forms of consultation. The degree of accomplishment of these procedures much depends on the political culture of each country. Such instruments are rarely applied in countries with strong traditions of representative democracy. State control of local government has also evolved. Administrative controls, which are carried out in most of the countries, are generally limited to legal checks and audits. The power of national or regional authorities to approve, amend or censure the acts of local governments still exists particularly in urban planning. Policies aimed at upgrading performance effectiveness and evaluation could lead to new forms of state control (Marcou and Wollmann, 2007).

The election of municipal councils, or more generally of community-level local governments, by direct, free and secret universal vote is today a reality in all the countries of the Council of Europe. A look back over even recent history is enough to show what important gains have been made. As far as intermediate-level local governments are concerned, the situation is a little more complex: In some cases, indirect elections seem to be a better option for linking intermediate-level tasks with local-level responsibilities (Marcou and Wollmann, 2008). This is desirable to prevent legitimate interests at the middle level from competing and conflicting with those of local councils, and also to protect the independence of the latter, as exemplified by regional authorities in Ireland, regional councils in Finland and Romania, and provincial delegations - "deputación provincial" - in Spain. The provincial delegations in Spain are considered part of the local level and are meant to serve the local councils. However, it was decided in Norway and Hungary not to use indirect elections for the county-level councils.

The most significant developments have taken place in the executive ranks of community - level local governments, namely for a certain personalization of the executive role and for direct elections. The most typical changes here occurred in Italy, Germany and the United Kingdom. In Germany, the former variety among municipal institutions has given way to a unique model, broadly speaking characterized by the election of mayors by direct universal vote, and the possibility of removing them from office. Italy has introduced the direct election of mayors, provincial presidents, and regional presidents. In the United Kingdom, following the election of a mayor of London by direct vote, the law has also provided for other cities to adopt a similar model, along two variant forms. In Central and Eastern Europe, mayors are elected by direct vote, except in the Baltic States, Poland, the Czech Republic and Croatia. The question is being debated in Belgium and the Netherlands. In the Netherlands, a draft bill to amend the Constitution to allow the election of burgomasters failed in 2005, so these officials continue to be appointed by central government on the basis of nominations from the municipal councils, but with the nominations being open to citizen consultations. Mayors continue to be appointed in Belgium and Luxembourg, but, as in the Netherlands, the executive body is a collegiate executive body whose other members are elected by the council (Marcou and Wollmann, 2008).

Behind all these developments and reforms, apparently very different in spirit, lies the same key goal: restoring or reinforcing political leadership in local governments, and above all at the municipal level. Of course this has not been an issue in countries like France or with the "Länder" in the south of Germany. In both places, the figure of a strong mayor is deeply rooted in history. But it should be noted that all of the Western European countries mentioned here have either traditionally had a collegiate local executive body, or have not had an executive body that was distinct from the council. In most countries in Central and Eastern Europe, it was the desire for democracy that drove the introduction of directly-elected mayors. However, it is clear that the various countries have very different approaches to this issue. In most cases, direct election of mayors has seemed the best way to guarantee political accountability, to the extent that their mandate is renewable. But in the Netherlands and probably in the United Kingdom, the preferred approach to reinforcing political leadership is to focus on strengthening the political role of the councils. This ambition was also in the background of the so-called "free community" reforms in the Nordic countries in the 1980s, which gave municipal councils the freedom to determine the internal organization of local government. Previously, the executive committees had been determined by law. The reforms meant that the councils could have their own choices on their administrative organization in relation to their functions; they have also reinforced the executive council's management lead role in the various specialized sectors.

For local assemblies, the changes are less clear. There appears to be a definite tendency toward what is called "parliamentarization." This condition is characterized by a reinforcement of the rights of councilors, and the possibility of calling the executive branch to account politically. This is particularly evident in Spain in the devolving of powers and responsibilities from the council to the mayor. One avowed aim of this reform is strengthening the executive branch's capacity for action, particularly in the major cities (laws of 1999 and 2003). Calling the mayor to account can in some countries require a procedure for recall by the citizens. This kind of procedure is seen in most of the German "Länder" as well as some Central European countries, including Poland, where several such cases have occurred. In a more general form, we are seeing political groups gaining official recognition in local assemblies of the larger local governments. As in France, these political factions have certain rights recognized by the law in larger councils. This is a form of legal acknowledgment of the role of political parties in the running of local institutions.

The increasing responsibilities of local governments have inevitably affected the status of elected officials (Guérin-Lavignotte and Kerrouche, 2006). In all of these countries, there is a clear trend toward professionalizing the status of local executive officers, and toward strengthening the professional safeguards necessary for the exercise of their mandate. This tendency to professionalize manifests itself also in the move away from a system of remunerative allowances to one of real salaries, complete with social security and pension rights. In tandem with this, there is a move toward preventing officials from assuming several executive roles (Marcou and Wollmann, 2008). In Central and Eastern Europe, the former classification of local executive officers as civil servants has acquired a particular relevance in the new institutional context. In Germany, a full-time mayor is classified as a public sector employee for the duration of his mandate; in most of the other countries, such status is only partial.

Despite all these reforms, one troublesome fact continues to haunt the modern electoral process: low voter turnout for local elections (Gabriel and Hoffmann-Martinot, 1999). Declining voter participation and stagnation in voter numbers reflect a worrying disaffection with politics at large. This new iteration of a kind of voter torpor appears to be more a response to high-level politics at national level and perhaps the international levels, rather than a widespread unhappiness with local authorities. An exception may be found in Central and Eastern Europe, where local elections provoke dramatically lower participation than national elections, perhaps reflecting a general feeling that local authorities don't have much of a role to play. Only three countries are bucking the trend: Hungary, Ireland and Switzerland. The United Kingdom is also seeing a rise in voter participation, albeit from a very low benchmark (Marcou and Wollmann, 2008).

Importance of Local Democracy and Local Services

Most countries have a system of local government for two reasons: as a manifestation of local democracy and a provider of local services. As an instrument of local democracy, councils of elected politicians make decisions on behalf of local communities, thus serving to safeguard against central government domination (Weeks, 2009). The strengths of local government as a democratic instrument are its closeness to the population, its elected status, its accessibility and the opportunity it provides for public participation in the democratic process (Callanan and Keogan, 2003). The European Charter on Local Self-Government (Council of Europe, 1985) signed by most European countries recognizes local government as an integral part of a democratic regime.

Local government is also a provider of public services on a localized basis, developing models of service provision appropriate to specific areas. The provision of services is probably the most visible function of local government. Notwithstanding the localized nature of services these should be delivered as efficiently as possible.

These two functions of local government can be contradictory. Efficient delivery of services can require larger or different geographic areas (sometimes these can be tied to specific geographies such as water catchment areas) but local democracy requires smaller units which facilitate citizen participation. There can also be conflict between national and local democracy (central control versus local autonomy).

Levels of Local Government

Local government is the generic term used to describe all levels of government lower than central government in countries. 'Municipality' is generally used to describe the lowest level of political authority. The municipalities provide basic services such as housing and other social services, water and waste collection. However, the form local government takes varies considerably across the European Union countries in terms of the levels of government, the services provided and the average size of municipalities.

7.1: EU Sub-national Governments

Country	1st Tier	2nd Tier	3rd Tier
Austria	1,357	9	
Belgium	589	10	6
Bulgaria	264		
Cyprus	254		
Czech Republic	6,250	14	
Denmark	98	5	
Estonia	227		
Finland	348	2	
France	36,682	100	26
Germany	12,379	301	16
Greece	1,034	54	
Hungary	3,175	19	
Ireland	114	8	
Italy	8,101	110	20
Latvia	118		
Lithuania	60		
Luxembourg	116		
Malta	68		
Netherlands	441	12	
Poland	2,478	314	16
Portugal	308	2	
Romania	3,180	42	
Slovakia	2,892	8	
Slovenia	210		
Spain	8,115	50	17
Sweden	290	18	2
UK	406	28	3
Source: CEMR-Dexia (2009) (with 2008 figures)			

As Table 1.1 above shows, eight countries including Estonia, Slovenia, Luxembourg, Malta, and Cyprus have only one level of local government, that of municipality. These countries tend to be geographically small or have a small population. Twelve, mostly medium sized countries have two levels of local government: municipalities and an intermediary level (typically counties or provinces). Although a small country in population and size, Ireland also has two tiers. The remaining eight countries, including Germany, France, Italy and the UK, have three levels of local government.

Local Governments' Reforms in Central Europe

If we look at the reforms of regional administration in Central Europe: Czech Republic, Slovakia, Hungary and Poland, the most of them suggested an adaptation to similar regional structure, as in the European Union. It was obvious that a degree of convergence was also taking place in these countries, which were not members of the European Union in the 1990s and already ten years after the fall of communism in Eastern Europe, a stable and often sophisticated framework of political and free market economic institutions was established in most of the countries of former Eastern bloc, especially in Central European countries. However, the systematic reform of the administrative system lagged behind, although the absence of administrative reforms means the continuation of one of the most severe legacies of the socialist system. The systemic administrative reform was belated, despite its earlier start and importance of the agenda. For example, in Poland local government reform was one of four main issues of the round table talk between February and April 1989. During eight months since formation of Mazowiecki's government the whole package of bills went through parliament and local elections took place on 27 May 1990. This election was a landmark, as it was the first free election since 1945 in Poland, and in the whole Central and Eastern Europe. Similar importance of local government for development of democracy was also in case of local government in Czechoslovakia and Hungary. In all these countries local governments' institutions were introduced only at commune level. Hungary introduced the most advanced local government reform at two levels: commune and districts, while regional divisions were preserved. By contrast, the other countries waited for the reform of district and regional administration - Poland until 1 January 1999 and the Czech Republic with Slovakia even longer.

There are two questions: why were the regional stages of local government reforms, which are important for economic development, and development of democracy, delayed in most of these countries? Why did they decide to start their adoption only ten years later? The answers are pretty simple: Although the reforms were recognized as important, the political argument was decisive and thus they were delayed. The introduction of these reforms was no doubt driven by primarily by expectation of EU membership and no doubt propelled by structural funds could be seen as a major incentive here.

A. *Development of Local Government in Hungary*

In Hungary, it is particularly significant that preparation for local government reform and political discussion had already begun in 1987. This fact had an impact on the shape of the reform, which was ratified by the Hungarian National Assembly as early as in May 1990. Fiscal reform, which created the basic tax structure of the state, had already been introduced before the political transition in 1989. In consequence, local government was assigned its own local tax bases and the share of national taxes. Second, the advanced state of preparation for reform was also reflected in their scale; since it was applied not only to communes, but also to districts, the next tier of administration. This distinguished the Hungarian reform from all other post-communist countries. The 1990 reform in Hungary established the elected and self-governing municipalities. For development at this level, of particular importance was the right of the former communes to claim municipal status; and this reversed the trend of socialist amalgamation. As a result, the number of municipalities doubled, which meant a substantial weakening of their opportunity to perform certain functions.

The decision not to abolish the decision was only resisted after a proposal to divide the tasks between municipalities and districts, and in this manner to establish a non-hierarchical relationship, in contrast to the previous system. Nevertheless, their position was weakened, since their assembly was to be elected indirectly by the representatives of local government. The persistence of the districts even in a weakened form enabled a transfer from the central administration of supra-local tasks such as; secondary schools, hospitals and social care institutions. This was in contrast to neighboring countries, where those tasks were still to be administered by an unreformed and distant central administration. According to Illner (1998) the Hungarian reform introduced in 1990 was the best prepared, the most comprehensive and the most liberal, when compared with reforms in the neighboring countries. However, several issues still remained outstanding, among them the strengthening of the district which took place in 1994.

The country was divided into eight regions, which were administrative units, without an elected body and each headed by Commissioner of Republic. He or she was the regional agent of central government and his or her task was to co-ordinate state administration within the region and to supervise the local governments.

An important stage in the development of administration was the parliamentary elections in May 1994, when the post-communists gained the majority. In September 1994, the parliament approved the amendments, which abolished the regions and instead, Public Administration Offices (PAO) were established in the 19 districts. In contrast to the former regions, the PAO became a full-fledged administrative institution with defined by the government responsibilities.

According to Davey (2006), Hungary's position at the forefront of local government reform was again strengthened in 1994, when they entered the second cycle of reform and when the position of the district was strengthened. The formation of the district, which took over supra-local tasks, ended the conflict over services between big towns and surrounding villages. The second problem was multiplication of special administrative units which were under direct control of these ministries and did not possess any real autonomy (vertical fragmentation). The solution to this problem was the strengthening of the role of the districts, what created the opportunity to integrate these decentralized agencies into district government. However, according to OECD report (1996), they were still critical and emphasized than decentralized units of government existed in districts in such areas as for example, employment, environmental protection, education, agriculture and construction. Moreover, they indicated that local government received a wide range of new powers but its financing mechanism was inadequate. Moreover, in contrast to Davey, they even saw the current situation as dangerous:

"Paradoxically decentralization could lead to a situation where the central state effectively strengthens its control. The establishment of de-concentrated units with the limited financial autonomy and the fragmentation of communities may help to maintain strongly vertical administrative structures." OECD (1996:24). The issue of vertical fragmentation of administration with maintenance of several units directly subordinated to ministries, is the legacy of communism in all Eastern European countries. However, in Hungary due to the formation of communes, district and regions in 1990, the vertical fragmentation was much smaller than in neighboring countries. Nevertheless, vertical fragmentation has been one of the problems of the regional policy planning, despite that the first regional development plans were prepared as early as in 1971 (Horvath, 1999).

However, these regional development plans were prepared according to several narrow sectoral-ministerial lines, according to which socialist economy was divided and the lacked territorial co-ordination. In 1996 Regional Development Act defined the institutional structure for formulation of regional policy. District Council for Regional Development became responsible for coordination local and regional development activities conducted by a range of actors: that include both the representatives of the central government end local authorities. They also include non-governmental regional organizations and Economic Chambers, Regional Development Agencies. However, the issue of the regional level administration returned. The solution to the problem of vertical fragmentation seems to be the formation of strong, big and thus self-reliant regional level, as a precondition to effective decentralization and opportunity for coordination of administration at this level. According to Horvath (1999), the weakest level is the region. Moreover, the regional development council has no scope of authority or resources and it can only perform tasks transferred to it by the district. Their formation of these regional councils is still incomplete and it creation is largely determined by the EU and resources expected to be provided by them. In a fact, the central authorities are not interested in substantial transfer of power to the regional level. There are still so many things to do for Hungary.

B. *Development of Local Government in Poland*

After the formation of communes in 1990 the next stage of administrative reform; districts and regions was prepared in 1993. However, the shift of power to ex-communist governments, there were many efforts to stop reform, as attitudes toward the administrative reform divided the post-communist coalition down the middle. Only the most advanced project of reform of Suchocka's government, the town-district bill, which was already enacted by the parliament, was finally introduced in a limited form.

The reform of districts and regions was the end one of the most sever administrative legacy of socialism (Gierek's reform from 1975), when 17 strong and independent regions, which could challenge the national elite position were replaced by 49 regions. The new regions had much more limited competencies and lost their political power. Even more disruptive was the abolition of districts the intermediate level of administration between regions and communes, which were historical units of local self-government. Replacement of strong regions by 49 small ones meant a change of their competencies and functions, as they were no longer able any to fulfill the 'ambitious' tasks which they had earlier performed. After the reform, these tasks were taken to the center. Instead, competencies of former districts were then taken by new small regions, and the former districts disappeared.

Since the middle of the nineties, delaying of district and regional reform has been the main obstacle to the further development of the Polish economy. It was suggested that although the district and regional reform was to be costly at the initial stage, in the long run the merging of the 49 "vojvodships" into 12 large ones seems to be necessary. Modern trends in Europe indicate that the creation of big decentralized regions could lead to cuts in costs, greater flexibility, and efficiency in governing (Hryniewicz, 1995). Moreover, the need for closer co-operation within the EU emphasized the role of strong regional units. The majority of Western European countries were divided into regions several times larger than the "vojvodships" in Poland at that time.

This suggested that regions similar in size to the German "Länder" or the French provinces should be created in Poland. These would enable them to be equal partners in regional exchange and would enhance co-operation (Hryniewicz, 1995). Furthermore, establishment of about 12 larger regions would break with a tradition going back to the socialist period, vertical fragmentation, which divided central administration into several narrow-sectoral ministries. As a result, several administrative units were created at regional and local levels which received orders directly from different ministries without coordinating with each other or informing the general administration of these levels of their actions. Thus, the reform meant not only delegating responsibilities from central administration to lower levels according to the principle of subsidiarity but also coordinating the whole district and regional policies from one relevant office.

The reform also intended to limit dramatically central level responsibilities and created the opportunity for them to concentrate on national policies, on the formulation of economic strategy, and on issues of preserving the unity and uniformity of the state.

This reform was also intended to stop central government interfering in local and regional issues, and to clarify the division of power between various levels of administration.

On 1 January 1999, 16 large regions were formed, and, at the same time, elective administrative units were established at district and regional levels, and finally, the significant decentralization of power from the central level was carried out. Nevertheless, the final shape of the reform passed by parliament was a compromise, which had a rather negative impact on the shape of the reform. For example, because of political bargains to gain deputies' votes the ambitious government proposal to form 12 strong regions had to be reduced in to 16 regions with very different sizes and artificial shapes, with, the Warsaw region twice the size of the smallest one. Regions also received tiny financial resources, and many of responsibilities which might have been transferred to this level of administration were preserved by the central administration 'lobbies'.

C. *Development of Local Government in the Czech Republic*

During the inter-war period, Czechoslovakia was divided into four lands enjoying a limited form of self-government. In the Czech part there was Bohemia and Moravia. The first administrative reform after the war in 1948, when the lands were replaced by entirely new subnational levels, "kraje", of which there were 19. As a result, much weaker administrative units were established (Surazka, 1997). This 1948 administrative reform is a typical example of socialist territorial fragmentation, and seems to have lasting effects ever after the fall of communism.

In 1960 the number of regions "kraje" was reduced from 19 to 10. Also at the lower level of administration districts – "okresy" – the number of units decreased substantially. Since then the reorganization of territorial structure has been very limited (Maurel, 1994). In Czechoslovakia, the political changes in 1989 came as a surprise to the national elite and the reform of local government started only after first free local election in November in 1990. Nevertheless, democratization was one of the most important demands of the Velvet Revolution.

The demand for democratization and decentralization and the short time, in which the local reform was introduced, meant that the reform was limited to the lowest level of administration, the commune. Communes had only limited influence on the higher levels, via the district assemblies they elected. The sensitive situation during the break up of Czechoslovakia also suspended any further attempts at administrative reform.

The significant problem of Czechoslovak local government, as in the case of Hungary, was its extreme fragmentation. For example, in the Czech part of the federation in 1990, the number of communes increased by 40 per cent, which oppose action to the policy of forced amalgamation of the socialist period. The other major challenge of this hastily prepared local government reform was the absence of tax system reform as a result of which local governments depended on centrally distributed grants until 1993.

In contrast to Hungary, in the Czech Republic the 1990 local government reform abolished the district level. The territorial reform stopped half way through, and then more centralist tendencies emerged in the middle of the nineties. Local government reform was conducted almost immediately after the collapse of communism, as it was believed that its postponement could have serious negative impact on economic and political transformation.

However, in contrast to local government reform, the district and regional reform was seen as less important for economic transition and democratization. The regional elite saw the district and regional reform as relevant for their own political interests and thus the prolonged bargaining delayed the reform. But, in late 1997, the constitutional amendment passed by parliament called for establishment of 14 regions and the process was finished in 2001 (see more in the next chapter).

D. *Development of Local Government in Slovakia*

The first attempt of local government reform in Slovakia was realized in 1996. Despite the veto of president of Slovakia a new territorial and administrative division was adopted. The higher levels of territorial administration were established: eight regions were formed and the number of districts doubled from 38 to 79. At first glance, it seems that Slovakia was quicker in overcoming the difficulties of reforming its territorial structure than its Czech counterpart.

Nevertheless, on further investigation, the new territorial model of Slovakia seemed to be negative. Analysis of territorial division of administration indicated centralization and the domination of political criteria, for example: the splitting up of several naturally-formed regions, the division of districts with a predominately Hungarian population, the selection of centers of districts and the numerous shifts of municipalities between neighboring districts. The 1996 territorial division significantly multiplied the number of districts, in which the former Prime Minister, V. Mečiar›s party (HZDS) had a strong support. After the parliamentary elections in 1998 new projects of territorial administrative reform was prepared and introduced (see more in the next chapter).

Lastly, we can say that the systemic administrative reform in all four Central European countries (Czech Republic, Slovakia, Hungary and Poland) indicate on similar developments. At the beginning of the nineties there was radical decentralization facilitated by the formation of self-governing administrative units at lower level of communes. However, gradually the further administrative reform was either stopped or impeded and the re-centralization appeared. Thus, only ten years after the transition began the second wave of reform in all four countries: districts and regions have appeared.

\References

Callanan, M. and Keogan, J. F. (2003). *Local government in Ireland. Inside out*. Dublin IPA

Conyers. D. (1983). Decentralisation: the Latest Fashion in Development Adminsitration. *Public Administration and Development* (3) 97-107

Council of Europe (1985). *European Charter on Local Self-Government*. Strasbourg. http://conventions.coe.int/Treaty/EN/Treaties/Html/122.htm

Davey, K. and Péteri, G. (2006). Taxes, Transfers and Transition: Adjusting Local Finance to New Structures and Institutions: The Experience of Czech Republic, Hungary and Slovakia. *Local Government Studies* 22 (5) 281-283

Gabriel, O. W. and Hoffmann-Martinot, V. (1999). *Démocraties urbaines [Urban democracies]*. Paris. L'Harmattan

Guérin-Lavignotte, E. and Kerrouche, E. (2006). *Les élus locaux en Europe. Un statut en mutation [Local authority elected officials in Europe. A changing status.]*. Paris. La Documentation Française « Etudes »

Hendriks, F. and Tops, P. (1999). Between democracy and efficiency: trends in local government reform in The Netherlands and Germany. *Public Administration* 77 (1) 133-153

Horváth, Gy. (1999). Changing Hungarian Regional Policy and Accession to the European Union. *European Urban and Regional Studies* 6 (2) 13-30

Hryniewicz, J. (1995). Kierunki rozwoju samorządności i demokracji lokalnej a reform terytorialnego podziału kraju. *Władza i społeczności lokalne a reforma samorządowa w Polsce.* Uniwersytet Śląski Katowice, 263-275

Illner, M. (1998). Territorial Decentralization: An Obstacle to Democratic Reform in Central and Eastern Europe?. *The Transfer of Power. Decentralization in Central and Eastern Europe.* Local Government and Public Service Reform Initiative, 7-43

Marcou, G. and Wollmann, H. (2007). Europe – Executive Summary. *Decentralization and Local Democracy in the World.* United Cities and Local Governments – First Global Report, 32-35

Marcou, G. and Wollmann, H. (2008). Europe. *Decentralization and Local Democracy in the World.* United Cities and Local Governments – First Global Report, 128-166

Maurel, M. C. (1994). Local government reforms and the viability of rural communities. Eastern Central Europe. *Local Government and Market Decentralisation. Experiences in Industrialised, Developing and Eastern Bloc Countries.* United Nations University Press, 16-24

Nyiri, Zs. (2003). *Decentralization and Good Governance: Ten Years of Hungarian Experience.* Storrs-Mansfield. University of Connecticut Press

OECD (1996). *Transition at the Local Level: the Czech Republic, Hungary, Poland, and the Slovak Republic* Paris. OECD Publishing

Regulska, J. (1997). Local Government Reform. *Transition to Democracy in Poland.* St.Martins Press, 113-132

Rondelli, D. et al. (1984). *Decentralization in Developing Countries.* Washington. World Bank

Surazka, B. et al. (1997). Towards regional government in Central Europe: Territorial restructuring of postcommunist regimes. *Government and Policy* 15 (4) 437-462

Vengroff, R. (1994). *Decentralization in Africa: A Review of the Experience Rural Development.* AID Commissioned Concept Paper

Weeks, L. and Quinlivan, A. (2009). *All politics is local. A guide to local elections in Ireland.* Dublin. Cork Collins Press

Chapter Eight

Local Governments in the Czech Republic and Slovakia

Peter Csanyi

Key words: local governments, Czech Republic, Slovakia, creation, development

Introduction

The creation of modern, democratic and effective local/regional, self-government system is still one of the main issues of public administration reforms in Central and Eastern Europe (CEE). Nevertheless the basic legal and financial basis for local self-governments was created in most of CEE countries (especially in all accession countries) very soon. Already in 1990, in countries like Czech Republic, Slovakia, Hungary, and Poland, the first local democratic elections were held. There was a set of new laws on local self-government, respecting basic criteria for this level of governance, as defined by the European Charter of Local Self-Government, which states in part as:

"Local self-government denotes the right and the ability of local authorities, within the limits of the law, to regulate and manage a substantial share of public affairs under their own responsibility and in the interests of the local population…The basic powers and responsibilities of local authorities shall be prescribed by the constitution or by statute. However, this provision shall not prevent the attribution to local authorities of powers and responsibilities for specific purposes in accordance with the law…Local authorities shall, within the limits of the law, have full discretion to exercise their initiative with regard to any matter, which is not excluded from their competence nor assigned to any other authority" (Council of Europe, European Charter of Local Self-Government, 1985: http://conventions.coe.int).

Other CEE countries, with some minor exceptions (like Ukraine, where local self-governments are still more formal) followed similar patterns in later years, and as of today, the existence of local and in most cases also of regional self-government, allocated by many own responsibilities and also own resources is almost the rule in the region. However, experience and especially outcomes show that not all positive expectations from decentralization and creation of local self-governing structures were fulfilled; on the contrary, region specific problems emerged (Nemec, 2007).

Decentralization According to the Conception of the European Union

Decentralization in CEE region is also based on practical reasons. The most important of them is the European Union (EU) public finance system. The large proportion of EU resources is used through structural and pre-accession funds, allocated mainly on regional principle.

To become eligible to use structural funds any EU member state must draft its National Development Plan, based on thematic areas given by the European Commission (EC) and especially on own needs and priorities. Draft Plan is discussed with EC and after its approval national and regional bodies realize its implementation. The implementation is based on the NUTS system ("Nomenclature of territorial units for statistics"), including the following levels:

1. NUTS 0, 1 – the country
2. NUTS 2 – regions with approximately 1-2 million inhabitants
3. NUTS 3 – lover regional tier
4. NUTS 4 – local units (micro regions)
5. NUTS 5 – municipalities

The existence of necessary effective regional structures, especially at NUTS 2 level is thus a pre-condition for the use of allocated funds. Regions shall be able to draft their regional development plans, decide on spending priorities; define programs and select projects, constituted preferably in the form of self-governing units (Nemec, 2007).

Decentralization Trends in Central and Eastern Europe

Processes of decentralization and development of local and regional self-governments are characterized by large time and scale differences among transitional countries in CEE. Some countries (Hungary, Poland) enacted a relatively comprehensive package of decentralization measures already in the first half of nineties. Others started with the second phase of decentralization much later (for example, Slovakia and the Czech Republic in late 1990s), and there are countries where massive decentralization started only recently (Macedonia) or is only starting in the near future (Ukraine).

All CEE countries promised to create real local self-governments; however the real level of respecting all signed principles still differs (seems that the most "out of date" country is Ukraine, where elected local governments do not have any own funds). The scale of responsibilities delegated to municipalities differs significantly between CEE countries and the amount of own resources of elected local units is lower than in "old" EU member states: "Local public government finance decentralization and building the capacity for local revenue rising abilities of local/regional self-governments reforms have been lagging behind all other reforms in CEE countries" (Sevic, 2005). In most CEE countries the share of municipal expenditures in total public expenditures is between 10 and 20 per cent and in some even below 10 per cent. Intergovernmental transfers are still the dominant or a very important resource source. This situation improves very slowly, even in some countries the trend is reverse – for example in Hungary the share of local government's expenditures in GDP decreased from 16,5 per cent in 1993 to 12,8 per cent in 2000. Due to many factors the size of local self-governments in CEE is highly fragmented, and in some countries there are hundreds or thousands of (too) small municipalities (Nemec, 2007).

Regional Self-government

On regional level the situation is more complicated. In spite NUTS 2 level is necessary for spending of EU funds, few countries created respective elected structures. In some CEE countries regional self-government units do not exist (even in EU member states, like Bulgaria, where six regions were created in 1999 as administrative and not real self-government units). This situation is connected also to unclear EU policy in this area.

The Draft European Charter on Regional Democracy was initiated by the Council of Europe's Congress of Local and Regional Authorities in Europe (CLRAE) in 1997. The original idea behind the Charter was to set out the key principles that should underlie effective regional democracy in Europe, covering areas such as financial autonomy and legislative powers. However, the Charter failed to attract the support of a sufficient majority of Member States at the Ministerial Conferences in Helsinki in 2002 and Budapest in 2005, with disagreements emerging over whether the instrument should be legally binding.

Additionally, in some countries, where regional self-government units were created, their territories are large enough to fulfill criteria for NUTS 2 (Slovakia, Czech Republic), causing increased transactions costs of management of EU funds and complicating execution of other responsibilities. Although this problem has already been well known and named, for example Slovenia wants to do the same as a part of the territorial structure reform package currently in discussion – as clear example of limited capacity of CEE states to learn on mistakes already done by others and to utilize positive reform outcomes from abroad (Nemec, 2007).

The Re-creation of Regions in the Czech Republic and Slovakia

The Czech Republic and Slovakia introduced regions and regional self-governments as missing links between central and local government on the one hand, between state administration and self- government on the other. In the wake of the democratic transition in Czechoslovakia, the national committees ceased to function as organs of Communist party rule on the regional and local level. Whereas democratic local self-government was established already in 1990, the new democratic elites did not create institutions of general territorial administration on the regional level (Illner, 1998). This was mainly due to the complexity of administrative reform and the lack of political consensus over the constitutional status of regions, the need for regional self- government and the administrative division of the territory. In the early 1990s, governments were preoccupied with re-organizing and dissolving the Czechoslovak federation as well as with economic reforms to create a market economy. The resolve to introduce "higher territorial (self-administrative) units" was declared in both constitutions of the new republics emerging in 1993, but attempts to realize these units failed until 1996-97. In both countries, the laws on regional self-government were preceded by laws that defined the new territorial-administrative division.

In March 1996, Slovakia's parliament adopted a law dividing the country into eight regions ("kraje"), following a proposal of the Mečiar government. The parliament also created regional offices of state administration as bodies of general territorial state administration and attached several de-concentrated units of sectoral state administration to these new "integrated" offices (Nižňanský and Kňažko, 2001). In the Czech Republic, the constitutional law on the creation of 14 regions ("kraje") was adopted between October and December 1997, during the government of Václav Klaus and the caretaker government appointed after Klaus' resignation. The self-governing institutions, their competences and resources and their relations with local self-government and state administration were codified by the successors of Klaus and Mečiar: the social democrat minority government of Miloš Zeman in the Czech Republic and the government of Mikuláš Dzurinda formed by the four-party coalition that had won the 1998 elections against Mečiar in Slovakia.

In May 1999, the Zeman government submitted a concept on the reform of public administration to parliament. The concept envisaged not only the creation of regional self-government, but entailed also reforms of central government, the civil service, territorial state administration and public finances (Vidláková, 2001). The majority of the Czech parliament endorsed the concept but induced the government to opt for an integration of regional self-government and state administration, contrary to the initial plan of the reformers in the Ministry of Interior. On the basis of the revised concept, the Czech parliament adopted the laws on regional self-governments and regional elections in March/April 2000. The Civic Democratic Party of Václav Klaus (ODS), which used to support the minority government in parliament, rejected the laws, but the so-called Quad coalition of center-right parties voted together with the social democrats. In the following months, the parliament adopted further laws that regulated the relations with local self- governments, the status of the district offices, the competences, property, budgetary organization and revenues of regions and the state support of regional development.

Regional self-governments were first elected in November 2000. Since the reform envisaged the phased dissolution of district offices at the end of 2002, a second package of new laws and amendments was needed to transfer their functions to the municipalities and regions. These laws were adopted by the Chamber of Deputies in March 2002.

In Slovakia, the Dzurinda government adopted a concept on the decentralization and modernization of public administration in April 2000, but did not submit the concept to parliament. One reason was that the parties of the governing coalition could not agree on the number of regions and regional self-governments. While the center-left parties SDL' (Slovak Democratic Left) and SOP (Party of Civic Understanding) wanted to retain the eight regions created by the Mečiar government, the center-right Slovak Democratic

Coalition (SDK) and the ethnic Hungarian party (SMK) intended to replace this division by twelve regions. Another conflict emerged over the creation of a region comprising the largest ethnic Hungarian settlement area around Komárno in south-western Slovakia, which was demanded by SMK but opposed by the other three governing parties. Despite these protracted disputes, the coalition parties managed to amend the constitution in February 2001 and to achieve a cabinet agreement about the bills on regional self-governments and regional elections in April 2001. The constitutional amendment gave regional self- governments a stronger legal status, similar to municipal self-governments. Although the bills adopted by the cabinet envisaged twelve regions and reflected a consensus in the governing coalition, it did not pass through parliament. When the laws were adopted by parliament in July 2001, SDL' and some SOP deputies together with the opposition supported an amendment that maintained the eight regions created by the Mečiar government (Nižňanský and Kling, 2002). The first elections of regional self-governments were held in December 2001.

A comparison of the sequencing of reforms in both countries shows that Slovakia established the new territorial units and the regional offices of state administration five years prior to the creation of regional self- government. The Czech Republic adopted the law on the territorial units 19 months later than Slovakia, but created regional self-governments after three years, one year earlier than Slovakia. The Slovak reform has not yet addressed the role of district offices of state administration, the revenues of regional self- governments and the status of the capital – issues that have already been codified in laws in the Czech Republic.

The political constellation differed in three respects: First, the Czech regionalization was an integral part of a comprehensive reform of public administration that was mainly driven by government experts and may be described as 'the state coming closer to the citizens'. On the whole, those political actors who were interested in maintaining universal administrative standards throughout the territory and a smooth co-operation between state administration and elected regional bodies proved stronger than actors who attempted to transfer more powers from state administration to self-government. In contrast, regionalization in Slovakia was a political project in its own right. It was advocated by the mobilized civil society that had backed the campaign against Mečiar, and it originated in the experience of the centralization and abuse of power that characterized the Mečiar period. Local self-government experts were the main proponents of the reform, and the political thrust of their efforts was 'expanding democracy vis-à-vis the state'. The different structures of Czech and Slovak regions can be attributed to these contrasting political logics underlying the reform projects.

Second, the Czech Republic succeeded in solving the problem of the territorial-administrative division prior to the problems of institutional arrangement. The constitutional law of December 1997 fixed the number and location of regions and enabled the incoming Zeman government to focus on their institutional set-up. Although ODS opposed the creation of regions more fundamentally than the major veto actors in Slovakia, the 1997 law became irreversible mainly due to the three-fifths majority threshold required to repeal the law together with the tight majority relations in the Chamber of Deputies. In Slovakia, the number and boundaries of regions set by Mečiar's law of March 1996 remained contested throughout the reform and dominated the debate on the institutional set-up of the regional self-government. Modifying the 1996 law was easier than in the Czech Republic since it required only an absolute majority in parliament. The major Slovak opposition party, the Movement for a Democratic Slovakia (HZDS), led by Mečiar, did not reject regionalization in principle and the SDL' was not principally against a model with 12 regions. However, the heterogeneity of the Dzurinda government together with the instable party system necessitated lengthy negotiation processes and impeded political agreement.

Third, the presence of ethnic Hungarian parties in Slovakia added an ethno-political dimension to the reform that did not exist in the Czech Republic, despite the emergence of Moravian regionalism after the political transition. Slovakia's political actors perceived the creation of regional self-government through the lens given by the ethnic cleavage and actively related the issues to this cleavage. In contrast, the Moravian-Silesian regionalist party was successfully marginalized by Czech parties with a country-wide constituency in 1996, and regional differences in electoral behavior declined between 1992 and 1998 (Kostelecký, 2001).

The new institutional arrangements on the regional level display several major differences: The relationship between state administration and self-government differs in so far as the Czech Republic set up an integrated model, involving the assembly and the board into the work of the regional office, while Slovakia established a fairly strict institutional separation between the regional assembly and the regional office. This difference between an integrated and a separated model is anticipated on the district level where local self-government participation has been institutionalized in the Czech Republic, contrary to the loose and informal involvement of local self-governments in Slovakia.

Whereas the Czech Republic chose for a collegiate executive of the regional self-government ("rada kraje"), Slovakia introduced a directly elected head of the region ("predseda kraja"). This difference is related to the different municipal constitutions of the two countries which correspond to the different models of local government prevailing in the Czech and Slovak Republic as well as in Northern and Southern Europe. Czech regional assemblies have the constitutional right to submit bills to parliament which constitutes an institutional trace of a federalist model that is also reflected in the existence of a second chamber of parliament.

Local and regional self-governments in both countries perform tasks on behalf of the state administration and tasks belonging into their own, independent competence. While not attempting to disentangle the relative weight of independent and transferred competences, the following table gives an overview on the competences of the new regions.

8.1: Areas Belonging to the Competencies of Refional Self-Government

Czech Republic:	Slovak Republic:
Development program of the region	Development program of the region
Transport infrastructure maintenance	Transport and communication infrastructure planning
Adoption and preparation of territorial planning documents (larger regions only)	Preparation and adoption of territorial planning documents
Economic management	Economic management
Secondary schools, special primary schools, educational consulting and training for teachers	Secondary schools, vocational schools, sport, culture
Preservation of historic and cultural monuments	Regional museums and galleries, cultural activities, libraries
Creation, maintenance and development of regional institutions of social care	Creation, maintenance and development of social care and social services
Creation, maintenance and development of in-patient health care institutions; protection against drugs	Creation, maintenance and development of in-patient health care institutions; control and co-ordination of pharmacies
Planning of waste management policy	
Participation in environmental impact assessment, strategies of conservation of nature, climate, collection of, access to information on the environment	
Civil protection, emergency situations	Civil protection
Source: Czech Republic: (Koudelka 2001); Slovak Republic: (Ministry of Education, Laws No. 302 and 416/2001)	

The size of the new units is roughly equal since Slovak regions have on average 672,000 inhabitants and a territory of 6,129 km² while Czech regions comprise 737,000 inhabitants and 5,633 km². Prior to the reforms, local administration in both the Czech and Slovak Republics was characterized by a low degree of fiscal decentralization: in 1998, the share of local government expenditure in general government expenditure amounted to 8 per cent in Slovakia (municipalities only) and to 21 per cent (municipalities + district offices) in the Czech Republic. While Slovak regions in 2002 still depended on allocations from the state budget, the revenue basis of Czech regions was strengthened in 2002, inasmuch as they were granted 3.1 per cent of the VAT, personal and corporate income tax revenues (Brusis, 2003).

Local Government in the Czech Republic

Local government and territorial public administration in the Czech Republic are based on long historical tradition. The first systems containing self-government elements were created as early as the Middle Ages in some Czech and Moravian royal towns.

More systematic attempts to form a modern concept of local government appeared in 1848, when the Kroměříž Congress of the anti-feudal, democratic strata of the population lobbied for the municipal self-determination, including proposals to elect representatives freely, to form municipal, police and to inform inhabitants on municipal economic activities. However the Constitution of the Austrian Habsburg Empire enacted only a limited number of these demands. The rules of municipal establishment enumerated by the constitution proclaimed a relatively significant number of rights for municipalities. The principal that the independent municipality represents the basic unit of the "free state" was implemented step by step, but in the 1850s, most democratic approaches were strictly suppressed until 1864, when these rules were specified in more detail for Bohemia and Moravia.

The 1867 Constitution of the Austro-Hungarian Empire determined other municipal competencies; local government and certain "transferred competencies" from some branches of the state administration to the municipalities were defined. Profit from business operations utilizing municipal real estate, a share of state taxes, communal housing rental and local taxes and fees were specified as revenues of municipalities.

The role of municipalities in the system of public administration was detailed further and strengthened from 1918 to 1938, during the existence of the Czechoslovak Republic between the two World Wars. This period played a very important role in the establishment of democratic principles of public administration in the independent Czechoslovakia. Three tiers of local government, each with its own elected bodies, were introduced: municipalities, districts and regions. Their independence from the state administration, competencies and duties were defined by the constitution and by different legislative acts.

The military occupation of Bohemia and Moravia by Nazi troops and the creation of the "Free Slovak State" from 1939 to 1945 interrupted this long-term democratic development (Lacina and Vajdová, 2000).

The principal aspects of the public administration system from 1945 to 1990 were the existence of local, district and regional national committees formed in April 1945 that theoretically united the activities of the state administration and of local government. After 1948, however, the local government system in the Czechoslovak Republic was completely annihilated. The rights of municipalities were restricted in many spheres, particularly with respect to independent decision-making concerning financial resources. A new democratic system of local government emerged after the fall of iron curtain.

The European democratic traditions of local government have developed in the Czechoslovakia and also in the Czech Republic since 1990. At that time important legislation creating the legal framework of local government was adopted. The Constitution of the Czech Republic was adopted on 16 December 1992, stipulating that "the self-administration of territorial self-governing unit shall be guaranteed". The municipality is defined as a principal local government unit comprised of territorial communities of citizens with the right to self-government. The constitution also guarantees the independent administration of the municipality by its elected assembly and council (Lacina and Vajdová, 2000).

The Constitution of the Czech Republic anchors the division of the Czech Republic into lower (municipalities) and higher (regions) territorial self-government units. Regional self-government is formed by 14 regions (since 1 January 2000), including the City of Prague (which is at the same time a municipality and a region). Municipalities administer their territories within the framework of independent competence. Besides, they execute delegated competences on behalf of the state. Within their self-competence, all municipalities and towns have equal rights and obligations. Execution of the delegated competences depends on the size of the municipality and the territory it administers. Municipalities are divided into three groups, according to the scope of delegated competences. «Classification of regional statistical units - CZ-NUTS» replaced the existing Nomenclature of Regions and Districts.

8.2: Administrative Map of the Czech Republic:

In 2000 along with the formation of 14 higher territorial self-governing units, Phase I of the regional public administration reform took place. Phase II of this reform took place in the end of 2002, the aim being the termination of district authorities' activities as at 31 December 2002. A significant part of their powers was delegated to the administrative districts of municipalities with extended powers, which began their activities on 1 January 2003.

Czech governmental and administrative systems, including the fiscal organization, were composed until recently of only two tiers, the national center and the municipalities. At the present moment, there are 6,250 independent municipalities in the Czech Republic, which is substantially more than were extant in 1989. Directly after the Velvet Revolution, small communities were permitted to assert their independence, and they did so with enthusiasm. The problem with this large number of small municipalities is that it is very difficult to provide competent administration for them. In the Czech Republic, this challenge seems to recommend either the administrative union of small groups of villages, and/or the establishment of an intermediate governmental tier to assist the municipalities with their administrative challenges. Czech authorities have recently addressed this problem by adopting regional administrative units, the "kraje", to assume some of the functions of the center and some of those of the municipalities.

The regional policy was developed in quite a complex manner in early 1990s. At that time, the governments of the Czech Republic paid major attention to solving transformation problems on the level of the entire state as these problems were of a mostly macro-economic character; also, once the transformation started, interregional economic and social differences in the Czech Republic, despite of their gradual deepening, were not as big as in the majority of the EU countries.

In the following period, approximately up to 1996, the regional policy was of marginal interest particularly due to proclaimed liberalism. The regional policy was therefore limited to regional support to small and medium-sized enterprises by means of improving their access to loans. Since 1996 the regional policy has been gradually actuated. Such development was triggered by both reasons arising from a changed economic and political situation of the CR as well as those related to the preparation of the Czech Republic for its accession to the EU. At that time, interregional differences in socioeconomic development increased, which resulted in a number of changes in the area of institutional provision of regional policy on the central level (e.g. establishment of the Ministry for Regional Development) as well as on the regional level. Changes occurred also in the area of legislative framework, by adopting Act No. 248/2000 Coll., on Regional Development Support; until 2000 regional policy had been conducted merely based upon several resolutions of the Government. Having adopted the Act, the Czech Republic substantially approximated the regional policy legislative framework to the EU.

There were other acts adopted in relation with the creation of regions in the Czech Republic, complementing the legislative framework of the regional policy in the Czech Republic. In this respect an important role is played by Act No. 129/2000 Coll., on Regions (Regional Organization), and Act No. 132/2000 Coll., on Amending and Canceling Some Other Acts related to the Act on Regions, the Act on Municipalities, the Act on District Authorities and the Act on the Capital City of Prague. The support of the regional development focuses on the development of business, human resources, research and technological development, development of tourism, improvement of the regional infrastructure, development of civil facilities, development of services of social and health care and measures leading to protection of the environment.

In late 1990s a whole set of program documents was drafted - starting from the central level (Regional Development Strategy of the Czech Republic) up to the local level (Municipalities Development Programs). The fundamental document of the regional policy is the Strategy of the Regional Development of the Czech Republic adopted by the Government in July 2000. This document includes in particular an analysis of regional development of the Czech Republic in the past period (both sectors and the individual regions), evaluation of the existing sectorial measures of the ministries and approach of regions, identification of weaknesses and strengths in the development of the individual regions and sectors, strategy of further regional development of the Czech Republic, identification of priorities and measures supporting development, identification of regions with focused state support.

Among major support programs with a regional impact there are also those aiming at the development of small and medium-sized enterprises. The Czech-Moravian Guarantee and Development Bank have been entrusted with providing specific assistance to entrepreneurs. The principal purpose of all the regional programs is to increase the number of employees besides their regional aspect - development of structurally affected and economically weak regions.

According to the Act on Principles of Government Regional Economic Policy from the year 1992, regional policy was defined as an activity of the state aimed at supporting the effective functioning of the market economy taking into account the regional economic differences. The policy was clearly oriented toward the support of small and medium sized enterprises and the improvement of the infrastructure and can be thus regarded as regional industrial policy. The role of the state remained essential even though it did not include proper co-ordination of the relevant ministries on regional issues. Partnership with regional or municipal level was similarly not a declared aim.

In 1996, newly formed Ministry for Regional Development was awarded a co-coordinating role in securing regional policy of the state. And it was only in April 1998 when the general rules governing the implementation of regional policy were set in the new Principles of regional policy. This document does not come with concrete solutions of regional problems; rather it replaces temporarily missing legislation. Compared to the government principles of 1992, a broader approach is proposed.

The regional policy of the Czech Republic was designed to respect the basic principles of the structural policy of the EU and the overall aim of economic and social cohesion. In this respect an allocation mechanism as part of the institutional framework has to be set up to enable the future use of structural funds.

Already The Principles of the Government Regional Policy define two types of problem regions - structurally afflicted regions and lagging regions (economically weak regions). Structurally afflicted areas were defined as regions with high concentration of traditional industry and high level of urbanization and unemployment. Lagging regions were characterized as regions with low standard of living, high share of employment in the primary sector, low population density and generally also above the average level of unemployment. These regions comprise mostly rural areas with lower level of urbanization and economic development and with rather preserved environment.

Moving to regional level, Regional Co-ordination Committees (composed of the representatives of the regions and state administration) were formed in 2006 to manage the preparation of regional development strategies and work closely with Regional Development Agencies. RDAs operated on the territory of almost all regions. It could be suggested that these regional committees acted as informal non-elected governments on the sub-national levels. Later, the Regional Development Strategies formed together with sectoral analysis of the economy, the National Development Strategy of the Czech Republic. This strategy of the Czech Republic was transformed at the end of 2007 into the National Development Plan and it became a background document for the transfer of resources from structural and pre-structural funds of the EU (LGI-Open Society Institute, http://www.osi.hu/lgi).

Local Government in Slovakia

Until its independence in 1993, the territory of Slovakia had been part of different larger state units. If oldest written documents are considered, already in 5th and 6th century large settlements had been formed, to which surrounding areas gravitated. Later, as part of Austro-Hungarian Empire, administration of local matters on the territory of Slovakia was more or less centralized, until 1860, when a reform of public administration formed 18 free royal cities and 164 district cities.

In 1918, the Czechoslovak Republic was formed, which initially kept all previous Austro-Hungarian administration laws in place (different in Czech and Slovak republics), to replace them later with a unified dual system of territorial administration based on the one in Czech Republic. This strengthened state power and reduced local self-government to a merely formal level. This process continued until 1947, when the communist party took over. Under this regime the dual system of public administration (state and local self-government) was completely eliminated. The whole public administration system was state controlled, organized in three levels, with government units in towns, districts and regions – all operating as long arms of central government. Between 1945 and 1989 several territorial reforms were undertaken without significant impact on the system of local government (Belajová and Balážová, 2004).

Local self-government in its true sense was renewed only after the fall of communism in 1990, the so-called 'Velvet Revolution'. This long-term reform process, divided into 3 phases, started in 1990, with its last part (financial decentralization), which took off in 2005. Phase 1 laid foundations for the present dual system of public administration, where state and local self-government share and independently take care of assigned public administration responsibilities. In 1992, Czechoslovakia was divided into two separate countries, Czech Republic and Slovak Republic. In the new constitution of Slovakia existence of independent self-government regulated by specific laws is inherent. From 1996 to 2000, reform phase 2 did not fulfill its aims completely and thus did not contribute much to strengthen self-government, but had been more focused on the new territorial organization of the local state government. Phase 3 of the reform (2000- 2004) focused on creating a regional tier of self-government, on decentralization of functions from the state onto self-government and de-concentration of function from central state bodies onto local state bodies. A symmetrical model of public administration was created, where state and self-government bodies operate in the same territories and tiers of government. A financial decentralization and modernization of public administration began, but were not carried out fully in this phase. In 2005, financial decentralization began, which focused on tax sharing and own tax levying powers for self-government.

The present dual and symmetrical model of public administration consists of both state and self-government. State government operates in two tiers – national and district offices plus specialized state agencies of different kinds. Self-government operates in two tiers – local and regional – independent of each other. Regional tier of self-government consists of eight regions; local tier of self-government consists of 2,892 local governments (138 cities and 2,753 villages). The capital city Bratislava and the eastern metropolis Kosice are governed by a separate law.

For the purposes of Eurostat, Slovakia is divided into five NUTS area levels, NUTS 1 being the whole territory of Slovakia; NUTS 2 being four large regional units (Bratislava, Western Slovakia, Central Slovakia and Eastern Slovakia); NUTS 3 being the eight regional self-government territories (see Table 1.2);; NUTS 4 being 79 state government districts; and NUTS 5 being the local self-government level (2,892 local governments).

8.3 Territorial Systemization of the Slovak Republic:

Unit:	Number of Territorial Units:	Territorial Unit/Units:
NUTS 1	1	Slovakia
NUTS 2	4	Bratislava Region Western Slovakia Central Slovakia Eastern Slovakia
BUTS 3	8	Bratislava Region Trnava Region Nitra Region Trenčín Region Banská Bystrica Region Žilina region Košice Region Prešov Region
Source: Ministry of Education, Government Resolution No. 157/2002		

The territorial organization of Slovakia has been subject to many political debates and changes. Even the current system of eight administrative regions and four NUTS 2 regional units does not copy the traditional ethno-cultural division among different territories of Slovakia. The most recent change, in 2006, was the abolition of eight regional state governments and the transfer of their powers to 79 district state offices. This change was meant to save administrative costs. It, however, did not have the expected financial impact, since most of the agenda and employees were transferred elsewhere rather than eliminated. In the light of this, further political debate, and possibly changes, may be expected.

As it was mentioned, Slovakia has 8 regions, 79 districts without an administrative role, and 2892 municipalities of which 138 have city status. The municipality is the basic unit of local administration, which is an independent and legal body. At the subnational level, the public administration has a system of self-government and a system of state administration. The reform of public administration has as objective to give more responsibilities from the central government to municipalities.

8.4: Administrative Map of the Slovak Republic:

The 1992 Slovak Constitution, last amended in 1999, institutes political rights such as the right to information, the freedom of expression, the right to petition, and the right to participate in the administration of public affairs directly or by freely elected representatives (Art. 26, 27 and 30). The Constitution also regulates the field of self-governing bodies, in its Fourth Part.

In 1990 the Law on Municipal Establishment was adopted. It was based on a separate (dual) model of securing public tasks, and it comprised/regulated: institutional division of the execution of state administration and self-government; decentralization; and the creation of mechanisms of cooperation between the state administration and the self-government.

The municipal authorities are: municipal office and mayor's office. Members of the municipal office, as well as the mayor, are directly elected by citizens at the local level. The mayor is the executive authority and he or she represents the municipality in all matters.

The municipalities finance their activities first and foremost by their own funds and by national subsidies. Not all revenue sources are owned by municipalities and, thus, they must fulfill specific expenditure obligations decided by the central government. Functional responsibilities, powers and financing sources have not been completely determined with regard to local governments in Slovakia. According to the 1996 legislation, municipalities have limited powers in deciding on their revenues. They can establish the coefficient and change property tax rate, within the limits set by the central government. Otherwise, the central government determines the tax revenues of the municipalities. Most fees are also determined by the center.

The Law on the Municipal System stipulates the right of municipalities to decide in all local matters with regard to its administration and property. Municipal authorities have been given rights such as:

- Compilation and approval of municipal budgets and final accounts;

- Organization of public discussions on issues of budgets and final accounts;

- Administration of local taxes and fees;

- Guidance of economic activities in the municipality (investment activities, the uses of local resources, etc.);

- Establishment, incorporation, cancellation, and control of their own budgetary organizations and subsidized organizations, and other legal entities.

Their responsibility areas are:

- Construction of housing and connected infrastructure;

- The maintenance and administration of public property;

- Local public transport (in big cities);

- Local roads and parking places, public space, public light, water supply networks;

- Municipal police forces and fire service.

The principle functions devolved to municipal governments were urban services, housing and physical infrastructure, utilities and local economic development, together with some cultural, sporting and social services (Nemec, 2000). Economic development became particularly important during the period of economic transition of the 1990s, with the collapse of many of the former state-owned businesses and rapid growth of unemployment. Municipalities are empowered to undertake a variety of activities in support of their local economy, including using their own resources to support companies located within their jurisdiction (Buček, 2005).

Other important local services, such as education and health, along with planning and other regulatory functions, remained with the state administration at regional and district level until 2003 (Davey and Péteri, 2006). This was in part because of disagreements about what to do with the intermediate tiers of government, and partly because most municipal governments were considered to be too small to manage services such as health and education.

Regions and districts remained a major part of the system of state administration for more than a decade after the reintroduction of local self-government. This was a major source of dispute within the Slovak system, until 2002 when the districts were abolished and new regional governments ("kraje") were established as elected bodies (Bryson and Cornia, 2004). Quite apart from the pressure from within the country to make that change, an elected upper tier was perceived as a necessary condition for EU accession. Ironically, however, the new regions are too small to constitute planning regions for EU structural fund purposes (Davey and Péteri, 2006).

As part of the reforms of 2002/3, responsibilities for primary education were transferred to municipalities, while secondary education remained with the regional governments. Increased powers for local economic development and territorial planning were also transferred to municipalities (Buček, 2005).

Fiscally, Slovakia remains quite centralized. Local budgets in 2001 represented only 14 per cent of the national budget, around half the proportion in the Czech Republic (Bryson and Cornea, 2004). In 1998, municipal revenues represented 4 per cent of GDP (Nemec, 2000).

The only tax available to municipal governments is the property tax, which contributes only 16 per cent of local revenues (Bryson and Cornea, 2004). Local taxes on alcohol and tobacco disappeared with accession to the EU. A further 5 per cent (on average) of local budgets comes from a variety of fees for permits and charges for local services. The main weakness of the property tax is that it is still based on floor area rather than property value. While there have been proposals for some time to introduce a valuation basis for the tax, which would greatly increase its potential, this has not yet happened. Municipalities have the right to set tax rates, but they have been reluctant to increase tariffs on domestic properties, preferring to increase them on business properties (Davey and Péteri, 2006). However, there are no local business taxes, and the government has been reluctant to assign additional revenue sources to local government, at least in part because of the huge differences in local fiscal capacity. The only significant fiscal change has been to assign motor vehicle taxes to the new regional level. However, the revenue from this is heavily skewed towards the capital city, since this is where most company-owned vehicles are registered.

There is also a system of intergovernmental grants, both general and specific. These represent around 17 per cent of local budgets – half the level in the Czech Republic (Bryson and Cornea, 2003). The main grant is for education, allocated on a per pupil basis. Other earmarked transfers are provided for public housing, public transport, and the administration of small municipalities. There are also a number of state funds available for projects to do with the environment, culture, housing and water (Nemec, 2000). Prior to 1990, the intergovernmental transfer system operated on the basis of gap-filling grants (i.e. grants making up the difference between revenues and expenditures), with minimal local discretion. From 1990, the system moved to a formula basis, with a significant degree of local discretion about use. However, national fiscal constraints have meant that the real value of grants has declined during a period of inflation. This has had a particular impact in relation to utilities like district heating, where costs have risen dramatically but subsidies have been reduced. The other weakness is the absence of any real equalization element in the grant formulae to offset the significant differences between jurisdictions in local revenue capacity (United Nations Development Program - UNDP, http://europeandcis. undp.org).

The Velvet Revolution opened up the possibility for decentralization and the re-establishment of democratic local government. However, there was limited preparation for the changes, so that the development of the system has taken longer and been less far-reaching than in some other countries of Central Europe. Despite the establishment of a very large number of elected municipal governments, the system remained highly centralized, at least until 2002/03, when the state administration at district level was replaced by an elected regional tier. This gave significant additional responsibilities to the municipal level. It seems that there are still significant weaknesses in intergovernmental fiscal arrangements, and in local level service delivery, but the situation is more positive in both countries than couple of years ago.

References

Belajová, A. and Balážová, E (2004). *Economics and Management of Local Government.* Nitra. University of Agriculture Press

Brusis, M. (2003). Regionalization in the Czech and Slovak Republics: Comparing the influence of the European Union. *The Regional Challenge in Central and Eastern Europe, Territorial Restructuring and European Integration.* Oxford. Peter Lang Publishing 131-150

Bryson, P. J. and Cornea, G. C. (2004). Public Sector Transition in Post-Communist Economics: The Struggle for Fiscal Decentralization in the Czech and Slovak Republics. *Post-Communist Economics* 16 (3) 125-176

Buček, J. (2005). The Role of Local Government in Local Economic Development - Slovakia. *Local Government and Economic Development.* Budapest. LGI Books, Open Societies Institute 107-134

Council of Europe (1985). *European Charter of Local Self-Government.* Brussels. http:// conventions.coe.int

Davey, K. and Péteri, G. (2006). Taxes, Transfers and Transition: Adjusting Local Finance to New Structures and Institutions: The Experience of Czech Republic, Hungary and Slovakia. *Local Government Studies* 22 (5) 281-283

Illner, M. (1998). Territorial Decentralization: An Obstacle to Democratic Reform in Central and Eastern Europe?. The Transfer of Power. Decentralization in Central and Eastern Europe. Local Government and Public Service Reform Initiative 7-43

Kostelecký, T. (2001). *Vzestup nebo pád politického regionalismu? Zmeny na politické mape v letech 1992 az 1998 - srovnání* České *a Slovenské republiky.* Prague. Sociologický ústav Akademie věd České republiky

Koudelka, Z. (2001). *Obce a kraje.* Prague. Linde

Lacina, K. and Vajdová, Z. (2000). Local Government in the Czech Republic. *Decentralization: Experiments and Reforms.* Budapest. LGI Books, Open Society Institute 257-295

LGI-Open Society Institute: http://www.osi.hu/lgi

Ministry of Education of the Slovak Republic (2008). *National Report of the Slovak Republic.* Bratislava. http://www.unesco.org/fileadmin/Slovakia.pdf

Nemec, J. (2007). Decentralization reforms and their relations to local democracy and efficiency: CEE lessons. *Uprava, letnik* 5 (3) 7-40

Nemec, J., Bercik, P. and Kuklis, P. (2000). Local Government in Slovakia *Decentralization: Experiments and Reforms.* Budapest. LGI Books, Open Society Institute 297-343

Nižňanský, V. and Kňažko, M. (2001). Public Administration. *Slovakia 2000. A Global Report on the State of Society.* Bratislava. Institute for Public Affairs 103-121

Nižňanský, V. and Kling, J. (2003). Public Administration. *Slovensko 2001. Súhrnná správa o stave spoločnosti.* Bratislava. Inštitút pre verejné otázky 183-200

Sevic, Z. (ed). (2005). *Fiscal decentralization and grant transfers: a critical perspective.* Bratislava. NISPAcee

United Nations Development Program – UNDP: http://europeandcis.undp.org

Vidláková, O. (2001). První desetiletí reformy veřejné správy v České republice. *Správni právo* 34 (7) 16-22

Chapter Nine

Economic Empowerment for Women in Petac and Tizimin, Yucatán Mexico [1]

Gabriela Miranda-Recinos

Key words: decentralization, women's empowerment, microcredit in Mexico, *Mundo Rural, Ayuda para Ayudar* (APA)

Introduction

Part of the rationale for decentralization in this chapter is that it has served, in the case of developing countries, to point out the need to reach several sectors of society in the delivery of local financial services to large populations through the use of loans given to municipalities and managed by local authorities (Litvack, Ahmad, & Bird, 1998). In the specific case of Mexico, one of its goals was to generate effective mechanisms to reach the country's poorest inhabitants to combat extreme poverty. As this idea gained momentum, several institutions decentralized its operations and focused its efforts to reach peripheral communities. One of the viable solutions recognized globally as an instrument for poverty alleviation and empowerment for women has been the use of microcredit. In 1997 under the auspices of then governor of Guanajuato Vicente Fox, financial credits were disbursed to several regions in that state. During that same year, the Microcredit Summit underlined the need to empower women economically through microloans. The Summit established that by this medium, women were to take control over their economic resources to make informed decisions; thus exercising an empowered position. Since then, many state and non-state organizations have made available small amounts of money to poor citizens. Albeit the goal of eradicating poverty, and extreme poverty in Mexico has been the focus of many governmental agendas, progress to regulate and coordinate programs and social policies has produced uneven results. It is incumbent on newly elected officeholders and appointed experts to extend and deepen these practices, as a way of strengthening the nation-state, and to contribute adequate and accountable mechanisms to find real, and tangible results to this situation.

This chapter observes and presents empirical data through a series of interviews with women currently participating with microcredit organizations. *Mundo Rural* headed by Jorge Anlehu Lara and *Ayuda para Ayudar* directed by the religious nun Mother Aurora del Rivero Heredia. As presented in this discussion, both institutions try to improve the socioeconomic circumstances and self-reliance of women in the municipalities of

153

Petac and Tizimin in Yucatán, and have performed as a vehicle to empower women economically in this state. Furthermore, this chapter captures a brief overview of the genesis of microcredit and its expansion in Mexico and the conceptualization of economic empowerment in diverse forums. Two important points are derived from the latter discussion, the conversations conducted with the women of those communities, and how participation in microcredit workshops allows them to concretize at different levels an opportunity for entrepreneurship and ultimately sustain the decision-making process regarding their own personal finances.

Decentralization and local development

In the early eighties, due to the economic crisis, Mexico backed away from a centralized economy and began to transfer their political, fiscal, and administrative power to sub-national levels of government. During this period those resources were gradually restructured and transferred to the state government and municipalities. In addition, the government assigned federal resources to establish a social emergency fund that attempted to alleviate the impact of the weakening economy on the poor. An example of this approach was the program PRONASOL (National Program of Solidarity) instituted during the Carlos Salinas' government in 1988. Initially, this plan was a huge success; however, the federal government managed all resources and the program overlooked those areas to which the fund was intended, states and municipalities. By 1995 PRONASOL was redesigned and a new program was created. PROGRESA (fully implemented until 1997), a scientifically oriented organization helped focus governmental goals of decentralization by creating criteria that would give resources to states and municipalities (Díaz-Cayeros & Silva Castañeda, 2004 p. 14).[2]

As previously observed, in the structure of the modern Mexican state and that of decentralization, one aspect that has been part of the discourse in political agendas and international forums since 1997, is the need to channel resources to the disenfranchised and to empower women economically. Two successful advantages in the use of non-centralized modes of operation are: first, the ability to access different sectors of society including those at the local level; and second, the faculty to adapt its methodology to serve and provide financial help to socioeconomic strata, generally excluded from the traditional banking system. Over the years women and men in situations of poverty have benefited from decentralized programs, and in several cases as it is examined in this chapter it has served as a tool to empower women. In spite of that reasoning, for many rural regions in Latin America progress has been slow, hence the need to reach more communities to strengthen and establish a series of core actions that find ways out of poverty.

Microcredit and Microfinance in Mexico

In developing countries, like Mexico, poverty is an endemic problem.[3] During the twentieth century two popular movements, whose objectives still resonate at the ontological and epistemological level, remind us that the stated predicament is still far from being resolved. Those movements were the Mexican Revolution of 1910, and the Zapatista Army of National Liberation (EZLN), who began their insurgency in Chiapas in 1994. Both events still linger in the collective memory of this country and are tangible evidence that the problems of poverty and discrimination, be it geophysical, linguistic, class, gender or economic, are still a reality.

At the turn of the century, attention was placed on improving the livelihood of the world's poorest citizens thus, several initiatives like those developed by the United Nations (UN) have been part of the agenda of state governments. In the year 2000 the UN Millennium Project (UNMP) concretized the goal "to halve [by 2015] the proportion of people whose income is less than one dollar a day" (UN Millennium Project, 2005, p xii). The latter emphasizes the urgent need to install and apply a strategic plan for poverty reduction in developing countries where sub-standard living conditions are still a reality. One measure taken to emphasize the significance of this pressing issue at the regional level is exemplified by the state of Chiapas, Mexico. Chiapas is the first local government to include in July 2009 a reform in their constitution that guarantees that the objectives set forth by the UNMP is to be fulfilled by the state's government and municipalities (Línea, 2010).

The gap between socioeconomic classes and the myriad issues surrounding poverty in Mexico are a point of debate and controversy inside and outside governmental circles. With the attention placed on the disenfranchised at the global and local level, one solution sought was the use of microcredit. Fundamentally, a microcredit makes available small amounts of credit to poor clients. For the most part the distribution of funds is in most cases managed by government run organizations, banks and NGOs. Microfinance includes other services such as insurance, savings, etc. Studies confirm that microcredit has gained acceptance worldwide as a tool for alleviation of poverty. It has been hailed as an important force to empower women in particular, by improving their socioeconomic circumstances and promoting participation in financial processes. [4] Furthermore, women have proven more likely to repay loans and to use their earnings for the family well-being than men. These microloans also contribute to strengthen the social power of women as they develop their own productive and organizational capacities.

For Mexico, microcredit and the allocation of financial resources for poverty alleviation in rural areas entered the national discourse in 1997. [5] At that time, the governor of Guanajuato and later president of Mexico, Vicente Fox, met with Muhammad Yunus, who designed the model that extends credit to poor people and who first implemented it, in partnership with Grameen Bank, in Bangladesh. Based on the data provided by Yunus, Vicente Fox drafted the "*Plan de Santa Fe*" (1997), and financial credits were given to the disenfranchised - mainly peasants and housewives. According to data released by the Fox presidency, the Santa Fe Program reached nearly 70,000 residents (Presidency of the Republic, 2003). It was not until Fox's term as President of Mexico (2000-2006), and a subsequent visit by Yunus in 2003, that nationwide programs were installed to aid women and men in situations of poverty. These organizations are the Microfinancing Fund for

Rural Women (FOMUR) (*Fondo de Microfinanciamiento a Mujeres Rurales*) and the National Financial Program for Micro Entrepreneurs (PRONAFIM) (*Programa Nacional de Financiamiento al Microempresario*). The latter, currently covers the national territory and has been in operation since the year 2000. This governmental institute, in conjunction with the private sector, manages microcredit, savings, cooperatives, and oversees distribution of funds to micro-financing institutions. In addition it grants financial aid and/or credits to targeted population - in most cases women.[6] The amount of micro-credits given by PRONAFIM in the year 2001 represent a total of 91,630 pesos in 2001 and 2006, 4,815,000 pesos (in today's rate exchange an equivalent of 7,000 and 370,000 respectively). More recently for the period of 2007-2010, close to five million micro-credits were distributed nationally by this institution (Portal de Microfinanzas, 2011).

Another initiative to promote savings among the general population is the *Banco de Ahorro Nacional y Servicios Financieros* (BANSEFI). In the year 2002, the bank began to offer competitive products generally, savings and credit to clients in different entities of the country. In a workshop given by economist Dr. Jorge O. Moreno, *Evaluating the Role of Microfinance Institution in Mexico* (2009), one of the points analyzed was the participation in the microfinance program instituted by BANSEFI in Mexico. This financial organization, according to the study, served 2000 municipalities and has provided more opportunities for credit to its users by decentralizing its traditional format. The role of centralized forms of financing is how traditionally members get credit, give credit, and set credit. Capacity of crediting and control are factors that eventually create negative effects in the number of participants. Thus, Moreno concludes, this bank has increased participation by decentralizing its operations. Many more micro-financing institutions (MFIs) like the BANSEFI now operate in Mexico offering services in rural areas.

At the non-governmental level, non-profit organizations operate in small sectors of the population and their terms, generally speaking, tend to be more client-friendly. Two non-profits are: the Grameen Trust and Kiva. The Grameen Trust whose name is affiliated with Muhammad Yunus, Nobel Peace Prize winner (2006), has been in Mexico since 1997. [7] This organization holds several local branches in different states in Mexico, including Yucatán. Another example is Kiva, a non-profit based in San Francisco, California. Kiva sends money of Internet lenders to field partners in Latin America and around the globe. Their mission statement is to "connect people through lending to alleviate poverty [. . .] individuals lend as little as $25 to help create opportunities." (Kiva, 2011). [8] While not a comprehensive list, it illustrates the diversified nature of microcredit groups operating in different parts of Mexico. In the conceptual map of the nation, and beginning with international models, microcredit and microfinance programs have rapidly expanded their reach from governmental to non-governmental institutions. These organizations still maintain, at their core system, the need to improve financial access and services for the country's poor.

Twentieth Century: Women in the History of Yucatán

Mexican women through the early 20th century have been active participants in the socio-historical processes of the nation. This is signified by the role of the *soldaderas* (women soldiers) of the Mexican Revolution (1910) whose contributions have been overshadowed and often ignored. Mexican intellectual Elena Poniatowska observes that in most of the arts and literature produced during the post-revolutionary period *soldaderas* were often portrayed as prostitutes or their presence was relegated to a peripheral role. However, Poniatowska has stressed and made abundantly clear their fundamental presence: "without the *soldaderas*, there is no Mexican Revolution — they kept it alive and fertile" (p.16). The latter quote echoes throughout the history of women's equality in Mexico and their unrelenting fight for new ground despite the myriad of obstacles presented to them.

At this historical juncture women in Yucatán were gaining public presence, this in turn, allowed them to underline and promote awareness to problems of equality and rights. Two moments chronicle the difficult and arduous road for women's equality: the military tribunals and the feminist movement. During this critical time rural and wealthy women, as established in court records, appeared in military tribunals insisting that revolutionary commanders investigated and paid attention to issues that affected women. For instance: rape, honor, domestic violence, deflowering, adultery, and divorce among others (Smith, 2009, p. 54-83). Another important marker was the First Feminist Congress in 1916, although Maya women were not represented it allowed for the gradual improvement of women's conditions. [9] One ramification of this meeting was the formation of The Article of Domestic Relations that was included in the Mexican Constitution of 1917, and which establishes basic rights for female citizens.

The importance, relevance, and presence of women in the public and political sphere are highlighted with those who first organized the *ligas feministas* - Elvira Carrillo Puerto, Rosa Torre and Genoveva Perez. These leagues addressed issues of literacy, hygiene, the right of women to vote, and birth control among other topics. By 1922 Rosa Torre became the first woman to have occupied a seat in Congress in Yucatán. This can be attributed, in part, to the modernist reforms installed by the governor, Felipe Carrillo Puerto (1922-1924). Carrillo Puerto's modernizing plan included a series of laws that improved the status of women, one of them being education. As a result of this reform many more women entered the teaching profession. After Carrillo Puerto's assassination the ground gained by feminist leagues soon dissipated and the new government limited the advancement of women.

The space achieved during the first two decades of the 20th century has continued despite the political agenda of national and state governments. Two cases in point illustrate the presence-absence binary for women; for instance, it is not until 1953 that suffrage was possible for all women in Mexico; second international attention to specific issues affecting all women became a reality until the mid-seventies. In the more recent history of Yucatán women have played a predominant and participatory role as public servants. Kathleen R. Martin discusses that during the early 1990s women won three key political seats in that state including Maya women. [10] By the late 1990s both Maya and non-Maya women had lost its centrality in the political arena of that state (Martin, 1998). The current Governor of Yucatán, Ivonne Ortega Pacheco (2007-2012) is the first woman elected for that position, and the second to serve in that post after Dulce María Sauri who was interim governor from 1991-1994. The recent integration of rural women to the political life of the state confirms the volatile relationship that still reigns regarding the role of women in public office. Although women's presence in the political sphere has not been continuous it has certainly set a precedent, as more women affirm their rights and reclaim a sociopolitical and economic space amidst the political shifts in Mexico. In the next section I will provide a broad summary of empowerment for women focusing on the economic empowerment of rural women participating in microcredit.

Women and the Conceptualization of Empowerment

Over the last few decades, the fight for women's rights and equality has championed significant changes in the socio-political and economic sector of developing countries. For Mexico, it is undeniable that women's rights and their empowerment are as much the result of women's struggle to obtain those rights, as they are a reflection of governmental reforms. During the last quarter of the century to the present, the United Nations, along with other important congresses, has been at the forefront to support plans of action and reforms for the advancement of women worldwide. The forums have allowed a space to address issues central to the rights and development of all women. One topic that has been present in these dialogues is the need to empower women in all areas.

The concept of empowerment - its gradual and real inclusion in the multiple social, historical, political, and economic processes in which women participate - has gained dialectical presence since 1975. At first little attention was paid to the issue. Starting with the First World Conference on Women (1975), held in Mexico City, the international community examined fundamental issues concerning the status of women around the world, and focused its efforts to bring about change at micro and macro levels. In this meeting, which unleashed controversies and differing points of view, the topics discussed ranged from poverty, education, health, violence against women and issues related to the protection and development of women of all ages. This meeting was followed by several conferences: Copenhagen (1980), Nairobi (1985), Beijing + 5(1995), Beijing + 5 (2000), Beijing + 10 (2005), the 15 year review of the implementation of Beijing Declaration in Beijing + 15 (2010), and the UN Millennium Project (2000). In fact, the objective of the UN Millennium Project considers empowerment and equity of gender issues preponderant in the fight to obtain women's equality (Fondo de Desarrollo de las Naciones Unidas para la mujer, 2005). Focal to the history of women's equality was the Convention on the Elimination of All Forms of Discrimination Against Women in 1979. The convention provided a reference point for programs and laws regarding women's equity. The document that was produced is now known as the "Bill of Rights for Women."

Certainly, one objective that has been articulated prominently in several platforms is the need to develop economic empowerment for females. For instance, in the World Summit for Social Development held in Copenhagen in 1995, the Third Preparatory Committee "adopted by the heads of state governments asserted that 'the most productive policies and investments are those which empower people to maximize their capacities and opportunities." (Deshmukh-Ranadive & Murthy, 2005, p. 45). Hence the need to reach women, provide viable resources and develop their own capacities for full participation in social processes. Another important meeting on economic empowerment was the World-Micro-credit Summit Campaign in 1997. In their 2nd "core theme" stresses the need to empower women through micro-credit:

> Women are a good credit risk, and that woman-run businesses tend to benefit family members more directly than those run by men. At the same time, through earning an income women achieve a higher status in their homes, their communities, and their nations (Microcredit, 2009).

It is interesting to note that although these campaigns have brought important improvements for the majority of females; it was not until the IV Conference in Beijing, sanctioned by the UN in 1995, that the needs of indigenous women - a group that has been marginalized from the public, political, and economic discourse- were clearly articulated (Calfio Montalva & Velasco 2006). One institution that addresses particular issues within these communities is the *Instituto para el Desarrollo de la Cultura Maya del Estado de Yucatán* (Institute for the Development of Mayan Culture in the State of Yucatán) or INDEMAYA (Spanish acronym) established in the year 2000. Its objective is, "to propel participation of the Mayan people in the construction of a State Policy [. . .] based on their *based on th*eir *cosmovisión* and with gender perspective; for the full exercise of their rights as it has been established in the legal framework at the state, national, and international arenas." [1]

In addressing the needs of women's equality in agricultural and rural development, organizations like the Food and Agriculture Organization of the United Nations (FAO), with its regional office for Latin America and the Caribbean, provide local resources to empower the country's poorest people. The FAO has also been active in defining gender equity for rural women by promoting programs, like the *Proyecto Estratégico de Seguridad Alimentaria Mexico* (Special Program of Food Security) PESA (Spanish acronym). The FAO-PESA alliance has been put into practice in several regions, including Mexico. In fact, one of the principle objectives is to provide communities with the tools necessary to find sustainable practices and viable economic resources that will ensure their survival (Ballara, 2006). In addition, the Economic Commission for Latin America (ECLA) holds a regional conference on women every three years. Some of the issues discussed revolve around the needs of indigenous and rural women. At the local level, Mexico has been involved with the FAO via a governmental organization the *Secretaría de Agricultura,*

---

1 My translation

Ganadería, Desarrollo Rural, Pesca y Alimentación SAGARPA (Spanish acronym) or the Ministry of Agriculture, Livestock, Rural Development, Fisheries and Food. Between 2005-2007 SAGARPA implemented the PESA project in several rural areas in Mexico. The results brought on by these conferences and organizations, can be underlined in the continued pressure placed on national and local governments to develop viable public policies and programs to benefit women across the globe.

Certain programs have placed particular importance on the issue of empowering women. Over the years, studies have questioned the validity of the claim that microcredit contributes to women's empowerment. Some research reports the negative impact of these microloans on female empowerment by pointing out that, "credit fails to alter, and sometimes reinforces, women's subordinate position" as in cases where males in the family pressure women to take loans against their better judgment (Sebstad & Cohen, 2001 p. 82). In an additional case study, researchers working with Indian women have found that at times large corporations can use females to promote their products and that the exploitation that is caused by this type of practice contributes to disempowered women. Another reason cited is that obtaining a microcredit and having the freedom to handle finances does not necessarily trigger the process of empowerment (Deshmukh-Ranadive & Murthy, 2005). On the other side of the argument several studies analyzed by Sebstad and Cohen (2001) bring attention to the fact that these loans raise the "standard of living of women and their families [. . .] women's economic contributions, women's decision-making power" (p.82). Furthermore the report observes that, "over time women's increased contributions to household income affords them more status and decision making control within their households" (p. 83). There is no doubt that these examinations have found many variables on how financial access can serve as an agent to empower women economically. My interviews on the other hand, as captured in these conversations, present a view that stands on the qualitative side of the argument. Although these exchanges are empirical and not statistical, they nevertheless indicate a trend that cannot be contradicted as such. Therefore, for this chapter women's empowerment can be understood according to the following paradigm - control over economic resources, as it allows women the power to make informed decisions. It is common practice among microcredit lending organizations to use the definition of the word to mean precisely that —women are to have access and control over their own economic resources. Moreover, in these conversations, I try to establish how access to a microcredit has initiated a process of empowerment and thus, has become a catalyst for change in their lives. The women beneficiaries interviewed from the organizations in the Yucatán Peninsula, *Mundo Rural* and *Ayuda para Ayudar*, present a good example of constructive practices and affirmative results, as their goal is to promote, provide access, and education and management of economic resources to rural women in the municipalities of Tizimin and Petac, respectively.

"Providing loans that help people"

Based on current models of microcredit lending, the organizations *Mundo Rural* and the NGO, *Ayuda para Ayudar* (APA),[11] have been servicing communities in two geographical areas in the state of Yucatán. As part of this research, the first community visited was the town of Petac; a municipality located about 30 minutes from the state's capital, Merida. Jorge Anlehu Lara, director of *Mundo Rural*, and a team of professionals in agricultural science and biology oversee operations for eight microcredit borrowers, six of which are women. Adjoining the neighboring state of Quintana Roo, Tizimin is situated in the northeastern part of the state, approximately two hours away from Merida. In the center of Tizimin is the *Ayuda para Ayudar* Foundation headed by Catholic nun from the Carmelite Order, Aurora del Rivero Heredia, who along with a group of experts, work to improve the lives of women and men in these communities. Of the many rural areas contained within this extensive municipality, I had access to two of them: San Luis and San Manuel, both of which are represented in the interviews conducted. The personnel involved in these organizations released general information concerning operations and local issues, as well as bridging communications with the women in the region.

Although microcredit has been seen as a tool to alleviate poverty, some banks servicing clients in semi-urban and rural areas have established loan terms that become difficult to repay, thus negating their very purpose. For example, some microcredit institutions set a high interest rate and late charges compounded by the hour. In addition, these predatory microcredit lenders force clients to travel long distances to make their weekly, biweekly or monthly payments at the local branch. This spatial geographical barrier, coupled with unfair banking practices render clients unable to repay the debt on time. These practices increase women's vulnerability and further contribute to the impoverishment of its borrowers.[12]

It is important to observe that, as in the case of *Ayuda para Ayudar* and *Mundo Rural*, geophysical barriers and inequitable banking practices are met with innovative solutions that save borrowers traveling time and money. In this case in particular, borrowers deposit their weekly payments with the female treasurer of the town and later an employee collects the fees. This system, that requires several traveling hours between towns, is a local strategy that has yielded results. To illustrate, in a meeting held July 2011, Mother Aurora pointed out that since the year 2009, when microloans were first distributed in Tizimin, they have had 100% repayment of that money. Institutions that provide loans that help people are this foundation's purpose, because it is not only necessary to raise people out of poverty but to educate them. As the name suggests "Help to Help" (*Ayuda para Ayudar*), establishes a synergistic system, a dynamic that is twofold; on the one hand a concerted effort to assist those in need and on the other allow and teach women to better their living conditions.

This foundation has benefited 350 females in this municipality, with continued efforts to expand and serve more clients in the community. The women, whom I had the opportunity to interview, are currently on their fifth micro-credit and according to their testimony, their quality of life and opportunities to better themselves; their family and economy have improved. In Tizimin, some of the projects supported through micro-credit are sustainable growth by independent producers of habanero chile and honey - two very profitable enterprises in Yucatán (Figueroa, 2010). [13] In Petac, San Luis and San Manuel, where the interviews were held, the projects supported range from horticulture, making textiles, hammocks and embroidery (items sold to stores that cater to tourists). Other enterprises funded are the purchasing of a refrigerator, merchandise for an existing business, raising chickens or other small animals, and self-sustenance. Equally important in this formula, is the need to educate borrowers at all levels of the process, which is to say that before a borrower receives a microcredit she/he participates in workshops dealing with a variety of topics.

Keeping up with current standard practices in the microcredit business industry and before disbursing any loans, these institutions employ strategic methodologies that are client friendly. Case in point is the aforementioned foundation APA. In the town of Petac, *Mundo Rural*'s personnel offered documentation regarding the local gatherings that promote and educate new and existing clients on microcredit. Some of the topics discussed are developing a business plan, money management and savings, strengthening their individual capacities, and lastly, an explanation of terms on loans, repayment dates, interest, and assistance in the collection of fees. One example that stands out in the documents provided by this organization, demonstrates how clients are guided to express verbally/visually and/or in writing their vision for a business plan. For APA, in Tizimin, Mother Aurora (personal communication, 15 July 2011) expressed that the courses cover various subjects that might begin with a fundamental class on organizational skills: how can women work together, what to do with their microcredit, and how to utilize their microcredit money in an effective manner. The course's teaching methodology is participatory and active in nature; women learn to verbalize their needs and work with other women in the community. In regard to the latter, Mother Aurora expresses:

> "We give them a training course. That class has a cost for us, because we go to their communities. Every eight days we go back to those communities for a follow-up. We have the picture of every woman and a short biography, their names, where they live, how old they are, number of children, what the husband does [for a living], and what are they doing with their microcredit. We have a database of each woman and every town. We teach women, in their condition of poverty, how to save money. Savings are for the their benefit, because these savings are not managed by us [APA] it is managed by the community's treasurer."

As observed, diverse methods are employed to inform and reach future borrowers and to increase women's participation and contribution in the household. It is my observation that through these education seminars a process of empowerment is set in motion. It begins with participation in workshops, then continues to develop when women in these communities are given the prospect to not only concretize a practical business and apply the knowledge, but also to sustain the decision-making process regarding finances which is one key factor in the newfound power for women.

In the interviews conducted in these communities, during the second week of July

2011, my purpose was to capture: how access to a micro-credit loan was used, if the program indeed has had a positive or negative impact in their lives, who decided to get a loan and why, what new skills have they learned, and what new insights they have gained. These inquiries can shed light onto the relevance of economic empowerment, as understood in this article, which grants women access and control of their economic resources to make informed decisions.

Women's testimony

On a hot mid-July morning, I had the opportunity to travel to Petac to speak to several women from this community. In the first interview with María Adolfina Canche Pat, currently a microcredit borrower with *Mundo Rural*, she commented how this money has helped her finance the construction of a small store:

> "Thanks to *Mundo Rural*, we have started to build this store. We have lots of plans right now. We are working on making textiles, embroideries and paintings. At the store we are planning to sell several things for example; arts and crafts, and we will also use it to sell food. At this moment, we are waiting to see if we can buy materials to construct the roof and, later on, the floor. Like I tell my daughters, we can do everything if we work hard."

Her self-reliance is noted in the fact that the decision to obtain a micro-credit was solely hers. She also supports other women in the community by teaching them how to sell and promote their arts and crafts. Fina, as everyone calls her, mentions that having the opportunity to obtain a microcredit has given her a new impulse, as she is now making the majority of economic decisions in the household.[14] This newfound role as a businesswoman has also brought her to the realities and challenges facing her small town; for that reason, she decided to run for the town's police commission. In our conversation she relates this experience with pride:

> "I thought. I will make Petac prosper. I want to make Petac prosper. At that time, I did not have a lot of money, nothing to count on to give people. Back then, I said I am going to put my name on the ballot for the post at the police station of Petac and I won. And not only because I now work here, I am going to be in Merida I am going to be here [. . .] I am managing things here and in other places for my people."

At the time this testimony was taped in July 2011 she had been in that post for eight months, and one year as a microcredit borrower. Of the ways in which she is helping Petac to become a better town, Fina has managed to get money from the local government and has made some improvements to the police station. In the not so distant past, this station was a shabby little office, now she has managed to add an open meeting space with a roof (something of a luxury) and a new jail. Even though this is an example independent of her microcredit, it serves to illustrate that her participation with *Mundo Rural* functioned as a conduit to broaden her current accomplishments.

One cannot leave this town without noticing the spatial linearity of its clean paved streets, the smell of food emanating from the orange colored houses, and the quietness of the place. Sadly, these elements reminded one of a reality constructed to please nostalgic tourists, nonetheless behind this families still struggle to make ends meet. [15] Further down the street, sat a brand new playground where children, unaware of the group of adults walking in the sweltering heat, carried on games and laughed at the mischievous dealings of a small half-naked boy. Not far from the playground stands a house with a small grocery store inside. A young girl and boy greeted us as we entered. In fact, all the women were very friendly and eager to share their experiences.

Maria Victoria Caamal Macias relates that when she received the microcredit, it was used to buy new merchandise for her store:

"We bought a few things and later we purchased more sodas and the refrigerator [. . .] My daughter and I requested the microcredit. My husband does not know it, he helps me, but he does not know anything about it. This was my decision and my daughter's."

—Who controls the economy of the house Maria?

"Well, I do. [. . .] I usually do not go out of the house, I like to stay here [. . .] the doctor says that because of my asthma I can't go to the fields or work too much."

—Then, because of your health your daughter helps you. What are the things that she does?

"She sells, attends to the store, if she needs something she tells me, if she has the money I say buy it. [. . .] I try to teach my other two daughters how to do this, how to manage a store and I explain it to them. I see that they like it. I also have two sons. One of them comes on the weekends and helps me stock up the store. He understands our job and tries to help, but the other one does not help me with the store."

—Maria, you teach them by example.

"Yes, I do."

In my visit with Paolina Chap Dzul, a shy middle-aged woman, answers my questions amicably regarding her experience:

"I had this business before my microcredit. With the loan, we bought a few   things for the store that we needed."

—Paolina, did you ask for permission from your husband to get a microcredit?

"No, I just went to get it. The decision was mine. The only thing I said to my husband - I am going to get a loan."

—If you decided to get a microcredit, who manages the money?

"I manage the money from both the store and the house. My husband helps me. He does not have a permanent job, but he helps."

The first town visited in Tizimin was the community of San Luis. This region is about 20 minutes away from the city and can be reached via a narrow paved road. In San Luis I spoke with Maria Esther Tamay, who along with her husband, own a well-dispensed convenience store:

"Between both of us, we assumed a responsibility to obtain a loan [. . .] If someday I am not here he has to take over the payments, because it is an obligation."

—Maria Esther, who is the person that administers the economy?

"My husband. Mmmm. Well, my husband and I. It is fifty-fifty.

—Before getting a microcredit, did you have your own business?

"Yes, I had a small store. Now thanks to God, we are adding more merchandise and provide a service to the community."

—Has a micro-credit changed your life? How?

"Yes. [. . .] Now that I have more revenue, I can give clients some merchandise on credit, and wait for them to pay me when they receive their bi-weekly salary. I do not see myself pressed to pay my distributors. [. . .] At the store, I offer a variety of products, groceries, sodas --I have a little bit of everything."

—How do you help other women in the community?

"Sometimes women come to ask for my help, for example if their kids are sick I help them. I lend them money. Of course there has to be a guarantee. [. . .] Some women say to me, "I do not have anything to eat can you give me credit," and I do. I try to encourage the women in my town so they can have the knowledge to move forward. Some of them are shy, but I tell them you cannot get mad with your husband. You have to think, develop yourself. If a woman is active, immediately money will come."

—How do you feel now?

"I feel like an accomplished woman, because I have more experience. If some women do not know something, I try to explain things to them so they can overcome their problems. Every week, I also visit the organization of women who work at the mill. I organized them back in 1979. We had a mill that did not work. I requested the federal and state government for a replacement. We obtained a new one and it is now located in the house that we have here. By the way, I am the president and organizer."

Around noon, we headed to the town of San Manuel. From San Luis we traveled 30 to 40 minutes on an old winding narrow road. San Luis is located close to the border of the state of Quintana Roo and, compared to the previous region, most houses here are huts and few of them are made out of bricks (a project that was supported by the government after hurricane Wilma in 2005). Its remoteness is confirmed when Teresa, my first interviewee and the community's treasurer, comments, "aside from APA very few people come to visit."

When Teresita de Jesus Contreras decided to get her first microcredit the business she had in mind was to own a butcher shop. Unfortunately, she did not know anything about the particulars of running that type of business. Thanks to APA, they made available workshops training courses from primal cuts on how to slaughter a pig. Now, San Manuel's residents save money since they no longer travel thirty minutes to the nearest meat store:

"Before microcredit, my family relied only on my husband's salary. It was very difficult and I decided to get a microcredit for this butcher shop. Today, I am in my fifth microcredit with APA. My husband is the one in charge of slaughtering the animals and my sons help too. I usually sell the meat and manage the store. When I first received my first loan in 2009, we used it to fix our property. Later on, we bought small animals and utilized what we earned. That is the way it is done. We now have a refrigerator and we sell meat products to our clients and they save money. [. . .] The money I make here is used for the family. I have a daughter at the Public University in Tizimin. She is not charged tuition because it is free; however, from time to time she needs cash to buy books or pay for transportation, I help her."

—Teresita, do you see you yourself as a businesswoman? How do you feel?

[Smiles] "I am a small storeowner. Yes, I do feel more confident to deal with other women in the community, because I am the treasurer. My job is not only to collect their money but I also talk to them to help them better themselves."

Dominga Cumul Balam, an older woman, tells me:

"I see that it has benefited us, the decision to ask for the microcredit was from both of us. I talk to others about my experience and I tell them the loan has helped me. With the first loan, I bought a few pigs and now I have a lot more, whenever I sell them, I make some money. I like to work in that manner. Today, I do not have too much money, but I do not have too little."

Ana Maria Herrera is the commissariat's wife, at the time this interview was taped the husband was present and he offered additional details on how he helps her in the business:

"My husband and I decided to get this microcredit for apiculture. Thanks to this business, we have a little bit more money."

The husband interjects:

"I basically get all the honey out and she is in charge of processing it - put the honey in the bottles, sealing it and of course selling it. I sell other things at the market, but she always sells more than I do. She is very well known, the clients like the honey she sells. From October to February is the best time to produce honey here in Yucatán. In the months we do not have production here, I take the bees to Quintana Roo where the climate is right, and we continue to produce honey. Because she already has her clients and they know we have a good   product."

—Ana, how many bottles of honey do you sell at the market?

"I usually sell thirty bottles every week at twenty-five pesos each [about two dollars]. I sell my honey and I feel happy because I have money to spend for all the things I need, before I did not have it, now I do."

Husband says:

"She has more money than I do. Really!"

Porfiria Gomez has never had a small business, but now with a microloan from APA she sells her embroideries to tourists.

"I learn to embroider just by watching other women. Now that I know how, I sell them. I buy all the materials I need to embroider napkins and I also make hammocks."

—Who made the decision to borrow a microcredit?

"It was my own, but I asked my husband first because if I do not have money to pay, he helps. I learned that APA worked with other women in the community and I was curious to know what it was."

—Who makes most of the financial decisions in the house?

"Well everything I make, I keep and if we need anything in the house I can buy it. Yes, my husband has his own salary and helps, but now I also help. I now do not ask for permission to buy things. If I need it, I buy it."

My next conversation was with Maria Rosaura Fernandez Tamayo she showed me some of the work in progress:

"I complete the embroidery on these napkins in two to three days. I already have clients that come and buy from me. This time around, I used the loan to buy materials for my embroidery business. I learned this trade from the nuns that came to give us workshops. [. . .] When speaking to my clients I feel less shy than before. Now I offer my work and I feel proud and satisfied. I also feel good around people, because they can tell me what they want. When I deliver my work, they say "how beautiful!" and I feel good and proud of what I did."

—You mentioned this last microcredit was used to buy materials. How about the others?

"The previous loan was used to buy some material and also pay for my son's education. He is nineteen years old and is studying Information Technology at the Technological University in Tizimin."

—Do you have any more children?

"Yes, one is already married, another one is sixteen. He only works and does not study the other kid is the nineteen year old, and two younger ones. If we get more help and my business grows, I can help them go to University."

As observed in the conversations with these women, the experiences with APA's microcredit program reiterates that through the use of these loans, not only are women able to sell and offer a variety of products to their respective communities, but through that process they have also gained a sense of accomplishment, which, in turn, affirms their economic empowerment. As shown in their testimony, they have made decisions for the household that go beyond the day-to-day, as they provide opportunities for younger generations through education. It is certain that the work carried out by Mother Aurora and that of *Mundo Rural* not only provide financial services, but recognizes the need to service the community by creating personal and intimate relationships that go beyond a micro-credit. This has been an important and determining factor in their success.

Conclusion

In Mexico, "decentralization was understood by the federal government as a way to rationalize spending and to generate a wider socio-political impact" (Díaz-Cayeros & Silva Castañeda, 2004, p. 12). That is social participation as a collective activity implicates that its citizens have the capacity and power to influence and take their own decisions, meaning that the most appropriate medium to strengthen such power is at the municipal level. Montecinos (2005) observes that in order to reach larger populations decentralization has to be in direct contact with local organizations to generate a wider accountability. As discussed in this chapter, micro-credit in Mexico, from its inception, has subscribed to the mobilization of those financial resources via governmental and non-governmental institutions. The pressing need to promote participation and opportunities for women entrepreneurs, and to improve women's lives economically, has been at the forefront of international and national dialogues; such is the case of the United Nations and the lasting contributions made by that democratic body.

In the 20th century, women in the state of Yucatán have set an example of strength and involvement in the decision-making process of the political, social, and economic life of that state. Despite the advances achieved by women the fact remains - poverty and extreme poverty affect women and their children more prominently. One strategy used as a tool to aid women in situations of poverty is microcredit. Studies made about micro-credit support that women borrowers are more responsible than men in repaying a loan on time and making informed choices regarding their economy. However, as certain institutions giving microloans applied unfair banking practices that further contribute to the impoverishment of their clients. Some organizations, like the ones visited, offer loans with simple straightforward terms, and have in turn presented women with the opportunity to develop income-generating enterprises. Fina, Maria Victoria, Paolina, Maria Esther, Teresa, Dominga, Ana Maria, Porfiria, Maria Rosaura represented in this chapter, and the many other women interviewed in Petac and Tizimin have always contributed to the well-being of the family and the household; now with the use of microcredit it has given them another way to participate in the collective operations of the community, to help their families, and support younger generations through example and courage.

ENDNOTES

1   Research for this chapter was supported by a grant from the Stephen F. Austin State University Research Enhancement Program. I would especially like to thank Jorge Anlehu Lara, Diana E. Cáceres and Wilson Palma from *Mundo Rural*; from *Ayuda para Ayudar* Mother Aurora del Rivero Heredia, and Claudiana Santiago Gutierrez for bridging communications and providing invaluable information for this chapter. I would also like to thank Dr. Rogelio Garcia-Contreras from University of St. Thomas for his generous time, and to all the women in these communities without whom this chapter would not have been possible.

2   In Yucatán, during the years of 1990-1992, PRONASOL distributed one hundred and fifty-three million pesos (approximately fifty-one million dollars). According to Marie Lapointe this program had various initiatives to promote a social development policy. Unfortunately, the efforts to carry out these strategies and implement them among those in need were not coordinate (2008, p 248).

3   The data gathered in a national multidimensional measurement of poverty presents staggering numbers. The study explains that the number of people living in poverty has risen from 44.5% in 2008 to a 46.2% in 2010. This is an increment from 48.8 million to 52.0 millions of inhabitants living in poverty. During the same period the report reveals that 11.7 million of people are living in extreme poverty; the data shows the extent of this problem and the challenges faced by regional and national entities. (Consejo Nacional de Evaluación de la Política de Desarrollo Social [CONEVAL], 2010).

4   See the following works Foschiatto and Stumpo (2006), Microcredit Summit (2009) and Sebstad, J. & Cohen, M. (2001).

5   In February 1997 the World Micro-credit Summit Campaign in Washington, DC held a conference to focus on the supply and demand of microcredit. In that summit two documents were drawn, the Declaration and the Plan of Action. Both offer a series of guidelines used by people who operate in this sector (Microcredit Summit Campaign, 2009).

6   In 2010 the General Coordinator of PRONAFIM, Dr. Maria del Carmen Diaz Amador, stated that 85 percent of the individuals who have used microcredits are women. (Programa Nacional de Financiamiento a Micro Empresarios [PRONAFIM], 2010).

7   By 2007, the Bangladesh Bank, Grameen Trust had 20 branches in several states in Mexico (Perez, 2007). In 2009, a partnership between Carlos Slim and Yunus was signed the alliance is known as Grameen-Carso (Slim & Grameen, 2009).

8   Ever since its inception in 2005 the repayment rate on loans has been 98.79%. For the latest statistics see: http://www.kiva.org/about

9   "The exclusion of Maya women from state-sponsored congresses positioned the Maya as inferior, backward, and distinctly separate from the more "forward-looking" modern women who attended the congresses, further solidifying ethnic differences in Yucatán, particularly among women." (Smith, p. 31)

10   Those serving public office in the 1990's were: Governor Dulce Maria Sauri de Riancho, Chief Justice of the State Supreme Court, Ligia Cortez Ortega and Mayor of Merida Ana Rosa Payan Cervera, and Maya women Araceli Cab Cumi in the State Congress. In the 1993 elections, a Maya woman was a candidate for Governor, 10 ran for Congress, and 14 for Mayors of Yucatec towns. In that state Maya women became the mayoral majority; 6 of 7 female mayors were Maya ("From the Heart

of a Woman", 1998, p. 570).

11   Part of the money disbursed through these organizations comes from the fundraising efforts of students at the University of St. Thomas in Houston, a program initiated by Dr. Rogelío García-Contreras in 2008.

12   Some of the local women in Petac and Tizimin confirmed that information as being accurate. Evidence of the abuses carried out by this type of industry is illustrated on the many reported investigations about the near collapse of the microcredit sector in India. One effort to take concerted action to improve the microcredit industry is Convergences 2015 forum. For more information see: http://www.convergences2015.org/en

13   In an industry plagued by transnational corporations, the role of independent producers of habanero chili is fully supported by Mother Aurora and her foundation. A concrete example of this effort is accounted in two newspaper articles entitled "La procesadora de chile, un sueño de los productores del oriente" (2010), and "Nuevo estandarte maya: primera plantación de habanero Mayapán" (2011) both comment about the processing plant where local women and men produce habanero salsa, as well as the new areas to cultivate habanero chile.

14   The latter trend, although not new for Mexican women in semi-urban areas, demonstrates the important changes and impact that economic participation has had on women's self-esteem.

15   An important economic component in this town is the Hacienda of Petac. It attracts foreign visitors from all over the world and provides jobs to several people in the community.

References

Ballara, M. (2006). Género y Globalización sus impactos en los sistemas de producción, la situación de las mujeres y los(as) jóvenes: un desafío para la seguridad alimentaria. *Agronuevo*, 2 (13), 67-87.

Calfio Montalva, M & Velasco L. F. (2006). Mujeres indígenas en América Latina: ¿brechas de género o brechas de etnia? *Pueblos indígenas y afrodescendientes de América Latina y el Caribe: información sociodemográfica para políticas y programas*. Retrived (2011, June 15) from http://www.eclac.cl/mujer/noticias/noticias/5/27905/FCalfio_LVelasco.pdf

Consejo Nacional de Evaluación de la Política de Desarrollo Social (CONEVAL). (2010). *Análisis y Medición de la Pobreza*. Retrived (2013, January 28) from http://www.coneval.gob.mx/Medicion/Paginas/Medición/Pobreza-2010.aspx

Díaz-Cayeros, A & Silva Castañeda, S. (2004). *Descentralización a escala municipal en México: la inversion en infraestructura social*. México, D. F.: CEPAL, Unidad de Desarrollo Industrial.

Deshmukh-Ranadive, J & Murthy K. (2005). *Micro-credit, Poverty and Empowerment*. New Delhi: Sage Publications.

Figueroa, MG. (2010, January 15). Darán microcréditos para proyectos de miel y chile habanero en Tizimín. *Punto Medio*. Retrived (2011, May 20) from http://www.puntomedio.com.mx/noticias/daran-microcreditos-para-proyectos-miel-chile-habanero-tizimin-4351/

Fondo de Desarrollo de las Naciones Unidas para la mujer (UNIFEM). (2005). *Camino a la igualdad de género: CEDAW Beijing y los ODM*. Retrived (2011, July 27) from http://www.unrol.org/files/PathwayToGenderEquality_spn.pdf

Foschiatto, P & Stumpo, G. (2006). El microcrédito: un instrumento para fortalecer las capacidades productivas locales. *Políticas municipales de microcrédito*. Santiago, Chile: CEPAL, Naciones Unidas.

Instituto para el Desarrollo de la Cultura Maya del Estado de Yucatan (INDEMAYA). (2000). *Decreto 293*. Retrived (2011, July 21) from http://www.indemaya.gob.mx/descargas/archivos/decreto-creacion-indemaya.pdf

Lapointe, M. (2008). *Historia de Yucatán Siglos XIX-XXI*. Mérida, Yucatán: Universidad Autónoma de Yucatán.

La procesadora de chile, un sueño de los productores del oriente. (2010, October 3). *Yucatán Ahora. com.* Retrived (2011, June 12) from http://www.yucatanahora.com/noticias/-procesadora-chile-sueno-los-productores-del-oriente-8036/

Línea Basal de los Objetivos de Desarrollo del Milenio para Chiapas. (2010). Tuxtla Gutiérrez, Chiapas. Retrived (2011, April 30) from http://www.ceieg.chiapas.gob.mx/home/wpcontent/uploads/downloads/2011/03/Linea-Basal-ODM.pdf

Litvack, J; Ahmad, J & Bird, R. (1998). *Rethinking Decentralization in Developing Countries: sector studies*. Washington, DC: World Bank.

Martin, Kathleen R. (1998). "From the Heart of a Woman": Yucatec Maya Women as Political Actors. *Sex Roles*. 39 (7/8), 559-571.

Microcredit Summit Campaign. (2009). *About the Microcredit Summit Campaign*. Retrieved (2011, April 8) from http://www.microcreditsummit.org/about/about_the_microcredit_summit_campaign/

Montecinos, Egon. (2005). Los estudios de descentralización en América Latina: una revision sobre el estado actual de la temática. *EURE*. 31 (93), 73-88.

Moreno, J & Harriman, L. (2009). Evaluating the Role of Microfinance Institution in Mexico. University of Chicago. Retrieved (2011, March 10) from http://www.youtube.com/watch?v=D1-w__hVAtg

Nuevo estandarte maya: primera plantación de habanero Mayapán. (2011, March 5). *Reporteros Hoy*. Retrieved (2011, June 12) from http://www.reporteroshoy.mx/wp/nuevo-estandarte-maya-primera-plantacion-de-habanero-mayapan.html

Poniatowska, Elena. (2006). *Las Soldaderas: Women of the Mexican Revolution*. El Paso, TX: Cinco Puntos Press.

Programa Especial de Seguridad Alimentaria (PESA) en México (n.d.). Antecedentes del PESA en México. Retrived (2011, June 24) from http://www.utn.org.mx/proyecto_pesa.html

Perez, MF. (2007, May 25). El programa de microcréditos de Bangladesh en México. *El Universal*. Retrieved (2011, May 23) from http://www.eluniversal.com.mx/articulos/40227.html

Portal de Microfinanzas. (2011). *PRONAFIM comparte sus éxitos de 10 años*. Retrieved (2011, June 23) from http://www.portalmicrofinanzas.org/p/site/s/template.rc/1.1.10807/

Programa Nacional de Financiamiento al Microempresario. (2010). *IX Encuentro Nacional de Microfinanzas*. Retrieved (2011, July 20) from http://www.encuentromicrofinanzaspronafim.com/CONFERENCIA%20DE%20PRENSA%20(3).pdf

Sebstad, J., Cohen, M., & Consultative Group to Assist the Poorest. (2001). *Microfinance, risk management and poverty: Synthesis study*. Washington: Consultative Group to Assist the Poorest (C.G.A.P), World Bank.

Slim y Grameen otorgan microcréditos en México. (2009, September 24). *El Universal*. Retrieved (2011, May 23) from http://www.eluniversal.com.mx/notas/628677.html

Smith, Stephanie J. (2009). *Gender and the Mexican Revolution: Yucatán women and the realities of patriarchy*. Chapel Hill, NC: U of North Carolina. Press.

United Nations Millennium Project. (2005). *Investing in Development: A Practical Plan to Achieve the Millennium Development Goals. Overview*. Washington, D.C.: Published by Communications Development Inc.

Chapter Ten

Decentralization in the United States of America

Lee W. Payne

Key words: decentralization, United States of America, federalism, local government, privatization

Introduction

The *Federalist Papers* specifies the foundation upon which the United States of America's federalist form of governance was constructed. Federal systems, unlike unitary systems, have different "levels" of government – federal, state, and local governments. These levels have different "reserved powers"[1] that sometimes come into conflict. At other times, levels of government can work together to solve pressing issues and serve the constituents.[2] After all, the constituents are the people and, as Madison suggested, the "ultimate authority ... resides in the people alone." What Madison was advocating in "Federalist No. 46" was decentralization of government, which is the topic of this text.

Not mentioned by Madison in Federalist No. 46 is local government – city, county, school district, etc. Madison's omission aside, the role of local government in the United States system of government should not to be marginalized. After all, local government is the level of government closest to the people. It is the level of government where problems, even problems identified on the federal or state level, are resolved. In addition, local government is the level of government where the people have the most input and, therefore, it is the most accountable as well. Given that local government is the most accountable, it is somewhat ironic that, in the United States, federal elections have the highest voter turnout while state and local election turnout drops precipitously.

Where government and decentralization is concerned, there are several public administration theories that can be applied. A fairly new concept in this area is collaborative public management, which is the focus of this chapter. These include a more in-depth treatment of federalism, efficiency versus effectiveness in the delivery of services, and privatization and accountability as a decentralization concept.

Federalism and Decentralization

Where unitary governments have centralized power and control over any and all sub-government units that may exist, federal governments reserve certain powers for the different levels of government and sub-units of government are semi-autonomous. For example, in the United States the federal government, through the Fifteenth,[3] Nineteenth,[4] and Twenty-Sixth[5] Amendments, has declared universal suffrage for citizens eighteen years of age and older. States, however, have the autonomy to restrict certain residents from voting based on criminal behavior. Several states disenfranchise felons who are incarcerated or who are on parole from voting and a number of states even restrict voting based on misdemeanor convictions. Other states, Oregon for example, allow incarcerated individuals to vote regardless of the type of crime committed – felony or misdemeanor. Finally, local governments have the autonomy to declare the method by which the residents will vote. Some municipalities or counties use computers, some use optical scanners, while other may use lever machines or punch cards. This illustrates how an issue like voting becomes decentralized at the different levels of government. The federal governments sets the baseline standard, state governments have the autonomy to restrict some from voting, and local governments (the level of government closest to the people) have the autonomy to implement the means by which residents vote. This is decentralization.

Given that decentralization is an intriguing concept that brings decision-making closer to citizens, it is interesting that most states (countries) have a unitary form of government. What makes some states adopt a unitary form of government while other states adopt a federal form of government? An answer to this question may be found in the geographic and demographic makeup of the state (Dikshit 1971; Fifer 1976; Kraynak 1987; Jenson 1990; Smith 1991; LaSelva 1993; Hochman, Pines, and Thisse 1995; Shroder 1995; Gibbins 2000; Mendelsohn 2000; Rodden and Wibbels 2002; Erk 2003; Strumpf and Oberholzer-Gee 2002; Rodden 2004; Bakke and Wibbels 2006; Levy 2007; Soss, Fording, and Schram 2008; Percival, Johnson, and Neiman 2009; Whitford and Wong 2009). Unitary states are typically geographically small and demographically less diverse, while federal states are typically geographically large and demographically diverse. For example, Austria, France, Switzerland, and Sweden are all unitary states, while Canada, India, Mexico, and the United States of America are all federal states. The unitary states listed are geographically small and largely homogeneous, while the federal states listed are geographically large and or heterogeneous.

Since unitary states tend to be geographically small and homogeneous, centralized control is feasible. The central government can exert substantial control over the sub-units of government because these states do not have a large diversity of needs. Conversely, a unitary form of government is not feasible in geographically large and heterogeneous states. Consider the United States, which is a large and diverse country. In the United States, a state like Texas is very different from a state like California. Not only are Texas and California in different regions (Texas is in the South and California is in the West), they have very different political cultures, demographics, industries, and governments.

175

Where political culture is concerned, Texas is considered a hybrid between individualistic and traditionalistic political culture, while California has a moralistic political culture (Johnson 1976). Individualistic political cultures believe that government should be limited to those areas that encourage private initiative and traditionalistic political cultures believe that the role of government should be limited to securing the maintenance of the existing social order. Both the individualistic and traditionalistic political cultures discourage political participation. Moralistic political cultures view government as a positive force and encourage political participation. Not surprisingly, California allows much more political input from citizens. For example, the California Constitution allows citizen initiatives,[6] referendums,[7] and recall elections,[8] while none of these forms of direct democracy are allowed on the state level in Texas.[9] In this comparison, California is more decentralized than Texas. That is, California allows much more input from its citizens than Texas.

Demographically, Texas and California have similar percentages (citizens) of Hispanics (37.6 percent in both states) but Texas has a higher percentage of African-Americans than California (11.8 percent and 6.2 percent respectively), while California has a larger percentage of Asians than Texas (13 percent and 3.8 percent respectively) (United States Census, 2000). Different demographics create different demands on state governments. For example, minority populations are linked to poverty levels – the higher the percentage of minorities in a state, the higher the level of poverty. Higher poverty rates create more demands on state resources in the form of Medicaid, school lunch programs, food stamps, and academic achievement, to name a few. In this regard, decentralizing the administration of these programs to the individual states is good policy. After all, depending on the demographic make-up of each state, the demands will be very different.

Where industries are concerned, historically Texas had a farming, ranching, and oil-based economy. While these industries are still strong, Texas is now moving toward high-tech industries in the medical and computer fields. California has strong high-tech ties to the computer industry (Silicone Valley), entertainment is a large industry, and California produces a great deal of the nation's fruits and vegetables. Considering these differences in industry, decentralizing economic control to the states makes sense. For example, regulations on the extraction of fossil fuels are more lax in Texas than in California. That said there are federal regulations regarding the extraction of fossil fuels that both states must adhere to.

Finally, where governments are concerned, Texas and California are very different. Texas has a constitutionally weak governor and a part-time legislature (the Texas Legislature only meets every other odd-numbered year for 140 calendar days), while California has a stronger governor and a full-time legislature. Reasons for the differences in Texas and California's governments are directly related to their political cultures. Texas has a hybrid individualistic and traditionalistic political culture; therefore Texas has a very limited and weak government. While California's moralistic political culture creates a friendly environment for stronger government. Whatever the political culture or government structure, decentralization allows the states to create the form of government that works best for its citizens. Furthermore, if residents of one state are unhappy with the form of government in the state they reside, they can vote with their feet.[10]

Given these differences, it should be evident that these states face different issues and have different needs. As such, centralized control from Washington D.C. is not practicable. The decentralized federal system of government in the United States allows states a level of autonomy to address their issues and demands in different ways. A good example of how the United States decentralized system works to allow states the autonomy to address their individual issues and demands, while still exerting federal standards, can be found in welfare reform.

In 1996 the Republican Congress passed, and President Clinton signed into law, the Personal Responsibility and Work Opportunity Reconciliation Act (PRWORA). PRWORA ended the Aid to Families with Dependent Children (AFDC) program and replaced it with Temporary Assistance for Needy Families (TANF). Two major, and somewhat controversial, components of TANF that distinguish it from the previous AFDC program are: first, recipients were life limited to 60 cumulative months of receiving benefits and, second, work requirements for continued assistance were established.[11] Further, TANF granted states the autonomy to "experiment" with welfare reform by allowing states the option of instituting additional, harsher, sanctions on welfare recipients.

There are three examples of options available to states under TANF: First, reducing the lifetime limit of 60 months' assistance that welfare recipients can collect benefits to fewer months, second, shortening the work requirement time limit, third, instituting "family caps" on recipients.[12] In addition to the new and creative sanctions introduced in TANF, it provided for performance bonuses to states that were successful in reducing welfare rolls by moving welfare recipients off welfare and into the workforce. This provision worried many that there would be a "race to the bottom" of benefits offered among states; the theory being that welfare recipients would leave states with harsher sanctions and take up residency in states with milder sanctions, which, in turn, would cause these states to adopt harsher sanctions in an attempt to reduce welfare rolls and further migration. Findings on whether welfare recipients actually migrate to "easier" states (voted with their feet) are mixed (Peterson and Rom 1989; Shroder 1995, Allard 2000, Berry, Fording and Hanson 2003), but the concept persists and may influence decisions made on welfare reform by state legislatures.

TANF allows states to experiment with their welfare benefits in an attempt to create a system that works best for their constituents. Since Texas and California have different demographics, they can adopt TANF benefits for their needs. In addition, states with similar demographics, cultures, etc. can learn from one another. For example, Texas and Louisiana are similar in demographics, culture (both are southern states), etc. Because states are allowed the autonomy to experiment with their welfare benefits, similar states can learn from one another. If Texas and Louisiana implement different welfare policies and one of the two states has more success at decreasing welfare roles than the other, the less successful state can adopt the welfare policies implemented by its neighbor. Although the states have the autonomy to implement harsher sanctions, the federal government has specified limits that states cannot exceed. That said, by allowing states the autonomy to create welfare policy that best suits their needs, the federal government has decentralized their ultimate control.

The TANF example leads to another aspect of decentralization in the United States – vertical and horizontal federalism (Smith 1991; Wood 1991; Schwager 1997; Cremer and Palfrey 1999; Gerber and Teske 2000; Prince 2001; Garman, Haggard, and Willis 2002; Rodden 2002; Rodden and Wibbels 2002; Rodden 2004; Volden 2005; Levy 2007; Soss, Fording, and Schram 2008). Vertical federalism is what usually comes to mind when considering federalism. Vertical federalism is hierarchical, top-down federalism. In this system, the federal government resides at the top of the hierarchical pyramid, the states are in the middle, and local governments are at the bottom. The voting and TANF examples illustrate this relationship well. The federal government adopts a standard but allows states and local governments the autonomy to tailor fit the federal policy to their individual needs. Horizontal federalism can be a form of decentralization of government sub-units at the same level – state-to-state or city-to-city.

Horizontal federalism has its roots in the Constitution and can be traced to the failed Articles of Confederation.[13] Article IV, Section 1 of the Constitution outlines the full faith and credit clause.[14] For instance, if a couple were married in Las Vegas, Nevada while on vacation, their home state would have to respect the Nevada marriage and offer the couple all of the benefits associated with getting married in their home state. Article IV, Section 2 of the Constitution outlines the privileges and immunities clause.[15] For instance, an individual from Florida who gets a speeding ticket in Georgia cannot be treated differently because they are not from Georgia. If the fine for driving 80 miles per hour in a 55 mile per hour zone is $200 for Georgia residents, the Floridian cannot be charged $300 for the same infraction. This Constitutional horizontal federalism has morphed into an informal decentralization between the states and local governments.

While decentralization between sub-units of government might appear counterintuitive, there are merits to this action. On the state level, states can enter into mutually beneficial agreements. For example, Northeastern states can experience substantial strain on their electrical systems during extremely cold winters as residents increase the heat in their homes. To keep power grids from becoming overly strained, Northeastern states might be forced to implement rolling brownouts and, in some cases, rolling blackouts during the winter months. A brownout is when electricity usage is limited; causing lights to dim, hence the term brownout. When brownout are insufficient in reducing electricity loads, complete blackouts, or shutting off electricity to certain areas at designated times, are implemented to reduce loads. Both actions inconvenience citizens and can lead to dissatisfaction with elected officials. As such, Northeastern states were desperate to find another solution to their problem. They found a solution several states away in Texas.

Texas is unique among the states because it has one power grid that supplies power to most of the state. This power grid is called the Electric Reliability Council of Texas (ERCOT). That Texas maintains its own power grid is another function of decentralized federalism. In 1935, President Franklin D. Roosevelt signed the Federal Power Act. The purpose of this act was to give the Federal Power Commission (now the Federal Energy Regulatory Commission) the authority to oversee and regulate interstate electricity sales. Because the Texas power grid is self-contained and does not cross state lines, Texas utilities avoid being subject to federal regulations.

ERCOT has ties to two of the Northeastern grids and is allowed to move power commercially or for emergency purposes without triggering federal regulations. Since Texas has mild winters and an abundance of power, Northeastern states can purchase or trade electricity with EROTC without federal interference when needed. This cooperative agreement benefits Northeastern states by providing much needed power to its citizens and benefits Texas' economy by allowing Texas to sell or trade electricity without federal interference. This is horizontal federalism and decentralization at its best – allowing states to engage in interstate trade without federal interference.

On the local level, cities and or counties can work horizontally as well. For example, if County A has an issue with jail overcrowding, it can work with County B to move some of their inmates to the neighboring county's facility. Horizontal decentralization arrangements can cross state lines as well, although not where inmates are concerned. For example, in the aftermath of Hurricane Katrina in September of 2005, New Orleans worked across state line to secure accommodations for refugees in sanctuary cities like Houston, Texas. What transferring inmates from one county to another and securing accommodations for refugees in another city across state lines have in common and why these are examples of decentralization, is that the decisions to engage in these arrangements are made at the local level, which is as close to the people as government can get.

Finally, where federalism and decentralization are concerned, the structure of the United States Government has strong decentralization underpinnings. After the Articles of Confederation failed, the Founding Fathers were tasked with creating a new constitution and a new form of government. They knew that a confederation was not feasible and they knew from their experiences with England that they did not want to create a unitary form of government – the citizens would never have approved of a unitary form of government because of the fear of too much centralized power. This left only one option – federalism. Knowing that they were going to create a federalist form of government did not end the debate about the new government though. There were conflicts between the Federalist[16] and Anti-Federalists,[17] between large states and small states, and between factions regarding how the different branches of government would be structured – would Congress be unicameral or bicameral or would there be a single executive or plural executive, for example.

Where the Federalists and Anti-Federalists were concerned, the pivotal sticking point between the factions was centralized versus decentralized control of the government – the Federalists wanted more centralized governmental control while the Anti-Federalists wanted decentralized governmental control. The Federalists argued that separation of powers[18] and checks and balances[19] would protect the people from too much centralized control. Further, the Federalists argued that each independent branch of government would represent a different aspect of the people – the Legislative branch would represent the people on the state level, while the Executive branch would represent the people on a national level. The Anti-Federalists argued that the new constitution gave too much power to the national government at the expense of the state governments, that the Executive branch held too much power, and that there was not a Bill of Rights included in the new constitution. How the two factions came together to adopt the new constitution was a compromise on the level of decentralization that would be allowed.

During the Constitutional Convention of 1787 the Federalists and Anti-Federalists each supported different plans for how they believed the new government should be structured. The Federalists largely supported the Virginia Plan, while the Anti-Federalists largely supported the New Jersey Plan. The Virginia Plan (also known as the Large-State Plan[20]) advocated for a bicameral, or two chamber, Legislative branch with both chamber's apportionment based on state population, one of these chambers would be elected by the people and it would then elect members to the other branch from nominations submitted by the state legislatures, and a single executive who was appointed by the legislative branch, to name a few of the provisions. While the New Jersey Plan (also known as the Small-State Plan) advocated for a unicameral, or one chamber, Legislative branch with equal representation elected by the people and a plural executive, to name a couple of the provisions.

The schism between the Federalist and Anti-Federalist boiled down to a debate on the level of decentralization the new government would have, with the Federalist advocating for more centralized control and the Anti-Federalist advocating for decentralized control. Anti-Federalists were concerned with several aspects of the Virginia Plan. Foremost among these concerns was apportionment based on population in the Legislative branch. They knew that the voice of the citizens of less populated states would be unrepresented if representation was apportioned based on population. They were also concerned with having the members of the second chamber elected by the elected chamber. Finally, they feared having an executive appointed by the Legislative branch. What these concerns have in common is the marginalization of the people's input at each stage. In the end, the members of the Constitutional Convention agreed to the Connecticut Compromise (also known as the Great Compromise) and a promise to the Anti-Federalists that a Bill of Rights would be proposed and offered to the states for ratification.

The Connecticut Compromise took parts of the Virginia and New Jersey Plans and melded them into the form of government still in place in the United States. Foremost among the compromises adopted was a bicameral Congress with the House of Representatives apportioned by population and the Senate apportioned based on equal representation – each state has two members in the Senate. This agreement gave small states protection against large states passing legislation harmful to less populated states. In addition, House of Representative members would be directly elected by the people and serve two-year terms, while Senate members would be elected by the state legislatures and serve six-year, overlapping terms.[21] It is important to recognize that House members only serve two-year terms. This made House members more accountable to the people. Finally, instead of having a plural executive or having the Legislative branch appoint the executive, the compromise established a single executive elected through the Electoral College. While the Electoral College removes the selection of the president from direct election by the people, and is still in use today, it moves the election of the president closer to the people. What is important to recognize in all of these compromises is that Anti-Federalists were successful at decentralizing control from the central government.

Outside of the Connecticut Compromise, the Anti-Federalists were adamant that a Bill of Rights be added to the Constitution to protect the people and the states from the overreaching power of the central government – in other words, the Anti-Federalists were advocating further decentralization of the central government. For their part, the Federalists argued that the state constitutions currently contained individual bills of rights and that having one at the national level was unnecessary. Because there were several states with anti-federalist sentiments, and these states could derail ratification of the Constitution, the Federalists agreed to add a Bill of Rights to the Constitution after its ratification.

The Bill of Rights consists of the first ten amendments to the Constitution. While most are familiar with aspects of the first eight of these amendments, which deal with matters of free speech, the free exercise of religion, the right to keep and bear arms, and a number of rights afforded to those accused of crimes, the Ninth and Tenth Amendments were critical for the Anti-Federalists. The Ninth Amendment specifies that, "The enumeration in the Constitution, of certain rights, shall not be construed to deny or disparage others retained by the people" (United States Constitution 1787). Basically, the Ninth-Amendment specifies that the people reserve rights other than those specifically granted to the people by the federal government in the Constitution. The Tenth Amendment specifies that, "The powers not delegated to the United States by the Constitution, nor prohibited by it to the States, are reserved to the States respectively, or to the people" (United States Constitution 1787). Here, the Tenth Amendment specifies that whatever powers not specifically granted to the United States by the Constitution belong to the states and/or the people. The importance of these two amendments cannot be marginalized in a discussion of decentralization. As mentioned previously, the foundation of the United States and its practical application of government is an example of decentralization. The Constitution mandates decentralization.

Effectiveness and Efficiency

Another important concept in the study of public administration that can be discussed in terms of decentralization is effectiveness and efficiency in the delivery of services (Rymes 1979, Lustick 1980, Meier 1980, Abney and Lauth 1987, Bowman and Keamey 1988, Neiman 1989, Li and Smith 2003, Rahn and Rudolph 2005, Soss and Lael 2006, Tavits 2006, Trounstine 2006, Kelleher and Wolak 2007). Effectiveness refers to how well the policy goals are met, while efficiency refers to how well the policy is implemented. Where public administrators are concerned, effectiveness of policy goals being met is usually more important than how efficiently they are met. This can be a source of contention and ridicule of those who believe that government is too big and spends too much money, especially in times of bloated deficits and mounting debt, as is the case in the United States of late. One way to make the delivery of government services more efficient may be through the decentralization of services.

Before discussing how decentralization may help government provide services more efficiently, it is important to understand why this dichotomy between effectiveness and efficiency exists. There is a reason why governments have historically been more concerned with effectiveness over efficiency – it is the job of government to supply services to constituents without concern for profit. Indeed, one of the major distinctions between the public and private sectors is that the public sector is not profit oriented while the private sector is. Because the private sector is driven by profits, it must be more efficient. If the private sector is not more efficient, it will lose money and fail.

Another reason for the difference in effectiveness and efficiency between the public and private delivery of services can be found in the constituents served by the two sectors. While the private sector will provide services as long as there is a profit to be made, by law the public sector is mandated to provide services where profits cannot be made. Medicare[22] is an excellent example of this distinction between the public and private sectors.

It can be argued that the most expensive year of most individuals' life is the last year of their life; this is especially true of the aged. This is especially true of the elderly because their last year of life can consist of serious health related issues that can require extensive medical expenses. As such, there is little to no profit to be made by the private sector to provide insurance to the elderly. There was no profit for the private sector to provide insurance to the elderly; they were being dropped from their insurance once they retired.

Before Medicare, medical expenses incurred by some of the elderly resulted in bankruptcies, the loss of life savings, and an increase in poverty for the elderly. As such, many elderly simply opted not to seek medical treatment for ailments and injuries, which resulted in shorter life expectancies. As a society, the United States decided that, although there was no profit to be made in insuring the elderly and disabled, insurance should be provided to these individuals. To this end, Medicare was signed into law in 1965. Is Medicare an efficient program? The simple answer is no, it is not. Medicare is one of the fastest growing federal programs in terms of expenses and, without serious restructuring; it will go bankrupt around the year 2024. Is Medicare an effective program? By most measures, it is an effective program. Prior to the enactment of Medicare, approximately 35 percent of those 65 and older lived in poverty; today only about 10 percent of those 65 and older live in poverty (United State Census). In addition, life expectancy has increased from 69.6 years of age in 1965 to 78.3 years of age in 2010 (United States Census).

Given the contrast between effectiveness and efficiency, and the governments' responsibility to provide services in an effective manner, efficiency may not appear possible. This is where decentralization can effectively increase the efficiency of government. As mentioned several times throughout this chapter, decentralization entails moving the decision making power of government closer to the people. Each step that government moves closer to the people – moving from the federal government to state governments to local governments – efficiency, as well as effectiveness, can be increased.

Law enforcement is a good example of how decentralization can increase efficiency as well as effectiveness. In the United States of America there are a multitude of law enforcement agencies at the federal, state, and local levels of government. For example, on the federal level the United States has the Federal Bureau of Investigation (FBI), the Bureau of Alcohol, Tobacco, Firearms, and Explosives (ATF), and the Drug Enforcement Administration (DEA), to name a few. These agencies are specialized to deal with specific crimes – the FBI has jurisdiction on any crime that crosses state lines, the ATF has jurisdiction on federal alcohol, tobacco, firearm, and explosives crimes, while the DEA has jurisdiction on federal drug related crimes. This specialization and division of labor allows for much more effective and efficient law enforcement on the federal level. On the state level Texas has the Department of Public Safety (DPS) and the Texas Rangers. While locally, there can be a county sheriff, city police departments, and university police departments depending on whether the city or town in question has a university within its jurisdiction. These law enforcement agencies can have primary or secondary (depending on what law is violated) jurisdiction and/or overlapping (again, depending on what law is violated) jurisdictions.

That the national law enforcement agencies are specialized is evidence of an attempt by the United States to make law enforcement more effective and efficient, but decentralizing law enforcement control makes law enforcement even more effective and efficient. To illustrate this, consider crimes that can be committed and the level of government law enforcement responsible for responding. For example, Student A is apprehended with marijuana on a university campus and charged with possession. The level of government involved in the apprehension, prosecution, and detention of Student A is dictated, in large part, by the amount of marijuana Student A was in possession of when arrested. In Texas, up to four ounces of marijuana is considered a misdemeanor and under local government jurisdiction, four ounces to five pounds is considered a felony and under state government jurisdiction, while any amount over five pounds can be considered the trafficking of marijuana and would be under federal jurisdiction.

Given the marijuana example, how does the decentralization of law enforcement result in more effectiveness and efficiency? Consider how ineffective and inefficient law enforcement would be if the DEA had to investigate every drug arrest that took place in the United States. The federal system would be stretched beyond its limits and paralyzed by the amount of casework involved – this would reach beyond the law enforcement agencies to the court systems as well. Similarly, if the state police agencies (the DPS and or the Texas Rangers in Texas for example) had to investigate every drug arrest of less than five pounds, the state system would be equally stretched and paralyzed. By allowing local law enforcement the autonomy to pursue drug crimes that consist of small amounts of drugs, which make up the bulk of drug crimes in the United States, all levels of law enforcement become more effective and efficient. The drug example can be expanded to include all manner of crimes where misdemeanor crimes are dispensed of locally, felony crimes are dispensed of on the state level, and federal crimes are dispensed of on the national level.

Privatization

The extreme form of decentralization is to move government functions and responsibilities to the private sector – privatization (Miller and Moe 1983; Feigenbaum and Henig 1994; Treisman 1999; Rodden and Wibbels 2002; Dowding and Mergoupis 2003; Remmer 2004; Magnusson 2005; Slantchev 2005). Privatization allows these functions to be carried out by businesses, community groups, cooperatives, private voluntary associations, non-profit organizations, and other non-government organizations. This text is about public administration and decentralization, the role that private business plays will not be discussed. Instead, the focus will be on non-profit organizations that fall under the purview of public administration. The reason non-profit organizations fall under the definition of public administration is because, much like government agencies, non-profit organizations are not driven by profit, which is one of the major distinctions between the private and public sectors. In addition, non-profit organizations receive special tax-exempt status and grants from the various levels of government (in addition to charitable contributions, which are tax exempt as well) to carry out their missions. These conditions make non-profits somewhat accountable to governments and, by extension, the voters; accountability, or the lack thereof, can be viewed as a major drawback to privatization (Bowman and Kearney 1988; Feigenbaum and Henig 1994; Lowry, Alt, and Ferree 1998; Stasavage 2003). After all, if functions that were once in the realm of government responsibility are privatized to non-governmental organizations, the line of accountability can be blurred.

One of the main reasons that non-profit organizations and the services they provide can be considered under the banner of decentralization is because these organizations are extremely close to the clients they service. Each non-profit organization has a specific "mission statement" that outlines the services they provide and the public that they cater to. Examples of non-profit organizations are plentiful and include international organizations like the Red Cross and Amnesty International, national organizations like Good Will and the Salvation Army, and local organizations like animal shelters and homeless shelters, to name a few. What all of these organizations have in common is that they deliver services in conjunction with, or in place of, governmental organizations. For more detail on how a non-profit organization delivers services to its clientele, a specific example follows.

Independence Manor I and II are non-profit organizations in Nacogdoches, Texas. Independence Manor I was established in 1981 and Independence Manor II was established in 1985. Both Independence Manor's mission statements are to provide accessible housing for persons with disabilities and limited incomes. To facilitate this outcome wheelchair accessible housing was constructed and residents of Independence Manor I and II receive the bulk of their income from federal government agencies – Social Security Disability (SSD), Supplemental Security Income (SSI), or a combination of the two. Another connection that Independence Manor I and II have to the federal government is with the Housing and Urban Development (HUD) agency. HUD provides the Housing

Choice Voucher Program (Section 8) to Independence Manor I and II residents to supplement their monthly rent to make their housing more affordable; the HUD supplements also allow Independence Manor I and II to provide housing at below market value for their residents.

What the Independence Manor I and II example should highlight is that this non-profit organization is providing a service to residents that the private sector could not or would not provide because there is no profit to be made in providing the service. It should also be noted that Independence Manor I and II are providing a service that would fall to the government if this non-profit organization did not exist. Finally, it should be obvious why this example illustrates decentralization. HUD does not interact with the residents of Independence Manor I and II. It is the job of the staff at Independence Manor I and II to annually evaluate the residents' income and level of disability to ensure that they qualify for the benefits provided. HUD benefits are based on the number of residents and their individual income and provided to Independence Manor I and II, which then adjusts the resident's rent accordingly. The staff at Independence Manor I and II are accountable to HUD, which is, in turn, accountable to elected officials.

Conclusion

This chapter outlined a detailed account of decentralization in the United States of America. It should be noted that the United States epitomizes decentralization by constitutional design. From its' founding, because of disagreements between the Federalists and Anti-Federalists, the United States established a system of decentralization. The federal government is given specific powers in the Constitution, while powers not specified in the Constitution to the federal government are reserved to the states and the people in the Ninth and Tenth Amendments. In other words, the Constitution created a federal system of government in the United States. Two characteristics of the United States that make the federal system work are: the United States is large geographically and second, the United States has a diverse population. Federalism allows individual states to implement federal government policies and create local policies in a way that best serves their citizens. In addition, local government (counties, cities, school boards, water districts, etc.) have the autonomy to create and implement local policies that best fit their citizens. This is decentralization at its best.

In addition to the discussion on federalism, this chapter outlined how decentralization can impact the effectiveness and efficiency of government services. Historically, the private sector has been more concerned with being efficient while the public sector has been more concerned with being effective. The distinction between the private and public sectors can be attributed to the pursuit of profits – with the private sector concerned with profits and the public sector concerned with delivering services. The private sector is driven by profit; therefore it has an incentive to be more efficient. Another reason for decreased efficiency in the public sector is that the public sector must provide services to constituents when profit is not only impossible, deficit spending are expected. The example used in the chapter was Medicare. Because the constituents served by Medicare are the most in need of medical services, the private sector will not provide medical insurance to these individuals – there is no profit to be made in doing so. Instead of letting the elderly and disabled go without insurance or be financially ruined by health issues, the government stepped up and provided insurance for these individuals. Medicare is far from efficient but it is very effective at keeping the elderly and disabled healthy and financially secure.

Decentralization can make the public sector more effective and efficient by concentrating the delivery of services closer to the people. In addition, specialization of government agencies can make the public sector more effective and efficient. Law enforcement was used as an example of levels of service delivery and specialization. While there are many overlapping law enforcement agencies that can respond to any crime, penal codes are in place to specify which level of law enforcement has primary jurisdiction on any crime. City and county violations are under the jurisdiction of city police departments and county sheriff agencies, state crimes are the jurisdiction of state level law enforcement agencies, and federal crimes are the jurisdiction of national law enforcement agencies. This division of labor makes law enforcement much more effective and efficient.

Finally, privatization was discussed in terms of decentralization. While privatization can create concerns with accountability, private entities can work in conjunction with different levels of government to deliver services to constituents in need. Accountability is a concern because privatizing out government services removes the delivery of services from those who are directly accountable to voters through elections – politicians. That said, with proper government oversight, concerns over accountability could be diminished. An invaluable government partner in the privatizing of government services is non-profit organizations. Non-profit organizations are one step removed from government and have a finger on the pulse of the constituents they serve. As such, they are in a unique position to supply services to constituents that the profit driven private sector will not provide and to act as advocates for the constituents the serve.

Decentralization is an important development in how governments function. Although the United States is decentralized by constitutional design, there are ways in which the United States can further decentralize. One option that has been discussed is to give the states much more control of the delivery of Medicaid[23] services. Those in favor of allowing states to have more control over Medicaid point to the success of the TANF welfare reform as evidence of decentralization success. Others worry, much like those who worried about a welfare "race to the bottom," that states would not provide sufficient services without strong federal oversight. This disagreement will play out in the political arena in the future. Regardless of individual concerns, when decentralization is done correctly, it can result in the more effective and efficient delivery of services and privatization is one option to facilitate this goal.

ENDNOTES

1   See Article I, Section Eight and the Tenth Amendment of the Constitution for examples of reserved powers.

2   Temporary Assistance for Needy Families (TANF) is an example of federal, state, and local governments working together.

3   The Fifteenth Amendment was ratified in 1870 and gave African-American males the right to vote.

4   The Nineteenth Amendment was ratified in 1920 and gave females the right to vote.

5   The Twenty-Sixth Amendment was ratified in 1971 and gave citizens eighteen years and older the right to vote.

6   Initiatives give voters the ability to enact legislation. In the last 20 years California initiatives have lowered property taxes, adopted a state lottery, adopted term limits for stat elected officials, and eliminated state affirmative action programs, to name a few.

7   Referendums allow citizens to veto legislation passed and the state legislature and signed into law by the governor. In 2010, Californians tried to legalize the recreational use of marijuana with Proposition 19. Although it failed at the ballot box, supporters plan to try to legalize the recreational use of marijuana again in 2012.

8   Recall elections allow citizens to remove an elected official prior to their term of office ending. Without the possibility of a recall election, citizens must wait until the elected official's term of office is over or they are impeached and removed from office. Californians successfully recalled Governor Gray Davis in 2003 and subsequently elected Governor Arnold Schwarzenegger.

9   Texas does allow voters the ability to vote in referendum elections to ratify state constitutional amendments, but these amendments are initiated through the Texas Legislature, not the citizens.

10 The term "voting with your feet" means that dissatisfied residents can move from one state to another as a means of expressing their dissatisfaction. These moves are evident with each new Census. For example, after the 2010 Census, Texas picked up four seats in the House of Representatives. This four seat pick up represented population shifts from several states to Texas. The states that had reduced populations lost seats in the House of Representatives.

11 Single parents must work at least 20 hours per week the first year, increasing to at least 30 hours per week by FY 2000. Two-parent families must work 35 hours per week by July 1, 1997.

12 Family caps placed limits on the number of additional children for which recipients can receive additional benefits.

13 Under the Articles of Confederation, the central government was very weak and ultimate power resided in the individual states. During this time the states were free to print their own money, have their own militias, engage in interstate economic warfare, etc. Shays' Rebellion (Daniel Shays openly thwarted the central government's ability to foreclose on property, which it was doing to recoup the costs of the Revolutionary War, by surrounding court houses and denying the magistrates access to the courts to hold foreclosure hearings) highlighted the weaknesses of the Articles of Confederation and lead to the adoption the current federal system of government in the UNITED STATES.

14 "Full faith and credit shall be given in each state to the public acts, records and judicial proceedings of every other state" (United States Constitution).

15   "The Citizens of each state shall be entitled to all privileges and immunities of Citizens in the several states" (United States Constitution).

16   The Federalist supported creating a new government with a stronger central government.

17   The Anti-Federalists supported the Articles of Confederation and were against creating a new government with a stronger central government.

18   Separation of powers means that the three branches of government (Legislative, Executive, and Judicial) would be independent and have no overlap and therefore, no one branch would have too much power. Juxtapose this concept with the English Parliament where the Prime Minister and his or her cabinet are sitting members of Parliament. In the UNITED STATES system, members of one branch of government cannot hold simultaneous office in another branch. For example, when Obama won the presidency in 2008, he still had two years left on his Illinois Senate seat. He could not hold both offices at once; he resigned from his Senate position.

19   Checks and balances mean that no one branch of government can implement government policy without the agreement of at least one other branch. For example, when the Congress passes legislation, it does not become law unless or until the president signs in into law. If the president vetoes the legislation, Congress can override his veto with a two-thirds vote in both chambers. Also, the president cannot appoint officials to bureaucratic or judicial positions, or enter into treaties with foreign countries, without Senate conformation of appointees or ratification of treaties.

20   Where the competing plans are concerned, Large-State and Small-State Plans refer to population size, not geographic size.

21   The 17th Amendment, adopted in 1913, established direct election of senators by popular vote. This Amendment is an example of further decentralization of the United States federal government.

22   On July 30th, 1965 President Lyndon B. Johnson signed into law the Social Security Act of 1965. The Social Security Act of 1965 expanded the original Social Security Act of 1935 (Old-Age, Survivors, and Disability Insurance) to include Medicare for persons 65 years of age or older and individuals with permanent disabilities. Medicare provided these individuals with government sponsored insurance to cover 80 percent of their medical costs. Originally, Medicare consisted of two parts – Parts A and B. Part A provided hospital insurance, while Part B provided medical insurance for outpatient care. Medicare Part C was added as part of the Balanced Budget Act of 1997 and gave Medicare recipients the option of receiving their Medicare through private health-insurance programs. Medicare Part D was enacted through the Medicare Prescription Drug, Improvement, and Modernization Act of 2005 and gave Medicare recipients the option of receiving prescription drugs through Medicare. Medicare is financed by a 2.9 percent pay-roll tax with 1.45 percent paid by the employee and matched by a 1.45 percent contribution from the employer.

23   Medicaid, unlike Medicare, is a means-tested program, which means that individuals or families must qualify for Medicaid services. To qualify, individuals or families must earn below a certain amount of income. Medicaid was created in 1965 through the Title XIX of the Social Security Act.

References

Abney, Glenn and Thomas P. Lauth (1987). Prescriptions of the Impact of Governors and Legislatures in the State Appropriation Process. *The Western Political Quarterly* 40 (2) 335-342.

Allard, Scott W. and Sheldon Danziger (2000). Welfare Magnets: Myth or Reality? *The Journal of Politics* 62 (2) 350-368.

Bakke, Kristin M. and Erik Wibbels (2006). Diversity, Disparity, and Civil Conflict in Federal States. *World Politics* 59 (1) 1-50.

Berry, William D., Richard C. Fording, and Russell L. Hanson (2003). Reassessing the 'Race to the Bottom' in State Welfare Policy. *The Journal of Politics* 65 (2) 327-349.

Bowman, Ann O'M and Richard C. Keamey (1998). Deminsions of State Government Capacity. *The Western Political Quarterly* 41 (2) 341-362.

Census Document: US Census Bureau. "2000 Demographic Profiles." Washington DC: Bureau of the Census, 2010. http://www.census.gov/census2000/demoprofiles.html (accessed August 22, 2011).

Cremer, Jacques and Thomas R. Palfrey (1999). Political Confederation. *The American Political Science Review* 93 (1) 69-83.

Dikshit, Ramesh D (1971). Geography and Federalism. *Annals of the Association of American Geographers* 61 (1) 97-115.

Dowding, Keith and Thanos Mergoupis (2003). Fragmentation, Fiscal Mobility, and Efficiency. *The Journal of Politics* 65 (4) 1190-1207.

Erk, Jan (2003). Federal Germany and Its Non-Federal Society: Emergence of an All-German Educational Policy in a System of Exclusive Provincial Jurisdiction. *Canadian Journal of Political Science* 36 (2) 295-317.

Feigenbaum, Harvey B., and Jeffery R. Henig (1994). The Political Underpinnings of Privatization: A Typology. *World Politics* 46 (2) 185-208.

Fifer, J. Valerie (1976). Unity by Inclusion: Core Area and Federal State at American Independence. *The Geographical Journal* 142 (3) 462-470.

Garman, Christopher, Stephan Haggard, and Elza Willis (2001). Fiscal Decentralization: A Political Theory with Latin American Cases. *World Politics* 53 (2) 205-236.

Gerber, Brian J. and Paul Teske (2000). Regulatory Policymaking in the American States: A Review of Theories and Evidence. *Political Research Quarterly* 53 (4) 849-886.

Gibbins, Roger (2000). Federalism in a Digital World. *Canadian Journal of Political Science* 33 (4) 667-689.

Hamilton, Alexander, James Madison, and John Jay. "The Federalists Papers," forward by Kathleen M. Sullivan. American Bar Association Publishing: Chicago, Illinois.

Hochman, Oded, David Pines, and Jacques-Francois Thisse (1995). On the Optimal Structure of Local Governments. *The American Economic Review* 85 (5) 1224-1240.

Jenson, Jane (1990). Representation in Crisis: The Roots of Canada's Preamble Fordism. *Canadian Journal of Political Science* 23 (4) 653-683.

Johnson, Charles A (1976). Political Culture in American States: Elazar's Formulation Examined. *American Journal of Political Science* 20 (3) 491-509.

Kelleher Christine A. and Jennifer Wolak (2007). Explaining Public Confidence in the Branches of State Government. *Political Research Quarterly* 60 (4) 707-721.

Kraynak, Robert P (1987). Tocqueville's Constitutionalism. *The American Political Science Review* 81 (4) 1175-1195.

LaSelva, Samuel V (1993). Federalism as a Way of Life" Reflections on the Canadian Experiment. *Canadian Journal of Political Science* 26 (2) 219-234.

Levy, Jacob T (2007). Federalism, Liberalism, and the Separation of Loyalties. *The American Political Science Review* 110 (3) 459-477.

Li, Quan and Dale L. Smith (2003). The Dilemma of Financial Liberalization: State Autonomy and Social Demands. *The Journal of Politics* 64 (3) 764-790.

Lowry, Robert C., James E. Alt, and Karen E. Ferree (1998). Fiscal Policy Outcomes and Electoral Accountability in American States. *The American Political Science Review* 92 (4) 759-774.

Lustick, Ian (1980). Explaining the Variable Utility of Disjointed Incrementalism: Four Propositions. *The American Political Science Review* 74 (4) 342-353.

Mendelsohn, Matthew (2000). Public Brokerage: Constitutional Reform and the Accommodation of Mass Publics. *Canadian Journal of Political Science* 33 (2) 254-272.

Meier, Kenneth J (1980). Executive Reorganization of Government: Impact on Employment and Expenditures. *American Journal of Political Science* 24 (3) 396-412.

Miller, Gary J. and Terry M. Moe (1983). Bureaucrats, Legislators, and the Size of Government. *The American Political Science Review* 77 (2) 297-322.

Magnusson, Warren (2005). Protecting the Right of Local Self-Government. *Canadian Journal of Political Science* 38 (4) 897-922.

Neiman, Max (1989). Government Directed Change of Everyday Life and Coproduction: The Case of Home Energy Use. *The Western Political Quarterly* 42 (3) 365-389.

Percival, Garrick L., Martin Johnson, and Max Neiman (2009). Representation and Local Policy: Relating County-Level Public Opinion to Policy Outputs. *Political Research Quarterly* 62 (1) 164-177.

Peterson, Paul E. and Mark Rom (1989). American Federalism, Welfare Policy, and Residential Choices. *The American Political Science Review* 83 (3) 711-728.

Prince, Michael J (2001). Canadian Federalism and Disability Policy Making. *Canadian Journal of Political Science* 34 (4) 791-817.

Rahn, Wendy M. and Thomas J. Rudolph (2005). A Tale of Political Trust in American Cities. *The Public Opinion Quarterly* 69 (4) 530-560.

Remmer, Karen L (2004). Does Foreign Aid Promote the Expansion of Government. *American Journal of Political Science* 48 (1) 77-92.

Rodden, Jonathan (2002). The Dilemma of Fiscal Federalism" Grants and Fiscal Performance around the World. *American Journal of Political Science* 46 (3) 670-687.

Rodden, Jonathan and Erik Wibbels (2002). Beyond the Fiction of Federalism: Macroeconomic Management in Multitiered Systems. *World Politics* 54 (4) 494-531.

Rodden, Jonathan (2004). Comparative Federalism and Decentralization: On Meaning and Measurement. *Comparative Politics* 36 (4) 481-500.

Rymes, T. K (1997). Money, Efficiency, and Knowledge. *The Canadian Journal of Economics* 12 (4) 575-589.

Schwager, Robert (1997). Redistribution and Administrative Federalism. *The Canadian Journal of Economics* 30 (4b) 1161-1183.

Shroder, Mark (1995). Games the States Don't Play: Welfare Benefits and the Theory of Fiscal Federalism. *The Review of Economics and Statistics* 77 (1) 183-191.

Slantchev, Branislav L (2005). The Political Economy of Simultaneous Transitions: An Empirical Test of Two Models. *Political Research Quarterly* 58 (2) 279-294.

Smith, David E (1991). Empire, Crown, and Canadian Federalism. *Canadian Journal of Political Science* 24 (3) 451-473.

Soss, Joe and Lael R. Keiser (2006). The Political Roots of Disability Claims: How State Environments and Policies Shape Citizen Demands. *Political Research Quarterly* 59 (1) 133-148.

Soss, Joe, Richard C. Fording, and Sanford F. Schram (2008). The Color of Devolution: Race, Federalism, and the Politics of Social Control. *American Journal of Political Science* 52 (3) 536-553.

Stasavage, David (2003). Transparency, Democratic Accountability, and the Economic Consequences of Monetary Institutions. *American Journal of Political Science* 47 (3) 389-402.

Strumpf, Koleman S. and Felix Oberholzer-Gee (2002). Endogenous Policy Decentralization: Testing the Central Tenet of Economic Federalism. *The Journal of Political Economy* 110 (1) 1-36.

Tavits, Margit (2006). Making Democracy Work More? Exploring the Linkage between Social Capital and Government Performance. *Political Research Quarterly* 59 (2) 211-225.

Treisman, Daniel (1999). Political Decentralization and Economic Reform: A Game-Theoretic Analysis. *American Journal of Political Science* 43 (2) 488-517.

Trounstine, Jessica (2006). Dominant Regimes and the Demise of Urban Democracy. *The Journal of Politics* 68 (4) 879-893.

Volden, Craig (2005). Intergovernmental Political Competition in American Federalism. *American Journal of Political Science* 49 (2) 327-342.

Whitford, Andrew B. and Karen Wong (2009). Political and Social Foundations for Sustainability. *Political Research Quarterly* 62 (1) 190-204.

Wood, B. Dan (1991). Federalism and Policy Responsiveness: The Clean Air Case. *The Journal of Politics* 53 (3) 851-859.

Chapter Eleven

Perspectives on Corruption: "He who pays the piper"

Heather Wyatt-Nichol and Ed Gibson

Key words: corruption, African countries, decentralization, anti-corruption initiatives

Introduction

Corruption is historical and global, existing in every society regardless of time and place. However, the extent and impact of corruption range from various acts of transgression in some societies to being deeply imbedded in the institutions of others. The consequences of corruption also vary from a mere loss of money for a few individuals to the loss of lives for entire groups of people. This chapter examines perceptions of corruption across various countries in Africa, taking into account the hegemonic discourse of Western nations, and offers contrasting instances of corrupt acts in U.S. municipalities.[1]

Among African countries, there are numerous examples of corruption that contribute to social injustice across the continent. For example, the Democratic Republic of Congo is a major oil producer in sub-Saharan Africa yet 70 percent of the population lives in poverty. In addition, one third of the oil revenue is unaccounted for (McFerson, 2009). Similarly, Angola annually produces over $1 billion (American dollar – USD) of oil – of which 25 percent is unaccounted for. The majority of the population lives on less than one dollar per day (McFerson, 2009). In the Nigerian Delta, oil and gas account for 85 percent of government revenues, but two-thirds of the population lives in poverty (McFerson, 2009).

An institutional perspective has been used as the framework for anti-corruption reforms in Africa. Studies have found that corruption is less likely to occur in affluent countries and more likely to occur in countries under authoritarian regimes with valuable natural resources (Chang & Godden, 2009; Treisman, 2000). There is also a common perception in the literature that corruption is less likely to occur in democracies due to factors such as freedom of the press, a well-informed public, equality, and openness (Triesman, 2000). When power is centralized, there is both motive and opportunity for corruption. Ayittey (2005) asserts, "The centralization of both economic and political power turns the state into a pot of gold that all sorts of groups compete to capture. Once captured, power is then used to amass huge personal fortunes, to enrich one's cronies and tribesmen, to crush one's rivals, and to perpetuate one's rule in office" (48). Research has demonstrated a relationship between corruption and centralized structures that afford discretion only among top leaders (Antwi-Boasiako & Bonna, 2009; Joaquin, 2004; Meagher, 2001). Considered a necessary element of democracy, decentralization is correlated with economic growth and deemed an indirect means to minimize corruption when transparency and participation are included in reform efforts (Antwi-Boasiako & Bonna, 2009; Joaquin, 2004). Yet decentralization, if it is to have effect, must provide for true independence of action and perspective, lest the corrupting influences of concentrated economic and political power find and exploit the ethical vulnerabilities of decentralized units of government.

Decentralization as Agent of Checking Corruption

The theme of decentralized authority runs strongly through the study of African democracies (Antwi-Boasiako, 2010). Although it is an infeasible and misguided enterprise to attempt to describe of the whole of an immense continent using a single governing framework, the tension in many of the countries between centralization and decentralization represents a potent issue. Moreover, African democracies offer important institutional factors, such as tribal structures and traditions (Antwi-Boasiako & Bonna, 2009), that bear on questions of governmental structure and capacity for official venues and procedures to operate without undue influence from traditional leadership sources.

The question of decentralization and corruption has been of keen interest to scholars, who have come down on both sides of the role of governmental structure in ameliorating corruption. Cross-national studies (Arikan, 2004; Fisman and Gatti, 2002) indicated that decentralizing governmental units could result in diminished corruption. Treisman (2007) argued that cross-national studies failed to take into account Protestant religious tradition and longstanding democratic governance. However, counterexamples in Box 1 drawn from U.S. localities provide qualitative evidence that Protestantism and long experience with democracy are hardly a panacea for the corrupting influence of concentrated unofficial power.

The notion that localized authority is more responsive to the voice of the citizenry has occupied broader comparative inquiries (Mikesell, 2007). The difficulty of concentrated power distancing public officials from concerns that legitimately should compel their attention has a number of roots. One cause of this distance is the absorption in bureaucratic issues that increases as administrative authority coalesces. Another rationale for separation of public officials from citizens' concerns is self-dealing, cronyism, or oligarchy that may follow non-transparent operation of government, obscured from popular observation.

Yet one aim for this chapter is the isolation of the structural factors that concentrate or distribute authority from the other influences—cultural, environmental, and institutional—on the level of de facto governmental decentralization. In the examples drawn from cases of U.S. corruption in local governments (see Box 1), apparent checks and balances due to structure appear to have been frustrated by concentration of unofficial, but very real, power in political parties, commercial interests, and personal networks.

Notwithstanding the apparent choice of decentralization, the premise drawn from a recent study of Ghana (Antwi-Boasiako, 2010) is that official barriers—such as the central appointment of a significant proportion of local positions—preclude even the possibility of developing structures accessible to local citizenry. The balance of this chapter focuses on the situation African democracies face in institutionalizing borrowed norms that may or may not successfully integrate with the structural residuum of the colonial era and the preexisting traditional institutions that contend with these official structures.

The Proliferation of Anti-corruption Initiatives in Africa

The institutional perspective of corruption has resulted in the proliferation of anti-corruption measures and reform initiatives. In 1991, the World Bank supported twice as many reform efforts than in the decade prior (Therkildsen, 2001). A few years later, "… the World Bank (1994:99) argued that the public sector lies at the core of the stagnation and decline in growth in Africa" (Therkildsen, 2001::5). By 1997, the Public Management Service (PUMA) division of the Organization for Economic Cooperation and Development (OECD) posited that an ethics infrastructure is necessary for public service integrity. Elements of the ethics structure include political commitment, legal framework, accountability mechanisms, codes of conduct, mechanisms for professional socialization, 'supportive public service conditions' (e.g., adequate pay, fair treatment), an ethics coordinating body, and 'an active civic society' (5).

Several measures have been developed to assess and compare corruption among countries. For example, Transparency International's (TI) Corruption Perception Index (CPI) is widely used among scholars and practitioners in the public and private sector. The CPI compiles data for 183 countries. CPI scores range from zero representing most corrupt to ten representing least corrupt. Corruption is considered serious challenge when scores are between three and five, and rampant when scores are below zero. Botswana is the only African country to receive a score above five. Table 1 provides data on the 2011 CPI ratings for countries in Africa.

According to the *East African bribery index* published by Transparency International (2011), Burundi, Uganda, Tanzania, and Kenya exhibit the highest prevalence of bribery.[2] Among the respondents who reported that bribes were requested in their interactions with institutions, Uganda residents reported 39percent, followed by Tanzania (32 percent), and Kenya (29 percent). Fifty-six percent of respondents from Tanzania who experienced bribery did not report it due to lack of confidence in the anti-corruption system, followed by Kenya (40 percent), and Uganda (36 percent). The most corrupt organizations included the Kenya Police and the Department of the Ministry, the Uganda Police and the Uganda Revenue Authority, and the Tanzania Police and judicial system.

The World Bank has developed *Worldwide Governance Indicators* (WGI) that includes voice and accountability, political stability, government effectiveness, regulatory quality, rule of law, and control of corruption. One report on WGI by Kaufman, Kraay, and Mastruzzi (2009) reported improvements in governance between 1998 and 2008:

- Ghana and Niger had demonstrated improvements in voice and accountability;

- Political stability had increased in Algeria, Angola and Sierra Leone;
- Government effectiveness and rule of law had improved in Rwanda;
- Control of corruption and rule of law had improved in Liberia;
- Improvements in regulatory quality were reported for the Democratic Republic of Congo and Libya.

In contrast, degeneration among governance dimensions was reported for Zimbabwe, the Cote d'Ivoire (Ivory Coast) and Eritrea.

The *Global Integrity Report* (2010) scores countries on a scale of 0 to 100 on internet censorship, access to government information, and professionalism of the civil service. In 2010, the following African countries received a 100 (no internet censorship): Nigeria, Somalis, South Africa, and Tanzania. Cameroon received a score of 63 and Ethiopia received a score of 25. The percentage of citizens with access to the internet was not included in the results. Regarding access to government information, five African countries were ranked as bottom performers—Somalia (17), Cameroon (8), Tanzania (6), Nigeria (2), and Egypt (0). Regarding professionalism of civil service, two out of four of the bottom performers were the African countries of Somalia (33) and Angola (30).

The International Monetary Fund (IMF) has developed the *Open Budget Index* (OBI) to assess budget transparency and accountability. Scores range from zero to 100 with 100 being the highest ranking. In 2010, South Africa received a score of 92 compared to the United States (82). The following African countries were placed in the third category as providing "some information": Uganda (55), followed by Ghana (54), Namibia (53), Botswana (51), Kenya (49), Egypt (49), Malawi (47), and Tanzania (45). Several African countries were also included in the "minimal category": Liberia (40), Zambia (36), Mali (35), Mozambique (28), and Angola (26). Half of the 22 countries that were categorized as providing "scant or no information" were in Africa: Nigeria (18), Rwanda (11), Sudan (8), Democratic Republic of Congo (6), Burkina Faso (5), Niger (3), Senegal (3), Cameroon (2), Algeria (1), Chad (0), Equatorial Guinea (0), and Sao Tome and Principe (0).

Assessing Anti-Corruption Initiatives

Most African countries have established anti-corruption laws and regulations as well as codes of conduct. For example, Zambia enacted the Corrupt Practices Act in 1980, the Parliament and Ministerial Code of Conduct Act in 1994, and the Anti-corruption Commission Act in 1996 ("Summary Report", 2007). Various countries have also been signatories to anti-corruption treaties such as the United Nations Convention against Corruption (UNCAC) and the African Union Convention on Preventing and Combating Corruption (AUCPACC) ("Summary Report", 2007). To the degree that anti-corruption reforms are linked to governance reforms, readers should be aware that in 1989 the majority of countries in Africa were either one-party states or military dictatorships (Meredith, 2005)—table 1 delineates current forms of government.

Despite reform efforts, some countries demonstrate little to no change in the perception and prevalence of corruption. For example, similar to the 2011 CPI results reported in table 1 of this chapter, Zimbabwe was a 2.1 and DRC was 1.9 in 2007 ("Summary report", 2007). Another example is found in Uganda—although the country has enacted several anti-corruption initiatives (e.g. Prevention of Corruption Act 1970; Office of Inspector General established in 1987; Code of conduct for civil servants), there is a major gap between what is on paper, and what is enforced (Global Integrity, 2009). According to Yeh (2011), "Ugandan IGG is appointed by and serves at the pleasure of the president; this substantially weakens its authority to investigate and prosecute corruption that may involve the president and loyal elites" (634). Similarly, Tanzania enacted the 1971 Prevention and Corruption Act; established an Office of Controller and Auditor General; a Permanent Commission of Inquiry; and a Prevention of Corruption Bureau, problems persist because most of the positions within these organizations are at—will, appointed by the president (Yeh, 2011).

Explanations for Ineffective Anti-Corruption Initiatives

Reform efforts have been ineffective for several reasons, including:
- a lack of political will to implement reform (Kalantari, 2010);
- multi-party systems provide more opportunity for corruption;
- lack of accountability in public procurement systems due to an absence of strong monitoring and enforcement mechanisms ("Summary report", 2007).

For example, Antwi-Boasiako and Bonna (2009) explain, "In Ghana, politicians who advocate for decentralization are sometimes skeptical in giving or sharing power with their subordinates as the concept is not well understood" (27). Similarly, Therkildsen (2001) indicates that considerable decentralization has taken place in Uganda, however, "practically all ministries put up silent or quasi-active resistance to letting go of many of the decentralized functions" (37). In addition, Transparency International found that corrupt judicial systems in the Democratic Republic of Congo and Zimbabwe often block anti-corruption reforms ("Summary report", 2007). Positing that stronger institutional reforms are in order, some scholars (DeSpeville, 2010; Yeh, 2011) have considered the "Hong-Kong Model" since it incorporates a three-pronged approach of prevention, education, and enforcement. Enforcement in this model is unique because it establishes an independent body, separate from domestic leadership, to investigate and enforce policy.

11.1: 2011 Corruption Perception Index Scores for Countries in Africa

Country, Year of Independence	Form of Government	Country Rank	CPI Score
Algeria, 1962	Multi-party republic, 2 legislative houses	112	2.9
Angola. 1975	Unitary multi-party republic, 1 legislative house	168	2.0
Benin, 1960	Multi-party republic, 1 legislative house	100	3.0
Botswana, 1966	Multi-party republic, 1 legislative house	32	6.1
Burkina Faso,1960	Multi-party republic, 1 legislative house	100	3.0
Burundi,1962	Republic, 2 legislative houses	172	1.9
Cameroon, 1960	Unitary multi-party republic, 1 legislative house	134	2.5
Cape Verde, 1975	Multi-party republic, 1 legislative house	41	5.5
Central African Republic,1960	Multi-party republic, 1 legislative house	154	2.2
Chad, 1960	Unitary republic, 1 legislative house	168	2.0
Comoros, 1975	Republic, 1 legislative house	—	—
Republic of Congo (Middle Congo), 1960	Republic, 2 legislative houses	154	2.2
Democratic Republic of Congo(Belgian Cong, Zaire), 1960	Unitary multi-party republic, 2 legislative houses	168	2.0
Djibouti, 1977	Multi-party republic, 1 legislative house	100	3.0
Egypt	Republic, 2 legislative houses	112	2.9
Equatorial Guinea, 1968	Republic, 1 legislative house	172	1.9
Eritrea,1993	Transitional regime, 1 interim legislative house	134	2.5
Ethiopia	Federal republic, 2 legislative houses	120	2.7
Gabon, 1960	Unitary multi-party republic, 2 legislative houses	—	—
The Gambia,1965	Multi-party republic, 1 legislative house	77	3.5
Ghana, 1957	Multi-party republic, 1 legislative house	69	3.9

Guinea, 1958	Republic, 1 advisory body		
Guinea-Bissau, 1974	Republic, 1 legislative house	154	2.2
Ivory Coast (Cote d'Ivoire), 1960	Republic, 1 legislative house	154	2.2
Kenya,1963	Unitary multi-party, 1 legislative house	154	2.2
Lesotho,1966	Constitutional monarchy, 2 legislative houses	77	3.5
Liberia	Multi-party republic, 2 legislative houses	91	3.2
Libya, 1951	Authoritarian state, one policy making house *	168	2.0
Madagascar,1960	Transitional regime, 2 legislative houses	100	3.0
Malawi, 1964	Multi-party republic, 1 legislative house	100	3.0
Mali (French Sudan), 1960	Multi-party republic, 1 legislative house	118	2.8
Mauritania, 1960	Republic, 2 legislative houses	143	2.4
Mauritius,1968	Republic, 1 legislative house	46	5.1
Morocco, 1975	Constitutional monarchy, 2 legislative houses	80	3.4
Mozambique, 1975	Multi-party republic, 1 legislative house	120	2.7
Namibia, 1990	Repbulic, 2 legislative houses	57	4.4
Niger, 1960	Republic, 1 legislative house	134	2.5
Nigeria,1960	Federal republic, 2 legislative houses	143	2.4
Rwanda, 1962	Multi-party republic, 2 legislative houses	49	5.0
Sao Tome and Principe,1975	Multi-party republic, 1 legislative house	100	3.0
Senegal, 1960	Multi-party republic, 2 legislative houses	112	2.9
Seychelles	Multi-party republic, 1 legislative house	—	—
Sierra Leone, 1961	Republic, 1 legislative house	134	2.5
Somalia	Transitional regime	182	1.0
South Africa, 1961	Multi-party republic, 2 legislative houses	64	4.1
Sudan, 1956	Military backed interim regime, 2 legislative houses	177	1.6
South Sudan, 2011	Republic, 2 legislative houses		

Swaziland, 1968	Monarchy, 2 legislative houses	95	3.1
Tanzania,1961	Unitary multi-party republic, 1 legislative house	100	3.0
Togo, 1960	Multi-party republic, 1 legislative house	143	2.4
Tunisia, 1956	Multi-party republic, 2 legislative houses	73	3.8
Uganda, 1962	Multi-party republic, 1 legislative house	143	2.4
Zambia (Northern Rhodesia), 1964	Multi-party republic, 1 legislative house	91	3.2
Zimbabwe, 1965	Transitional regime, 2 legislative houses	154	2.2
Sources: Data compiled from Transparency International, CPI and the Time Almanac, 2012. http://www.ethicsworld.org/publicsectorgovernance/ticpi. php#2011cpi			

Therkildsen (2001) contends that by taking a top-down approach, many reform initiatives ignore the importance of street-level bureaucracy—the relevance of villages, community groups, and citizens through their interactions with public servants has been omitted. In contrast, Pope (2007), once an advocate for strong institutions, contends the emphasis on standards needs to shift to an emphasis on people and ethical values in order for anti-corruption reforms to be effective:

> However, the more TI worked on trying to strengthen those institutions and to implement the international standards that we had helped create—frequently in alien settings and where others (including Western corporate interests) were seeking to undermine them—the greater the consciousness that, at the end of the day, it really does not matter how strong one's institutions are if the wrong people are inside them (76).

Examination of the U.S. examples of municipal corruption in Box 1 reinforces Pope's emphasis on personal values and his wariness about the influence of corporate interests. The example of Palm Beach County, Florida illustrates the capacity for concentrated economic interests to undermine nominal checks and balances provided by divided political power and structural distribution of authority. Cuyahoga County, Ohio responded to apparent abuses of political power in a modern-day "machine" by adopting a county executive form of government. Yet, the conviction of the previous county executive of Prince George's County in a "pay to play" scheme calls into question the reliance on governmental structure alone to ward off corruption. A second Maryland example, in Baltimore, reiterates the potential for concentrated political power—in this case from the Democratic Party—coupled with entrenched commercial interests to put susceptible individuals in power and exploit their ethical lapses. Thus, this examination of corruption in U.S. municipal governments ends where it began, with the pervasive power of commercial interest able to introduce its influence wherever unethical officials can be located and their avowed service in the public interest corrupted.

In addition, several scholars (Antwi-Boasiako & Bonna, 2009; Haruna, 2008; Kalantari, 2010) have noted the importance of socio-cultural, historical, and political factors in developing strategies to curb corruption and have highlighted the importance of situational perspectives to understand the root causes of corruption, particularly the fact that the history of colonialism shapes public administration in Africa:

> From some individuals' perspective, African countries may see themselves as independent sovereign nations; but the shackles of colonialism and evils of slavery continue to haunt them as the colonizers and slave masters have developed new political policies to financially control these nations. Some have argued that when sub-Saharan Africans fought for independence in the 1960s and 1970s, they kept their masters' political structures with very little understanding of how these structures function (Antwi-Boasiako & Bonna, 2009:14).

Power was distributed between colonial appointees and a small number of local chiefs as a means to reinforce the objectives of colonial governments (Antwi-Boasiako & Bonna, 2009; Yeh, 2011). Some scholars (Theobold, 2008; Yeh, 2011) contend that such practices institutionalized patrimonial structures where politics and power are embedded in the policy process, leading to weak administrative structures that reflect patronage and abuse of public power for personal gain. As a result, many African leaders have been resistant to reform—"By the end of the 1980s, not a single African head of state in three decades had allowed himself to be voted out of office. Of some 150 heads of state…only six had voluntarily relinquished power" (Meredith, 2005:379).

Several African countries are also described as a "paradox of plenty" (McFerson, 2009), characterized by extreme poverty surrounded by a wealth of natural resources such as gemstones, minerals, oil, and gas. Although the number of African countries categorized by Freedom House as "not free" decreased from 25 in 1977 to 14 in 2007, "…all but one of the resource-rich countries is found in the "not free" category" (McFerson, 2009:1530). Beneath the surface, we are forced to confront the undesirable question of whether reform initiatives are authentically concerned with citizens or with capital. With the exception of economic regulation in terms of property registration, contract enforcement, and credit access, Angola and Equatorial Guinea consistently receive low rankings (McFerson, 2009). The World Bank advocates the view that economic development is important to reduce corruption and frequently collaborates with IMF, the European Investment Bank, and the United Nations (Michael, 2004). Sometimes monetary assistance counters the efforts reform by providing resources to sustain authoritarian regimes (Yeh, 2011). At other times, donor sponsored initiatives may distort accountability by leaving agencies accountable to their domestic constituents rather than to the intended recipients (Therkildsen, 2001). Although many of us may agree with proverb, "He who pays the piper calls the tune", we also need to question the extent to which donor sponsored initiatives have contributed to the hegemonic discourse of western ideas over traditional values throughout Africa.

Box 1

Corruption in U.S. Municipal Governments under a Variety of Structural Alternatives

Implementing a decentralized structure is viewed as a check on the capacity of a corrupt core to act with impunity (Bagchi, 2007). Yet the cases of U.S. local-level corruption described below reveal a basis for concentrated power that transcends structural factors. The subject cases of local government corruption occurred in the city of Baltimore, Maryland and the counties of Palm Beach, Florida, Cuyahoga, Ohio, and Prince George's, Maryland. The following sketches of these cases, some still being in adjudication, show how unethical individuals can coordinate corrupt efforts through the organizing aegis of concentrated political power or the concerted efforts of powerful commercial influences. It also helps to emphasize that unethical behavior and official corruption are enduring aspects of first-world governance rather than being the sole province of the developing world.

This examination of U.S. local government corruption begins in Palm Beach County, Florida, notorious as the "new capital of Florida corruption" after losing its third county commissioner in the span of two years, attributable to "a culture of graft that has plagued Palm Beach over the years" (Florin, 2009). The pay-to-play development environment later ensnared "mid-level bureaucrats" in a "six-year-long scheme that generated 77 criminal charges against 13 individuals..., which alleges everything from racketeering to money laundering to unlawful compensation" (Beall & Roldan, 2011). Despite the division of political power between political parties and rotation of personal power through term limits, the pro-development stance of the Palm Beach County Commission appears to reflect continued influence by powerful economic interests (Engelhardt, 2010).

Cuyahoga County, Ohio, contains Cleveland, a Democratic Party stronghold. Like Palm Beach County, an elected Board of County Commissioners governed the county. A successful ballot initiative, prompted by a massive corruption scandal, changed Cuyahoga County's system of government by instituting the elected county executive and council system in 2011. At the center of the scandal was County Commissioner Jimmy Dimora, described as "the most powerful man in Cuyahoga County politics" because of his position heading the county's Democratic Party organization (Brown, 2010). Along with Dimora, indictments targeted judges, the County auditor and a number of business owners and labor union officials.

Unlike the cases in Ohio and Florida, which are well known as "swing" states in American politics, where single-party domination is usually localized and/or transitory, Maryland is one of a handful of "true blue" (Democratic Party dominated) states in the Eastern U.S. The two cases of corruption occurred in Democratic Party strongholds, even by Maryland standards, both with "better than 8 to 1 Democratic to Republican margins" (Smith & Willis, 2011:54). Prince George's County, Maryland, houses many commuters to Washington, D.C. Its form of government, elected county executive and county council, mirrors the structure that Cuyahoga County adopted in reaction to endemic corruption. County Executive Jack Johnson had been the State attorney for Prince George's County prior to his election in 2002. He was completing his last term (prevented from running in 2010 by term limits) when charged and eventually convicted, in 2011, on bribery and extortion charges stemming from a public housing development (Castaneda & Spivack, 2011).

The mayor of Baltimore, Maryland "heads an extremely strong an extremely strong and centralized mayoral system" (Smith & Willis, 2011:291). As chair of the City Council, Sheila Dixon automatically became mayor in 2006 when her predecessor, Martin O'Malley resigned the office after being elected governor and was elected in her own right in 2008 (Smith & Willis, 2011:293). Yet the embezzlement conviction for which forced Dixon to resign her office covered misdeeds when she chaired the City Council (Urbina, 2010). Her solicitation and misappropriation of gift cards from Baltimore developers reflected, "a cozy relationship between developers and politicians in this town" (Rohrbauch in Urbina, 2009:A16). Despite her distance from the structural power of then-Mayor O'Malley's administration, apparently endemic corruption found its way to a less powerful, though still influential position.

ENDNOTES

1. While it is unwise to place all African countries "under one umbrella" due to historical, cultural, geographical, governmental, and ethnic differences, our intent is to provide examples in a broader context.
2. TI defines bribery prevalence as "likelihood that an individual will be required to pay a bribe to access services at the national level" ("East Africa", 2011, p. 1).

References

Antwi-Boasiako, K. (2010) "Administrative decentralization: Should districts and regions elect their own Leaders in Ghana?" African Social Science Review 4(1), article 3. Retrieved February 14, 2013, from http://digitalcommons.kennesaw.edu/assr/vol4/iss1/3.

Antwi-Boasiako, K., & Bonna, O. (2009). *Traditional institutions and public administration and democratic Africa*. Xlibris.

Arikan, G. G. (2004). "Decentralization: A recipe for corruption?" *International Tax and Public Finance* 11 175-195.

Ayittey, G.B.N.(2005). *Africa unchained: The blueprint for Africa's future*. New York: Palgrave Macmillan.

Bagchi, (2007). Combating corruption in state and local revenue administration. In Anwar Shah (ed.), *Local Budgeting* (pp. 105-128), Washington: The World Bank.

Beall, P. & Roldan, C. (2011, March 18). 13 Arrested in massive Palm Beach County public corruption case. *Palm Beach Post*. Retrieved from http://www.palmbeachpost.com/news/13arrested-in-massive-palm-beach-county-public-1330041.html

Brown, T. (2010, September 15). Jimmy Dimora at center of one of biggest local corruption cases in U.S. history. Cleveland Plain Dealer. Retrieved from http://www.cleveland.com/countyincrisis/index.ssf/2010/09/county_commissioner_jimmy_dimo_1.html

Castaneda, R. & Spivack, M.S. (2011, May 17). Jack Johnson pleads guilty. *Washington Post*. Retrieved from http://www.washingtonpost.com/blogs/crime-scene/post/jack-johnson-pleads guilty/2011/05/17/AFIofq5G_blog.html.

Chang, E.C. & Godden, M.A. (2009). Sources of corruption in authoritarian regimes. *Social Science Research Network Paper Series*.

De Speville, B. (2010). Anticorruption commissions: The 'Hong Kong Model' revisited. *Asia Pacific Review* 17(1) 47-71.

East African bribery index (2011). Transparency International. Compressed download available at http://www.tikenya.org/index.php?option=com_docman&task=doc_download&gid=85&Itemid=146

Engelhardt, J. (2010, July 28). Palm Beach County: Where R's are D's and D's are R's. *Palm Beach Post*. Retrieved from http://www.palmbeachpost.com/opinion/columnists/engelhardt- palm-beach-county-where-rs-and-ds-828664.html

Fisman, R. & Gatti, R. (2002). "Decentralization and corruption: Evidence across countries." *Journal of Public Economics* 83(3) 325-345.

Florin, H. (2009, January 10). Palm Beach: The new capital of Florida corruption. *Time*. Retrieved from http://www.time.com/time/nation/article/0,8599,1870853,00.html

Global Integrity Report (2010). Retrieved October 15, 2011, from http://www.globalintegrity.org/report/findings#best

Global Integrity Report, Grand Corruption Watchlist (2009). Retrieved October 15, 2011, from http://report.globalintegrity.org/globalindex/2009_Key_Findings.pdf

Haruna, P.S. (2008). Recovering integrity in Ghana's governance: A transcultural study in public service ethics. *Public Integrity* 10(2) 113-132

Joaquin, E.T. (2004). Decentralization and corruption: The bumpy road to public sector integrity in developing countries. *Public Integrity* 6(3) 207-219.

Kalantari, B. (2010). Corruption in the public and private organizations: Causes, consequences, and remedies. *International Journal of Ethics* 6(4) 301-313.

Kaufman, D., Kraay, A., Mastruzzi, M. (2009).*Governance matters VIII: Aggregate and individual governance indicators,* 1998-2008, World Bank Policy Research Working Paper No. 4978.

McFerson, H.M. (2009). Governance and hyper-corruption in resource rich African countries. *Third World Quarterly* 30(8) 1529-1548.

Meagher, P. (2001). Devolution, quality of governance and corruption. Center for Institutional Reform and the Informal Sector, University of Maryland. Retrieved January 15, 2011 from http://www.iris.umd.edu/Reader.aspx?TYPE=FORMAL_PUBLICATION&ID=760f4bad-62f0-4659-b631-b6a849552a6d

Meredith, M. (2005). *The fate of Africa: A history of fifty years of independence.* New York: Public Affairs, Perseus Books Group

Michael, B. (2004). What do African donor-sponsored anti-corruption programs teach us about international development in Africa? *Social Policy & Administration*, 38(4), 320-345.

Mikesell, J. L. (2007). "Fiscal administration in local government: An overview." In Anwar Shah (ed.), *Local Budgeting* (pp. 15-52), Washington: The World Bank.

Open Budget Index (2010). Retrieved January 2, 2012 from http://internationalbudget.org/what-we-do/open-budget-survey/rankings-key-findings/rankings/

Pope, J.D. (2007). The third phase in the fight against corruption: Implementation and comparative administrative ethics. *Public Integrity* 10(1) 75-83.

Public Management Service Policy Brief (1997, February). Managing government ethics.

Organization for Economic Development and Cooperation (OECD). Retrieved October 10, 2011 from http://www.oecd.org/dataoecd/59/60/1899269.pdf

Smith, C. & Willis, J.T. (2011). *Maryland politics and government: Democratic dominance.* Lincoln:University of Nebraska Press.

Summary report of national integrity system studies of DRC, Mauritius, South Africa, Mozambique, Botswana, Zambia, and Zimbabwe. (2007, November). Transparency International Retrieved October 10, 2011, from http://www.transparency.org/content/download/28102/423254/file/Southern_Africa_NIS_overview_2007.pdf

Theobald, R. (2008). Polishing up the steel frame: Will more bureaucracy help contain the problem of petty corruption in Sub Saharan Africa? *Commonwealth & Comparative Politics* 46(2) 157-176.

Therkildsen, O. (2001). *Efficiency, accountability and implementation: Public sector reform in East and Southern Africa.* Democracy, Governance and Human Rights Programme Paper Number 3, United Nations Research Institute for Social Development.

Time Almanac (2012). London: Encyclopedia Britannica, Inc.

Treisman, D. (2000). The causes of corruption: A cross national study. *Journal of Public Economics* 76(3) 399-457.

Treisman, D. (2007). *The architecture of government: Rethinking political decentralization.* New York, Cambridge: Cambridge University Press.

Urbina, I. (2009, November 9). Trial begins for Baltimore mayor." *New York Times* A16.

Urbina, I.. (2010, January 6). Mayor agrees to step down in Baltimore in theft case. *New York Times* A20.

World Bank, *Worldwide Governance Indicator Project* (WGI). Retrieved January 2, 2012, from http://info.worldbank.org/governance/wgi/index.asp

Yeh, S. (2011). Ending corruption in Africa through United Nations inspections. *International Affairs* 87(3) 629-650.

Chapter Twelve

DEVOLUTION OF WATER POLICY IN THE AMERICAN SOUTH: THE CASE OF THE ACT AND ACF WATER WARS

James Newman

Key words: devolution, water policy, American South, political culture, interstate negotiations

Atlanta's regional population approaches five and a half million residents (United States Census, 2010). The Chattahoochee River and Lake Lanier, a reservoir along the Chattahoochee River north of Atlanta, are increasingly inadequate to meet water demands as the region's primary source of fresh water. Concerns over water may seem unusual given the region's annual rainfall average of about fifty inches and notoriously high levels of humidity (www.noaa.gov). However, the city is located near the origins of its source of freshwater and not the mouth of the river. Compounding the problem, water authorities in the metropolitan area of Atlanta cannot access an underground aquifer. Access to freshwater is limited to a river, therefore the region relies exclusively on surface freshwater. This strain on the river's freshwater impacts downstream individuals in different cities and states. This chapter will discuss attempts at creating a regional water policy involving a web of three states, a few federal agencies, and numerous stakeholders.

History of Regional Water Negotiations

The origin of the water wars can be traced to 1990 when interests within the state of Georgia believed building a reservoir along the Tallapoosa River would assist in meeting future water demand, and the Army Corps of Engineers recommended that some of the water in Lake Lanier be reallocated to municipalities in the Atlanta region. Interests downriver in Alabama sued to prevent development of the reservoir. This event sparked an ongoing 'water war' between interests in Alabama, Florida, and Georgia. The 'water wars' provide a unique case study in which to view water allocation policy in the Southern United States. A lack of federal and state law governing water allocation rights, and a hostile political culture relating to federal involvement in this area, create a unique environment in which to study development of water allocation policy.

Despite over twenty years of negotiations and lawsuits, the three states are not closer to a regional water policy involving water allocation in the Alabama-Coosa-Tallapoosa and Apalachicola-Chattahoochee-Flint River Basins. To understand why an agreement is elusive, a discussion of the region's political culture and historical development is beneficial in understanding motivations behind what may seem to be a simple concern over allocation of a natural resource.

While Atlanta can trace its humble beginnings to a junction of two major railroads, Atlanta's status has risen to that of an internationally recognized city with approximately 5.5 million residents in the metropolitan area (United States Census, 2010). The city has hosted The Olympic Games (1996), is home to the world's busiest airport, headquarters for several large multinational corporations, and home to the region's first franchises in major professional sports teams (the National Football League, National Basketball Association, and Major League Baseball). Its desirability as a home to these events, teams, and corporations stems not only from its large population and healthy economy, but the city's progressive image relating to racial acceptance and a motto of being "too busy to hate". As one of the earliest cities in the Deep South to show acceptance for the civil rights of African Americans, corporations and professional sports teams were eager to take up roots in this growing New South city.

A city's residential growth requires access to natural resources, in particular, fresh water. The Deep South's environment is characterized by high levels of humidity, large rivers, hot summers, and mild winters. Consequently flooding is more of a concern for southern cities than limited access to fresh water. However, most large southern cities are located near the mouth of a river, not approximately 300 miles upstream from the navigable head of a river or its mouth, as is the case with Atlanta. The Atlanta area also has the unfortunate distinction as being one of the few regions in the Deep South that does not have easy access to an underground aquifer. Yet, few observers would confuse the climate and landscape of Atlanta with that of Phoenix, Arizona. So, why is the Atlanta area in a dispute with its neighbors lasting longer than twenty years over fresh water? The answer is not a simple one. Comprehending why water stirs such controversy within the region, requires one to understand the culture of the region and how water is viewed through a uniquely southern lens. In addition to practical reasons such as sustaining human life and transporting goods and people, rivers occupy a romantic role in Southern literature. Mark Twain's classic works evoke a romantic view of young boys enjoying the independence and simplicity of travel offered by the Mississippi River. Images of riverboat gamblers and steamboats, lumbering along a wide river lined with large leafy trees laced in Spanish-moss, create a uniquely Southern mystique.

Use of rivers and their water became synonymous with economic prosperity. Consequently, southerners saw rivers as vehicles of economic development. While this is not a unique concept, it was viewed as the primary source of wealth for settlers in the pre-industrial revolution era. With few natural resources below ground, sediment laden topsoil and access to a major river were essential in gaining access to wealth. Unlike more arid regions of the United States, the thought of a river's water disappearing or shrinking beyond useful levels did not exist. Concern for water quality was non-existent. Viewing rivers simply as vehicles for economic development was commonplace for generations.

To many Southerners, environmentalism conjures images of individuals protecting rare species, or trees, sometimes at the expense of badly needed jobs. Often, persons supporting these concerns are considered to be outsiders. While conducting interviews to determine the scope of regional water issues, many of the individuals moved from other regions of the country after reaching adulthood. Several moved to the region to retire. This supports a general view that people active in regional environmental issues are outsiders of the region. The viewing of those not raised in the South as outsiders dates back to Reconstruction, when people from the North came south to take advantage of the region's natural resources, which were needed to support industry in the early days of the Industrial Revolution. Southerners are typically not open to attitudes and ways of thinking, which do not agree with the region's traditionalistic culture. Environmentalists often pride themselves in being 'activists'. In traditionalistic political cultures, activism is not a shared value. Leaving governing to societal elites while most citizens possess low levels of political participation is more in tune with political behavior in a traditionalistic culture. One individual interviewed who advised governors on environmental issues was told by a Democratic governor running for re-election, "it is your job to make sure I do not get the environmentalists' endorsement." While it may seem unusual for a politician to not want a group's endorsement, being endorsed by 'outsiders' is usually not good campaign strategy.

The lake owner groups, cognizant of the label, 'outsider' and the region's traditionalistic culture, are careful not to be lumped into the 'extreme environmentalist' group. While interview subjects from the lake groups were concerned about safe drinking water and having a healthy ecological balance, they clearly stated they supported economic development and protecting the value of lakefront property. One lake side home owner in Alabama who served as president of a 'friends of the lake' group went so far as to say, "I am not one of those tree huggers or frog kissers." (interview with author).

Adam Snyder, then-executive director of the Alabama Rivers Alliance, relayed a story of his efforts in persuading state legislators to support a bill prohibiting interbasin transfers of water. Snyder approached the legislators from the standpoint of how interbasin transfers would damage a region's ecological balance. After discussions with several legislators, Snyder realized this approach may not be the most effective way to persuade them. In explaining this bill to an Alabama state legislator, the legislator interrupted, "Do you mean to tell me they (opponents of the bill) want to undo what God has done (take water from one river basin and place it in another)?" Snyder replied, "Well, yes." The legislator promised to vote for the bill (interview with author).

Discussion of Political Culture

To gain a better understanding of political culture on the impact of governing, Daniel Elazar (1966) creates a classification of political cultures. Elazar classifies Alabama as having a traditional political culture. Traditional cultures have comparatively lower political participation than regions with other political cultures. Therefore, most citizens are less likely to show interest in following issues of public policy, which are not essential to daily life, as would citizens in nontraditional political subcultures. Unless a neighboring river or reservoir is suffering from a severe drought, most citizens are not interested in issues related to water policy and environmentalism. A common criticism of environmental policy studies is its elitist nature. Public policy issues such as poverty, education, and crime are viewed as more pressing among non-elites because of the desire to meet the most basic needs of survival. Issues relating to endangered species are not important to a person below the poverty line lacking the basic necessities of life.

Political Culture in Alabama

When the 'water wars' began, Alabama's government did not have an existing state government agency qualified to represent the state's interests. Therefore they created an agency to address environmental concerns and represent Alabama in negotiations of interstate compacts addressing water allocation issues among Alabama, Florida, and Georgia. However, the state government did not feel comfortable enlisting existing state employees to manage the agency. Consequently, Alabama looked toward an interest group, Alabama Power, for assistance. The state's first negotiator was a former Alabama Power employee who provided the technical knowledge necessary to present Alabama's needs. In sum, the state of Alabama was represented by an Alabama interest group during negotiations with other states regarding issues of water allocation. Local governments in Alabama appear to have little concern over issues of interstate water allocation and do not address the issue. Interviews suggest local governments were content with allowing an electrical power company to represent their interests.

In Alabama, awareness of issues surrounding the 'water wars' is low. Few newspapers and television news programs devote much editorial space or time to the issue. In examining media outlets and through contacting interview subjects, a pattern emerged in which the further away from Georgia the citizen, the less concern and awareness the person possesses about 'water war' issues. Part of this can be explained by traits of the traditionalistic political culture in which most citizens prefer to put governing in the hands of the region's elites. One representative with a lake protection group near Montgomery was asked why interest in the water issues decreases further down the Coosa River from Georgia, he replied, "I don't think it [extremely low water levels] will get this far down. Alabama Power won't let it get that bad for us."

Leaders in the lake and river interest groups in Alabama, that are a few hundred miles downstream, are quick to acknowledge the lack of awareness and interest among their groups' membership in issues involving regional 'water wars'. To combat this, some of the leaders devoted a great amount of time explaining to members the threats to wealth and livelihoods that could be caused by reduced water levels. This argument is believed to be the most effective in prompting action among residents and members of lake protection groups along the Coosa and Tallapoosa Rivers.

The lack of awareness applies not only to citizens but to state legislators in Alabama. If the lack of water flowing into Alabama from Georgia is perceived to be harmful to economic development, some concern would likely be expressed to state legislators by the affected cities. However, no Alabama municipality representatives expressed public interest in the negotiations. Despite being located on the banks of the Alabama River, which originates at the intersection of the Coosa and Tallapoosa Rivers, interest and legislators from Montgomery and Mobile did not express concern about water withdrawals from any entity in the state of Georgia. A county environmental manager upstream on the Coosa River indicated his county commission directed him that the compacts were not something his office should closely follow.

Throughout the state, environmental activists believe their legislators are not only unaware of the compact negotiations, but they also do not want to become aware. "This just isn't on their radar screen," is a common remark from activists in Alabama. One legislator reinforced this sentiment, "When I talk with other legislators about interbasin transfers [of river water], they begin to get a glazed look in their eyes. I don't consider myself an expert on water. I am a lawyer, but I don't practice environmental law."

States that are more rural, have legislatures that are dominated by one party, are relatively poor, and are more agrarian, are less likely to have interest groups dominating public policy than states with opposite characteristics (Froman, 1966). This axiom explains that Alabama is ripe for domination from a particular interest group on a particular issue of public policy. Alabama is a state with one of the nation's lowest per capita incomes, few major urban centers, a state legislature controlled by the Democratic Party from Reconstruction to 2010 (Book of the States, 2010), and an economy heavily dependent on agriculture as its top industry. (United States Census, 2010). This scenario contains all elements for Alabama Power to be the dominant interest group. Georgia, predominately a rural state outside of the Metropolitan Atlanta area, is dominated by agricultural interests except for the city of Atlanta. In contrast, Atlanta is dominated by many interest groups with the same goal, fighting off any threat to the area's growth. "This is really a negotiation among four states: Alabama, Florida, Atlanta, and the rest of Georgia," remarks one Florida stakeholder (personal interview with the author). While competing interests clearly exist in Georgia, interest groups in other states feel a clear and monotone message is sent by the state of Georgia as to its needs. The message is that the Atlanta area's needs are Georgia's primary concern.

Political Culture in Georgia

The economic development interests in the Atlanta area also have a history of being able to exert a great amount of influence over public policy issues in Georgia. The reasons for this can likely be explained by having access to many economic and political resources as well as great levels of cohesion in their desired outcomes regarding issues of water allocation. One stakeholder in the Atlanta region places the importance of freshwater access hand-in-hand with economic development, "There is no natural boundary for

Atlanta's growth, no ocean, no mountain, no desert, no other big city to bump into, just cheap land. The only thing that can restrict Atlanta's growth is lack of water." (personal interview with the author). A Georgian stakeholder in downstream Columbus echoes this observation, "Atlanta has been growing for years, now it is our turn to grow." (personal interview with the author). Clearly, the implication is that if the Atlanta area is forced to limit its water intake, then businesses and industries would be more inclined to locate elsewhere. This regional divide plays out in other policy areas besides water allocation. "It is politically fashionable in some Georgia circles to bash Atlanta," comments one Atlanta area stakeholder (personal interview with the author). This statement could not be truer than in Georgia's intrastate battle over water.

Despite the long contentious history of arguing among Alabama, Florida and Georgia, there is virtually no desire expressed by any elected official, or interest group supporting the involvement of a federal agency in negotiations. During the existence of the interstate compacts the federal government played only a minor role in the negotiations. Today, only the federal courts are playing a role and that role is a result of the Constitutional requirement of the courts when one state sues another state or a federal agency such as the Corps of Engineers (COE). No individual interviewed suggested increased involvement from the federal government would be desired. Some cited mistrust of federal agencies, in particular the COE, among citizens and elected officials of both states. Others sited the longstanding views of suspicion or outright hostility among citizens and state governments toward involvement from the federal government. Alabama's motto, "We dare defend our rights" comes to mind.

In addition to the uniqueness of the region's political culture, the differences in water law between the eastern and western regions of the country are a reflection of the resource's availability in the different parts of the country. The lack of federal laws concerning water rights and allocation, therefore states have been left to develop these laws. States in the eastern portion of the country have developed water policy reflecting water allocation provisions prevalent in the United Kingdom during the settlement of the United States. Because many of the European settlers on the east coast were from the United Kingdom, the states adopted similar water laws. Due to an abundance of fresh water in the United Kingdom and the southeastern United States, the laws have received only slight modifications. Water law in arid western portions of the nation; reflect a 'first in time, first in right' rule that governs access to river water and underground aquifers (Shurts, J. 2000, Dellapenna, J. 2002, Ruhl, J. 2003).

Because of the scarcity of water in arid western states, laws concerning water rights are more detailed and tested than water laws in eastern states. The sheer volume of water available to users in eastern states creates conditions favorable to many uses of water without consideration of available quantity. Therefore, laws governing allocation and sharing of water resources are few, young, and often untested in the judicial system. Existing laws in the East are more likely to have been born out of concern for pollution of the water than allocation of the resource.

Disagreements over rights to water allocation in western states have existed since white settlement in the West, so most existing laws arose from customs set in the 19th century. Interstate compacts involving water allocation in western states, as is true with water law in general, are more detailed, court-tested, and older than compacts in eastern states. In addition, compacts involving western states are more likely to have a governing commission making decisions involving water allocation than compacts involving states east of the Mississippi River. One key assumption among interstate river basin compacts in the West is that states have addressed issues of intrastate water management and allocation and have the capacity to manage these issues in the future.

Water Quality versus Water Quantity

With respect to water policy development in the South, river water is considered a private good (Shurts, J. 2000, Dellapenna, J. 2002, Ruhl, J. 2003). This label is true for the quantity as well as the quality of water; therefore, negotiations regarding water allocation are actually over two private goods. Some interest groups, such as Alabama Power Company, do not seem to be concerned about water quality as much as it is quantity. However, several lake and river protection groups throughout Alabama believe water quality is directly affected by quantity. The higher the volume of water, the quicker and more thoroughly water can dissolve harmful bacteria, chemicals, and other pollution that the downriver users of the water would have to filter. Florida users of the Apalachicola River as well as non-Atlanta area water consumers downstream on the Chattahoochee River, are also concerned about water quality. With the headwaters of the Chattahoochee River originating in extreme north Georgia, the Atlanta area is the first major metropolitan area to use the river. The head waters of the Flint River are immediately south of the Atlanta airport.

Rapid Growth of Atlanta Garners Attention

The metropolitan area surrounding Atlanta has grown rapidly with no sign of decrease. Much of the growth can be attributed to the increase in population of the suburban areas surrounding Atlanta, regions with few zoning ordinances or plans addressing water as a limited resource. This growth has created a strain on the ability of counties and municipalities to maintain an infrastructure that adequately supplies water to their new residences and industries. Many of the longtime residents of the Atlanta area are accustomed to using water in ways that reflect the perceived abundance of this natural resource in the southeastern United States. Residents who have migrated to Atlanta have also noticed the quantity of rain and use water in ways that assume plentiful resources.

Immediately following the Second World War, at the urging of Atlanta's mayor Hartsfield, the Corps of Engineers (COE) built a dam along the Chattahoochee River and created the Lake Lanier Reservoir. The dam was built in response to the growing water demands of the Atlanta area and in anticipation of the area's future growth. The 1950 Census indicated about 400,000 people living in the Atlanta area. Lake Lanier Reservoir begins north of Atlanta near the headwaters of the Chattahoochee River with few strong feeders into the river. According to the dam's license, Lake Lanier was created for three reasons. The first was to create an inexpensive power source. Hydroelectric power created by Buford Dam would be used to supply the growing metropolitan area surrounding Atlanta. The second was to improve navigation along the Chattahoochee River. While Lake Lanier is not used for commercial shipping, lower sections of the Chattahoochee River are used for commercial navigation. Regulation of Lake Lanier's water level affects water levels in lower portions of the Chattahoochee River. The third purpose was to prevent flooding. While not listed as a specific purpose in the dam's license, over time, the lake served as a freshwater source for municipalities in the growing metropolitan area of Atlanta and as a destination for recreation. As the Atlanta area grew, concern about the ability of Lake Lanier to provide drinking water for the many citizens and industries prompted several different water analysis studies to be completed during the 1970s. These studies indicated a need for an additional water source in the near future, so local government agencies asked the COE to build another reservoir that could service the growing thirst of the Atlanta area.

By the late 1980s, the COE announced plans to construct a dam about fifty miles southwest of Atlanta along the Tallapoosa River. The plans initiated a lawsuit, filed by the state of Alabama against the COE in 1990, with a goal of preventing the creation of the dam. The reservoir, which would be located entirely within the state of Georgia, would be upstream from reservoirs built by Alabama Power that are located entirely within the borders of Alabama. The compact negotiations began in this litigious setting, but as a condition of entering into compact negotiations, the state of Alabama suspended its lawsuit over the proposed reservoir along the Tallapoosa River against the COE. Alabama, Georgia, and Florida began to discuss usage of river water within the ACT and ACF River Basins outside the court system. By 1997, the states of Alabama, Georgia, and Florida asked Congress to create the ACT and ACF River Basin Compacts, which were signed into law within the year.

Interstate Compact Negotiations Begin

The compacts provided for one chief negotiator and one alternate negotiator from each state and the federal government. Although the compacts were distinct and separate, the same eight commissioners represented the federal government and each state in both compact negotiations. Each state commissioner also had one vote on both compacts with the exception of Florida's commissioner not voting on the ACT compact since none of the ACT basin was in Florida's boundaries. Formally, each state's chief commissioner was its governor; however, the state's alternate commissioner represented the state at the negotiation meetings and voted. The governors appointed the alternate commissioner. By all accounts, each governor's role was more ceremonial than substantive. None of the states' governors attended a public meeting. Most quotes available in media outlets cited an appointed alternate commissioner, not the governor.

From the outset, the federal government's formal role in the negotiation process was minimal. While each state's commissioner had one vote and veto power over the compacts, the federal commissioner did not vote at all. According to one state commissioner, "Their role was to observe and ensure that federal laws were not being violated." To fully understand why the lack of federal involvement, the historical background of the states involved in the compacts must be considered. While each state negotiator interviewed had a slightly different explanation for why there was so little federal involvement, each commissioner emphasized a common theme of mistrust toward the federal government, in particular the COE.

Devolution Becomes the Preferred Path

Alabama's the lack of trust in the COE stems from the fact that Alabama resented the COE for wanting to construct a dam on the Georgia side of the Tallapoosa River without any prior consultation or consent. "Before the compact was created, Alabama felt the COE was running things," said one person familiar with the process of creating the compacts. Alabama was appeased by not giving the federal government a vote in the compact negotiations. Throughout the negotiations, the COE was deemed the face of unwanted federal involvement among many interest groups in Alabama. A state commissioner concurred that Georgia is suspicious of the role of the federal government because of fear that the Environmental Protection Agency (EPA) might have reservations with Georgia's view about the quantity of the Chattahoochee River's water flow once the river left the state. However, little evidence exists that the EPA made a direct impact on the negotiations. With its role reduced to providing advice instead of actively participating in decision making the EPA's influence on the negotiations was minimal, as was true with all federal agencies. One characteristic of the federal commissioner, Lindsey Thomas, who was originally appointed by President Clinton and reappointed by President Bush, not overlooked by Alabama and Florida was his residency. The federal commissioner lived in Georgia, was a former Georgia congressman, and served two years as president of the Georgia Chamber of Commerce during his tenure as the federal commissioner. Commissioners and interest group members in Alabama and Florida felt that created a conflict of interest or at the very least, gave appearance of possible impropriety. As one stakeholder from Alabama remarked, "[Federal Commissioner] Lindsey was a good guy, very bright. But no matter how hard he tried, there was always the appearance of a conflict of interest."

Each state feared the federal government, acting on behalf of a federal agency, would side with one state and requires other states to agree to a compact that was harmful. This mistrust prevented the federal government, or any federal agency, from becoming an active partner in the formal negotiation process. A skeptical view of involvement from individuals outside the three states also prevented the possibility of an objective fourth party having meaningful influence. A member of Florida's negotiation team echoed this point when asked why the compacts ultimately failed. He indicated a lack of willingness among the negotiators of each state to allow the involvement of individuals familiar with water negotiations in other regions of the country. This sentiment was supported by interviews from other state negotiators and representatives of interest groups in each of the three states.

In January of 2003, all three states had Republican governors, a first since Reconstruction. The common political ground brought hope that an agreement would occur once the three governors collaborated. In May of 2003, all three governors signed a memorandum of understanding; however, the memorandum of understanding only stated that the governors would work together to reach an agreement. Georgia sent a proposal to Florida, with Alabama's consent, hoping to obtain the final signature. By 2003, the Apalachicola River Basin area of Florida had gained political clout with the governor. After the redistricting that followed the release of the 2000 U. S. Census data, the Apalachicola River Basin area became a part of the district of the Speaker of the Florida House. The Speaker, a fellow Republican, was a long-time ally of then-Florida governor Jeb Bush. Once the stakeholders of the bay area saw Georgia's proposal, they contacted the Speaker and urged him to discourage the governor from signing the agreement. The governor did not consent to the proposal that was deemed favorable to Georgia at the expense of Florida because Georgia would not guarantee a minimum water flow at the state line.

From the outset, Governor Bush was skeptical of Georgia's desired compact outcomes. One member of Florida's negotiation team indicated they had spent millions of dollars over several decades purchasing land in the Apalachicola Bay. The land was used to create several state parks with the purpose of protecting the bay area's estuary from commercial development and ecological change. The same negotiator also indicated how this spending took on increased importance with members of the state's government who did not want to see the Apalachicola Bay area erode in the same fashion as the Everglades in the southern portion of the state. In this sense, the state became an advocate for the Apalachicola Bay area and supported the goals of the individuals and interest groups associated with the bay who were involved in the negotiation process.

After nearly six years of negotiations and extensions, the states decided to end negotiations, and the ACF compact expired June 30, 2003. Since some of the provisions of the ACT compact were contingent on water access within the ACF Basin, Alabama and Georgia decided to discontinue negotiations of the ACT compact. The ACT compact expired June 30, 2004. With the goal of negotiating an agreement that left the natural flow of the Apalachicola River unaltered, Florida believed it could protect its interests as long as it possessed veto power, because the compacts' design allowed each state to be treated as equals and prevented federal involvement from being able to override a state (interview with a member of the state's negotiation team). When asked if the compact negotiation was a failure, a member of Florida's negotiation team replied, "No. It was not a failure because we did not sign a bad agreement."

Devolution Continues After Interstate Compacts Expire

Three major events have occurred since the end of the compacts: 1) a severe drought in 2007, 2) a ruling by Federal Judge Magnuson that Buford Dam's purpose is not to provide a source of water for Atlanta area water authorities, and 3) Judge Magnuson's ruling overturned by a federal court. Each event created change in discussions of water allocation in the region.

The drought of 2007 created a water shortage in the South, the severity of which had not been seen in decades (www.caes.uga.edu). Typical annual rainfall data for the Atlanta area is around 50 inches. However, water levels had not been especially strong in recent years. During 2006, rainfall for the region was 40 inches (www.caes.uga.edu). Traditionally wet spring weather and the dry summer of 2007 were worse than normal. No official figures were created to determine a dollar value in the loss of tourism to areas such as Lake Lanier, but many businesses dependent on water such as golf courses or marinas servicing reservoirs experienced a reduction in business and in extreme cases, a complete shutdown of operations. The Atlanta region depends on the Chattahoochee River and its northern most reservoir, Lake Lanier, as its primary water source. Since Lake Lanier's creation shortly following World War II, the region's population grew from under one million residents to almost five million by 2007. The 2010 United States Census indicated over five million residents in the region; approximately three million residents depend on the Chattahoochee River and Lake Lanier for water, with about half a million depending on surface water in the Flint River. The remaining one and a half million residents in the northeastern region of metropolitan Atlanta depend on surface water from the Etowah and Coosa River Basins.

Following consecutive years of reduced precipitation, Lake Lanier was vulnerable to drought conditions in 2007. Much of the region experienced drought conditions deemed 'exceptional' (meaning drought conditions of once every 100 years) with other portions experiencing 'extreme' (once every 50 years) or severe (once every 20 years) (www. georgiafaces.caes.georgia.edu). Many measuring stations in Georgia found 2007 to be the driest or second driest year on record (www.georgiadrought.org). In August of 2007, 51 counties were experiencing exceptional drought conditions. Lake Lanier resembled a muddy plain surrounding a creek and was no longer navigable by most any means. This status did not dramatically change until spring precipitation. The lake did not reach full pool until the spring of 2009.

As a result of severe drought of 2007, state and local governments scrambled to determine how to balance water demand with fewer water supply options. Because of the dependency on surface water throughout North Georgia and few strong water flows due to its approximation to the foothills of the Appalachian Mountains, drastic measures were taken to protect remaining freshwater resources. Initially, elected officials asked citizens to conserve water. Later, ordinances were passed prohibiting watering of lawns and reducing operations of water intensive businesses such as car washes. The responses were not sufficient to slow a shrinking supply of water in Lake Lanier. Water quality became a concern throughout the Chattahoochee River Basin as less water became available to dilute pollutants and other chemicals used to treat waste water. Municipalities down river such as Columbus needed to spend more time and money treating water to bring it to a level suitable for human consumption. Policy makers became painfully aware existing solutions were not solving the problem.

This drought was on the heels of a drought in 2006. While not as severe as the drought in 2007, an accident by the United States Army Corps of Engineers (COE) created more distrust of the federal and other state governments as thousands of gallons of water were released from Lake Lanier. It was later learned the decision to release the water was caused by reading a faulty gauge (accessnorthga.com). At a time when cooperation among levels of government would be helpful or prove useful in solving water allocation issues during a drought, suspicion and hostility ran high. After a few months of precipitation close to historical norms Lake Lanier's level began to rise, and the sense of emergency began to subside for many citizens as media attention to the issue decreased. By 2009, with Lake Lanier near full pool, attention shifted to changing economic conditions and an emerging recession.

A lasting impact of the drought was awareness of vulnerability to water shortages in the region. The inadequate responses to the crisis indicated other solutions would be needed in order to prevent abysmal water quality conditions and an outright lack of water to meet basic human needs for millions of residents. Despite the increased awareness, there is little evidence of change in water usage policies other than an increase in attempts to find additional water sources in other states and create more reservoirs along existing rivers. While Alabama and Florida were able to weather the drought more effectively, due to smaller populations of citizens withdrawing water and being located downstream with higher volume water flows, neither state was immune to its impact. In Alabama, production of electricity from Alabama Power's dams was threatened by a reduction in water flow along the Coosa and Tallapoosa Rivers. This reduction forced a rare lowering of reservoir pools during the summer months. Typically, regional electric power companies producing electricity from hydroelectric generators reduce a reservoir's pool in the fall and winter with anticipation of seasonal winter rains. Winter's bountiful precipitation usually more than replaces a seasonal reduction in the reservoir's pool. However, 2007 was different. Due to lower summer pools created by lower levels of water flowing downstream and higher than average demand of electricity to cool homes that resulted from higher than average summer temperatures, electric power companies did not need to reduce the reservoir levels during the fall to prevent possible flooding during the seasonally higher precipitation months in the winter and spring. Because precipitation was less than normal in the winter and spring, reservoir levels were unseasonably low going into the dryer summer season.

Tug-of-War over Water

In the South, the peak season for electricity demand is the summer. As temperatures rise and residents seek to cool their homes and places of work, demand for electricity increases. In this regard, the summer of 2007 was especially brutal. Several days of temperatures hovered over 100 degrees Fahrenheit, excessive even for a region accustomed to high summer temperatures with ample humidity. With much of the region dependent on hydroelectric power for electricity generation, tension between the need to increase release of water to generate electricity and the need to hold water for human consumption. The reduced release of water flowing through turbines meant electric power needed to be generated from other sources such as coal burning and nuclear facilities. While coal burning facilities are not dependent on water levels, the same cannot be said for nuclear power generators. Reduced water flow is problematic for generating electricity using nuclear power. Nuclear reactors need to be cooled. A common practice is to cool reactors by running large amounts of freshwater over the reactors. During sweltering summer months, water was not cool enough to reduce the reactor's temperature. With reduced water levels in the Chattahoochee River, the deepest portion of the river is closer to the surface, receiving more sunlight and exposure to hot air. To compound matters, record electricity demand occurred during this time because of the need to run air conditioning in buildings to combat high temperatures. Although only one nuclear reactor is located along the Chattahoochee River, near Dothan, Alabama, the lack of water to produce electricity by hydroelectric dams increased the importance on other sources of electrical production to compensate for a reduction of hydroelectric power generation. To this end, the region's dependence on coal burning to produce electricity increased which caused pollution concerns and challenged compliance with federally mandated air quality standards.

Despite these concerns major water authorities and municipalities in the portion of the basin in Alabama did not feel the need to adopt and enforce restrictions on water usage. Notable exceptions include municipalities such as Birmingham and surrounding suburbs depending on the Cahaba River. With no reservoirs along the river, and the only major reservoir being Lake Purdy, water usage was restricted throughout much of the drought in 2007 in central Alabama.

In Florida, harvesting of oysters and shrimp suffered. Because of the reduction in freshwater flows from the Chattahoochee and Flint Rivers, the Apalachicola River could not provide adequate freshwater to sustain a viable ecosystem for seafood in Apalachicola Bay. In the absence of a harvest, a vital revenue source did not materialize. Because the bay's ecosystem was damaged, repair was slow and tedious. Normal harvests did not return until 2009. Because of the small population in the Apalachicola Basin, water withdrawals from water authorities did not face increased regulation during the drought.

Federal Courts Intervene

On July 17, 2009, Senior United States District Judge Paul Magnuson determined Buford Dam, which creates the reservoir known as Lake Lanier, was not created to supply drinking water for metropolitan Atlanta. Therefore, municipalities surrounding Atlanta did not have a right to continue withdrawing water at current levels (Rankin 2009). The judge ruled the dam's purpose was to provide electricity, flood control, and assist in navigation. Judge Magnuson gave state governments in Alabama, Georgia, and Florida or United States Congress three years from the date of his ruling to reach an agreement for water sharing. If no agreement is reached, withdrawal levels for metropolitan Atlanta will return to levels not seen since the 1970s when the river and its reservoir, Lake Lanier, supplied water to almost half the number of current users. Currently approximately three and a half million people receive drinking water from the Chattahoochee River (Scott 2010). Judge Magnuson further iterated only water authorities in Gainesville and Buford, Georgia are authorized to withdraw water from Lake Lanier to meet current and future water needs. However, this ruling was rendered moot in June of 2011 when a three judge panel from the 11th United States Circuit Court of Appeals overturned the ruling. Attorneys from Alabama decided to appeal the ruling. After twenty years of negotiations and lawsuits, the promise of any regional water agreement remains elusive.

Discussion of tapping into the Tennessee River Basin made its way through the state legislature. With only a small portion of the basin within Georgia's boundary, the state tried to argue over the exact boundary with neighboring Tennessee. The goal was to move the boundary north into existing Tennessee with the goal of increasing access to surface water. By increasing access to more water in the Tennessee River Basin, water could then be transferred to neighboring basins such as the Chattahoochee and Coosa. This option is, at best, a long shot that will likely see numerous court challenges over several years should the state of Georgia pursue the issue. Even the option of transferring water from existing portions of the Tennessee River Basin within Georgia's boundary is more complicated than placing a pipe into the Tennessee River's tributaries and sending it south. Because the water in the Tennessee River and its reservoirs are owned and managed by a federal agency, Tennessee Valley Authority, water authorities seeking to make withdrawals from the basin must secure permission from the federal government before making the withdrawal. Nonetheless, this is not deterring Georgia state legislators. During the 2011 legislative session, bills allowing for interbasin transfers and reservoir creation along tributaries in the portion of the Tennessee River Basin within Georgia's boundaries were introduced. At the end of the 2011 session, none of the bills became law. No bill regarding water withdrawals from the Tennessee River or changing state boundaries was introduced in the 2012 session.

Conclusion

With the Republican midterm election sweep in 2010, two new Republican governors were inaugurated in Alabama and Georgia. Initially, this brought a plan to renew negotiations between the two governors. However, hopes were quickly dashed as the governor of Georgia, Nathan Deal, proposed to create more reservoirs in portions within Georgia's boundaries of the Coosa and Etowah River basins. Alabama governor Harold Bentley viewed this as a topic that should be included in negotiations between the two states and not a matter solely for debate in the Georgia state legislature. Frustrated by this impasse, the Alabama governor withdrew from negotiations. The two states do not appear to be close to an agreement in the foreseeable future.

Water wars in the Deep South provide a unique and intriguing lens in which to view southern culture. This uniqueness renders analogies and solutions that are applicable in other regions of the country, largely fruitless. Because of the region's lack of interstate cooperation, a desire to not lose versus give a little to get a little, and a view of river water as a good for all to use rather than a commodity to be owned, hopes for an agreement are slim. Baring an edict from the federal courts or Congress, states in the Deep South will continue to argue over water allocation for decades to come.

References

Dellapenna, J. (2002). "The Law of Water Allocation in the Southeastern States at the Opening of the Twenty-First Century". *University of Little Lock Law Review*, 25(9), 9-88.

Froman, L. (1966). "Some Effects of Interest Group Strength in State Politics." *The American Political Science Review*, 60(4), 952-962.

Ruhl, J. (2003). "Equitable Apportionment of Ecosystem Services: New Water Law for a New Water Age" *Journal of Land Use and Environmental Law*. 19(1). 47-54.

Shurts, J. (2000). *Indian Reserved Water Rights, The Winters Doctrine in its Social and Legal Context, 1880s – 1930s*. Norman, Oklahoma. University of Oklahoma Press.

United States Bureau of the Census. 2011. Census 2010. Washington D.C. Author.

Website
www.noaa.gov
http://www.srh.noaa.gov/ffc/?n=rainfall_scorecard (Accessed February 11, 2013)

Chapter Thirteen

IMPLEMENTATION OF DECENTRALIZATION IN GHANA: ISSUES AND CHALLENGES

Kwame Asamoah

Key words: decentralization, Ghana, local governance, implementation, challenges

Research Design

The study is purely qualitative and uses the content analysis technique for the research. Secondary data was obtained from intensive evaluation of textbooks, journal articles, and working papers from the Ministry of Local Government and Rural Development, Balme Library of University of Ghana, Institute of Local Government Library, Institute of African Studies Library, and Ghana Institute of Management and Public Administration (GIMPA).

Objective

The study rests on the premise that attempts to utilize decentralization policy in Ghana have not yielded the expected results due to administrative and logistical constraints.

Literature Review

Decentralization as a system of governance has received much scholarly attention the world over and has been recommended by both developed and developing countries as a policy that can help bring about sustainable national and local level development.

Decentralization as a developmental policy is aimed at bringing governance to the doorsteps of the citizens in a country. The success of this policy largely depends on the modalities of its implementation. The extent to which the various institutions that are responsible for implementation of decentralization are resourced in terms of powers and capacity to be able to operate freely are critical to its success. Decentralization has been regarded by many as a panacea for economic development and growth as it brings governance to the people and gets them involved in all aspects of governance (Crook and Manor, 2000). The central and paramount objective of decentralization is to ensure participatory government. It is within this context that various attempts in Ghana have been made to develop a system of local government that would properly allow the citizens to participate in local governance.

Decentralization is often seen as a way of increasing the ability of central government officials to obtain better and less suspect information about local or regional conditions, to plan local programs more responsively, and to react more quickly to unanticipated problems that inevitably arise during implementation (Maddick, 1963). In theory, decentralization should allow projects to be completed sooner by giving local managers greater discretion in decision-making to enable them to cut through the "red tape" and the ponderous procedures often associated with over-centralized administration (Rondinelli, 1981).

The World Bank (2000), embraced decentralization as one of the major governance reforms on its agenda (World Bank, 2000; Burki, Perry and Dillinger, 1999). Decentralization refers to a worldwide practice of 'devolving the responsibilities of centralized governments to regional or local governments' with the rationale to improve upon efficiency (by way of inter-governmental competition and fiscal discipline) and democratic voice (through informed local control over service rendering). The fiscal aspect has to do with giving tax and expenditure authority to local units of government to ensure efficiency in the internal revenue mobilization and expenditure control. This definition adds that decentralization performs better in environments that have an enlightened democratic credentials and professionalism of personnel at its peak within the sub -national government circles. Care must therefore be taken in situations where these factors stated are not practiced with imbalances in regional set-ups, pervasive corruption, and weak management abilities (Cornell University, 2006).

Tresiman (2007) argues that decentralization is a process in which a central government delegates power to the local government. To Ribot (2001), decentralization "is any act in which a central government formally cedes powers to actors and institutions at lower levels in a political-administrative and territorial hierarchy." The United States Agency for International Development USAID (2009), on the other hand, defines decentralization as the "transfer of power and resources from the national governments to sub national governments or to administrative units of national governments". This basically has to do with the reassigning of authority to the various levels of the central government which include, regional, sub regional, districts, towns and local unit committee levels.

The fiscal federalism literature suggests that decentralized and shared governance ensure a more efficient delivery of public goods, limits government intervention in the economy, brings decision making closer to citizens, and encourages the emergence and maintenance of effective markets, because of the competitive pressures that decentralized governments place on each other and national governments (Tiebout, 1956; Oates, 1972; Inman &Rubinfeld, 1997).

After a long period of concerted efforts and advocacies to bring about efficiency and competency within government's officialdom and leadership, partisanship still exhibits its influence on all governmental institutions. As many individuals felt that they could not get their views represented on all policies originating from the main organs of the state which affect them as stakeholders, hence, the call for a shift from a fragmented administrative system of government to a decentralized form of governance. Also, the ever increasing numbers of organizations in every sphere of life needed a model of representative leadership that could be adhered to current development of economic, social, and political nature (Kaufman, 1969).

As part of the democratization processes, some level of decentralization is necessary to actually get citizens involved in the policy-making process. When people participate in all processes of a policy, it makes them own such programs as such they offer their technology, labor, and support of all kinds to enable the attainment of the needed results.

It is therefore, not surprising that the New Public Management(NPM) as a management culture, has put much premium on decentralization as one of its major principles, aimed at management and control of public institutions and to make them more competitive at all levels (Economic Commission for Africa, 2004) .

Forms of Decentralization

Decentralization has been categorized into four forms, which are deconcentration, delegation, devolution, and privatization.

Deconcentration is defined as "the reassigning responsibilities of central government to the field offices of national ministries, departments, and agencies without placing these offices under the control of sub national government" (USAID, 2009). Deconcentration is thus the handing over of some amount of administrative authority or responsibility to lower levels within central government ministries and agencies. It is a shifting of the workload from centrally located officials to staff or offices outside of the national capital. Deconcentration, when it is more than mere re-organization, gives some discretion to field agents to plan and implement programs and projects, or to adjust central directives to local conditions, within guidelines set by central ministry or agency headquarters (Rondinelli, Nellis and Cheema, 1983). This means that all the ministries, departments, and agencies of the central government have their sub-offices to perform various functions at various levels. It ensures that the central government gets all its activities to all parts of the country and to respond rapidly to emergency cases. For instance, in the Ghanaian situation, the National Disaster Management Organization (NADMO) does not have to send officials from the national headquarters in Accra to a flooded area in a District since they have sub-units at all levels of governance throughout the country.

Delegation constitutes "a greater degree of change in the distribution of power relative to deconcentration because it shifts responsibility for specifically defined functions to sub national governments or sub national administrative units" (USAID, 2009). Delegation transfers managerial responsibility for specifically defined functions to organizations that are outside the regular bureaucratic structure and that are only indirectly controlled by the central government. Delegation has long been used in administrative law. It implies that a sovereign authority creates or transfers to an agent specified functions and duties, which the agent has broad discretion to carry out. However, ultimate responsibility remains with the sovereign authority.

In developing countries, responsibilities have been delegated to public corporations, regional development agencies, special function authorities, semiautonomous project implementation units, and a variety of parastatal organizations to perform some specifically defined functions (Rondinelli, 1981a). In other words, it involves the practice by which functions are transferred to lower levels of government, public corporations, or any other authority outside the proper sphere of regular political-administrative structure, to implement programs on behalf of a government agency. It is regarded as a way of developing the capacity of decentralized governments and administrative units; and their personnel for upward level and other national government responsibilities; and services delivery to the doorsteps of the citizenry.

In Ghana like most East African countries, delegation has been used extensively. Public corporations and special authorities have been used to finance, construct, and manage physical infrastructure projects such as highways, dams, hydroelectric facilities, railroads, and transportation systems, and to organize and manage large-scale agricultural activities such as cotton growing in the Sudan and tea raising in Kenya (King 1967; Khalil 1970).

Devolution is the creation or strengthening financially or legally of sub-national units of government, the activities of which are substantially outside the direct control of the central government. Under devolution, local units of government are autonomous and independent, and their legal status makes them separate or distinct from the central government. Central authorities frequently exercise only indirect, supervisory control over such units. Normally, local governments have clear and legally recognized geographical boundaries within which they exercise an exclusive authority to perform explicitly granted or reserved functions. They have corporate or statutory authority to raise revenues and make expenditures. They should be perceived by local citizens as organizations providing services that satisfy their needs, and as governmental units over which they have some influence (Rondinelli, 1981a).

Privatization involves a total transfer of government services and functions to private (profit or not-for-profit) institutions. Privatization ranges from total transfer of state services to be executed by the non-governmental organization to public-private-partnerships where both the government and private sector forge alliances to execute services or goods. The concept can involve "allowing private enterprises to perform functions that had previously been monopolized by government, contracting out the provision or management of public services or facilities to commercial enterprises"   (Kobia, 2011, p.7). Such private enterprises operate rural development projects and community self-help programs that provide social-overhead capital--roads, water tanks, irrigation canals, sanitation facilities, and wells. Many provide working capital for local, small-scale agricultural and handicraft projects and market outlets for the goods produced in villages (James 1982). A typical example involves the contracting out of management functions of water delivery in Ghana to Aqua Vitens Rand in 2005 and Zoomlion in the area of sanitation.

Justification for Decentralization

In the era of modern organizational management structure, a function that ought to be centralized or decentralized depends largely on the size and the number of activities to be supervised. Where the area of operation is large with a multiplicity of activities, decentralized administrative structure is the answer. Bhattacharya (2006) viewed decentralization in the light of decision-making in institutions with an avalanche of complex activities that need quicker decisions to achieve efficiency. He has also suggested that the degree of decentralization is greater under the following conditions:

(I) Greater number of decisions are made at lower levels of management;

(ii) Decisions made at lower level are important;

(iii) Various organisational functions are more influenced by decisions made at lower levels;

(iv) There is less monitoring of decisions made by managerial personnel.

In Ghana, there are two main fundamental aims for the implementation of decentralization system of governance. These are:
1. To strengthen and expand local democracy and; 2. To promote local, social and economic development, thereby reducing poverty and increasing choices of people (Ghana Society for Development Dialogue Publications (GSDDP, 2008).
The above conditions confirm the fact that when people participate in decision-making process, they feel ownership of the programs and therefore offer local support to enable sustainability of developmental activities. Rapid response is also given to emergency situations as well as reductions in time spent to take decisions from the central government level.

The Myth of Decentralization and the concept of Subsidiarity

The concept of decentralization appears to be rich or full of substance in theory but its practice makes it a two-edged sword. Technically, it ends up perpetuating the very social evil or canker it sought to correct (Ostrom, 1989; Stone, 1997). This point has forcefully been brought home by Conyers (2000) that "most decentralization efforts have both explicit and implicit objectives; those objectives likely to appeal to the general public, such as local empowerment and administrative efficiency, are generally explicitly stated, while less popular ones, such as increasing central control and "passing the buck", are unlikely to be voiced" (p. 9).
It therefore, appears that Governments use decentralization for "political purposes" rather than economic and social development interests and Ayee (1999) refers to the phenomenon as "decentralized centralization". Oyugi (2000) goes as far as saying that "the

legal-political design of local government in Africa tends to weaken the cultivation of a democratic culture at the local level as well as weaken the ability of local authorities to take initiative in the field of service provision". Asibuo (1991) argued that decentralization is about distribution of power in society and hence nobody would like to implement a program that will disadvantage him in terms of sphere of influence and power. This to him has been a major obstacle to effective decentralization which to the third world was supposed to "suggest the hope of cracking open the blockages of inert central bureaucracy, curing managerial constipation, giving more direct access for the people to the government and the government to the people, stimulating the whole nation to participate in national development plans (Mawhood, 1983 cited in ibid).

Furthermore, the statutory books of Ghana contain a lot of centralizing factors (most of them colonial and early post-colonial baggage) that have hindered effective and autonomous local government and have sought to make the District Assemblies more subservient to the centre.

Per the Local Government Act, Act 462, all by-laws are approved by the Minister of Local Government and Rural Development (LGRD); the President has the power to dissolve defaulting or non-performing District Assemblies without consulting the electorate; the Minister of LGRD has power to issue guidelines, in respect of fees to be charged by the District Assemblies for the service and facilities provided, licenses and permits issued/ rates levied; According to Section 88 of the Local Government Act, Act 462, the District Assemblies require central government guarantee to raise loans in excess of GhC 25,000.

Brief History of Decentralization in Ghana

Ayee (2008) points out that the history of decentralization in Ghana is traced back to the introduction of indirect rule by the British colonial authorities in 1878, lasting until 1951. Ghana the then Gold Coast, has its local government system dating back in the colonial era which was in the form of " Indirect Rule" which featured 'native authority' who were not only corrupt but inefficient, undemocratic and above all interested in helping the colonial masters to institutionalize colonization. In 1859, the Municipal Council Ordinance established municipalities only in major coastal towns with seven members each elected by their own people. The rest of the country was governed by the State Councils and Native Authorities system.

Before independence in 1943, a new Ordinance set up elected town councils in the major cities with the District Commissioner as the president. Following the Report of the Coussey Committee, the Municipal Councils Ordinance was passed with five-six members elected by the electorate and one-sixth nominated by the State Council in charge. Apart from these Ordinances, several other Native Ordinances such as; the Native Treasuries Ordinance (1936), Native Administrative Treasuries Ordinance (1939) and the Local Government Ordinance (1951) also existed (Ahwoi, 2010).

Ghana, since independence, has had successive governments going through a series of efforts to decentralize authority to the local units of government. Regional and districts devolution were the main targets for public administration of which little impact was felt. In the 1970s, the system was then reconstituted into a four-tier structure consisting of Regional, District, Local Councils and Town and Village Development Committees with the district councils being the focal point of local governance (Administrative and Executive power).

As part of government's efforts to decentralize governance, a comprehensive policy was drafted and the Local Government Law, 1988 was enacted. The modalities in the policy document were discussed with the various stakeholders of the country as to direction of the decentralized system of governance. The main policy included a drift from 'command approaches' to amore consultative and participatory atmosphere, devolution of power and all other resources to the district level with the implementation been supervised by a high powered Committee with oversight responsibilities controlled by the Cabinet. Under the current system, the Ministry of Local Government and Rural Development has responsibilities over the system.

Article 240 (1) of the 1992 Republican Constitution clearly states how the local government and administration should be decentralized while Article 240 (2) stipulates the features the system should operate within. As it stands, the guiding principles and modalities about the implementation processes of the decentralized system of governance in Ghana are found in the Local Government Act, 1993, Act 462, the District Assembly Common Fund Act, 1993, Act 455.

Decentralization, the Local Government System and the 1992 Constitution

Decentralization as a concept has a series of principles and policy guidelines. The policy in general has political and administrative under-tones and the process in the Ghanaian contest is extremely political. The system in Ghana involves a number of issues which include:

The Framework: In the 1992 Constitution of the Republic of Ghana, Article 240 made the provisions for decentralization and Article 240 (1) has it that local government and administration should, as far as practicable, be decentralized while Article 240 (2) specifies that features that the decentralized local government system should operate within.

Coordination of Transfers within the various system: Parliament is the legitimate body as stipulated by Article 240 (2) (a), responsible to enact the right legislation to ensure that the functions, powers, responsibilities, and all other resources are made available to the local government units in a coherent and organized manner. In furtherance of the processes of transfers, the Local Government Act, 1993, Act 462 and the District Assemblies' Common Fund Act, Act 455, was passed to take care of the transfer of functions, responsibilities and resources to the District Assemblies.

Planning within the system: With regard to planning, Article 240 (2) (0) requires that "Parliament shall by law provide for the taking of such measures as are necessary to enhance the capacity of local government authorities to plan, initiate, co-ordinate, manage and execute policies in respect of all matters affecting the people within their areas, with a view to ultimately achieving localisation of activities"

To get this done, the National Development Planning Act was passed in 1994 to provide the legislative framework for decentralized planning by creating the District Assemblies Planning Authorities. The functions of development planning capacity have been transferred to the District Assemblies with offices created known as the District Planning Coordinating Unit manned by the District Planning Officer.

Financing of the Local Government Units: The 1992 Constitution Article 240 (2) (c) provides that "there shall be established for each local government unit a sound financial base with adequate and reliable sources of revenue". It is this same provision that grants the enactment of the district Assemblies' Common Fund Act and the other legislation regarding the revenues of local government. One major source of transfers of resources to the District Assemblies is the payment of salaries and emoluments of their (D.A) staff as recurrent expenditure.

Competence level of Personnel: Requirements for personnel of the local government units states "as far as practicable, persons in the service of local government shall be subject to the effective control of local authorities". Section 37 (2) of the Local Government Act, Act 462, has a provision that "a District Assembly shall have such staff as may be necessary for the proper and efficient performance of its functions". However as far as the control of staff is concerned, the Local Government Service Act, 2003, Act 656, appears to have vested all powers of appointment of the staff of the Local Assembly Service including the staff of District Assemblies, in the president with an exception under sub-section (4), where the president can delegate such powers. This situation does not ensure an effective decentralization since power is much vested in the President.

Participation at the Local Government Level: Participation at the local level is very necessary that it has to be encouraged. As a results of this, Article 240 (2) (e) provides that "to ensure the accountability of local government authorities, people in particular local government areas shall , as far as practicable, be afforded the opportunity to participate effectively in their governance".

Several mechanisms have been put in place to make sure that the aims of decentralization are realized. To qualify to take part in the local government level elections, one has to meet the normal residence requirement. The elections are supposed not to be state-sponsored and non-partisan to ensure that participation is done by people whose lives are directly affected by decisions and projects of the local authorities.

The Districts of Local Government: For the purposes of the districts of the local government, Article 241 (1) of the 1992 Republican Constitution, "... Ghana shall be deemed to have been divided into the districts in existence immediately before the coming into force of this Constitution". However, Article 241 (2) provides that "Parliament may by law make provision for the redrawing of the boundaries of districts or reconstituting the districts" and this has been provided for in the Local Government Act of 1993, Act 462, by vesting that power in the President by Executive Instrument on the recommendation of the Electoral Commission. After the re-demarcation the responsibility for the establishment of the District Assemblies falls on the Minister of Local Government under section 3 of

Act 462. The Minister of Local Government subsequently issues the necessary Legislative Instruments for the establishment of the creation of new districts.

The Composition of District Assemblies: With regard to the composition of the District Assemblies, seventy percent (70%) of members are popularly elected by the various electoral areas; this is to ensure that the local electorates are politically represented. Again, another thirty percent (30%) are appointed by the president in consultation with stakeholders of the respective metropolitan, municipal or District Assemblies. The rationale of this 30% appointment was to objectively select personnel with the requisite knowledge, skills and abilities (KSAs) as well as other expertise to augment the various Assemblies. However, it appears this provision is abused to fill party fanatics into the various District Assemblies whilst competence and expertise seem to be relegated to the background.

Again, Members of Parliament (MPs) from the various constituencies in the respective Districts, the District Coordinating Directors, Heads of the various Departments and Agencies of the central government are members without voting rights (ex officio members). The Metropolitan/Municipal/District Chief Executive (MMDCE) is also a member and experts and opinion leaders could be called upon to participate if the need arises.

The District Chief Executive: Article 243 (1) of the Constitution gives the President the power to nominate the District Chief Executive (DCE) and must be approved by two-thirds of the members of the Assembly present and voting. The Constitutional basis for the appointment of a District Chief Executive can be found in Article 243 of the 1992 Constitution. It provides as follows:

> There shall be a District Chief Executive for each district who shall be appointed by the President with prior approval of not less than two-thirds majority of the members of the Assembly present and voting at a sitting specifically convened for the purpose.

The method of appointment of the DCE has generated a lot of arguments which makes it necessary for a critical assessment.

Successes of Decentralization System of Local Governance in Ghana

Ghana has made significant strides in terms of the decentralized system of local governance in spite of certain constraints. For instance, from the perspective of the *New Legon Observer*, (2008), the numerous reforms have made a significant improvement in terms of political and administrative institutions to ensure successes of the decentralised process. These include;

i. The Metropolitan, Municipal and District Assemblies serve as training grounds for people to start their political career. One of such persons is Dr. Paa Kwesi Nduom who started as an Assembly member in the Komenda-Edina-Eguafo-Abirem District, became a Member of Parliament, a Cabinet Minister of State and eventually a Presidential candidate for the Convention Peoples Party (CPP) and Progressive People's Party during the 2008 and 2012 General elections respectively.

ii. The increase in the number of districts from 65 in 1988 to 170 in 2008, has improved administration as well as deepened democracy and governance, ensures equitable distribution of the nation's resources and above all acceleration of the overall national developmental agenda. For instance, after gazetting on March 9, 2012 for the creation of 42 additional districts, the government devoted about "GH¢43 million for the new assemblies and has also made provisions under the District Assemblies Common Fund to provide them with solid foundations from which to execute development project.

iii. There has also been a significant increase in the District Assemblies Common Fund (DACF) from 5% to 7.5% in recent times and this has improved the financial capacity of District Assemblies to undertake and complete many of their projects. Most of the District Assemblies do not have enough sources of funds or internally generated funds (IGF), therefore the increment in the DACF has to an extent enhanced financial positions

iv. There has been a series of local level elections from 1994, 1998, 2002, 2006 and in 2010 at both the District Assembly and Unit Committee levels. This gives the people the chance to be part of the decision-making process and to decide on their priorities as a people.

Implementation Challenges

Although governments of developing countries have offered a wide range of justifications for decentralizing, the results have been mixed. Governments of these nations have faced myriad problems in designing and implementing programs for decentralizing development administration. Even where the programs have been relatively successful, not all of the anticipated benefits have accrued due to problems relating to either central or local administrative units (Cheema and Rondinelli, 1983).

Despite the several successes and benefits of decentralized system of governance together with the broad objectives of the system, there have been some implementation challenges. Despite adherence to the rhetoric of decentralization, the political commitment of national governments to the devolution of power to local authorities is often limited. It is evident that the autonomy of local government is compromised and undermined in a number of ways, indicating that central control still remains very real.

Local government financing has been a major concern of most developing countries. District authorities basically have three main sources of revenue: the District Assemblies' Common Fund, ceded revenue, and their own internal fund generation through taxation. The District Assemblies Common Fund is the main source providing a constitutionally guaranteed minimum share of government revenue, and thus some financial independence. Yet evidence of its workings is somewhat mixed. The five percent minimum of national revenue to the District Assemblies' Common Fund is clearly insufficient given the broad range of responsibilities devolved to district assemblies. Given the extensive responsibilities of about 86 functions to be executed by District Assemblies, it is generally recognized that their financial position is weak. Local government has little fiscal independence, remaining overwhelmingly dependent on central government for its financial resources, with limited revenue generating ability.

Oyugi (2000) suggests that the dependence of local authorities on central government funding leads to a loss of operational autonomy, with local initiatives undermined. What perhaps seems more problematic about the DACF might not necessarily be with the amount but with the 'how and when' of the disbursement. Evidence suggests that most of the Assemblies receive their share of the Common Fund very late and tends to affect their planning processes and execution of developmental projects. In most cases, deduction at source greatly affects the net disbursements to the respective Assemblies. Before, the funds are released to the Assemblies; there is deduction ostensibly to purchase some items for the Assembly or other purposes by the central government. These deductions cumulatively take a large chunk of the DACF from the Assemblies. Besides, even though the legal framework of decentralization argues that central government ought to provide some ceded capital to the assemblies, empirical evidence suggests that these funds are hardly released.

The information and accounting systems as well as mechanisms of monitoring public bureaucrats are much weaker in low-income countries, and Ghana is not an exception to the rule. In the standard literature on decentralization and fiscal federalism, the focus is on allocation of funds, and it is implicitly assumed that allocated funds automatically reach their intended beneficiaries. This assumption needs to be drastically qualified in developing countries, where attention must be paid to special incentives and devices to check bureaucratic corruption-and thus the differential efficacy of such mechanisms under centralization and decentralization becomes important. This point has been brought home by Ahwoi (2011) that power decentralized to District Authorities as has been done in Ghana reveals 212 officials to be "inefficient, administratively unjust, incompetent and corrupt. It is therefore important that systems to check all those abuses are replicated at the destinations of the decentralized transfers. Unfortunately, central officials often use reasons of cost, human resource and logistical unavailability to fail or refuse to set up such systems, with the result that decentralized local authorities end up as inefficient, administratively unjust, incompetent and corrupt agencies of state power"(p. 7).

Another major issue of decentralization in Ghana is how to finance decentralization given the low levels of revenue for central government and low household incomes for the population. The decentralization process involves revenue mobilization from development partners to support its take off, and at the same time to be used as a strategy for local revenue generation to support sustainable local governance. Section 88 of the Local Government Act, Act 462 enjoins the District Assemblies not to raise draft or loan above GHC2000 without permission from the Minister of LGRD. This affects the ability of the District Authorities to be administratively responsible to the needs of the constituents.

Passivity and dependency syndrome on central government and external sources among the local population is a major drawback of decentralization in Ghana. It has been observed that because of the past experiences of dependence on central government, the majority of the population is passive and tend to depend on central government intervention or external assistance to solve problems pertaining to their communities for them.

Crawford (2004) observed that there is no commitment on the part of the central government to devolve power to the local government units. There is therefore much to prove that the 'autonomy' of local government is being compromised and undermined in several ways as the central government's control is obvious in many instances. This point has similarly been stressed by Ahwoi (2011) that lack of political will on the part of central government to cede adequate powers and financial resources to local authorities is done ostensibly hiding behind some unsubstantiated points such as lack of local capacity which to him can easily be addressed if the commitment is there. He therefore, puts it forcefully "The truth is that 'letting money go' within the public service is almost like committing bureaucratic suicide" (p. 7)

The issues of elected representative and the Presidents' appointment of thirty percent of District Assembly members as well as the appointment of the District Chief Executive (DCE) do not follow truly democratic principles. The fact that the District Chief Executive is the most powerful person and has oversight responsibility of the Assembly means that he/she will be influenced by the President and for that reason, policies and programs will be geared towards satisfying the President. The will of the people ultimately suffers under an appointee of the President who has his own agenda (Crawford, 2004).

The decentralization literature typically assumes that different levels of government all have similar levels of technical and administrative capacity with other professionals. It is an undeniable fact that efficient and professional cadre of local government staff is essential for local government to ensure high quality service delivery. It is important to note that qualified personnel to operate the various decentralized offices at the local level are inadequate. Most of the Assemblies find it difficult to recruit high quality personnel due to the under-developed nature of such Districts. Apart from the urban centers, the rural areas are unable to get personnel with the requisite skills and abilities (Hoffman et al., 2010). It is also evident that some level of local control of executive staff is essential for local accountability of staff and autonomous and responsive local government. However, local level control of staff has some underlying risks. The bias in selection of staff according to local preferences without due consideration to professional competencies and rather on familial relations is a serious threat to decentralization. Excessive local recruitment drives and non-payment of staff salaries or pension contributions, which leads to accumulated debts that ultimately may have to be carried by the central government undermine the decentralization effort.

Fiscal decentralization has also been an issue of much concern to many Assemblies in Ghana, especially those in the rural areas. There are not many businesses operating in the rural areas as compared to their urban counterparts who have a lot of economic activities going on. This makes the Assemblies in those rural communities difficult to raise the much needed revenue from taxation to support their developmental activities as well as to attract highly skilled personnel (Hoffman et al., 2010).

The Future of Decentralization in Ghana

In Ghana and Africa in general, decentralization by the colonial masters was not a conscious effort to really give self-determination and autonomy to the people at the local level but for administrative convenience. However, upon independence these same structures were inherited with minimal incremental efforts and reforms. Though some marginal successes are being achieved, it appears the local governments of Ghana still lack some considerable amounts of administrative responsibility.

Ahwoi (2011) provides some guiding principles for the future of African decentralization to be shaped around the following important canons:
- to make local governments more democratic and accountable
- emphasise decentralization as an essential component of the reforms
- the form of decentralization must be more of devolution than any of the other forms of decentralization such as de-concentration or delegation
- shift focus from the law and order local government systems of the first fifty years of independence to decentralized, "functional development" oriented local government systems (p.10)

A cursory diagnosis of pipeline projects and commission's reports seem to propose a better future for real political decentralization in Ghana. The argument and reality is that, the proper forms of decentralization in Ghana appear to be in the books, draft and always at the proposal stages which seem not to reach the implementation stage even after several years' of submitting commissions' reports. However, Sapru (2004) has argued that no matter how good the intention of any policy if it does not reach the implementation stage, it is as good as a 'dead lion' and of no effect.

The executive summary of the final report submitted by the Ghana Decentralization Policy Review (2007) has in it some useful proposals for proper sense of decentralization. Below are some of the proposals to shape the future of decentralization in Ghana.

i. decentralization must promote increased democratization of MMDAs: in the future the 30% appointments by the President into the various Assemblies and that the MMDCEs are to be elected by the people

ii. In the future accountability in decentralization must be clear and should be downward to the local electorates through their elected representatives

iii. The sub-district structures must properly be rationalized, their functions, membership and modes of election must clearly be known. They are to be adequately resourced.

Recommendation

Based on the study and the realization that the concept of decentralization is paramount and necessary for the development of the nation, these recommendations have been suggested to improve the efficiency of the system.

Financial issues should be given a second look into as the constitutional provisions place a ceiling on how much District Assemblies can borrow from financial institutions. Government should also ensure that an enabling business environment is created in the rural areas in order to attract many businesses to such areas. This will help increase the tax base of rural areas and their ability to fund and undertake many developmental projects. The principles and factors used in the sharing of the DACF should also be considered such that less developed Assemblies can be given enough funds to actually bridge the gap in terms of development between the urban and rural communities.

Furthermore, the powers that are conferred on the President with regard to the appointment of the District Assemblies, in addition to 30 percent of Assembly members should be reconsidered as this does not actually give the local people full control over how and what to use their resources for. Election of the DCE and all the assembly members will ensure that the local people take full control of their own developmental needs and to give their full support to projects undertaken. Participation of all stakeholders in every issue lends support of various forms especially the local people who can provide local data, communal labor and several others things which can reduce cost. In the current trend of appointments, where most Assembly members are not supportive of appointees by the President, it makes it difficult for such officers to perform creditably in ensuring quality development in their areas of jurisdiction. This point has forcefully been articulated by Antwi-Boasiako (2010, p. 174) that "allowing locals to elect their own political leaders is more likely to force local public officials to perform since failing to do so, may result in the electorates rejecting them in future elections"

Most District Assemblies are faced with the challenge of recruiting personnel with the requisite technical and managerial skills, aptitudes, knowledge and experiences to diligently discharge their assigned responsibilities dispassionately. It will be expedient and prudent for Assemblies to collaborate with the various tertiary institutions of learning to recruit some of their brilliant students especially those with specialization in public administration to work with the District Assemblies. Assemblies could also sponsor their own staff members to undertake some relevant courses that will enable them to perform creditably on the job.

All stakeholders should also be duly consulted and brought on board to seek diverse opinions in terms of planning and implementation of projects and programs of the Assembly. Politicians and the central government officials must also stop interfering in the work of the Assemblies and allow the local people to make decisions that best meet their local needs. Responsibilities given to local officials should come with the necessary authority and resources to ensure that they discharge their duties without problems.

For local government and decentralization system of governance to achieve the desired impact, authority, resources, and a well-planned checks and balances system must be put in place. The central government must be prepared to make the resources available in the right amount and at the right time. Several policies such as the appointment of the DCE's, appointment of 30% assembly members to the District Assemblies, the guidelines on fiscal decentralization, DACF and others should be looked at with all seriousness to ensure that decentralization in Ghana becomes a reality. Deductions at source of the DACF must not be encouraged and even in the extreme case where it is done, it must seek the overwhelming approval of the Assembly. The Assemblies must be given enough autonomy to use the Fund based on locally planned objectives, priorities and projects in order to meet the needs of the local community. This would encourage the concept of administrative responsibility where the Assemblies would be accountable and responsive to the needs of the local people in service provision.

References

Ahwoi, K. (2010). *Local Government and Decentralization in Ghana*, Accra, Ghana: Unimax, Macmillan.

Ahwoi, K.(2011). Challenges to effective decentralization in Africa. *33rd AAPAM Annual Roundtable Conference , Lilongwe: Malawi.*

Ahwoi, K. (2010), *Local Government and Decentralisation in Ghana.* Accra-Ghana: Unimax Macmillan Publishers Limited.

Antwi-Boasiako, K.B.(2010). "Public administration: Local government and Decentralization in Ghana." *Journal of African Studies and Development* Vol. 2(7), pp. 166-175

Asibuo, S.K. (1991). "Case Studies of African Experience in Decentralization in the 1970s and 1980s: Lessons for the 1990s." *The Journal of Management Studies. 3rd Series Vol. 7 pp 45-52*

Ayee J.R.A. (2008). Governance and Decentralization in Ghana-Retrospect and Prospects, Legon, University of Ghana.

Ayee, J.R.A.(1999). Ghana. In Public Administration in Africa: Main Issues and Selected Country Studies. Adamolekum,L(ed), 250-74. Boulder, CO: Westview Press.

Bhattacharya, M. (2008). *New Horizons of Public Administration.* New Delhi: Jawahar Publishers and Distributors.

Burki, S. J, Perry, G and Dillinger, W. (1999). *Beyond the Center: Decentralizing the State.* Washington D.C.: World Bank.

Cheema, G. S. and Rondinelli, D. A. (1983) 'Introduction' in G. S. Cheema and D. A. Rondinelli (eds), Decentralization and Development: policy implementation in developing countries (Sage, Beverly Hills, 1983), pp. 3-11

Constitution (1992). Constitution of the Republic of Ghana. Tema, Ghana Publishing Corporation.

Conyers, D. (2000): as cited by Ribot J. (2002) Ribot, J.C., 2002, *African Decentralisation: Local Actors, Powers and Accountability,* UNRISD Programme on Democracy, Governance and Human Rights Paper 8, Geneva: UNRISD.

Cornell University, (2006), "Decentralisation," Restructuring Local Government Home.United States Agency for International Development, (2009), Democratic Decentralization Programming Handbook, Washington, DC. Pg.9-16.

Crawford, G. (2004), Democratic Decentralisation in Ghana: Issues and Prospects (Working Paper No. 9). Leeds University, School of Politics and International Studies.Economic Commission for Africa. (2004). Public Sector Management Reforms in Africa: Lessons Learned (ECA/DPMD/PSM/TP/03/1). Addis Ababa: Ethiopia. Development Policy Management Division (DPMD).

Ghana Society for Development Dialogue Publications, (2008). Decentralization, Cities and Development: Some Retrospective Issues and Challenges. *The New Legon Observer*, *Vol.2.No.3.p1-5.*

Ghana, Republic of (1993). Local Government Act (Act 462). Accra.Government of Ghana and Development Partners.(2007). Decentralization Policy Policy Review. http://dege.dk/assets/files/DecentralizationPolicyReview.pdf.

Inman R, and Rubinfeld, D. (1997). "Rethinking federalism." *J. Econ. Pers, Fall: 43–64*James, E. (1982). "The Nonprofit Sector in International Perspective: The Case of Sri Lanka." *Journal of Comparative Economics*, vol. 6, no. 2 : 99-129.

Kaufman, H. (1969). Administrative Decentralisation and Political Power, In Tatom, D. , D. Bush, and H. Hogan (Ed), Classics of Public Administration (pp. 185-294). Wadsworth/ Thomson, U.S.A.

Khalil, H. (1970). "The Sudan Gezira Scheme: Some Institutional and Administrative

Aspects." *Journal of Administration Overseas*, vol. 9, no. 4: 273-85.

King, J. (1967). Economic Development Projects and Their Appraisal. Baltimore: Johns Hopkins University Press.

Kobia, M. (2011). Enhancing Public Service Delivery through Decentralization. *33rd AAPAM Annual Roundtable Conference , Lilongwe: Malawi.*

Maddick, H. (1963). *Democracy, Decentralization and Development*. Bombay: Asia Publishing House.

Mahwood, P.(1983). *Local Government in the Third World: The Experience of Tropical Africa.* John Wiley & Sons Limited, Chichester.

Oates W. (1972). *Fiscal Federalism*. New York: Harcourt, Brace, Jovanovich Ostrom, V. (1989). *The Intellectual Crisis in American Public administration.* Tuscaloosa: University of Alabama Press.

Oyugi, W. O. (2000): 'Decentralisation for Good Governance and Development: The unending debate." Regional Development Dialogue, Vol. 21, N0 1, spring, p.3-22.

Ribot, J.C. (2001). "Local Actors, Powers and Accountability in African Decentralization: A Review of Issues, *International Development Research Center*, Canada.

Rondinelli, D. A. (1981a). "Government Decentralization in Comparative Perspective: Theory and Practice in Developing Countries." *International Review of Administrative Sciences, XLVII (2): 133-145.*

Sapru, R.K. (2004). Public Policy: *Formulation, Implementation and Evaluation.* 2nd Ed. Sterling Publishers Private Limited. New Delhi.

Stone, D. (1997). Policy Paradox: The Art of Political Decision making. New York, W.W. Norton and Company.

Tiebout C. M. (1956). "A pure theory of local expenditure". *J. Polit. Econ.* 64:416–24

Tresiman, A. (2007*). Decentralization and Development Policy Implementation in Developing Countries. Decentralization in Ghana.* Beverly Hills: Sage.

United States Agency for International Development. (USAID). (2009), *Democratic Decentralization Programming Handbook.* Pennsylvania Avenue, NW Washington, DC. Office of Democracy and Governance (DG) of the U.S. Agency for International Development (USAID).

World Bank. (2000). *Entering the Twenty-First Century.* Oxford and New York: Oxford University Press.

Chapter Fourteen

MEDICAID: THE DECENTRALIZATION OF HEALTH POLICIES IN THE UNITED STATES AND PUERTO RICO

Minerva Cruz

Key words: health policy, decentralization, United States of America, Puerto Rico, Medicaid program

Introduction

The Social Security Amendments of 1965 created two programs, Medicare and Medicaid, to provide medical and health related benefits to people in the United States. Medicare provides benefits to older adults and disabled citizens. Medicaid covers the health care needs of individuals and families with low-income. Although some regulations from the Medicaid program work in a decentralized manner, in which the Federal and state governments share some responsibilities, both Medicaid and Medicare operate initially under a centralized system established by the Federal government. A centralized system is best understood as a legal authority with the power of making all major decisions related to a policy or program. Here, the concentration of power resides with the top management. In a decentralized system, however, the power of decision-making is shared between the higher and lower levels. The most important decisions may still be made at the top level, but the lower levels decide about how to better implement a policy or program according to their own needs. Yet, the authority delegated to the lower levels will depend in great part on the amount of power reserved at the top levels. This chapter focuses on Medicaid. It provides an overview of decentralization of policies involved with the Medicaid program in the United States and Puerto Rico and examines how the program works under the American Federal system.

In 1898, Puerto Rico became a territory of the United States, and in 1917, the United States Congress granted citizenship to all Puerto Ricans. By 1952, Puerto Rico achieved commonwealth status, which guarantees most of the benefits provided to other citizens. Therefore, Puerto Rico, as well as the states within the United States, enjoys Medicaid benefits. Although the Federal Government creates the Program and establishes general guidance for its administration, states and territories are allowed to decide about their specific criteria for eligibility. This allows localities to better address their specific needs. However, allocation of funds for the Medicaid Program is a great concern. The Federal Government shares the administration of the Program with the states and Puerto Rico and decides about the distribution of funding for the Program. Moreover, the Federal Government utilizes different criteria to allocate funds to Puerto Rico, compared to the states. As this chapter will show, the disparity of funds for the Medicaid Program limits the Puerto Rican government's ability to provide the health services needed in the country.

Decentralization is defined and the division of power between the Federal Government and localities is discussed. Next, an overview of the Medicaid Program in Puerto Rico and the United States is outlined. Then, the Medicaid services provided in Puerto Rico and Indiana are delineated. Indiana is used as a comparative study to show how the Medicaid Program in Puerto Rico compares to those in the states due to demographic differences between the two. Finally, the chapter discusses inadequate allocation of Medicaid funds to Puerto Rico and provides recommendations to improve the Program.

Decentralization in Government

Decentralization is defined by context. In terms of government procedures, the concept may be applied to the division of powers between the central government (e.g. federal government) and its localities (e.g. states). The literature popularly defines decentralization as a "transfer of planning, decision-making, or administrative authority from the central government to its field organizations, local administrative units, semi-autonomous and parastatal organizations, local governments, or nongovernmental organizations" (Rondinelli & Cheema, 1983, p. 18). It has also been defined as the "transference of power from larger to smaller units of government" (Yin, 1978, p. iii). Despite a variety of definitions, the concept of decentralization in government is usually employed to facilitate the distribution of power between the center of government and the different levels of government that exist in a particular country.

In a federal system, power is most often divided between the central government and state governments. The main objective is to guarantee the well-being of citizens, where each level of government carries out specific responsibilities within its own agencies. When the central government creates policies and calls for these policies to be implemented in an equitable manner, then the states are granted a level of decentralization in the implementation process, though they tend to carry them out following the specific terms and intentions defined by the central authority. While some policies cannot be changed or modified by localities, other policies can be created autonomously by the central authority for localities to implement according to their particular needs. Still other policies may be both created and implemented by localities (without any intervention from the central authority) to address the specific needs of constituents. In such cases, the national government may contribute financially for those policies to be successfully implemented. However, a disagreement between the central government and a locality may occur when each understands that it is directly responsible to the constituents. Here both face a difficulty, namely should policies be decentralized so that citizens are closer to government or should the centralized government apply policies uniformly despite the unique needs of constituents.

Stewart (1985, p. 26-27) developed a model to explain the relationship between the central and local governments. This model consists of several assumptions: First, central government has broad and different interests while subject to a diversity of pressures. Second, central governments cannot be considered as having a clear set of policy aims. Third, the different departments of central government cannot be considered as possessing clear aims for a large range of their activities, instead they are pleased to deal with issues "'on their merits'" (p. 27). Fourth, the balance of power of the different interests between and within departments of central government varies. Fifth, the policy instruments of central governments to control local authorities are often not designed for the objectives for which they are used. Lastly, the information available to guide central government to use policy instruments is fragmented.

The perceptions between the central and local governments as to how they might better respond to their constituents remain unclear. The proposal may come from the national government, which may create a policy and require localities to implement it, while retaining the fiscal control over that policy. Alternatively, the national government may allow localities to create and implement policies with the locale authority retaining responsible for controlling both the taxing and spending powers. In such cases, decentralization is perceived as a means to divide the power concentrated in the central government to encourage broader citizen participation.

Proponents of decentralization point out several advantages of this approach. Decentralization allows average citizens better access to the state and ensures a counterbalance to the abuse of power by national leaders (Selee, 2004, p. 4). In addition, decentralization in government allows for speed in the decision making process, since decisions are made according to local conditions and local situation (Baum, 1961). Decentralization also promotes more participation in democratic governance ("Fiscal decentrali[z]ation, now," 2011, p. 1). For instance, acting President John Nkomo from South Africa supported the decentralization of services in government and indicated that decentralization will make it possible for individuals not to go far to Harare each time to get simple things that are essential (e.g. birth certificates). He stated, "'[g]overnment departments and various administrative structures should be all over the country so that people access them and feel that they are part of governance'" ("No to devolution," 2011, p. 1). Hence, policies that are decentralized seek to better serve local needs.

Rondinelli, Nellis, & Cheema (1984, p. 5-9) point out several objectives that decentralization in government expects to fulfill:

> (1) Decentralization will reduce overload in the channels of administration and communication. That is, there is an expectation that delays will be minimum and that administrators will satisfy the needs of their clientele.
> (2) Decentralization is a means to manage national economic development more effectively.
> (3) Decentralization is a way to provide support for national development policies by making them better known at the local level.

(4)   Decentralization can create larger numbers of skilled administrators and managers, since those skills are strengthened when administrators have meaningful responsibilities in management.

(5)   Many functions carried out by central governments are poorly performed because of the inconvenience of extending services from the center to the localities. Decentralization will improve those services.

Decentralization of policies is intended to better serve the needs of their recipients. However, the process of decentralization may not fulfill its objectives when the center and localities do not work together or share the same priorities. The different priorities that sometimes exist between the central government and localities may affect both the efficiency and effectiveness of policies during implementation (see Webb & Wistow (1985) for a comprehensive evaluation of policies between the center and locality in the area of social services). In addition, policies may fail when there is not an appropriate balance of power, resources, and incentives between the central and local governments (see Stoten (1985) for an assessment of health policies between central and local governments).

Health policies in general often offer examples of decentralization. Medicaid is an appealing program to observe in evaluating decentralization, particularly because it allows for the examination of the division of power between the center and localities, namely the Federal Government and states in the Union and Puerto Rico. In addition, since Puerto Rico is a territory, it will be interesting to assess how the Medicaid Program works in a territory as compared to states.

Medicaid Program in Puerto Rico

Christopher Columbus discovered Puerto Rico for Spain on November 19, 1493. In 1898, under the provision of the Treaty of Paris, Spain ceded the country to the United States, and Puerto Rico became a territory. In 1917, Puerto Ricans became citizens of the United States, and by 1952, the country became a Commonwealth (*Estado Libre Asociado* in Spanish). Puerto Rico is subject to most federal laws and policies and it is thus entitled to most of the rights and benefits enjoyed by citizens of the states. Lewis (1953) describes the relationship between Puerto Rico and the United States:

The people of Puerto Rico, organized politically as the Commonwealth of Puerto Rico, will be able to satisfy their nationalist aspirations at the same time that they retain their membership in the Union as American citizens. They become a "free associated state"; that- is, a political society enjoying full local self-government and associated with the United States by a contractual union to which they have given their formal consent (p. 42).

English and Spanish are both official languages in Puerto Rico, though Spanish has remained the primary spoken language in the country (see Morris [1995]) for additional information related to culture, politics, and identity in Puerto Rico). Most Puerto Ricans consider themselves Hispanic, are Catholics, and share values of family unity and protection of family members (see Table 1). According to the U.S. 2010 Census, the total population in Puerto Rico is 3,725,789 (http://www.census.gov/geo/www/guidestloc/st72_pr.html) and approximately 45% of the total population is below poverty levels (www.census.gov/prod/2011pubs/acsbr10-01.pdf).

14.1. Main Characteristics of Puerto Rico

Ethnicity	Predominantly Hispanic
Language	Spanish
Values	Community-oriented Family unity, support, cooperation, and protection of family members*
Religion	Mainly Catholic

*Sources. Zayas, L. H., & Palleja, J. (1988). Puerto Rican familism: Considerations for family therapy. *Family Relations*, 37, 260-264. (Table adapted from Cruz, M. (2011). Are older adults satisfied with the implementation of federal programs to serve aging populations? A case study policy implementation. *Home Health Care Management & Practice*, 23(6), 404-411).

On January 1st 1966, the Medicaid Program began in Puerto Rico. The Program works as a health care delivery system that is publicly-owned and centrally administered (Pagan-Berlucchi & Muse, 1983). Known locally as *Mi Salud* ("My Health"), it provides services to low-income individuals. In each municipality of the country, a local Medicaid office decides eligibility and applies regulations to beneficiaries. To be eligible for these services, individuals must have American citizenship. Foreigners permitted to live in the United States are also eligible for the Program in Puerto Rico (Cruz, 2011). As of July 1, 2010, there were 1,037,552 people enrolled in Medicaid in the country[1]. This accounts for 27.8% of the total population in Puerto Rico.

Medicaid in the United States and Puerto Rico

Despite Puerto Rico being a territory and its citizens enjoying most rights granted to other citizens, the Medicaid Program in Puerto Rico operates in a distinctly different way from the programs on the mainland. In the states, the Program does not work as a government health insurance providing benefits to low-income people through a 'universal plan system.' Indeed, each state decides how to better serve the needs of their low-income people. For instance, contrary to Medicaid in Puerto Rico where the Program is largely 'one size fits all,' Medicaid in Indiana offers several program options to meet the needs of its different groups of people. Each of these options offers different healthcare solutions and has different requirements (http://member.indianamedicaid.com/programs--benefits. aspx). Some of the programs available are: *Hoosier Healthwise, Presumptive Eligibility, Care Select, Healthy Indiana Plan (HIP), Traditional Medicaid, M.E.D. Works, Waivers, Medicaid Pharmacy Benefits*, and

Family Planning Eligibility Program.

The "Hoosier Healthwise" program is designed for low-income families, children, and pregnant women. It provides medical care like prescription medicine, mental health care, doctor visits, surgeries, hospitalizations, and family planning at little or no cost to the individual. The program covers children under the age of 19, pregnant women, and parents or guardians of children under 18 years old. Beneficiaries will choose a health plan and the health care providers participating in that plan. The health plans available are: Anthem, MDwise, and Managed Health Services (MHS).

The "Presumptive Eligibility" program covers pregnant women who are low-income and are applying for Medicaid. Through this program, women receive temporary coverage of important prenatal care while waiting for the Medicaid application to be approved. Pregnant women needing assistance from Medicaid should contact their doctors or clinics to ask for assistance applying for this program and Medicaid. Women who are already receiving Medicaid services or living in another state than in Indiana cannot apply for this program.

The "Care Select" program covers beneficiaries with special health needs or who required specialized attention (e.g. blind, disabled, and aged). It also covers people with certain medical conditions, such as asthma, diabetes, depression, severe mental illness, and heart disease. The beneficiary chooses a doctor and a health plan from the Care Management Organizations (CMOs) contracted with the State. Some of the services covered under the Care Select plan are: preventive services, disease management, eye care, home health care & services, transportation, dental, pregnancy care, emergency care, inpatient and outpatient hospital care, and behavior and mental health services.

The "Healthy Indiana Plan (HIP)" is designed for people who do not live with a dependent child and parents with income less than $44,000 annually for a family of four, without insurance for six months and without insurance from an employer. The plan was created by Governor Daniels and the Indiana General Assembly in 2007 to benefit uninsured people in Indiana between 19-64 years old. It covers health benefits, such as hospital services, mental health care, prescriptions, physician services, and diagnostic exams.

The "Traditional Medicaid" provides health care coverage to people with low-income. It covers a variety of expenses, such as doctor visits, dental and vision care, family planning, mental health care, surgeries, prescription drugs, and hospitalizations. This program covers people from the following categories: blind, aged, Medicaid waiver program recipient, undocumented aliens, members in the hospice program, physically or mentally disabled, dually eligible for Medicare & Medicaid, and members in nursing homes, intermediate care facilities for the mentally retarded and state-operated facilities.

The "M.E.D. Works" plan, Medicaid for Employees with Disabilities, covers working people with disabilities. It allows disabled persons to be employed without losing health care benefits, by paying a small monthly premium based on income. To receive benefits, people must: (1) be between 16 and 64 years old, (2) be working, (3) meet the definition of disability according to Indiana's definition, and (4) meet income and assets guidelines according to the 'Poverty Guidelines for the 48 Contiguous States and the District of Columbia.' The program provides the same services as the regular Medicaid. Thus, people receiving Medicaid because of their disability can work and receive benefits under M. E. D. Works.

The "Waivers" program helps certain groups of people (e.g. aged and disabled, developmentally disabled) to live in a community setting thereby avoiding institutional placement. Under this program, people are not required admission into an institution for Medicaid to pay Home and Community-Based Services (HCBS). The waiver programs are operated by the Office of Medicaid Policy and Planning (OMPP). There are five waiver services programs: (1) Aged and Disabled Waiver, (2) Traumatic Brain Injury Waiver, (3) Community Integration and Habilitation Waiver, (4) Family Supports Waiver, and (5) Psychiatric Residential Treatment Facility (PRTF) transition waiver.

Medicaid Pharmacy Benefits are provided through several major pharmacies in Indiana (e.g. CVS, Rite Aid, Walgreens Pharmacy, Wal-Mart Pharmacy, Kroger, K-Mart, and Marsh). Medications can be obtained in two ways: the doctor can write a prescription and contact the pharmacy or the beneficiary can take the prescription directly to the pharmacy. The chosen pharmacy must accept Indiana Medicaid.

Finally, the Family Planning Eligibility Program provides services and supplies to women and men to prevent or delaying pregnancy. Some of the covered services are: Pap smears, tubal ligation, vasectomies, annual family planning visits, follow-up care for complications associated with contraceptive methods, hysteroscopy sterilization with an implant device, and initial diagnosis and treatment for sexually transmitted diseases and sexually transmitted infections if medically indicated. It does not cover services such as: abortions, artificial insemination, fertility drugs, and other services unrelated to family planning.

Compared to most states, Puerto Rico has a significantly higher number of people below the poverty level. By July 2010, the U.S. Census Bureau reported that 45% of Puerto Rico's 4 million people were below the poverty level (www.census.gov/prod/2011pubs/acsbr10-01.pdf). Mississippi, listed as the poorest state (by percentage of population) in the Nation has a total population of 2,979,000 (https://www.census.gov/popest/data/national/totals/2011/index.html), but experienced only about half that percentage at 22.4% (www.census.gov/prod/2011pubs/acsbr10-01.pdf), a difference of 23% of the total in Puerto Rico. Compared to Mississippi, the territory of Puerto Rico has almost 2 million people considered below the poverty level, while the poorest state totals about a million. Additionally, the median household income in Puerto Rico in 2010 was $18,862, while in Mississippi the median household income was $36,851 (http://www.census.gov/prod/2011pubs/acsbr10-02.pdf), a difference of $17,989, almost double the income in Puerto Rico. Other states with populations similar to Puerto Rico appear to have higher median household incomes but fewer people below the poverty level (see Table 2). Regarding this situation, Congressman Pedro R. Pierluisi[2] (2012) stated:

> The Federal government pays a significant share of the program's cost in the states—and up to 80 percent in the poorest states. By contrast, federal law imposes a cap on funding to Puerto Rico. Before 2009, Puerto Rico's cap was so low that the federal government paid under 20 percent of the program's costs on the Island each year. This has made it difficult for Puerto Rico to provide quality health care to our most vulnerable residents. It has also required the Puerto Rico government to spend a tremendous amount of its own funds to compensate for the shortfall in federal dollars, which has caused damage to the Island's fiscal health" (p. 2).

14.2: People in Poverty and Median Household Income for Selected States and Puerto Rico

Location	Population[a] April 1, 2010	Median Household[b] Income 2012 (in $)	Below Poverty[c] In 2012 (in %)
Connecticut	3,574,097	64,032	10.1
Iowa	3,046,355	47,961	12.6
Kentucky	4,339,367	40,062	19.0
Mississippi	2,967,297	36,851	22.4
Oklahoma	3,751,351	42,072	16.9
Oregon	3,831,074	46,560	15.8
Perto Rico	3,725,789	18,862	45.0

Sources: [a]U. S. Census Bureau; Population Division. (2011, December). *Annual estimates of the population for the United States, regions, states, and Puerto Rico: April 1, 2010 to July 1, 2011*. Retrieved March 6, 2012, from https://www.census.gov/popest/data/national/totals/2011/index.html

[b]U. S. Census Bureau; 2009 and 2010 American Community Surveys, 2009 and 2010 Puerto Rico Community Surveys. (n.d.). *Median household income and Gini index in the past 12 months by state and Puerto Rico: 2009 and 2010*. Retrieved March 6, 2012, from http://www.census.gov/prod/2011pubs/acsbr10-02.pdf

[c]U. S. Census Bureau; 2009 and 2010 American Community Surveys, 2009 and 2010 Puerto Rico Community Surveys. (n.d.). *Number and Percentage of People in Poverty in the Past 12 Months by State and Puerto Rico: 2009 and 2010*. Retrieved March 6, 2012, from www.census.gov/prod/2011pubs/acsbr10-01.pdf

Coady et al[3] also explain the Federal financial 'cap' for Medicaid in Puerto Rico this way:

> Unlike the 50 states and Washington, D.C., the amount of Federal Medicaid funding which Puerto Rico can receive is subject to a statutory cap. The ceiling was $250.4 million in Federal fiscal year (FFY) 2007. By statute, the Federal medical assistance percentage for Puerto Rico is 50 percent. Based on data from CMS' New York Regional Office, total State and Federal Medicaid expenditures in Puerto Rico for FFY 2007 were $1,103,720,336. Of this figure, the allowable Federal financial participation (FFP) was $390,696,174, or 35 percent (p. 4).

Although Puerto Rico's Medicaid Program operates under a financial 'cap' created by the Federal Government, laws recently enacted now make it possible for the Program to receive additional federal contributions. Indeed, in 2009, the American Recovery and Reinvestment Act (ARRA) was created as an economic stimulus package to assist Americans during the recession in areas such as education, health, and jobs creation. ARRA provided additional funds to the Medicaid Program in Puerto Rico. The Act raised the annual federal contribution to the Medicaid Program in Puerto Rico by 30 percent, which represented more than $185 million in additional federal funding for the health care program in Puerto Rico ("Pierluisi highlights the positive impact," 2010). The Education Jobs and Medicaid Assistance Act extended that 30% for an additional six months, until June 30, 2011 (Ibid). In addition, the Affordable Care Act of 2010 increased federal funding for Medicaid in Puerto Rico, and was enacted as a health care law to improve the current health care system in the United States and to provide new protections for individuals with health insurance. Regarding the Affordable Care Act, Pierluisi (2012) states, "[u]nder the Affordable Care Act, federal funding for Puerto Rico's Medicaid program, *Mi Salud*, will essentially triple over the next decade, from $3.1 billion dollars to $9.4 billion dollars. Instead of receiving about $300 million dollars a year, [Puerto Rico] will now receive over $1 billion dollars annually (p. 3). The funding will be provided until fiscal year 2019 ("Speaker Pelosi briefed," 2010).

Medicaid: Policy Implications and Recommendations

Based on the available data, one can safely conclude that Puerto Rico does not receive a typical state's share in Federal contributions for its Medicaid Program. However, because of recent legislation, the Medicaid Program in Puerto Rico will receive additional funding from the Federal Government, until fiscal year 2019, with most funds injected into "*Mi Salud*". But, what will happen after fiscal year 2019? It appears that prior to fiscal year 2019, Puerto Rican representatives in Washington will again need to negotiate with the Federal Government to receive the additional federal funding necessary for Puerto Rico's Medicaid Program to retain its now quasi-equitable status. Given the unfavorable economic conditions in the country, the Puerto Rican government will continue to face difficulties providing affordable health care to low-income individuals without the equitable contributions due from the Federal Government. Moreover, the situation may be further exacerbated if the unemployment rate in Puerto Rico remains high and the median household income remains below the poverty level.

An important characteristic of decentralized systems is that the central government encourages local participation. Since 1965, the administration of the Medicaid Program in the United States has operated following a decentralized approach. The Federal Government creates regulations but allows localities to choose the best way to implement the Program according to their needs. As such, each state and Puerto Rico implement the Program differently. As previously shown, the services that localities offer under Medicaid depend in great part on the Federal contributions received to administer the Program.

Because of the federal spending caps applied to the territories, the Puerto Rican government does not have the opportunity to choose, and thus, cannot offer certain health care services under its Medicaid Program that states may offer. For instance, Puerto Rico has designed a health care system "*Mi Salud*" to afford its Medicaid and to respond to the needs of its beneficiaries on the Island while Indiana can provide several types of programs to low-income individuals under its Medicaid Program. The Federal Government shares the administration of the Program with states and Puerto Rico but maintains the power to control the financial resources to fund the Program. If the intention of the Federal Government is to effectively decentralize Medicaid, then more power in the decision making process and the allocation of funds should be given to localities.

Rondinelli, Nellis, & Cheema (1984, p. 46) propose four main factors affecting the successful implementation of decentralization:

1.Support from central political leaders to decentralization and the organizations to which responsibilities are transferred, 2. Dominant behavior, attitudes, and culture are conducive to decentralized decision making and administration, 3. Policies that are designed and organized to promote decentralized decision making and management, and 4. Adequate human, financial, and physical resources that are made available to the organizations to which responsibilities are transferred.

Therefore, to implement decentralized policies successfully, the American Federal Government should support its localities by making adequate financial resources available to them. As Rondinelli, Nellis, & Cheema (1984) put it, "[d]ecentralization policies that transfer adequate financial resources as well as powers and responsibilities will be more successful than those that merely call for consultation with or participation of local officials or citizenry" (p. 75).

Conclusion

This chapter has provided an overview of how the Medicaid Program operates in states and territories of the United States. Medicaid is a health care program that provides benefits to low-income individuals in the United States and its territories. Because of the political relationship between Puerto Rico and the United States, citizens of Puerto Rico are entitled to most of the benefits enjoyed by citizens of the states. As shown, the administration of the Medicaid Program works in a decentralized way, where the Federal Government designs policies but allows localities to implement such policies according to their particular needs. Yet, it begs the question of equity between the central government and the state/territorial governments.

The Medicaid Program in Puerto Rico works differently from those in the states, as federal regulations have created a "cap" in the Federal contribution to the Medicaid Program in the Island. Because of the limited amount in Federal contribution, the Puerto Rican government utilizes that contribution to provide health care through a health care plan, "*Mi Salud*". To effectively carry out the objectives involved in decentralization, the Federal Government should review its intentions of decentralizing Medicaid policies by providing localities with more power and financial resources.

ENDNOTES

1   See (http://www.google.com/url?sa=t&rct=j&q=&esrc=s&frm=1&source=web&cd=2&sqi=2 &ved=0CDoQFjAB&url=http%3A%2F%2Fwww.cms.gov%2FResearch-Statistics-Data-and-Systems%2FComputer-Data-and-Systems%2FMedicaidDataSourcesGenInfo%2Fdownloads%2F20 10July1.pdf&ei=w2w5UdSYL8y60QGd9YDQDA&usg=AFQjCNGM5al1Osp_7xtvpj0BooG3nH3 keA&sig2=-pbOozJNByb21kQ29RHgHw)

2   Congressman Pierluisi is the Resident Commissioner of Puerto Rico to the United States Congress. He has delivered several speeches related to the contribution of federal funding in Puerto Rico.

3   Coady, J., Charleston, M., Fitzpatrick, R., Jackson, T., & Mateo, M. (http://www.google.com/url?sa= t&rct=j&q=&esrc=s&frm=1&source=web&cd=1&sqi=2&ved=0CDIQFjAA&url=http%3A%2F%2 Fwww.cms.gov%2FMedicare-Medicaid-Coordination%2FFraud-Prevention%2FFraudAbuseforProf s%2FDownloads%2FPRfy08.pdf&ei=efg5UbS9HeS20QHbzYDACw&usg=AFQjCNHC7CanqYtF VuyCAf8gZPOQpNI8lw&sig2=1QQgD960lys3gviFs6QzAQ&bvm=bv.43287494,d.dmQ)

References

Baum, B. H. (1961). *Decentralization of authority in a bureaucracy.* Englewood Cliffs, NJ: Prentice- Hall, Inc.

Centers for Medicaid and Medicaid Services.(2012). *Medicaid Managed Care Enrollment As of July 1, 2010.* Retrieved March 6, 2012, from http://www.google.com/url?sa=t&rct=j&q =&esrc=s&frm=1&source=web&cd=2&sqi=2&ved=0CDoQFjAB&url=http%3A%2F% 2Fwww.cms.gov%2FResearch-Statistics-Data-and-Systems%2FComputer-Data-and-Sy stems%2FMedicaidDataSourcesGenInfo%2Fdownloads%2F2010July1.pdf&ei=w2w5U dSYL8y60QGd9YDQDA&usg=AFQjCNGM5al1Osp_7xtvpj0BooG3nH3keA&sig2=-pbOozJNByb21kQ29RHgHw

Cruz , L. (2011). *Working together to serve our beneficiaries. Medicaid eligibility, Medicaid/ASES.* 2011 Medicare Symposium- Puerto Rico, p. 1-8.

Cruz, M. (2011). Are older adults satisfied with the implementation of federal programs t o serve aging populations? A case study policy implementation. *Home Health Care Management & Practice, 23*(6), 404-411.

Department of Health and Human Services; Centers for Medicare & Medicaid Services. Coady, J., Charleston, M., Fitzpatrick, R., Jackson, T., & Mateo, M. (2009, September). *Medicaid Integrity Program. Puerto Rico comprehensive program integrity review. Final report.* Retrieved March 7, 2012, from http://www.google.com/url?sa=t&rct=j&q=&esrc=s&fr m=1&source=web&cd=1&sqi=2&ved=0CDIQFjAA&url=http%3A%2F%2Fwww.cms. gov%2FMedicare-Medicaid-Coordination%2FFraud- Prevention%2FFraudAbusefor Profs%2FDownloads%2FPRfy08.pdf&ei=efg5UbS9HeS2 0QHbzYDACw&usg=AFQjC NHC7CanqYtFVuyCAf8gZPOQpNI8lw&sig2=1QQgD96 0lys3gviFs6QzAQ&bvm=bv.4 3287494,d.dmQ

Fiscal decentrali[z]ation, now. (2011, May 30). *The Friday Times*, Retrieved from ProQuest Newsstand database.

Indiana Medicaid. (2012). *Programs and benefits.* Retrieved March 14, 2012, from http://member.indianamedicaid.com/programs--benefits.aspx.

Morris, N. (1995). *Puerto Rico: Culture, politics, and identity.* Westport, CT: Greenwood Publishing Group, Inc.

No to devolution of power, says Nkomo. (2011, June 22). *AllAfrica.com.* p. 1-2. Retrieved from ProQuest Newsstand database.

Pagan-Berlucchi, A. & Muse, D. N. (1983). The Medicaid Program in Puerto Rico: Description, Context, and Trends. *Health Care Financing Review, 4*(4), 1-17.

Pierluisi highlights the positive impact of federal health care reform in Puerto Rico. (2010, August 13). *Targeted News Service.* Retrieved from ProQuest Newsstand database.

Pierluisi, Pedro R. (2012). *2012 Puerto Rico health & insurance conference, economic transformation in health*. Conrad San Juan Condado Plaza, p. 1-7.

Rondinelli, D. A. & Cheema, G. S. (1983). Implementing decentralization policies. An introduction. In G. S. Cheema & D. A. Rondinelli (Eds.), *Decentralization and development: Policy implementation in developing countries* (pp. 9-32). California: Sage Publications.

Rondinelli, D. A., Nellis, J. R., & Cheema, G. S. (1984). *Decentralization in developing countries. A review of recent experience*. Washington, DC: The World Bank.

Selee, A. (2004). Exploring the link between decentralization and democratic governance. In J. S. Tulchin & A. Selee (Eds.), *Decentralization and democratic governance in Latin America* (pp. 3-36). Washington, DC: Woodrow Wilson International Center for Scholars.

Speaker Pelosi briefed on Puerto Rico's use of federal ARRA and Affordable Care Act funds. (2010, September 27). *Targeted News Service*, Retrieved from ProQuest Newsstand database.

Stewart, J. (1985). Dilemmas. The dilemma of local government. In S. Ranson, G. Jones, & K. Walsh (Eds.), *Between centre and locality. The politics of public policy* (pp. 23-35). London: George Allen & Unwin Ltd.

Stoten, Bryan. (1985). Health. Introduction: Centre-local dilemmas in the NHS. In S. Ranson, G. Jones, & K. Walsh (Eds.),*Between centre and locality. The politics of public policy* (pp. 225-239). London: George Allen & Unwin Ltd.

U. S. Census Bureau; 2009 and 2010 American Community Surveys, 2009 and 2010 Puerto Rico Community Surveys. (n.d.). *Median household income and Gini index in the past 12 months by state and Puerto Rico: 2009 and 2010*. Retrieved March 6, 2012, from http://www.census.gov/prod/2011pubs/acsbr10-02.pdf.

U. S. Census Bureau; 2009 and 2010 American Community Surveys, 2009 and 2010 Puerto Rico Community Surveys. (n.d.). *Number and Percentage of People in Poverty in the Past 12 Months by State and Puerto Rico: 2009 and 2010*. Retrieved March 6, 2012, from www.census.gov/prod/2011pubs/acsbr10-01.pdf.

U. S. Census Bureau; Geography Division. (2011, September). *Puerto Rico*: Basic information. Retrieved March 7, 2012, from http://www.census.gov/geo/www/guidestloc/st72_pr.html

U. S. Census Bureau; Population Division. (2011, December). *Annual estimates of the population for the United States, regions, states, and Puerto Rico: April 1, 2010 to July 1, 2011*. Retrieved March 6, 2012, from https://www.census.gov/popest/data/national/totals/2011/index.html.

Webb, A. & Wistow, G. (1985). Social services: Introduction. In S. Ranson, G. Jones, & K. Walsh (Eds.), *Between centre and locality. The politics of public policy* (pp. 207-223). London: George Allen & Unwin Ltd.

Yin, R. K. (1978). *Decentralization of government agencies: What does it accomplish?* California: The Rand Cooperation.

Zayas, L. H., & Palleja, J. (1988). Puerto Rican familism: Considerations for family therapy. *Family Relations, 37,* 260-264.

Chapter Fifteen

CLUSTER POLICIES IN THE U.S. STATES: THE EFFECTS ON JOB CREATION AND FIRM FORMATION IN HIGH-TECH INDUSTRIES

Alexandra Tsvetkova

Key words: clusters, cluster policies, job creation, high-technology sectors

Introduction

The American federal system allows states to pursue their own economic development (ED) policies in accordance with current demands and available resources. States frequently become 'laboratories of democracy', as they try novel social and economic experiments in a search for their own response to external and internal economic and political pressures (Gray & Hanson, 2008). In the case of success, such experiments may become the models for other states with similar conditions. Sometimes federal programs use successful state policies as a template.

In his seminal book on city politics, Paul Peterson (1981) argues that cities seek to pursue their economic goals and to enhance their economic status, while citizens choose among local jurisdictions as postulated by Tiebout (1956). Hwang and Gray (1991) contend that Peterson's logic extends to any set of sub-national units in competition with one another. States try to maximize their economic interests by adopting various policies within certain limits imposed by the structure of the national economy. Peterson (1995) argues that state and local governments should assume primary responsibility for enhancing their competitiveness. In his view, lower tiers of government are best equipped to design and administer ED programs because of pressures from both market and political forces. The federal government, in contrast, often lacks the ability to perceive market signals that may help it choose among alternative development proposals.

States may employ various approaches to boost their economic performance. Cluster-based initiatives became very popular in the last two decades (Solvell, Lindqvist, & Ketels, 2003). Some scholars argue, however, that successful cluster examples are the result of a particular and unique set of underlying characteristics that happen to work together towards a vibrant cluster formation by pure chance (Wolfe & Gertler, 2004). Skeptics doubt policy-makers' ability to understand how clusters work and to design wise programs conducive to sustained growth of a cluster (Aziz & Norhashim, 2008). Palazuelos (2005) acknowledges the potential of cluster policies to bring about desired results; yet, he finds no systematic empirical support for cluster superiority. He argues that few regions have preconditions for flourishing clusters.

The existing evidence on the achievements of the clustered sectors and industries is largely based on the "natural" clusters, which emerged and developed under the influence of market forces. One should not readily take such evidence as a proof that cluster policies inevitably lead to formation and development of successful clusters. Instead, further research distinguishing the effects of "natural" clusters and cluster policies on state economic performance is needed.

This chapter contributes to the literature by testing empirically the effects of cluster policies, in addition to the effects of clusters, on job creation and the number of firms in four U.S. high-technology industries. The results of panel data estimation suggest no positive relationship between state cluster initiatives on the one hand, and employment and the number of firms on the other. The research points out the limits of the U.S. states' ability to influence economic performance in selected industries by supporting high-tech clusters.

The chapter is organized as follows. The next section is devoted to economic development policies in general. It briefly discusses various levels of government and their role in economic development. Section 3 describes two major types of state ED programs, locational and entrepreneurial. Section 4 reviews cluster theory and cluster policies. Section 5 takes a closer look at high-tech cluster policies in the U.S. Sections 5 and 6 introduce research design, estimation results, and discussion followed by conclusions.

Levels of Government and Their Role in Economic Development

Cities, states, and national governments differ in their ability to implement various policies (Peterson, 1981). Local governments cannot declare war, erect tariff barriers, and prevent people from moving to their jurisdictions. Natural limits of power require that each level of government concentrates on the policies that it performs the best. Economic development policies in the U.S. are widely designed and implemented at all levels of the government. So, what level is the most appropriate for ED policies? There is no unequivocal answer to this question. Design and implementation of economic development policies at each level of the government have their advantages and limitations.

Delegation of responsibility for economic growth to the lower levels of government goes in line with economic efficiency argument. The closer the design of a policy to the market, the stronger the market's signals are. This ensures sensitivity of a program to existing demands and an opportunity for faster adjustments if something goes wrong. On the other hand, successful economic development efforts often require recourses available only at higher levels of government. Besides, efficiency considerations call for internalization of externalities, both positive and negative, associated with economic growth. If ED policies are implemented at lower levels of government, such internalization may be impossible. In general, an optimal level of government to develop and implement an economic development policy depends on the policy at hand, its scope, required resources, and other characteristics.

Federal level. The federal government has always been an active player in economic development and planning on a national scale, as well as in specific states and localities. The government performs the 'framing' functions by establishing legal, business, and regulatory frameworks. It is solely responsible for monetary policy that influences macroeconomic performance of the country. In addition, it is involved in a variety of specific economic growth programs and initiatives through numerous grants, usually intended for building physical infrastructure, such as highways, housing, and airports (Drabenstott, 2006). Nevertheless, the federal government is not well suited for the purposes of specific ED initiatives and programs. Peterson (1981) shows that it is better equipped to deal with redistributive functions due to its ability to control movement of people, capital, goods and services and to minimize efficiency loss resulting from such policies.

Local level. Public choice literature, very influential in the 1960s and 1970s, makes perhaps the strongest case for provision of public goods at a local (city, municipality, community) level. Economic growth is considered a public good by this tradition (Logan & Molotch, 1987); therefore, locality is best suited to design and implement ED programs. The logic of the public choice view is rather straightforward. Because residents are presumed to 'shop' around communities to find the one best serving their needs (Tiebout, 1956), communities and localities constitute something like a competitive market. Residents choose a place to live rationally taking into account the ratio of costs and benefits associated with a bundle of public services offered by a community (Peterson, 1981). Likewise, elected officials, being aware of such considerations, attempt to tailor the supply of public services and goods in a way that maximizes their jurisdictions' wellbeing by attracting desired types of residents. The jurisdictions constantly compete for wealthy residents and businesses (Basolo, 2003). To succeed, cities and municipalities have to concentrate on economic development programs, which respond to the existing demands and utilize local resources. Community residents (interested in their property values) can be expected to pressure the governments to use resources efficiently. At the same time, local governments have strong incentives to gather information on the optimal ways of public service provision.

Regional level. Regional approach offers yet another level for the design and implementation of economic growth initiatives. Regional level usually embraces several jurisdictions such as a central city with its suburbs, or several municipalities. Typically, there is no governmental structure in place to govern such a region. Often regional efforts, including those related to economic development, rely on cooperative agreements and *ad hoc* arrangements. One municipality may be a part of different regions for the purposes of various initiatives. The constituent parts of a region do not compete among themselves; they rather unite to provide a unified delivery of certain services based on economies of scale and efficiency. This stands in sharp contrast to the public choice theory, which champions competition among localities[1].

State level. Practically all arguments for local governments as the best designers of ED policies are applicable at a state level (Hwang & Gray, 1991). Even Peterson (1995), furthering his argument for superiority of the city (or the lowest possible) level when it comes to ED initiatives, refers to changes in federal vs. *state* expenditures on developmental and redistributive policies. At any rate, states are perhaps the most active players in the field of economic development, which has been an important part of state planning for more than thirty years (Peters & Fisher, 2004). By implementing various economic growth programs, state policy-makers attempt to increase employment, enhance economic activity and welfare in their jurisdictions. If successful, ED policies attract capital to a state, amplify its visibility and bargaining power *vis-à-vis* the federal center, and increase state politicians' chances to be reelected.

States have the advantages of (relatively) 'small is better' approach to economic growth as compared to the federal level. At the same time, states have more power and resources to implement economic strategies compared to cities. Greater resources allow states to be engaged in various types of developmental polices (infrastructure-related, locational, and entrepreneurial). States build infrastructure, such as highways, bridges, sewers, and waste treatment plans, in order to provide necessary conditions for business to flourish (Saiz & Clarke, 2008) Locational incentives seek to attract new industries and enterprises to an area by offering tax breaks and other incentives (Turner & Cassell, 2007). Entrepreneurial strategies attempt to 'self-generate' industrial capital formation by promoting firms' growth potential (Hart, 2008; Teitz, 1994).

Locational vs. entrepreneurial ED policies

Over the years, ED programs have been extensively implemented all over the country, while continuously evolving in nature and scope in response to new challenges. The "locational" ED strategies have the longest history in the U.S. state policy-making and are still the most widely used. Peterson (1981) refers mainly to this type of actions when he speaks about developmental policies. These policies aim at attracting new business or retaining existing ones through employment tax breaks, subsidies, and other means. The locational ED policies often start as relatively small enterprise zone programs, and extend to a state level after some time.

With more states involved in the inter-state competition for businesses, costs of successful projects soar. The so-called "smokestack chasing" is often characterized as a "race to the bottom" because the price of attracting high-profile projects might be too high (Hart, 2008)[2]. This at least partially explains the fact that expenditures on locational programs are the major part of state economic development budgets in the U.S. (Turner & Cassell, 2007).

Despite long history of implementation, and ample attempts to empirically detect the impacts of locational programs on regional economic performance, there is no unanimous opinion on the effectiveness of these policies. Overall, attitudes used to be more optimistic in the 1980s and 1990s than now. Current research tends to find a smaller (or even a negative) impact of locational programs on economic growth, job creation, and business activity (Gabe & Kraybill, 2002).

Recently, however, the focus of economic initiatives has shifted from "locational" programs to entrepreneurial ones (Hart, 2008; Hofe & Chen, 2006; Palazuelos, 2005). In contrast to locational programs, entrepreneurial growth policies target high-growth firms or economic sectors. These initiatives typically build firms' and workers' ability to participate in innovative economic activities via best-practice sharing, training, and leveraging private investment capital with public funds (Hart, 2008). State support for industrial and innovation clusters (also called technopoles, business agglomerations, or spatially concentrated high-technology clusters in the literature) is an example of entrepreneurial ED policies[3].

Cluster theory and cluster policies

Cluster theory, quite popular with policy-makers nowadays, is mainly associated with Michael Porter, who introduced and promoted it the 1990s. The roots of the concept, however, can be traced at least a century back[4]. Many researchers acknowledge the role of Alfred Marshall who first elaborated on the positive effects of agglomerations on economic growth (Newlands, 2003; Palazuelos, 2005). In the 1970s, Krugman introduced the "new economic geography" that described the relationships between agglomeration, specialization, and trade using formal economic analysis (Krugman, 1998)[5]. Although Krugman did not use the term "cluster", his work is widely accepted as a building block of the later cluster theory (Cumbers & MacKinnon, 2004). Porter (1998:78) defines 'clusters' as

...geographic concentrations of interconnected companies and institutions in a particular field [which] encompass an array of linked industries and other entities important to competition.

During the 1990s and 2000s, cluster theory was extended considerably. Porter points to at least three potential advantages of clusters. First, proximity to inputs and customers, and associated with it cost minimization, should lead to productivity gains. Next, clusters may promote enhanced innovation and flexibility, faster adaptation to demand, and production of customized goods and services resulting from proximity to consumers. Finally, clusters should attract new businesses due to locally available information on the existing opportunities within a cluster.

Clusters come in various forms. One classification divides them into agglomerations, industrial complexes, and social networks (Gordon & McCann, 2000; McCann & Sheppard, 2003). Agglomerations are the clusters consisting of atomized competitive firms and dynamic environment with externalities available to all firms in the area. Such clusters offer the advantages of qualified labor pool, skill development, local knowledge accumulation, appropriate infrastructure, and services. They also facilitate information flows (Palazuelos, 2005). Industrial complexes are club-like groups, which consist of the firms belonging to an industry. These firms have long-term, stable, and predictable relationships. In order to become a part of an industrial cluster, a firm undertakes significant investments, primarily into infrastructure and capital. The benefits of participation in an industrial complex usually accrue to its members only. The network cluster definition relies on inter-firm personal relationships based on trust. Members of such clusters benefit from good communication with their peers, as well as with other national and international nodes.

The theoretical developments in cluster theory have promptly made their way into actual policy-making. Clusters, named sometimes "economic weapons" of a country, have become a mantra of the contemporary debates on urban and regional economic growth (Aziz & Norhashim, 2008; Cumbers & MacKinnon, 2004). Policy-makers all over the world appear to believe strongly in clusters' ability to provide better (or cheaper) access to land, information and knowledge; as well as faster (or cheaper) access to the suppliers of inputs, institutions, and to public goods for the firms (Oerlemans, Meeus, & Boekema, 2001). The common expectations are that all those characteristics of clusters would inevitably translate into technological spillovers with increased innovation and productivity (McDonald, Tsagdis, & Huang, 2006).

Glavan (2008:43) observes that Porter's influence is "phenomenal throughout the world". In 2003, the Global Cluster Initiative Survey identified 500 cluster initiatives globally. In the U.S., the National Governors' Association, in cooperation with the Council on Competitiveness, has been active in promoting the idea of cluster-based economic growth. The NGA called for greater application of cluster concepts as a way to increase state competitiveness in the global economy (Finkle, 2002). The Association released *A Governor's Guide to Cluster-Based Economic Growth* (Rosenfeld, 2002), and *Cluster-Based Strategies for Growing State Economics* (Rosenfeld, 2007), which provide instructions about sustaining and growing a successful cluster.

The set of specific actions, which can be termed "a cluster policy", is surprisingly broad. This grants state agencies substantial discretion in the way they can implement cluster approach to promote economic growth of their region. *A Governor's Guide to Cluster-Based Economic Growth* names four major policy options to support competitive clusters. Organization of state service delivery around clusters involves collection and aggregation of information by clusters, creation of cross-industry quick-response teams, and a range of measures to encourage multi-firm activities. Targeted investments into clusters call for channeling funds into cluster R&D parks to support clusters' entrepreneurial activity, and cluster promotion in order to create markets for clusters' products. Network strengthening includes facilitation of cluster external linkages, encouragement of communication channels, and recognition or establishment of cluster associations and alliances. Lastly, human resource development entails establishment of cluster skills training centers, which would prepare specialized labor force, and support regional skill alliances.. Given the broad nature of cluster guidelines, a substantial part of contemporary ED initiatives and policies may easily fall into one or more of these categories.

The seeming fascination with clusters may lead one to believe in cluster approach as a universal remedy to all growth problems at urban, regional, and national levels. Scholars' opinion on this issue, nevertheless, is divided. The recent literature highlights a number of problems associated with clusters and cluster-based economic policies. Despite logical clarity and appeal of the cluster theory, several researchers point out the negative factors associated with proximity and agglomeration. Overcrowding of businesses often leads to increased costs of labor, land, environmental damages and free-riding problems (Palazuelos, 2005). At the same time, networks, sometimes termed the arteries of a viable cluster (Aziz & Norhashim, 2008), may result in higher dependence, potential constraints on future development strategies, and stickiness of knowledge (Oerlemans et al., 2001).

High-tech clusters and cluster initiatives in U.S. states

The cluster concept has become increasingly associated with "knowledge economy" or "new economy" (Martin & Sunley, 2003). Indeed, the very notion of a successful cluster rests on its ability to generate new ideas and innovative entrepreneurial practices, which are supposed to spill over to other firms in proximity. High-technology industries in a number of states, such as California, New York, and Massachusetts, are the prime examples of vibrant clusters, which serve as models for replication elsewhere.

Academic literature does not give a definitive opinion on the ability of policy-makers to shape high-technology growth in a region. Some argue that technology is an extremely path-dependent process and cannot be significantly influenced exogenously (Mayer & Cortright, 2001). On the other hand, active policies that support high-tech industries, despite alleged inability to influence innovation and invention *per se*, should foster high-tech firm formation, thus increasing chances of innovation. Other researchers believe that state initiatives are able to promote high-tech firm growth (Clarke & Gaile, 1989). Jenkins, Leicht, and Jaynes (2006) argue that the increased share of high-tech employment is a critical maker of the "new economy". They find positive effect of public venture capital, business innovation research programs, technology grants, and research parks on share growth of high-tech employment.

There is some ambiguity in the literature as to what industries can be termed the "high-tech". The definitions may be industry-based, firm-based, product-based, and life cycle based (Steenhuis & Bruijn de, 2006). The American Electronics Association, for example, includes electronics manufacturing and software into its list of high technology industries. It excludes, though, other high-technology industries such as biotechnology and aerospace (Jenkins et al., 2006).

This chapter concentrates on the industries that represent manufacturing (aerospace and defense manufacturing, and computer manufacturing), services and information (software), and research (biotechnology research). These four industries nest several large clusters throughout the U.S. and are popular targets for state cluster policies.

About forty U.S. states have firms in aerospace and defense manufacturing. The industry is most concentrated in California, Florida, Texas, Kansas, and Washington, while only Arizona, Connecticut, California, and Washington have clusters, according to the Institute for Strategy and Competitiveness at Harvard Business School. Clusters in these four states have formed before 1996. The California and Washington aerospace clusters rank among the top ten in the world. Two state programs, *Arizona Strategic Partnership for Economic Development (ASPED)*, and *Joint venture: Silicon Valley Network*, support clusters in Arizona and California respectively.

Nearly every U.S. state manufactures various types of computers and electronic components. The number of establishments in this industry grew in the 1990s to reach 617 in year 2000. It plummeted to 370 in 2001, and then resumed growth to 530 by 2004[6]. According to the Institute for Strategy and Competitiveness, four states (California, Texas, Massachusetts, and Minnesota) had computer-manufacturing clusters on the brink of the century. In California, two policy initiatives supported the cluster, *Joint Venture: Silicon Valley Network* and *Collaborating to Compete in the New Economy. Twin Cities Industry Cluster Project* played the same role in Minnesota. No state programs were identified for the industry in Texas and Massachusetts.

Companies in all U.S. states design, develop, and publish software. California, Texas, Massachusetts, Illinois and Florida are the national leaders in the number of software establishments. The Institute for Strategy and Competitiveness recognizes only six state clusters (Arizona, California, Minnesota, New York, Oregon, and Washington). The former three have implemented state policy initiatives, which support clusters in software industry (*ASPED*, *Joint Venture*, and *Twin Cities* projects).

Biotechnology and biotech research is clustered in Arizona, California, Connecticut, Indiana, Ohio, Kentucky, Maryland, New Jersey, North Carolina, and Texas. The first three states on this list support their biotechnology industries through state programs.

Research design and estimation

Logical model and hypotheses

According to cluster theory, clustering should contribute to cost minimization, productivity gains, innovation and flexibility, and informational and technological spillovers. These benefits of clusters should improve firm performance and increase their profits. For policy-makers, however, job creation and firm formation are arguably the most important outcomes (Figure 1).

15:1 The logical model

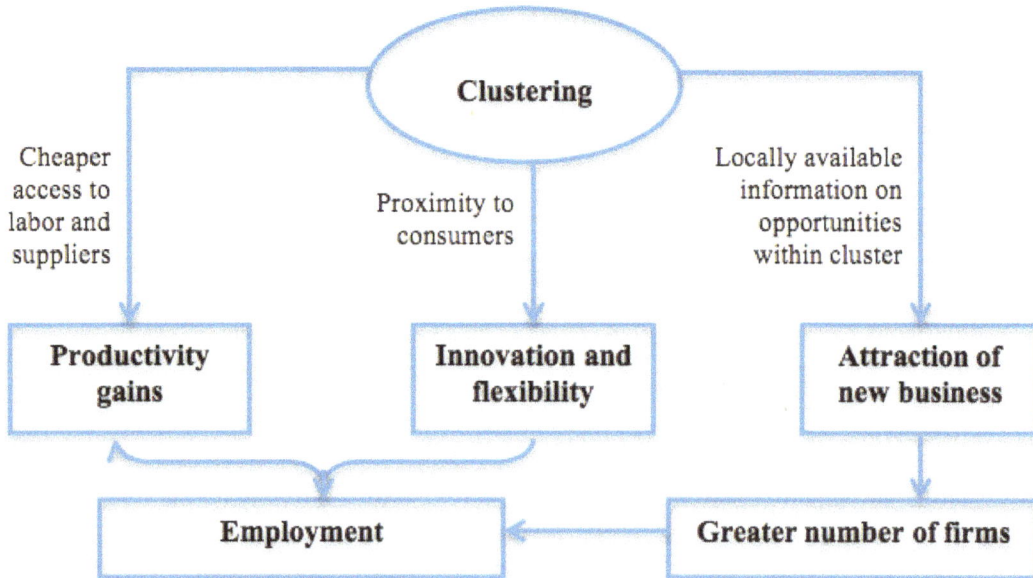

Figure 1 demonstrates how advantages of a cluster accrue through several channels. Public policy programs and initiatives have no specified place in the chart. They are intended to strengthen the natural advantages of clusters, and to contribute to job and firm creation. The primary means of such contribution are internalization of businesses' transaction costs associated with information gathering, employee training, and networking.

The exact meaning of the boxes and arrows in Figure 1 is likely to depend on the industry. For example, for aerospace and defense manufacturing, proximity to consumers is less likely to be important because of large-scale and highly standardized processes employed in this industry. On the other hand, software development and publishing should be sensitive to consumers' demand. To account for industry-related variations, the following hypotheses are tested separately for each industry:

H1. Cluster policies lead to higher employment in high-tcch industries, *ceteris paribus*;

H1.a. Clusters are associated with higher employment in high-tech industries, *ceteris paribus;*

H2. Cluster policies lead to a greater number of establishments in high-tech industries, *ceteris paribus*;

H2.a. Clusters are associated with a greater number of establishments in high-tech industries, *ceteris paribus.*

Econometric model

This chapter focuses on four industries that belong to high-technology sectors (Jenkins et al., 2006) and correspond[7] to the clusters identified by the Institute for Strategy and Competitiveness: (1) aerospace and defense manufacturing (Aerospace Product and Parts Manufacturing, NAICS3364); (2) software design, development, and publishing (Computer Systems Design and Related Services, NAICS5415, and Software Publishers, NAICS5112); (3) computer and electronic component manufacturing (Computer and Peripheral Equipment Manufacturing, NAICS3341); and (4) biotechnology and biotechnological research (Research and Development in the Physical, Engineering, and Life Sciences, NAICS541710). For each industry, two unbalanced panel data equations are estimated using robust random effects model. Model 1 estimates the effect of the main explanatory variables on population-adjusted employment in a given industry:

$$Employment_{it} = \alpha + \beta Policy_i + \theta Cluster_i + \delta' X_{it} + \varepsilon_{it}$$

Model 2 estimates the effect of the same variables on the population-adjusted number of establishments in a given industry:

$$Establishments_{it} = \alpha + \beta Policy_i + \theta Cluster_i + \delta' X_{it} + \varepsilon_{it}$$

In both models α is the intercept, β and θ capture the effect of variables *Policy* and *Cluster* respectively, δ is a vector of coefficients of the control variables constituting the matrix X. The matrix includes state demographic characteristics (population, percentage of Black, and educational attainment), population density, R&D expenditures, number of patents per 1,000 residents, and gross regional product per capita. All variables, except for dichotomous *Policy* and *Cluster*, enter the models in logarithmic form.

Data and variables

The data set includes states that have clusters, and states that do not have clusters in the industries under consideration[8]. Some of those clusters (but not all) are associated with state policy initiatives aimed at cluster support and development. This allows capturing the effects of both cluster policies and clustering in the high-technology industries. The data span the 1998-2004 period. All clusters and policy initiatives had been in place for at least two years by 1998 (many of them had been in place for five years or more).

Dependent variables

This chapter empirically estimates the ability of state cluster-based ED programs to influence employment and the number of establishments in four U.S. high-technology

264

industries. The two dependent variables are (1) the natural logarithm of the number of employees in the industry of interest per 1,000 residents, $Employment_{it}$, and (2) the natural logarithm of the number of firms in the industry of interest per 1,000 residents, $Establishments_{it}$.

The U.S. Census Bureau County Business Patterns program is the data source for both variables. This program collects and publishes annual industry level statistics, which includes payroll, number of workers, and number of establishments. In compliance with the non-disclosure laws, exact employment information is not available for the industries that have small number of establishments in a state. Instead, the program reports the exact number of firms and size brackets these firms fall into. In such cases, variable $Employment_{it}$ was imputed by multiplying the number of establishments in each size category by the median number of workers in a corresponding category, and summing over the categories[9]. Another dependent variable, $Establishments_{it}$, is used as reported by the program.

Explanatory variables

There are two explanatory dichotomous variables, $Policy_i$ and $Cluster_i$. The former equals one if a state has a cluster-based ED policy (or a cluster initiative) targeted at the industry of interest, and zero otherwise. The latter equals one if there is a cluster in the industry being considered, and zero otherwise.

The data come from the Institute for Strategy and Competitiveness at Harvard Business School, which provides information on clusters and cluster policies. Between years 2002 and 2004, the Institute has conducted a cluster meta-study project that traced and documented all clusters throughout the globe using open data sources. The study resulted in profiles (with varying degree of details) of about 500 clusters[10]. For the U.S., the Institute has documented 143 clusters in 34 states, spanning 36 industries with more than a dozen of state cluster policy initiatives.

Control variables

The models include several variables that control for state major characteristics related to demography, innovative activities, and economic performance in order to isolate the relationship of interest. Demographic composition determines availability and quality of the labor pool that high-tech firms may use. In general, employment tends to follow the patterns of population growth or decline (Acs & Armington, 2004). $Population_{it}$ is the estimated number of residents in a state, in thousands. The conclusions of Acs and Armington about the association between employment and population size may not be applicable to the high-tech industries. Intuitively, such industries should be more sensitive to the quality of a labor pool, rather than its size. $Education_{it}$ approximates the level of educational attainment in a state measured by percentage of adult population with a bachelor degree or higher. Percentage of Black population in a state, $Black_{it}$, captures the effect of racial composition on state economic performance. As the literature suggests, its influence may be both positive and negative. Markusen, Hall, and Glasmeier (1986) find a negative relationship between percentage of the black population and high-technology employment growth. In contrast to these findings, Florida (2002) argues that racial heterogeneity attracts young, highly educated workers who contribute to economic growth. Jenkins and co-authors (2006) find no effects of racial composition on high-tech employment in the U.S. metropolitan areas. $Density_{it}$ is the measure of population density in a state. The U.S. Census Bureau is the data source for all demographic variables.

High-tech employment and firm formation is likely to be related to the "innovativeness" of a state economy. Markusen and colleagues (1986) discover a positive effect of four-year higher education institutions on high-tech employment, while Jenkins et al. (2006) fail to find any significant relationship. Goldstein and Renault (2004) maintain that university R&D leads to knowledge spillovers and is positively related to average wage change. R&D expenditures by colleges and universities per 1,000 residents, $RDit$, and a number of patents per 1,000 residents, $Patents_{it}$, are included in the models in order to capture the state innovative environment. The National Science Foundation (NSF) is the data source for the variable RD_{it}[11]. The U.S. Patent and Trademark Office provides information about patenting in the U.S. states, which is the data source for the variable $Patents_{it}$[12].

GSP_{it}, per capita Gross State Product, is the size of a state economy that roughly approximates the resources available to businesses in a region. The data for this variable are available from the State Politics and Policy Quarterly Data Resource[13].

Results and discussion

Tables 1 and 2 report the results of the study. The most notable conclusion is that cluster policies, in the majority of cases, are not statistically associated with employment and the number of establishments in the industries they are targeting. Clusters, on the contrary, have a positive effect in two industries. The tables also demonstrate that the relationships between the dependent and independent variables are industry-specific.

Table 1 presents estimation results for employment. State-level cluster initiatives appear to be unable to increase the population-adjusted number of employees in the industries considered. Presence of a cluster is statistically associated with higher employment in aerospace and defense manufacturing, and software design, development, and publishing. In the latter case, though, the effect is significant only at the 0.1 level. In the other two industries, computer and electronic component manufacturing, and biotechnology and biotech research, clusters have no effect on employment.

15.2: Estimation results for Model 1

Variable	Aerospace & Defense Manufacturing	Software Design, Development & Publishing	Computer & Electronic Component Manufactuting	Biotechnology & Biotech Research
Policy	-2.239 (1.604)	-0.541 (0.414)	0.694 (0.871)	-0.207 (0.275)
Cluster	4.645*** (1.467)	0.716* (0.381)	-0.269 (0.927)	-0.024 (0.259)
Population	0.966** (0.463)	0.130 (0.108)	0.378 (0.301)	0.227** (0.091)
Education	-1.677 (1.053)	1.562*** (0.565)	0.834 (0.941)	-0.272 (0.379)
Black	-0.049 (0.064)	0.088 (0.092)	-0.237 (0.175)	-0.113** (0.054)
Density	-0.873** (0.420)	-0.012 (0.105)	-0.055 (0.180)	0.052 (0.088)
R&D	0.908*** (0.343)	-0.003 (0.033)	-0.989* (0.529)	0.504** (0.217)
Patents	0.021 (0.016)	1.064*** (0.292)	1.526*** (0.327)	-0.038 (0.122)
GSP	-0.691 (1.430)	-3.130*** (0.583)	-0.509 (1.292)	2.722*** (0.570)
Constant	-4.560 (5.661)	2.058 (2.785)	-12.802 (6.409)	-11.251 (2.437)
Observations	284	349	306	349
Groups	44	51	40	50
Wald Chi2	303.6	105	61.46	82.05
Prob>Chi2	0.0000	0.0000	0.0000	0.0000

Dependent variable: Number of jobs in a corresponding industry per 1,000 residents, logged
*** - significant at 0.01%; ** - significant at 0.05%; * - significant at 0.1%

The effects of other state characteristics on employment differ by industry. While aerospace and defense manufacturing tends to employ more people in more populous but less dense states with greater R&D expenditures, software design, development and publishing does the same in more educated and inventive states with smaller size of economies as measured by the GSP. Computer and electronic component manufacturing provides more employment in the states with smaller university expenditures on research and development but greater patenting activity. Employment in biotechnology and biotech research is positively associated with population, university R&D expenditures, and GSP. The proportion of African-American population in a state appears to have a negative effect on employment in this industry.

Table 2 demonstrates estimation results for the population-adjusted number of firms as the dependent variable. The table implies that there is a statistical relationship between cluster policies and the number of businesses only in one industry, aerospace and defense manufacturing. In this industry, state initiatives to promote clusters seem to reduce the number of firms. One plausible explanation is the potential for a reactive nature of state cluster policies. Perhaps states, traditionally strong in aerospace and defense manufacturing, started to lose firms in this industry. To reverse this trend, state governments initiated cluster policies. If this is the case, this study suggests that the cluster initiatives are either ineffective, or need more time for the desired results to be achieved. The second explanatory variable, *Cluster*, is positively related to the number of firms in aerospace and defense manufacturing, and software design, development and publishing. It has no statistically significant effect on the number of firms in computer and electronic component manufacturing, and biotechnology and biotech research.

15.3. Estimation results for Model 2

Variable	Aerospace & Defense Manufacturing	Software Design, Development & Publishing	Computer & Electronic Component Manufactuting	Biotechnology & Biotech Research
Policy	-1.180**	-0.111	0.304	0.232
	(0.485)	(0.172)	(0.868)	(0.251)
Cluster	1.715***	0.486***	-0.180	-0.038
	(0.426)	(0.168)	(0.443)	(0.185)
Population	0.011	-0.088	-0.838***	-0.057
	(0.135)	(0.093)	(0.065)	(0.049)
Education	-0.378	0.613*	0.502	-0.034
	(0.279)	(0.339)	(0.385)	(0.122)
Black	0.001	-0.009	-0.052	-0.044**
	(0.023)	(0.046)	(0.058)	(0.019)

Density	-0.441***	0.117*	0.057	0.018
	(0.115)	(0.064)	(0.068)	(0.043)
R&D	0.307***	0.003	0.115	0.385***
	(0.111)	(0.021)	(0.210)	(0.087)
Patents	0.013	0.442***	0.496***	0.020
	(0.015)	(0.125)	(0.143)	(0.063)
GSP	-0.287	-0.912***	-0.702**	0.921***
	(0.472)	(0.273)	(0.324)	(0.227)
Constant	-2.401	-2.004	6.596	-4.831
	(1.730)	(1.581)	(2.332)	(1.072)
Observations	284	349	306	349
Groups	44	51	40	50
Wald Chi2	303.6	145.9	246.47	140.6
Prob>Chi2	0.0000	0.0000	0.0000	0.0000

Dependent variable: Number of firms in a corresponding industry per 1,000 residents, logged
*** - significant at 0.01%; ** - significant at 0.05%; * - significant at 0.1%

Table 2 indicates that aerospace and defense manufacturing firms tend to locate in less dense states. In contrast, software design, development and publishing industry gravitates to densely populated regions. This industry has more firms in the states with smaller economies but greater educational attainment and patenting. The number of firms in computer and electronic component manufacturing industry is positively related to patenting activity and negatively related to the size of the economy. Finally, biotechnology and biotech research firms are attracted to states with greater university spending on R&D, higher GSP, and with smaller proportion of African-American population.

Conclusion

A government based on federation principles is a good illustration of how decentralization and centralization co-exist. The U.S. government is rather decentralized when it comes to economic development policies. Although the national government participates in ED projects in various states and localities, states and municipalities actively design and implement economic development initiatives. These lower levels of government are better suited to shape economic performance, as policy-makers at those levels are more perceptive to local demands, market signals, and are effectively disciplined by political pressures.

The results of ED efforts at state and local levels depend on many factors and may drastically differ depending on specific circumstances. This chapter empirically tests the effects of state cluster initiatives in four U.S. high-technology industries during the period 1998-2004. The results suggest that the optimism about the ability of state policy-makers to form successful clusters, which contribute to policy-relevant outcomes, may be premature. While clusters are found to have a significant positive effect on employment and the number of firms in aerospace and defense manufacturing, software design, development and publishing industry, the presence of a cluster is not related to these outcomes in computer, electronic component manufacturing, and biotechnology with biotech research. There is no statistically significant relationship between employment in the four industries and state-level cluster initiatives. In addition, cluster policies are not a significant predictor of the population-adjusted number of firms in software design, development and publishing industry, computer and electronic component manufacturing, and biotechnology and biotech research industries. In aerospace and defense manufacturing, cluster policy initiatives appear to have negative effect on the number of firms. The negative effect, however, is likely to be caused by the reactive nature of state support for this traditional industry.

Overall, this chapter demonstrates opportunities and limitations of state government policies in economic development. State governments have the freedom to devise and put into action a wide range of economic development programs in accordance with the state needs and resources. This does not guarantee the ability to shape economic landscape of any industry in a desired way. Cluster initiatives appear to be an example of ED policies that, despite the reported success of clusters and much guidance provided to policy-makers, have yet to prove their ability to boost employment and firm formation.

ENDNOTES

1   The desirability of intercity competition was questioned on the grounds of equity and efficiency long ago. Logan and Molotch (1987) contend that competition leads to the 'growth machine' approach to development, which imposes substantial costs. Growth does not necessarily improve living standards; it may exacerbate problems of segregation and inequality. Peterson (1995) calls regional income inequalities the main cost of federalism. In addition, regional growth initiatives are able to account for and to internalize both negative and positive externalities from these activities, thus, enhancing overall efficiency.

2   The "expensive" projects include $410 million package granted to Kia for its location in Georgia; $300 million to United Airlines in Indiana; $250 million to Mercedes-Benz in Alabama, and $125 million to Toyota in Kentucky.

3   In some cases, cluster policies may incorporate traits of both entrepreneurial and locational policies.

4   Some authors track the origins of the cluster theory to the 1826 Von Trunen's model of the relationships among markets, production, and transportation (Hofe & Chen, 2006).

5   Paul Krugman received 2008 Nobel Prize in Economics "for analysis of trade patterns and location of economic activity".

6   County Business Patterns, available at a state level for years 1986 – 2010 at http://www.census.gov/econ/cbp/download/index.htm

7   The best effort was made to find NAICS industry definitions that match exactly the clusters identified by the Institute for Strategy and Competitiveness. This was not possible in all cases. For example, in addition to biotechnology research, NAICS541710 includes research in agriculture, bacteriology, biology, protein engineering, DNA recombination, and other research

8   The cluster initiatives considered in this chapter are implemented at a state level. This determines the level of analysis performed in the chapter.

9   Imputing 'expected employment' introduces a measurement error; however, this error has the effect of increased variance but it should not bias estimation results (Wooldridge, 2003).

10   Cluster profiles are accessible at http://data.isc.hbs.edu/cp/index.jsp

11   The tables *R&D Expenditures at Universities and Colleges, by State, Control, and Source of Funds* are available at NSF website http://www.nsf.gov/statistics/rdexpenditures/ for years 1992 – 2008.

12   The variable *Patents$_{it}$* is extracted from the table *Extended Year Set - Patent Counts by Country/State and Year, Utility Patents Report* at http://www.uspto.gov/web/offices/ac/ido/oeip/taf/reports.htm#by_hist.

13   http://academic.udayton.edu/SPPQ-TPR/tpr_data_sets.html

References

Acs, Z. J., & Armington, C. (2004). Employment growth and entrepreneurial activity in cities. *Regional Studies, 38*(8), 911–927.

Aziz, K. A., & Norhashim, M. (2008). Cluster-based policy making: Assessing performance and sustaining competitiveness. *Review of Policy Research, 25*(4), 349-375.

Basolo, V. (2003). U.S. regionalism and rationality. *Urban Studies, 40*(3), 447-462.

Clarke, S., & Gaile, G. (1989). Moving towards entrepreneurial local development strategies: Opportunities and barriers. *Policy Studies Journal, 17*(3), 574-598.

Cumbers, A., & MacKinnon, D. (2004). Introduction: Clusters in urban and regional development. *Urban Studies, 41*(5/6), 959-969.

Drabenstott, M. (2006). Rethinking federal policy for regional economic development. *Economic Review - Federal Reserve Bank of Kansas City, First Quarter*, 115-142.

Finkle, J. (2002). New economic development strategies for the states. *Spectrum: The Journal of State Government, Summer*, 23-25.

Florida, R. (2002). *The rise of the creative class and how its transforming work, leisure, community and everyday life*. New York: Basic books.

Gabe, T. M., & Kraybill, D. S. (2002). The effects of state economic development incentives on employment growth of establishments. *Journal of Regional Science, 42*(4), 703-730.

Glavan, B. (2008). Coordination failures, cluster theory, and entrepreneurship: A critical view. *Quarterly Journal of Austian Economics, 11*(1), 43-59.

Goldstein, H., & Renault, C. (2004). Contribution of universities to regional economic development: A quasi-experimental approach. *Regional Studies, 38*(7), 733-746.

Gordon, I., & McCann, P. (2000). Industrial clusters: Complexes, agglomeration and/or social networks? *Urban Studies, 37*(3), 513-532.

Gray, V., & Hanson, R. (2008). Preface. In V. Gray & R. Hanson (Eds.), *Politics in the American states: A comparative analysis*. Washington, DC: CQ Press.

Hart, D. M. (2008). The politics of "entrepreneurial" economic development policy of states in the U.S. *Review of Policy Research, 25*(2), 149-168.

Hofe, R. v., & Chen, K. (2006). Whither or not industrial cluster: Conclusions or confusions? *The Industrial Georgapher, 4*(1), 2-28.

Hwang, S.-D., & Gray, V. (1991). External limits and internal determinants of state public policy. *The Western Political Quarterly, 44*(2), 277-298.

Jenkins, C., Jaynes, A., & Leicht, K. (2006). Do high technology policies work? An analysis of high technology employment growth in U.S. Metropolitan areas, 1988-1998. *Social Science Quarterly, 89*(2), 456-481.

Krugman, P. (1998). What's new about the new economic geography? *Oxford Review of Economic Policy, 14*(2), 7-17.

Logan, J. R., & Molotch, H. L. (1987). *Urban fortunes. The political economy of place*. Berkerley: University of California Press.

Markusen, A., Hall, P., & Glasmeier, A. (1986). *High tech America: The what, how, where, and why of the sunrise industries*. Boston: Allen & Unwin.

Martin, R., & Sunley, P. (2003). Deconstructing clusters: Chaotic concept or policy panacea? *Journal of Economic Geography, 3*(1), 5-35.

Mayer, H., & Cortright, J. (2001). High tech specialization: A comparison of high technology centers *Survey series*. Washington, DC: Brookings Institution.

McCann, P., & Sheppard, S. (2003). The rise, fall and rise again of industrial location theory. *Regional Studies, 37*(6-7), 649-663.

McDonald, F., Tsagdis, D., & Huang, Q. (2006). The development of industrial clusters and public policy. *Entrepreneurship and Regional Development, 18*(6), 525-542.

Newlands, D. (2003). Competition and cooperation in industrial clusters: The implications for public policy. *European Planning Studies, 11*(5), 521-532.

Oerlemans, L., Meeus, M., & Boekema, F. (2001). Firm clustering and innovation: Determinants and effects. *Papers in Regional Science, 80*(3), 337-356.

Palazuelos, M. (2005). Clusters: Myth or realistic ambition for policy-makers? *Local Economy, 20*(2), 131-140.

Peters, A., & Fisher, P. (2004). The failures of economic development incentives. *Journal of the American Planning Association, 70*(127-37).

Peterson, P. (1981). *City limits*. Chicago: The University of Chicago Press.

Peterson, P. (1995). *The price of federalism*. Washington, DC: The Brookings Institution.

Rosenfeld, S. (2002). *Governor's guide to cluster-based economic growth*. Washington, DC: National Governors' Association.

Rosenfeld, S. (2007). *Cluster-based strategies for growing state economies*. Washington, DC: National Governors' Association.

Saiz, M., & Clarke, S. (2008). Economic development and infrastructure policy. In V. Gray & R. Hanson (Eds.), *Politics in the American states: A comparative analysis* (9th ed.). Washington, DC: Congressional Quarterly Press.

Solvell, O., Lindqvist, G., & Ketels, C. (2003). The cluster initiative greenbook Retrieved February 15, 2013, from http://www.isc.hbs.edu/pdf/Greenbook_presentation.pdf

Steenhuis, H.-J., & Bruijn de, E. (2006). *High technology revisited: definition and position*. Paper presented at the IEEE International Conference on Management of Innovation and Technology, Singapore, China.

Teitz, M. B. (1994). Changes in economic development theory and practice. *International Regional Science Review, 16*(1&2), 101 - 106.

Tiebout, C. M. (1956). A pure theory of local expenditures. *Journal of Political Economy, 64*(5), 416-424.

Turner, R. C., & Cassell, M. K. (2007). When do states pursue targeted economic development policies? The adoption and expansion of state enterprise zone programs. *Social Science Quarterly, 88*(1), 86-103.

Wolfe, D. A., & Gertler, M. S. (2004). Clusters from the inside and out: Local dynamics and global linkages. *Urban Studies, 41*(5&6), 1071-1093.

Wooldridge, J. (2003). *Econometric analysis of cross section and panel data*. Cambridge: The MIT Press.

Chapter Sixteen

Public Administration, Decentralization, and Elections in Africa: Ghana, A Case Study

Kwame Badu Antwi-Boasiako

Key words: Ghana, public administration, decentralization, elections, development

Introduction

To fully understand public administration, decentralization, and governance in Africa, one has to study each of the over fifty countries on the continent. Despite the similarities in the form of administration in Africa both military and democratic administrations, one should expect conspicuously distinct differences employ by each country. That is, the evolution of public administration in Africa would be a collection of traditional and contemporary administrative history of each country. Africa is very deficient in recorded history as outsiders documented greater part of its history. Such deficiency in the data makes it difficult in the chronological and/or longitudinal analysis of public administration and governance in Africa. But public administration and governance in Africa "has been with us as long as recorded history" (King and Chilton 2009: 29). The Great Empires of Africa and Ancient Civilizations including Egypt, China, and Rome did require their citizens to build cities and other public goods such as roads and palaces as symbols of unity and power. Similarly, traditional administrative leaders in Africa also utilized communal labor for public projects while contemporary political leaders rely on taxes to build public goods.

The administrative process required leaders the need to plan, organize, staff, direct, coordinate, report, and budget. Luther Gulick in the 1930s referred to this administrative process as POSDCORB. In fact, Gulick's acronym had been in existence even before recorded history therefore the POSDCORB concept is not a new phenomenon to traditional societies and administrations. The great empires had fully understood the concept of decentralization as conquered cities, tribes, and villages did control themselves but took instructions from a central authority (the conqueror). The conquered were also made to pay taxes for the upkeep of the central authority, a concept the European colonial powers adopted to rule the conquered colonies in Africa and elsewhere. Public Administration therefore is a process of manipulating the human capital to increase productivity to improve our environment for a better quality of life. So administration is not a new phenomenon in African history as the kings, chiefs, and opinion leaders did plan, organize, mobilize, and got their subjects ready for communal labor including fighting wars. This chapter attempts to define public administration, decentralization and administration, and the need for local elections. It uses Ghana as a case study.

Evolution and Definition of Public Administration

The genesis of public administration is academically unknown and any attempt to reject that premise could be seen as an intellectual dishonesty. The evolution of public administration varies from nation to nation as the great empires of Africa had solid but different administrative structures with unit heads. Over the centuries, the field of public administration has transformed itself from a centralized standard of operation to a more decentralized concept giving more power to the people, at least in theory as its practical benefits could be debated. It also has to conform and adapt to the changing political environment as each generational shift comes with redefining the old definition to address public interest (Shafritz, Russel, and Borick, 2013:23-24: King, and Chilton, 2009: 29-45).

So where do we begin the discussion of the evolution of public administration in Africa? This is where oral history (tradition) plays a very significant role in conceptualizing how administration was effected in the various empires. For example, Ntsebeza (2004) noted the traditional administrative structures of land acquisition had been in place for long time. "These structures, which were made up of chiefs, headmen and councilors and a tribal sectary…" (77) help in acquisition of property: Land. The problem with contemporary administration in Africa is that postcolonial leaders have failed to fully accommodate the known traditional practices to the borrowed practices of the colonizers, hence the administrative uncertainties in democratic Africa. Ntsebeza found that "the major stumbling block to implementing democratic decentralization is the unresolved question of the roles, powers and functions of traditional authorities in land, and local government reform" (87).

Credit must be given to those who attempted to introduce structure and organization into the field public administration. Hence the pioneering work in the field as an academic discipline would always remember the likes of the Woodrow Wilsons, Frank Goodnows, Leonard Whites, and others. Woodrow Wilson whom the public administration literature claims to be the father of the discipline because of his 1887 publication, *The Study of Administration,* actually initiated the examination of the field, which hitherto had been considered a subset of political science. From a broader perspective there is an enormous public administration literature on Europe, the United States, and other areas but the same cannot be said about public administration literature on Africa. Robert Denhardt (1995) noted that the beginning of public administration in the U.S. dates back to Woodrow Wilson's though some studies did question his influence yet his reformist ideology and pragmatic approach to address inefficiencies on corruptions in government was symbolic. So who does Africa look up to as the initiator of contemporary structured administrative practices?

This means that for lack of well documentation of traditional administration in Africa, intellectuals and politicians have, by and large, considered the theoretical consideration of the discipline from afar neglecting the cultural aspect of the African administrative practices. The unfortunate story of African administrative practices is that the narratives of public administration in Africa do not consider local cultures by incorporating African symbols, customs, and other attributes to meet the practical need of the administrative challenges that confront African countries. It would be myopic on my part to ignore the attempts made by some African intellectuals. For example, Ogwo Jombo Umeh and Greg Andranovich in 2005 published *Culture, Development, and Public Administration in Africa*. Such an attempt is not only encouraging but it brings to light the integration of the African cultural context into the studying of public administration with better understanding from our traditional upbringing and poltical environment. The overreliance on foreign models and concepts in the field does not translate into pragmatic solutions for Africa hence the need for an integrated definition and approach to public administration on the continent. I am, however, not arguing for a complete rejection of the public administration literature of Western narratives. In fact, I am rather looking for the amalgamation of narratives from all cultures that can be utilized to work in the African political and administrative environs. For example, the core concept of seeing the public "administrator as an impartial implementer" (Holzer and Schwester, 2011:31) as advocated by Woodrow Wilson and Frank Goodnow needs a deeper scrutiny to fit the needs of each country on the continent of Africa.

Affirming my argument that defining public administration in the African context may increase administrative productivity clearly shows that there is lack of conscious in defining the field. The pioneers insisted for a "distinction between the functions of politics and the administration of government, noting that politics had to do with policies and the administration dealt with their execution" (Holzer and Schwester, 2011:31). This dichotomous argument where administrative practices are completely separated from the politics of the day will simply not work in Africa as the culture is intertwined with individuals' daily activities. For example, religiosity is part of the African regardless of ones accepted religious practice. The African leader does not leave his or her beliefs as one ascends the role of leadership.

According to Holzer and Schwester public administration has severally been defined among many deceptions (31-32). This statement could be interpreted as lack of common agreement in defining public administration as noted above. Kettl and Fesler (2009) categorically state that "scholars have never agreed on a common definition" and see the field as suffering from "crisis of identity" (29). Most studies provide characteristics needed to define public administration but fail to offer one for the fear of criticism and where one is provided, an attempt to incorporate all the characteristics makes the definition too long to make sense. Here, for example, is Holzer and Schwester definition:

The formation and implementation of public policy. It is an amalgamation of management-based strategies such as planning, organizing, directing, coordinating, and controlling. It incorporates behaviorally based practices adopted from fields such as psychology and sociology. All of those strategies and practices are utilized within a democratic framework of accountability. The formation and implementation of policy, while formally controlled by government managers, has since been expanded to include the nonprofit and for-profit communities (2011:32).

Such a long definition further complicates ones understanding of the field as it tends to incorporate almost everything but lacks specificity.

Defining Public Administration in Africa

While the above definition may be considered comprehensive other studies might take a different approach. Wilson in his 1887 essay has argued that administration finds its roots throughout Europe meaning that other parts of the world did not have administrative structures. But Peter Guys (1990) who rejects that premise, is of the opinion that meaningful comparative analysis of public administration is needed and realizes how difficult it would be to do such a study therefore the study of public administration must be a country specific phenomenon. If that argument by Guy holds then what happens to international organizations? So confining to one strategic definition for the whole of Africa clearly defeats Guys assertion. It could also be argued that public administration is not scientific as proclaimed in the literature but an art or a combination of both. In fact, public administration is define here as a scientific, artistic, and personality attributes of individuals to utilize both human and capital resources for the benefit of the public. These characteristics must include accountability, probity, and transparency.

Post-colonial African countries have become proclivity for experimentation on issues including economic, political, and administrative initiatives or laboratories for investigations (Ayee, 2008). Public administration is an art because all the African leaders, like leaders in other parts of the world, exhibit different leadership styles. For example, Nelson Mandela's leadership qualities and style is different from John Mahama (Ghana), Robert Mugabe (Zimbabwe), Julius Nyerere (Tanzania), Yayi Boni (Benin), Nelson Mandela (South Africa) and Jonathan Goodluck (Nigeria). Even military dictators such as Jerry John Rawlings (Ghana), Idi Amin (Uganda), Mobutu Sese Seko (Congo), Murmur Al Gadhafi (Libya), Blaise Compaore (Burkina Faso) and a host of others have different leadership skills, which affirm the diverse administrative styles of public administrators. Fortunately, for Africa, its administrative system regardless of the political system revolves on its traditional administrative institutions: Chieftaincy. To better understand decentralization and traditional institutions first a brief discussion of decentralization in Ghana is provided.

The Conundrum of Decentralization in Ghana

The concept of decentralization is as a component of democratic societies, which is widely being adopted in emerging democracies in African countries to make their administrative systems more efficient. However, there is a large body of scholarly literature that provides conflicting effects of decentralization on effective public administration (Faguet 2008; Kim et al. 2005). In Ghana, politicians who advocate for decentralization are sometimes skeptical in giving or sharing power with their decentralized leaders as the concept is not well understood in its theoretical form. This could be that because of the unitary political system in Ghana it makes it difficult for the central government to fully rely on district heads who may not share the same political ideology with the former. In a unitary system, unlike a federalist system, the central government has direct say in who is appointed or elected, if allowed, as district head.

In fact, the literature on decentralization as diverse as it may be, according to constitutional law specialists, tries to avoid the problem of confining decentralization to "legal models of government relations" (Cohen and Peterson 1999:19). The authors define it along the principal distinction between unitary and federal-based systems like federation, confederation, unions, and leagues. Decentralization, as they put it, is therefore a community having legally specified sovereignty over the identified public sector tasks in a well-defined territorial jurisdiction (19–22). Ghana's political structure falls into the unitary political category where the executive holds the power of nominating or appointing district and regional leaders. Hence, the governed in these units have no or very little input in the selection of who leads a district. This modern political structure is directly contradictory to how chief under traditional administration is selected. In the case of traditional administration, the community is aware of the royal family and would have idea of who might become the next chief.

Ghana, the first country south of the Sahara to attain political independence has become a model of democracy in Africa. Since the Fourth Republic of Ghana in 1992, despite the accusations of electoral frauds, election manipulations, intimidations, and irregularities during general elections by the two leading political parties New Patriotic Party (NPP) and National Democratic Congress [NDC]) in the country, one can argue that Ghana has enjoyed successful general presidential elections. It should, however, be noted that in the 2012 presidential election, though the opposition NPP rejected the results declared by the Electoral Commission (EC), the NPP abiding by Ghana's Constitution, regarding general elections, did file its objection to the results as announced by the EC to Ghana's Supreme Court for redress. This process, undeniably, makes Ghana a more politically matured and stable country compared to some of its neighbors over the same period. Kenya also settled its 2013 presidential election results in court another sign of political maturity on the continent. The irony of Ghana's political system is that notwithstanding the form of government the country has, military or democratic, the role of the executive remains the same regarding the appointments of the heads of local governments. This practice, arguably, provides little or no local power to the grassroots. It therefore minimizes the otherwise political difference between a military and democratic regime. In fact, decentralization, like democracy, mean several things to may people, hence the importance in understanding the theoretical argument underpinning decentralization as a concept of development and political empowerment.

The Theory of Decentralization

What is theory and where does decentralization come in? Many studies have argued that decentralization at best solidifies the core of democratic principles, which present the idea that government must be chronologically be responsive to the desires and interest of its citizens. So in making a theoretical argument for or against decentralization, what set of principles is use to analyze the relations among the principles to explain the decentralization phenomenon? The literature defines decentralization in a variety of ways by the degree of delegation and autonomy of local actors (Assibey-Mensah 2000; Fesler 1965; Werlin 2003), which presents conflicts and dilemmas in the concept and its impact (Faguet 1997; Hommes 1995). Empirical literature does not agree on the benefits of decentralization, as different studies are poles apart in their conclusions. For example, there are two schools of thought when it comes to decentralization; while Olowu and Wunsch (1990), Putnam (1993), and World Bank (1994) argue that decentralization makes governments more responsive, Faguet (2008), Tanzi (1995), Prud'homme (1995) and Samoff (1990) think otherwise. In fact, Faguet maintains, "local governments are too susceptible . . . to local demand" (1101). Ghana's 1992 constitutional recognition for decentralization did renew political interest in decentralization. The concept remotely but pragmatically contributed to citizens of Ghana often rejecting leaders appointed by the central government (Ayisi 2008).

So is decentralization only beneficial to politicians or citizens? While economists focus on efficiency and equity, public administration scholars are also interested in the distribution of power, responsiveness, transparency, and accountability (Klingner and Nalbandian 1998). The literature affirms that macroeconomic function must remain with the central government, suggesting that local governments must deal with program specificities for local demand. Oates' (1993) analysis of over fifty countries confirmed a positive relationship between decentralization and economic growth. But if decentralization is defined through the Matthew Effect (ME) theory, then districts with more resources are more likely to develop faster than the deprived ones.

The concept of ME has more pragmatic approach to development where the intervention of the central government is needed to help less developed regions. The traditional understanding of decentralization was that the conquered where spread all over the territories the empire therefore the only effective way of administration was decentralize some of the centralized responsibilities to the conquered. The theoretical argument for fiscal decentralization is dated going back to the days of James Madison and Rousseaus in the seventeenth and eighteenth centuries (Wolman 1990) though they had different reasons for decentralization. For example, in the *Federalist Papers No. 39*

(FP39), Madison argued that leaders must derived their powers "directly . . . from the great body of the people," which means that locals and "not inconsiderable . . . handful of . . . nobles exercising their oppression by a delegation of their powers" (Rossiter 1961, 241). Though decentralization is not specifically mentioned in FP39, Madison believes that the people must be given the mandate to elect their leaders as "composing the distinct and independent" region, "which they respectively belong" (243).

Rousseau also favored small government. To him, "rulers over burdened with business, see nothing for themselves: clerks govern" (1762: 59–50). Using Poland's political system, Rousseau, who advocated for a political reformation, instructed the Poles to perfect and extend the authority of their provincial parliaments to avoid the dangers of larger state bureaucracies (1772, 183–184). By this assertion, Rousseau was insisting on the essentials of local representation: decentralization. According to Wolman, small democratic (local) governments were the fundamental hopes of the people as most of them distrusted the activities of the central government. The debate for political decentralization is inconclusive in the literature as both proponents and opponents provide different findings in their studies (see for example Putnam 1993 and Prud'homme 1995).

Though decentralization is primarily a strategy for transferring authority and responsibility from the central government to subnational (regional and district) levels of government (Ostrom 1989; Stone 1997), many African leaders only adopt the concept in theory but fail to delegate powers to the districts and regions. Some studies maintain that the concept is not easily defined; therefore, it has several dimensions and a wide variety of institutional restructuring, which encompasses the term *decentralization*. Though some scholars see it as a simple term, they argue that its simplistic generalization is sometimes too broad. According to Fesler (1965), decentralization is a term of rich conceptual and empirical meaning, "which can designate static fact and dynamic process and it can refer to pure ideal-type and to moderate incremental change" (536) when the rational theory of decentralization is understood in all compartments.

Forms of Classical Decentralization

Decentralization (*political/administrative*, *deconcentration*, *devolution*, and *delegation*) as used in this chapter comes in different forms. Definition is provided based on the degree of discretion and responsibility delegated by the central executive. The literature shows that developing countries have addressed decentralization in different ways: a reflection of the history, politics, and the culture for administrative and economic efficiency, but more importantly, the role of district and regional leaders in focusing on the needs of their constituencies. However, the concept of the decentralization/development dichotomy has not yielded the desired results in other parts of the world (Kettl 2000), including Ghana.

Political/Administrative Decentralization

Political and administrative leaders are used interchangeable in this chapter though each could be distinctively define by other studies. Political decentralization, which is manifested in the degree and types of political autonomy and accountability, is of greater importance to this study. A fully developed system of political decentralization in Ghana is a situation where local people in the districts and regions elect their own legislative and executive personnel so that these units will be able to hire, pay, and dismiss administrative personnel without reference to central authority.

This gives citizens and their elected representatives' power in the public decision-making process. Political decentralization is associated with pluralistic politics and representative government. But it can also support democratization by giving citizens or their representatives more influence in the formulation and implementation of policies (Furniss 1974; Harrigan 1994) in their electoral areas. Political decentralization often requires constitutional or statutory reforms. Such a reform may force elected officials in their constituencies to be more accountable to the electorates instead of satisfying the wishes of a distant executive. This empowerment, unfortunately, is lacking in the current political process where the executive has the exclusive power to appoint district and regional leaders. The literature affirms that "political appointees are subject to the whims" (Klingner and Nalbandian 1998, vol. 43) of the central government.

Empirical studies generally tend to favor political decentralization over centralization in terms of innovation, leadership accountability, and responsiveness (Taylor 2003). This assertion, according to Taylor, has "become a sort of accepted wisdom among social scientists" (231). Nevertheless, given the theoretical support by social scientists, a general correlation between political decentralization and innovation is yet to be firmly established. Treisman (2007) argues that self-governing is the core aspect of modern democratic nations where the people must elect their own leaders. To Treisman, political decentralization is good for its facilitating features. These include but not limited to administrative efficiency, check on central government abuses, and policy experimentation. While it satisfies geographically concentrated ethnic groups, it can also prompt locally elected officials to be unsupportive to central government by "play[ing] the ethnic card" (15) to distort fiscal distribution. Political decentralization oftentimes leads to another form of decentralization; deconcentration.

Deconcentration

A form of network of central power and substate institutions comprising the elites of these constituencies give birth to deconcentration. As Assibey Mensah (2000) puts it, deconcentration is a power-sharing strategy where power is transferred from central-operating agencies to regional ones. The central government under such a concept uses the local governments to improve efficiency and effectiveness of delivering services (Cheema and Rondinelli 1983, 79–81). Rondinelli et al. (1981) argue that deconcentration takes place as long as central government disperses certain responsibilities of services to regional and local governments.

Devolution

Another division of decentralization is devolution. The theory behind this stipulates that it is non-incorporation with the districts. The central authority does not exercise any authority, and the regions are left alone in their operations. It is the transfer of service responsibility from the central government to autonomous units of local government with some corporate status. Devolution is a radical political concept that involves the creation of independent units at the subnational level. These autonomous entities function on their own accord to signify separation from the central authority.

For example, Conyers (1984) argues that it is the legal establishment of locally and democratically elected political authorities; but other scholars, Prud'homme (1995) and Samoff (1990), do question the viable policy process for development. Conyers is more likely to argue that poor districts and regions in Ghana, for example, may not benefit from the central government assistance if decentralization is adopted, making these areas less likely to develop. According to Cohen and Peterson (1991), the concept represents separateness of structure within a political system. But Esman and Uphoff (1984), argue that devolution and decentralization are two different issues, which should not be discussed together for any comparison. They argued that decentralization has relations to a central authority, but devolution is a unit of its own and not accountable to any authority.

This concept of decentralization describes an intra-organizational pattern of power relationships and should be seen as such. Esman and Uphoff contend that the institutional separation from other levels of the government only succeeds in rendering the local levels impotent. For example, the poor districts in the northern part of Ghana cannot raise enough revenue for development since there are no significant industries and businesses to provide employment in these districts. There are various interpretations of devolution in the literature as Uwadibie (2000) maintains that local autonomy "does not create incentives for development [but] only creates a network of organizations to promote development . . . by the central authority" (58).

Kincaid (1998) describes devolution as a revolution that must make state and local governments more efficient and effective in service delivery. He identifies the objectives of devolution to include (1) more efficient provision and production of public services; (2) better alignment of the cost and benefits of government for a diverse citizenry; (3) better fits between public goods and their spatial characteristics; (4) increased competition, experimentation, and innovation in the public sector; (5) greater responsiveness to citizen preferences; and (6) more transparent accountability in policymaking. Kincaid argues that these are ambitious objectives with no apparent direction but occurs in the context of vertical intergovernmental relations with some constitutional changes. In countries where devolution has been used, the central government still retains some authority. In Ghana, regardless of which type of decentralization the central government adopts, the executive will still control well over the districts and regions because of the dire financial conditions of some of the districts.

Delegation

The fourth and final form of decentralization discussed in this chapter is delegation, which seeks to transfer service responsibility from central government agencies to specialized organizations with some degree of operating autonomy (Ayee 2000). Apart from devolution, which is expected to stand on its own, the other forms of decentralization discussed above tend to overlap in the execution of responsibilities between the centralized authority and district or regional representatives. The theory of decentralization obviously presents a problem for a country with a unitary political system like Ghana because of its political and legal structures where the central government has all the administrative powers. In a Federalist country like Nigeria, the states responsibilities are clearly defined in its constitution but that is not the case for unitary countries.

Decentralization: Now and Then

Since the overthrow of the first president of Ghana, Osagyefo Dr. Kwame Nkrumah, almost all the governments from 1966 to 2012 have embraced decentralization in principle. For example, the National Patriotic Party (NPP), under John Agyekum Kufuor's presidency, like his predecessor, Jerry John Rawlings of the National Democratic Congress (NDC), promoted the decentralization concept as one of his administrative goals. But how will an administration choose one strategy over another as discussed above remains a matter of preference and interest of that administration. Though the constitution provides the structure of decentralization in Ghana (see Ghana's Constitution, Chapter 20, *Article 240 [A-E]*), it does not allow the locals to elect their political leaders. For example, *Article 243 (1)* states that regional and district political leaders "shall be appointed by the President." Undeniably, democratic deficits are associated with the ongoing decentralization reforms in Ghana. One can argue that decentralization has not succeeded since it does appear to adopt the characteristics discussed in the literature. The concept of political decentralization in Ghana has negative implications since some districts have over the years resisted the appointments and nominations of their leaders by the central authority.[1]

A detail discussion of the complexities that faced political leadership in Ghana, including the Kufuor administration, regarding decentralization is beyond the scope of this

---

1　　In his article, "Politics of inclusion, development planning, decentralization," Dr. Gabriel A. Ayisi argues that Ghana's democracy is at a learning curve as long as the president continues to appoint district and regional leaders. He refers to such practice as "politics of exclusion." He rejects the situation where the leadership is only comfortable dealing with only those in its political party. (http://www. ghanaweb.com/GhanaHomePage/features/artikel.php?ID=147006).　See also "Ghana's decentralization programme is failing." Retrieved from http://www.ghanaweb.com/GhanaHomePage/NewsArchive/artikel. php?ID=147630　on January 20, 2009.

chapter. However, some understanding of the concept from a historical background may help to explain the quandary of the executive. The literature on this topic considers the colonial British' indirect rule through the local chiefs as the genesis of decentralization in the then Gold Coast (Ghana). Decentralization thus became a political tool for the British through the chiefs and their elders to reinforce the wishes of the British government. As Bamfo (2000) noted, those chiefs who cooperated with the British were rewarded. And the uncooperative ones were punished. Such an authoritative implementation of the concept created fear among the chiefs and the locals.

Ghana's political independence in March 1957 did little to change the political structures established by the colonizers. As a result, many studies have described postcolonial decentralization ineffective as regime change through military coups became the order of the day after Kwame Nkrumah was ousted in 1966. It was during the mid-1970s under Lt. Col. Ignatius Kutu Acheampong's military regime where the government tried to empower the locals (Nkrumah, 2000). The history of contemporary decentralization in spite of Acheampong's attempt is credited to the Provisional National Defense Council (PNDC) regime under Jerry John Rawlings' administration (Assibey-Mensah 2000). Assibey-Mensah noted that after the passage of the 1987 local government law, PNDC Law 207, "110 District Councils and their respective District Assemblies (DAs) were set up" (17) to ensure local participation in the decision-making process. This led to the formation of the defunct People's Defense Committees (PDCs) in communities to identify each area's needs instead of relying on the central government to make every decision and try to solve local problems from the Castle.[2] Research shows that the PDC concept created grassroots interest in local administration as district elections during the PNDC regime were the highest ever recorded for the decades in the late 1980s. Assibey-Mensah also noted that "official reports indicated that 58.9 percent of registered Ghanaian voters cast their ballots in the local elections, and the turnout was the highest of any district-level election over the past 30 years" (200, 17).

The PDCs, made up of locally self-identified defenders of the PNDC revolution, effectively took over local government responsibilities, though often limited to mobilizing the implementation of local self-help projects, while the deconcentrated ministries played a more significant role. Ayee (1994) notes that despite the PNDC's rhetoric, its interest in decentralization reflected that of previous regimes, thus, a curiosity in the administrative decentralization of central government and not the devolution of political authority to the local level. Additionally, Ayee (2000) perceives a key feature of local governance, through the PDCs for example, in the pre-1988 period as a dual hierarchical structure in which central and local government institutions operated in parallel, but with encroachment at times by better-resourced central government on the roles and responsibilities of under-resourced local revolutionary activists (49–50). The PDC concept of decentralization became a legitimate revolutionary political institution under the PNDC military administration. Was there any legal or constitutional backing to decentralization in Ghana?

---

2   The Castle is the seat of government of Ghana. It is located in the national capital, Accra, and was built by the Europeans for trading on the West African Coast.

Decentralization before the 2000s in Ghana

Though decentralization has been a component of democratic Ghana, its history goes back to the colonial and military regimes. The PNDC government introduced a legislative reform, the local government law (LGL) or PNDC Law 207 in 1988, which led to the creation of 110 designated districts within Ghana's ten regions. Nonpartisan district assembly (DA) elections were held for the first time in 1988/89 under the PNDC and subsequently every four years (1994, 1998, 2002, 2006, and 2008). The law provides in part that two-thirds of DA members will be elected on an individual nonpartisan basis where one-third is appointed by the central government including a district chief executive (DCE) for each of the 110 districts. The 1988 LGL was to promote grassroots, citizen participation, and ownership of the machinery of government by devolving power, competence, and means at the district level. The PNDC decentralization exercise, through the PDCs, was to satisfy the demands of the revolution and not in the interest of democratic principles. Ayee argues that the decentralization policy under the second Rawlings regime had self-serving motives.

The military administration of the PNDC's decentralization policy was, therefore, seen by critics, as an effort to increase the legitimacy of Rawlings second revolution, which ruled Ghana from 1982 through 1992. After eleven years of dictatorship under Rawlings (1981–1991), the 1992 Constitution provided a transition from a military rule to multiparty democracy at the national level, which also authorized the 1988 LGL reforms. It consolidated the aim of decentralization within the overall context of a liberal democratic constitution; yet essential democratic elements remained compromised, especially through the retention of presidential appointments instead of local elections in the districts. The objective of decentralization was laid out specifically in the 1992 Constitution[3] under "Decentralization and Local Government." Here the constitution states categorically in *Article 240[1]* that "Local government and administration . . . be decentralized," and that the "functions, powers, responsibilities and resources should be transferred from the Central Government (*Castle*) to local government" constituencies (*Article 240[2]*).

The independent role of local government, with discretionary powers at the grassroots, was subjected to a provision in article 240[2][b], which states that "measures should be taken to enhance the capacity of local government authorities to plan, initiate, co-ordinate, manage and execute policies in respect of matters affecting local people." The principles of participation in local government and accountability to the locals were also emphasized in *Article 240[2][e]*, which states, "To ensure the accountability of local government authorities, people in particular local government areas shall, as far as practicable, be afforded the opportunity to participate effectively in their governance." There is a contradiction here. For example, during the eras of the Rawlings and Kufour's administrations, the locals rejected their leaders. But the executive rejected the cry of the locals.[4]

---

3   See chapter 20 of Ghana's constitution. The chapter discusses how decentralization should be implemented in Ghana.

4   See, for example, how districts have rejected appointments of the president over the years; yet those officials end up as district executives because the people have limited power in rejecting the president's nominations.http://www.ghanaweb.com/GhanaHomePage/NewsArchive/artikel.php?ID=83836. Retrieved November 2 , 2008

It is a common practice for the central government to appoint someone the people have rejected in parliamentary elections to become the senior administrator in the same constituency. In 2005, several of such appointments were made and the trend did not change. Critics argue that "in the first place, *such practice* amounts to undermining democracy, because these were people who were rejected by their own constituents at an election and the government is recycling them by using the 'back door' to now impose them on the people as their political heads." [5] Without a doubt, the democratic intent in the decentralization requirements are provided in article 35[6][d] that the "State shall take appropriate measures by decentralizing the administrative and financial machinery of government to the regions and districts and by affording all possible opportunities to the people to participate in decision-making at every level of national life and in government." The 1992 Constitution preserved some of the PNDC 1988 reforms of nonpartisan local-level elections and presidential powers of appointment. The DAs comprised 70 percent elected members and 30 percent of members appointed by the president "in consultation with traditional authorities and other interest groups in the district" (*Article 242[d]*). For example, the appointment of a district chief executive (DCE) by the president is retained, with at least the approval of 66 percent of the DA members (*Article 243[1]*). The DCE is the political head of the local executive, centrally involved in decision-making, with a district coordinating director (DCD) as the highest-ranking civil servant. The constitution also provides guidelines for the local government on finances and clearly states that the DAs "should have sound financial bases with adequate and reliable sources of revenue" [*Article 240(2)*], with an attempt to secure this through the establishment of the district assembly common fund (DACF). This is determined annually by the legislature but with appropriation "not less than five per cent of the total revenues of Ghana" [*Article 252(2)*]. The proceeds of the DACF are divided between DAs on the basis of a revenue-sharing formula approved by the legislative. *Article 240* provides reforms of the civil service with local government authority that states, "as far as practicable, the persons in the service of the local government shall be subject to effective control of local authorities" [2][d]). The irony of article 240 is that it is focused extensively on the districts with no mention of the responsibilities of regional leaders. For Ghana to benefit from the decentralization concept, it will largely depend on the vision of the leadership and constitutional amendment to empower the electorates.

The Crossroad of Decentralization

The process of getting an individual elected to public office, electioneering, is more of an elite democracy, which limits the electorates' role of choosing their leaders. In democratic Africa core party members choose candidates. The unfortunate situation

---

5   The central government forces public administrators on the district through the back door, which most locals disagree but have no choice of questioning the government.
See   http://www.ghanaweb.com/GhanaHomePage/NewsArchive/artikel.php?ID=82223.   Retrieved   on October 29, 2008

in African politics is that each party has completely different agenda. Thus, there is no national agenda, which is embraced by ruling and opposition parties. In terms of policy issues and nation building, Ghana's political administrations lack continuity. The road to Ghana's independence was brutal and nasty, as the British did not want to relent its power over the occupied colonies. The military and democratic mix of Ghana's political system since independence has given leaders cause to be cautious of how they share power at the regional and district levels. Since the military ousted the Convention People's Party (CPP) under Kwame Nkrumah's administration in 1966, democratically elected leaders like Dr. K. A. Busia (1969–1972), Dr. Hilla Limann (1979–1981), J. J. Rawlings (1992–2000), J. A. Kufour (2001–2008), and Professor Evans Fiifi Atta-Mills (2008-2012) have always suspected some individuals who may influence the military in coup plots. Busia and Liman became victims of military coups in 1972 and 1981 respectively while the Kufour administration accused some individuals of plotting to overthrow his administration. For example, several media reports quoted President Kufour, "that ex-President Rawlings *was* planning a coup to topple his government."[6] How does this play into decentralization? Given the above discussion, leaders tend to delegate responsibilities and government duties to individuals who are loyal to a ruling party instead of allowing the grassroots to elect their own leaders to ensure security. It can be argued that such appointments do not consider the interest of the ruled who oftentimes reject the presidential appointees.

On four different occasions (1966, 1972, 1979, and 1981), the Constitution of Ghana was suspended as a result of military coups. Such political instability has forced democratic leaders, arguably, to act like military leaders where the executive tends to hold on to power while the regional leaders become extensions of the executive branch without any significant power. Democratic and undemocratic changes of government in Ghana affect local political structures.

For example, the fall of Nkrumah's CPP saw the collapse of the Young Pioneers[7] while the PDCs vanished with the defunct PNDC as grassroot political structure. Ghana's political history shows that decentralization is a concept used by governments to reflect the leaders' political ideologies as seen under Nkrumah, Rawlings, Kufour, Atta-Mills administrations. But the actual implementation of the concept under any of these leaders is

---

6   An internet search on Rawlings coups in 2006 in ghanaweb.com provided eighty different stories. See also http://www.ghanaweb.com/GhanaHomePage/NewsArchive/artikel.php?ID=113201, retrieved November 4, 2008. Though none was found to be true, several media reports alleged that there are possibilities that Rawlings might oust the Kufour administration.

7   The Young Pioneers was the youth branch of the CPP especially among elementary and middle school students to propagate the ideology of Nkrumahism. It was used to cement the "physical presence" of Nkrumah in the districts and regions. The main purpose of the Young Pioneer Movement was to train the youth of Ghana to be up to their civic responsibility. To imbue them with a sense of patriotism, Nkrumah wanted the youth to be selfless in serving their nation but also dedicate them to building Ghana, in particular, and Africa, in general, where loyalty would not be to self, clan, or tribe. These objectives were in line with Kwame Nkrumah's vision of a free continent that would have a unitary government, a common market, a borderless Africa, technologically advanced and industrialized continent.

far from how the literature defines it. Politically, whether civilian or military, the executive has always appointed favorites as political leaders in the regions and districts with little input from the local electorates.

Presidential and Local Elections in Ghana

Do tribes play a role in African elections? This a very hard question to answer but one could easily argue that tribalism is a key factor in African elections. If tribalism is a factor then political ideology is equally an important variable in electing a leader. Elections in the Fourth Republic of Ghana reject the popular notion in the literature that Africans elect their leaders based on tribes. For example, the first two presidential elections (1992 and 1996) in the Fourth Republic, which elected Rawlings on both occasions was attributed, in part, to his popularity and charisma. Some critics have also argued that the long ban[8] on political party activities in the country as a result of the 1981 military coup seemed to have disorganized the opposition parties as some of their key party members were in either in exile or lost interest in active politics.

Ethnicity, Youth, and Voting

Critics of Rawlings regimes argued that he was voted to power because Ghanaians feared he might not have given up power in event of losing the general presidential elections in 1992. Though the opposition parties, especially the NPP, argued that the 1992 election was stolen by the NDC, the parties realized they had to unite to beat the NDC[9] in the 1996 election. The NPP and other political parties in opposition at the time lamented that the only way for the opposition win was "to *come in* terms with the fact that they have to unite or fall, there is every indication that the country is set to see one election, which in more ways than one will define greatly the future of the country."[10] It took the opposition nearly eight years to organize itself and confront the NDC on issues of interest to the people rather than ethnicity. Paul Nugent (2001) observed that the NPP, a leading opposition party from 1992–2000, was "more exposed to the charge of ethnic bias, given a heavy predominance of Akans within the leadership" (3) mostly from the Ashanti and Eastern regions. The NPP was seen as a two-region party and does not represent the rest of the country. In fact, it was not seen as a broad base party.

The results of both the 2000 and 2004 general presidential elections illustrated Ghanaian electorates will vote for someone they see competent, dedicated, and visionary—

---

8   Political parties activities were banned every time (1966, 1972, 1979, and 1981) there was a military coup in Ghana.

9   The NDC complained bitterly that the 2004 general election was stolen by the NPP and the Kufour administration.

10   The opposition parties decided to unite and remove the NDC from power since such a move would ensure the needed votes. See http://www.ghanaweb.com/GhanaHomePage/NewsArchive/artikel.php?ID=394. Retrieved on October 25, 2008.

not just a tribesman. Nugent noted "the distinctive characteristic of the 2000 elections *for example*, is that ethnicity did not feature particularly overtly in the campaign" (3). This means that Ghanaians are looking for and interested in good leadership. Therefore, the electorates will vote for anyone who they deem exhibits the qualities that will set the country on the economic path for growth. For example, when Ghanaians were not completely pleased with Rawlings and the NDC after the birth of the Fourth Republic in 1992, the party was voted out eight years later. Figures from the 2000 and 2004 elections indicate that the flag bearer of the NDC, Professor Evans Atta-Mills, a Fanti from Cape Coast, *Central Region*, could not win his own region during these elections.[11] Kufour carried the *Central Region* with over 60.2 and 58.8 percent against Atta-Mills' 39.8 and 38.9 percent in 2000 and 2004 respectively of the total votes cast. This analysis is focused only on the two leading parties, NPP and NDC, since the remaining parties were statistically insignificant in the voting results. Nugent noted that in 2000, the youth determined the outcome of the presidential election as it voted for a change and not on ethnic issues.

The youth considered the NPP as an instrument for change because of the party's endless promises for change, transparency, zero tolerance for corruption, and more vibrant economic growth. He argues that "each of the major parties *has support* across the length and breadth of Ghana" (3). Therefore, ethnicity was not a compelling issue in the general elections. On his third attempt to the presidency in 2008, John Evans Fiifi Atta-Mills' (NDC) strategic door-to-door campaign paid off against Nana Akufo-Addo's (NPP presidential candidate for 2008) big musical rallies, which drew both voting and nonvoting citizens to rallies. But the 2008 general election again established Nugent's (2001) argument that Ghanaians vote on issues and not on ethnicity.

While this assertion may be debatable, one can argue that the Kufour administration distance itself from the people as most of the ministers, including the president, exhibited a luxurious lifestyle without accounting for where they got their wealth. Many Ghanaians, not all, believed the wealth of some politicians were ill-gotten, not legally acquired. Apart from convincingly capturing the NDC stronghold, the Volta Region, Atta-Mills also made an impressive surge in the Asante and Eastern Regions, which were believed to be the Mecca for the NPP party. Overall, the NDC won eight out of the ten regions during the 2008 presidential run-off election[12]. A comparative analysis of the general election results provided by the Ghana Electoral Commission over the last three (2000, 2004, and 2008) presidential elections showed that Atta-Mills made significant gains over those years to eventually win the presidency in 2008.

Some Ghanaians found the Kufour administration as corrupt and non-accountable to

---

11   See the results of Ghana's presidential results for 2000 and 2004. Results were retrieved from http://www.ghanaweb.com/GhanaHomePage/election2000/ and http://www.ghanaweb.com/GhanaHomePage/election2004/election.results.php. 29 October 2008.

12   The run-off, which was held on December 28, 2008, became possible after each candidate failed the needed 50 plus percent needed for a candidate to win presidential election in Ghana. The run-off was statistically in a dead heat as Atta-Mills had 50.23 percent and 49.77 percent. See http://www.ghanaweb.com/GhanaHomePage/election2008/presidential2.php. Retrieved January 20 , 2009.

the electorate as it failed to account for the exact amount spent on Ghana Jubilee House (The White House of Ghana) and the fiftieth anniversary celebrations of Ghana. Several media reports during the transitional period from the Kufour's administration to the Atta-Mills administration exposed gross financial misappropriation.[13] Former ministers tried to legally, though through the back door, reward themselves. But such personal rewards were condemned by most Ghanaians and some of the notable NPP members.[14]

Elections and Democracy in Africa

Election is defined here as the act of casting one's vote to elect a preferred individual for a vacant position. Though elections may involve local or national, public or private, formal or informal depending on the type of position an individual is casting a vote for. Unfortunately, most African elections do not bear strong resemblance to the classical democratic understanding of elections. It could be argued that African voters either lack the needed information to elect their leaders or vote for groups to which they belong. They clinch to their strong held positions, which makes it an unwilling compromise during elections to change the minds of the electorates. Voting in any African formal elections such as presidential and parliamentary start with registration followed by a period of endless campaign where individuals contesting for any vacant position are expected to communicate with the electorates. These campaigns are suppose to discuss policy issues, visions of candidates, and their future plans. Unfortunately, campaigns on the continent have become personal attacks and insults, which make it difficult for the electorate to scrutinize the different policy positions presented by the candidates, if any.

Voters are bombarded with party slogan, misinformation about their opponents, and false promises. However, in any matured democracy, the people govern themselves or play a significant role in the governing process through elections. The theory of modern representative democratic systems provide that the core of popular participation is voting, therefore an elected candidate will represent the voice of the governed. The gap created through legal and constitutional backing for not electing district chief executives (DCEs) and regional ministers (RMs) in Ghana has been highlighted in this chapter. The actual challenge is on government (parliament) to realize this loophole in the country's constitution by legally and procedurally amending the constitution for elections in the district to elect individuals of their choice. A weak democratic constitution is better than the strongest authoritative decree since the former avails itself for amendments as they become necessary through the will of the ruled and their representatives while the latter presents the wishes

---

13   Though the seat of government, Jubilee House, was officially "outdoored" during the final month of the Kufour administration, the Atta-Mills found the building internally uncompleted and costing more than what Ghanaians were told. In addition, the fiftieth anniversary celebrations was found to be in arrears while some of the numerous vehicles imported for the celebrations were also missing. See http://www.ghanaweb.com/GhanaHomePage/NewsArchive/artikel.php?ID=156786

14   Some Ghanaians found President Kufour's extravagant, self-rewarding ambition as greed. See also http://www.ghanaweb.com/GhanaHomePage/NewsArchive/artikel.php?ID=156476

of an individual or the privileged few of an authoritative government. At least there is an iota of accountability in democratic system. However, the effectiveness of the process will depend on the viability of the institutions and citizens participation to ensure transparency.

The 1992 Constitution came into being after over a decade of military rule. It can therefore be argued that the absence of honest and prolonged discussion in the writing of this constitution before its adoption may have represented the views of a few who belong to the military class with their authoritative ideology despite several years of constitutional assembly meetings. Twenty years into the Fourth Republic is considered young in the political literature. However, it seems to be the ripe time for rigorous debates to amendments if the constitution will be able to stand the test of the years ahead as Ghana snails into a well-established democracy.

The government must devise new strategies for managing public programs as it critically evaluates policies regarding issues like health, education, the national economy, elections, and transportation. With anticipated growth in the economy and other sectors, it is obvious that the central government may not be able to police every sector of the economy at large, especially in the regions. Hence, the importance of decentralization as discussed earlier in this paper. Most government bureaucracies in Ghana remain structured and staffed to manage the traditional pre-independence political programs with the central government in control of every activity.

As the country has undeniably accepted democracy as the way toward viable political and economic development, government strategies and tactics must also change especially its structures and process in the area of human resource management. Regrettably, such centralized bureaucratic structures of the executive-appointed leaders in the regions and districts have not changed significantly in line with democratic principles. Though the district and regional leaders' appointments by presidents have constitutional backing, this paper advocates for a constitutional amendment to allow locals in electing their leaders instead of the central government. Admittedly, since the 1990s, Ghana has undergone a steady but often unnoticed transformation such as policies toward improved health care, education, transportation, and economic growth. However, in all these sectors, a decentralized management system could have provided a better sense of local ownership, which would have led to an improved maintenance of facilities and government assets through transparency and accountability on the part of the elected. Locals' direct involvement in electing their leaders is more likely to improve government efficiency and responsiveness, which will also ensure both regional and district accountability where the locals will have the mandate to replace or retain their leaders through elections based on the leaders' performance during their term.

Conclusion

Several conclusions can be drawn from the preceding narratives. Not much has changed since independence in terms of political structures in most African countries including Ghana. Despite the democratic structures, which on the whole are preferred by Ghanaians traditional structures of administration continue to prevail and politicians count on those structures for votes. Traditional, religious, and ethnicity interact in various ways leading to uncertainties in the democratic process. But for now Ghana, like Unganda, has successfully held a number of elections despite accusations of electoral irregularities and fraud by losing parties. Public administration and governance under the concept of decentralization were discussed. The theory of decentralization seems appealing, but countries are not sure, which type should be utilized. Decentralization enjoys both legal and constitutional guarantees with strong multiparty support as some scholars argue that decentralization ensures responsibility, efficiency, and accountability through participatory democracy.

The post-independence history of decentralization in Ghana has come with criticisms as the executive tends to appoint only party loyalists: the spoils-system concept. Such executive power, as enshrined in the constitution, does not ensure participatory democracy "unless the right, interest and involvement . . . [of] . . . society at large are taken into consideration [through] elections (Loh 2008, 128). Allowing locals to elect their own political leaders is likely to force local public officials to perform since lack thereof may result with the electorates rejecting them in future elections. The success of democracy is dependent on transparency, accountability, trust, and citizens' engagement in the process.

Many African countries have experienced decentralization especially under the traditional or tribal administrative system. In fact, most locals prefer to elect their immediate leaders who are aware of their needs instead of appointed officials by the central government. The implication of the decentralization model as understood in the literature shows that the central governments are not able to effectively provide and monitor services. Though local governments may lack the resources to fully provide for their citizens, they are responsive to the needs of their people. For example, fiscal decentralization is known to increase productivity at the local level where the locals instead of central government officials monitor accountability. However, it should be noted that there is no simple uniformity in decentralization. In incorporating decentralization in policies each country on the continent must understand the tradeoffs in the process to tailor the process to address the needs of the governed.

Decentralization continues to expand political participation in democratic African countries as both in theory and practice some bottlenecks in decision-making are avoided in the interest of the locals. It reduces bureaucratic red tape in addressing local needs through religious, ethnic, and political diversity and stability. Despite the theoretical advantages of decentralization, one must not see the concept as a panacea to lack of development on the continent. The Matthew Effect theory shows that political units with weak administrative, financial, and human resources are more likely to remain under served if the central government does not intervene. A balance between locals and central government is needed for decentralization to succeed.

References

Assibey-Mensah, George, O. 2000. Decentralization on trial: The case of Ghana's district assemblies. *Western Journal of Black Studies*, 24 (1) 16–23.

Ayee, J.R.A. 2000. Decentralization and Good Governance in Ghana. Unpublished paper of May 2000 prepared for the Canadian High Commission, Accra, Ghana.

———. 1994. *An anatomy of public policy implementation: The case of decentralization policies in Ghana.* Avebury, Aldershot.

Bamfo, Napoleon 2000. The hidden elements of democracy among Akyem chieftaincy: Enstoolment, destoolment, and other limitations of power. *Journal of Black Studies* 31 (2) 149–173.

Bennet, R.J. 1990 *Decentralization: Local governments and markets.* London: Clarendon Press.

Cheema, G. Shabbir, and Dennis A. Rondinelli 1983. "Implementating decentralization policies: An introduction." In *Decentralization and Development: Policy Implementation in Developing Countries* (9-34). Edited G. Shabbir Cheema and Dennis A. Rondinelli. Beverly Hills; New Delhi: Sage Publications.

Cohen, John M. and Stephen B. Peterson 1999. *Administrative decentralization: Strategies for developing countries.* Hartford, Connecticut. Kumarian Press, Inc.

Conyers, D. 1984. Decentralization and development: A review of the literature. *Public Administration and Development.* 4: 187–197.

Esman, M.J. and N.T. Uphoff (1984). *Local organization: Intermediaries in rural development.* Ithaca: Cornell University Press.

Faguet, Jean-Paul (1997). Decentralization and local government performance: A Report- Technical Consultation on Decentralization. FAO, Rome 16–18 December 1997. Working Group 6: Decentralization and Natural Resources Management.

_____ 2008 Decentralization's effect on public investment: Evidence and policy lessons from Bolivia and Colombia. *Journal of Development Studies* 44 (8) 1100–1121.

Fresler, James 1965. Approaches to the understanding of decentralization. *Journal of Politics* 27 (3) 536–565.

Furniss, Norman 1974. The practical significance of decentralization. *The Journal of Politics.* 36 (4) 958–982.

Ghana 2005. *Economic Aspects of Good Governance: Public Financial Management* Retrieved March 3, 2005 from: http://www.ghana.gov.gh./index.php

Harrigan, John J. 1994. *Politics and policy in the states and communities* (5th ed.) Glenview, ILL: Harper Collins College Publishers.

Hommes, Rudolf 1995. Conflicts and dilemmas of decentralization. *The World Bank Research Observer* 295–316.

Howell, J.M. and Avolio, J.B. 1993. Transformational leadership, transactional leadership, locus of control and support for innovation: Key predictors of consolidated-business-unit performance. *Journal of applied Psychology* 78 (6) 891–902.

Kettl, Donald F. 2000. *The global public management revolution: A report on the transformation of governance.* Washington DC: Brookings Institution Press.

Kettl, Donald F., and James W. Fesler (2009). *The politics of the administrative process.* Washington, D.C. CQ Press

Kim, P.S., Halligan, J., Cho, N., Oh, C.H. and Eikenberry, A.M. 2005. Toward participatory and transparent governance: Report on the sixth global forum on reinventing government. *Public Administration Review* 65 (6) 646–654.

Kincaid, John 1998. The devolution Tortoise and the centralization Hare." *New England Economic Review*, Vol. 00284726.

King, Stephen M. and Bradley S. Chilton 2009. *Administration in the public interest: Principles, policies, and practices.* Durham, NC. Carolina Academic Press.

Klingner, Donald E. and John Nalbandian 1998. Public personnel management: Contexts and strategies. Upper Saddle River, NJ. Prentice Hall.

Loh, Francis Kok Wah 2008. Procedural democracy, participatory democracy and regional networking: The Multi-terrain struggle for democracy in Southeast Asia. *Inter-Asia Cultural Studies*. 9 (1) 127–141.

Nkrumah, S.A. 2000. Decentralization for good governance and development: The   Ghanaian experience' *Regional Development Dialogue 21* (1) 53–67

Ntsebeza, Lungisile 2004. Democratic decentralization and traditional authority: Dilemmas of land administration in rural South Africa. *European Journal of Development Research*, (16) 1: 71-89.

Nugent, Paul 2001. Ethnicity as an explanatory factor in the Ghana 2000 elections. *African Issues* XXIX/1&2 2–7.

Oates, Wallace E. 1977. *The political economy of fiscal federalism.* Lexington, Massachusetts: Lexington Books.

Olowu, D. and Wunsch, J.S. 1990. *The failure of the centralized state: Institutions and self-governance in Africa.* Boulder, CO: Westview Press.

Ostrom, Vincent 1989. *The intellectual crisis in American public administration.* Tuscaloosa : University of Alabama Press.

Porter, M. 1980. *Competitive strategy.* New York, NY: Free Press.

Prud'homme, Remy 1995. The dangers of decentralization. *The World Bank Research Observer* 10 (2) 201–220.

Putnam, R.D. 1993. *Making democracy work: Civic traditions in modern Italy.* Princeton NJ: Princeton University Press.

Reese, L. 1994. The role of counties in local economic development. *Economic Development Quarterly* 8:28–12.

Rondinelli, Denis (1981). Government decentralization in comparative perspective: Theory and practice in developing countries. *International Review of Administrative Science* 47 (2) 133-145.

Rossitter, Clinton 1961. *The federalist papers: Hamilton. Madison. Jay.* NY, New York: Penguin Books.

Rousseau, Jean-Jacques 1762. *The Social Contract.* Trans Frederick Watkins (1986), Madison, University of Wisconsin Press.

_____ 1772. Considerations on the government of Poland and its proposed reformation. Trans; Frederick Watkins (1986), Madison: University of Wisconsin Press.

Shafritz, Jay M., E. W. Russel, and Christopher P. Borick. 2007. *Introducing Public Administration* New York, New York, Pearson: Longman.

_____2013. *Introducing Public Administration* New York, New York, Pearson: Longman.

Stone, Deborah 1997 *Policy paradox: The art of political decision making.* NY, New York: W.W. Norton and Company.

Tanzi, Vito 1995. Fiscal federalism and decentralization: A review of some efficiency and macro-economic aspects. *The World Bank Research Observer* 295–316.

Taylor, Mark Zachary 2003. Political decentralization and technological innovation: Testing the innovative advantages of decentralized states. *Review of Policy Research* 24 (3): 231–257

The World Bank. 2005. *Development report: A better investment climate for everyone.* Washington DC: The World Bank.

Treisman, Daniel 2007. *The architecture of government: Rethinking political decentralization.* NY, New York: Cambridge University Press.

Uwadibie, Nwafejoku Okolie 2000. *Decentralization and economic development in Nigeria: Agricultural policies and implementation.* NY, New York, University Press of America.

Werlin, Herbert H. 2003. Poor nations, rich nations: A theory of governance. *Public Administration Review* 63 (3) 329–342.

Wolman, H 1990. Decentralization: What it is and why should we care. In *Decentralization: local governments and markets* (29-42). R J. Bennet. London: Clarendon Press.

CONTRIBUTORS

Kwame Badu Antwi-Boasiako, PhD, is the Chair of the Department of Government and Associate Professor in Public Administration and Political Science at Stephen F. Austin State University, Nacogdoches, Texas, where he teaches Public Policy, Program Evaluation, Research Methods, and American Government. His primary research interests include traditional institutions and democracy in Africa, decentralization, terrorism, teaching public administration, and diversity in the public sector.

Kwame Asamoah is a Lecturer in the Department of Public Administration and Health Services Management at the University of Ghana Business School. He holds a Ph.D. in Public Administration from Jackson State University. He teaches Public Policy, Issues in Public Administration and Public Sector Human Resource Management. Currently, he is the Ph.D. Coordinator of Department of Public Administration and Health Services Management of University of Ghana Business School. His main research interest includes Public Policy, Decentralization, Human Resource Management, and Organizational Behavior.

Minerva Cruz is an Assistant Professor in the Department of Public Administration at Kentucky State University. She holds a Ph.D. in Political Science with a specialization in Public Administration and Public Policy from Purdue University. She also specializes in Quantitative Methods, Political Economy, Organizational Behavior and Human Resources and has a M.A. in Public Administration from the University of Puerto Rico. She teaches both at the graduate and undergraduate levels: Human Resource Management, Organizational Behavior, Nonprofit Organizations, Comparative Policy, Aging Policy, and Ethics. Dr. Cruz research interests include Health Care Policies, Public Policy Implementation, Comparative Studies, and Culture. She authored the article "Are Older Adults Satisfied With the Implementation of Federal Programs to Serve Aging Populations? A Case Study Policy Implementation," *Home Health Care Management & Practice* (2011). Cruz would like to acknowledge Robert Lancaster of Kentucky State University for his valuable comments and suggestions to this chapter.

Peter Csanyi has a Ph.D. in Political Science from Comenius University in Bratislava, with a specialization in Theory of Politics. He is currently an Assistant Professor and Vice-Chair for International Relations in the Department of Linguistics and Translation Studies at University of Economics in Bratislava, Slovakia. He teaches Comparative Politics, Theory of Political Systems and International Relations at graduate and undergraduate levels. His research interest covers political systems of Central and Western European countries, comparative politics and international relations. Prior to that he was the Vice-Director at the Institute of Political Science of Pan European University, where he directed the international and research activities of the institution. He has given lectures at several European and American universities. He is also a General Editor of an international journal – *Journal of Comparative Politics*.

Ed Gibson has a Ph.D. in Public Administration and Public Affairs from Virginia Polytechnic Institute. He is an Assistant Professor in the School of Public and International Affairs at the University of Baltimore. His entry into academia followed a 25-year career in the information technology (IT) field, ultimately consulting on acquisition-related issues for the federal government as a contractor. Gibson teaches courses in public finance and organization theory at the master's and doctoral levels. His research interests include trends in local government finance, performance management, and public organization studies. His article "Admitting a Bad Influence: Contracting the Public Service" explores the unexamined premises and unintended consequences of rampant contracting within the federal government. Gibson is the author of articles in Administration & Society, International Journal of Public Administration, International Journal of Organization Theory and Behavior, and other public administration journals.

Ahmed Mustafa Elhussein Mansour is a Full Professor in the Department of Political Science, United Arab Emirates University, Alain, Abu Dhabi, United Arab Emirates. He teaches Public Policy, Local Government and Administration and Governmental Budgeting. His research interest covers privatization, public policy, decentralization, total quality management in the public sector and e-government. Some of his recent publications include *"Is Total Quality Management Feasible in a Developing Context? The Employees' Perspective in the United Arab Emirates Public Sector"*, The International Journal of Public Administration (2013), *"E- Government in the Gulf Cooperation Council Countries (GCC): A Comparative Study"*, Journal of Social Sciences (2012), *"The Use of 'Policy Analysis' to Improve the Quality of Policy-Making in Government and Non-Governmental Organizations"*, Current Issues of Business and Law, *(2011), "The Style of Decision-Making in the United Arab Emirates Federal Budgetary Process"*, Journal of Public Budgeting, Accounting and Financial Management (2010), *"The Impact of Privatization on the United Arab Emirates Federal Public Sector"*, International Public Management Review.

James A. Newman is an assistant professor at Southeast Missouri State University where he teaches courses in public policy, public administration, state and local government and program evaluation. He has authored a chapter in an edited book on southern environmental policy that considers the impact of political culture in decision making by states regarding water policy. He has a forthcoming book with Cambria Press addressing interest group influence in the development of interstate water policy in the Southeastern United States. He received his Ph.D. in public policy and administration from Mississippi State University.

Heather Wyatt-Nichol, PhD, is the MPA program director and an Assistant Professor in the College of Public Affairs at the University of Baltimore in Maryland, where she teaches Diversity Management, Public Personnel, and Public Organizations. Her research interests include diversity management, ethics, family friendly-workplace policies, organizational behavior, and social equity.

Hong Pang has a Ph.D. in Politics and International Relations and an M.A. in Economics from the University of Southern California, with a specialization in international political economy and comparative politics. She is currently an Assistant Professor of the Department of History and Political Science, Utah Valley University, Orem, Utah, USA. Prior to the current position, she briefly taught at the School of International Relations at the University of Southern California. She teaches Introduction to Political Science, Introduction to Comparative Politics, Introduction to International Relations, and International Negotiation. She is also developing courses on Chinese Political Economy and Chinese Politics. Her research interests cover domestic compliance of international commitments, international negotiation, the evolution of international institutions, and Chinese politics. The author thanks the US-China Institute, the Dana and David Dornsife College of Letters, Arts and Sciences, the School of International Relations, and the Center for International Studies at the University of Southern California for their generous financial supports for her field work.

Lee W. Payne, PhD, is an Assistant Professor of Political Science and Public Administration at Stephen F. Austin State University, Nacogdoches, Texas, USA. He teaches US Congress, Public Opinion, Media and Politics, Applied Methods for Public Administration, and undergraduate statistics in Political Science. His research interests are public policy, public opinion, party polarization, and environmental politics. Some recent publications include: "The Transition of a Texas County from 'Dry' to 'Wet' and a Comparison of DWI Arrest Rates Before and After" (co-authored with Walt Scalen), *South-Western Journal of*

Criminal Justice (2011), "Constitution of the United States of America," *Social History of Crime and Punishment* (2012), "The Tragedy of the Commons and Climate Change," *Towards a More Livable World: Social Dimensions of Sustainability* (2012), and "Judicial Selection in Texas: A study of General Election Outcomes, 1988-2004" (co-authored with Billy Monroe), *Journal of Political Science* (2013).

Gabriela Miranda-Recinos has a Ph.D. from the University of California Riverside. She is currently an Assistant Professor in the Department of Languages, Cultures, and Communication at Stephen F. Austin State University in Nacogdoches, Texas, USA. Her research area is Latin American literature with a strong emphasis on socio-historical, economic and geo-cultural processes of the region. She teaches Research Methods and Contemporary Literary Theory, and Attitudes and Tendencies in Post-ideological Latin American Literature in the masters program. At the undergraduate level, she teaches literature, history, and language. Her publications "La espera: espacio inoperante en *El coronel no tiene quien le escriba"* in the compilation *Tradition, Transition and Identity* (2012), and a forthcoming article "Las palabras también están en situación: proyecto de revistas en el medio siglo en México y Colombia" in *Alba de América* (2013).

José Neftalí Recinos is currently an Assistant Professor of Spanish and the appointed Latin American Studies Program Coordinator at Stephen F. Austin State University in Nacogdoches, Texas, USA. He has a Ph. D from the University of California Riverside. His research area is Latin American literature and specializes in Mexican and Central American cultural production of the 20th and 21st century. He teaches seminars on Twentieth Century Latin American Literature, and Testimonial and Post-testimonial Literature from Mexico and Central America in the MA program at the Department of Languages, Cultures, and Communication. He writes creatively and on a variety of contemporary compelling cultural issues from the Central American isthmus. Currently, he is working on a book length study about animal representation in Central American literature of the Post-war. He has published "Actitudes de post-guerra: La nostofobia en *El asco* de Castellanos Moya" in the compilation *Tradition, Transition and Identity* (2012).

Alexandra Tsvetkova holds a Ph.D. in Public Policy from the University of North Carolina – Charlotte. She is a Policy Fellow at George Mason University School of Public Policy. Her research interests center around determinants of regional economic growth, including economic development policies, with specific focus on innovation, entrepreneurship, and the role played by individual firms.

Abdulfattah Yaghi is an Associate Professor of Public Administration and Public Policy in the Department of Political Science at the United Arab Emirates University. He teaches in the Master Program of Governance and Public Policy as well as in the undergraduate program. Some of the courses he teaches are local administration, research methods, public governance, budgeting, public policy, policy evaluation, and international political economy. He is the author of two books, "Public Policy: Theories and Applications" and "The Political System and Public Administration in the United States of America." His research appears in journals such as; Journal of Political Science Education, Arab Journal of Administrative Sciences, Asian Journal of Social Sciences, Journal of Public Affairs Education, Muslim Minorities Affairs, Dirasat, International Journal of Rural Administration, Journal of Human Resource Development Quarterly, South Asian Journal of Management, Nonprofit Management & Leadership, Asian Journal of Management, Human Resource Development Quarterly, and International Review of Administrative Sciences.

Acknowledgments

Since we started this project three years ago, a sizable cadre of individuals has helped us in various phases of the undertaking. It has been a long process, but it was worth it. *The Theories of Decentralization and Local Government: Implementation, Implications, and Realities. A Global Perspective* would not have been published without the generous support and friendship of many people. We were fortunate to have these talented professionals at our side throughout the long ordeal required to produce this book. We approached the writing of Decentralization from Global Perspective text with more than a little trepidation and our anxieties persisted during the seemingly endless episodes of writing and editing that were necessary to combine analytical rigor and readable prose. Finally, we made it and we are grateful to all those people, who helped us to achieve our goal. We are also indebted to Miro Haček, *University of Ljubljana*, for his contributions to this project. Two of our contributors also conducted their fieldwork through a grant from *Stephen F. Austin State University Research Enhancement Program*, which provided financial assistance to Gabriela Miranda-Recinos and José Neftalí Recinos in completing their chapters. We are equally grateful to Stephen Hutchinson, a graduate assistant in the MPA program at Stephen F. Austin State University.

We are indebted to individuals including, Al Bavon, *University of Arkansas*, David Owusu-Ansah: *James Madison University, Virginia, USA*, and Robert Lancaster of *Kentucky State University* who offered numerous constructive criticisms, comments, and suggestions during the preparation of the various chapters in the book.

Finally, we would like to thank the following contributors, whose hard work helped to publish this book: Kwame Asamoah, *University of Ghana,* Minerva Cruz, *Kentucky State University,* Ed Gibson, *University of Baltimore,* Ahmed Mustafa Elhussein Mansour, *United Arab Emirates University,* James A. Newman, *Southeast Missouri State University,* Heather Wyatt-Nichol, *University of Baltimore,* Hong Pang, *Utah Valley University,* Lee W. Payne, *Stephen F. Austin State University,* Gabriela Miranda-Recinos, *Stephen F. Austin State University,* José Neftalí Recinos, *Stephen F. Austin State University, and* Abdulfattah Yaghi, *United Arab Emirates University*

Kwame Badu Antwi-Boasiako and Peter Csanyi

Kwame Badu Antwi-Boasiako, PhD, is the Chair of the Department of Government and Associate Professor in Public Administration and Political Science at Stephen F. Austin State University, Nacogdoches, Texas, where he teaches Public Policy, Program Evaluation, Research Methods, and American Government. His primary research interests include traditional institutions and democracy in Africa, decentralization, terrorism, teaching public administration, and diversity in the public sector.

Peter Csanyi has a Ph.D. in Political Science from Comenius University in Bratislava, with a specialization in Theory of Politics. He is currently an Assistant Professor and Vice-Chair for International Relations in the Department of Linguistics and Translation Studies at University of Economics in Bratislava, Slovakia. He teaches Comparative Politics, Theory of Political Systems and International Relations at graduate and undergraduate levels. His research interest covers political systems of Central and Western European countries, comparative politics and international relations. Prior to that he was the Vice-Director at the Institute of Political Science of Pan European University, where he directed the international and research activities of the institution. He has given lectures at several European and American universities. He is also a General Editor of an international journal – *Journal of Comparative Politics*.

www.ingramcontent.com/pod-product-compliance
Lightning Source LLC
Chambersburg PA
CBHW080245030426
42334CB00023BA/2704